212 -
998 -
2575

2546
800 - 996
NYUr
- 6987

IFAD Studies in Rural Poverty No. 3

RURAL INDONESIA:

SOCIO-ECONOMIC DEVELOPMENT IN A CHANGING ENVIRONMENT

RURAL INDONESIA:

SOCIO-ECONOMIC DEVELOPMENT IN A CHANGING ENVIRONMENT

Erik Thorbecke
and
Theodore van der Pluijm

With a Foreword by Idriss Jazairy

Published for the
International Fund for Agricultural Development
by New York University Press

© 1993 by the International Fund for Agricultural Development (IFAD)

The opinions expressed in this volume are those of the authors and do not necessarily reflect official views or policies of the International Fund for Agricultural Development, except as explicitly stated.

The designations employed and the presentation of material in this publication do not imply the expression of any opinion whatsoever on the part of the International Fund for Agricultural Development of the United Nations concerning the legal status of any country, territory, city or area or of its authorities, or concerning the delimitation of its frontiers or boundaries.

Library of Congress Cataloging-in-Publication Data

Thorbecke, Erik, 1929-
    Rural Indonesia: socio-economic development in a changing environment / Erik Thorbecke and Theodore van der Pluijm.
        p.   cm. — (IFAD studies in rural poverty: no. 3)
    Includes bibliographical references (p.337) and index.
    ISBN 0-8147-8197-7 (cloth: acid-free paper)
    ISBN 92-9072-002-6
    1. Rural poor—Indonesia. 2. Rural development—Indonesia.
3. Indonesia—Rural conditions. 4. Agriculture—Economic aspects—
Indonesia. I. Pluijm, Theodore van der. II. Title. III. Series.
HC450.P8T45   1993
307.1'412'09598—dc20   91-40766
                                                              CIP

New York University Press books are printed on acid-free paper, and their binding materials are chosen for strength and durability.

Manufactured in the United States of America

Contents

Tables and Figures

Tables

Weights and Measures

1 square kilometre	=	100 ha = 0.39 square miles
1 kilometre (km)	=	0.62 miles
1 hectare (ha)	=	2.47 acres
1 acre	=	405 ha
1 kilogramme (kg)	=	2.20 pounds
1 tonne	=	2 200 pounds

Currency Equivalents

Currency Unit		Rupiah (Rp)
US$ 1.00	=	Rp 1 125.0 (1985 average)
US$ 1.00	=	Rp 1 132.0 (end August 1986)
US$ 1.00	=	Rp 1 633.0 (end September 1986)
US$ 1.00	=	Rp 1 639.5 (end April 1987)
US$ 1.00	=	Rp 1 669.0 (17 May 1988)
US$ 1.00	=	Rp 2 010.0 (February 1992)

Fiscal Year
1 April to 31 March

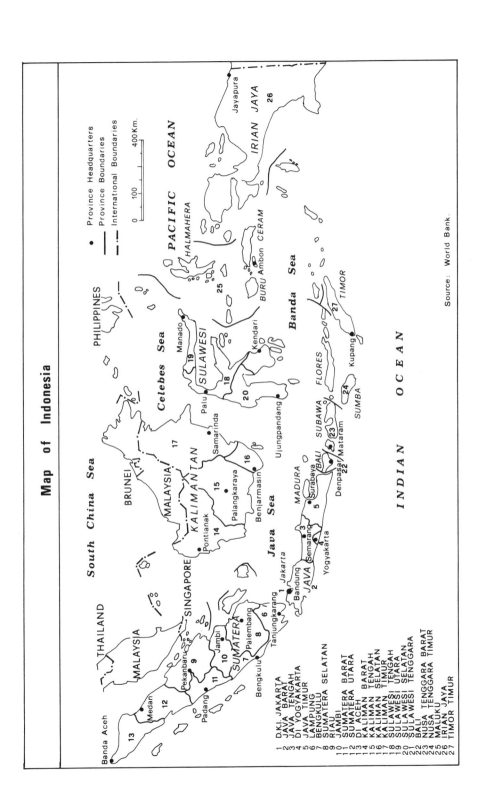

Map of Indonesia

Province Headquarters
Province Boundaries
International Boundaries

0   100   400 Km.

Source: World Bank.

THAILAND

MALAYSIA

SINGAPORE

South China Sea

BRUNEI

MALAYSIA

PHILIPPINES

PACIFIC OCEAN

Celebes Sea

KALIMANTAN

SUMATERA

Java Sea

JAVA

MADURA

BALI

SUBAWA

FLORES

SULAWESI

HALMAHERA

Banda Sea

SUMBA

TIMOR

IRIAN JAYA

INDIAN OCEAN

Banda Aceh
Medan
Pekanbaru
Padang
Jambi
Palembang
Bengkulu
Tanjungkarang
Jakarta
Bandung
Semarang
Yogyakarta
Surabaya
Pontianak
Palangkaraya
Banjarmasin
Samarinda
Ujungpandang
Manado
Palu
Kendari
Denpasar/Mataram
Kupang
Ambon
Jayapura

BURU CERAM

1   DKI JAKARTA
2   JAVA BARAT
3   JAVA TENGAH
4   DI YOGYAKARTA
5   JAVA TIMUR
6   LAMPUNG
7   BENGKULU
8   SUMATERA SELATAN
9   RIAU
10 JAMBI
11 SUMATERA BARAT
12 SUMATERA UTARA
13 DI ACEH
14 KALIMAN BARAT
15 KALIMAN TENGAH
16 KALIMAN SELATAN
17 KALIMAN TIMUR
18 SULAWESI TENGAH
19 SULAWESI UTARA
20 SULAWESI SELATAN
21 SULAWESI TENGGARA
22 BALI
23 NUSA TENGGARA BARAT
24 NUSA TENGGARA TIMUR
25 MALUKU
26 IRIAN JAYA
27 TIMOR TIMUR

Preface and Acknowledgements

In July and August of 1986, an IFAD Special Programming Mission visited Indonesia. The purpose of the Mission was to formulate a rural development strategy particularly oriented towards improving the employment prospects and the standard of living of the rural poor. Our approach from the outset was that the suggested strategy should be as consistent as possible with economic growth and efficiency.

In the light of the size and diversity of the Indonesian economy and agricultural sector, extended field trips appeared desirable to acquaint mission members with the underlying conditions. The Mission split up into two teams to visit, respectively (a) Sumatra (from North to South); Java (from West to East) and Bali; and (b) South, South-East and East Kalimantan, most of Sulawesi, Lombok and Bali. In addition, the whole Mission spent valuable time consulting with government agencies, donor organisations, private institutions and universities in Jakarta, Bogor and Yogyakarta.

The report is based on the contributions and finding of the members of the Mission: Erik Thorbecke (Professor of Economics and Food Economics, Cornell University, Ithaca, USA; Mission Leader); Thomas Cobbald (Agriculturalist and Agricultural Engineer; Consultant); Roger Downey (Professor of Economics, Sophia University, Tokyo; Consultant); Hiroyuki Nishimura (Professor of Agricultural Economics, Kyoto University; Consultant); Diva Sanjur (Professor of Nutrition, Cornell University, Ithaca; Consultant); Willen Wolters (Professor of Economic Anthropology, Catholic University of Nijmegen; Consultant); Theodore van der Pluijm (Senior Economist, Asia Region, IFAD); and Claus Jorgensen (Associate Expert, Danish Government, IFAD).

The Mission benefited greatly from the presence of the late Dr. A. T. Birowo during much of the field trips. He shared his valuable knowledge of Indonesia's rural economy with us and drew our attention to numerous issues. Without his professional dedication the Mission could not have attained its multiple objectives.

The Mission also wants to express its thanks to Dr. Hidajat Nataatmadja from the Centre for Agro-Economic Research in Bogor and to Mr. Hari Susanto of the Bureau of Foreign Cooperation, Ministry of Agriculture (MOA), both of whom accompanied the

Sumatra-Java team, and to Dr. Pantjar Simatupang, also of the Bogor Centre, and Mr. I. Wayan Sidhya of the Bureau of Planning, MOA, who were the counterparts of the other team. In particular, Dr. Hidajat contributed considerably to the Mission's work by writing a report on thematic and area-specific issues observed during the field trip.

During the Mission's field trip through Central Java, it benefited from an exchange of views on rural credit issues with Mr. Jeremy Wall (Project Controller, IFAD) and Mr. M. Alamgir (Consultant).

Towards the end of its stay in Indonesia, the Mission had two useful meetings with H.E. Minister Emil Salim of Population and Environment, and Mr. Syarifudin Baharsyah, Secretary General of the MOA, and their senior staff. The Mission owes a debt of gratitude to the Central Bureau of Statistics (BPS) for help in providing data on a multitude of issues. At the National Development Planning Agency (BAPPENAS), Dr. Ir. Alirahman, Head of the Agriculture and Irrigation Bureau, gave valuable advise on current and prospective issues.

The secretarial staff of IFAD, and in particular Ms. Susana Palacios, provided efficient and timely help.

Most figures in the text refer to the period when the IFAD Mission visited Indonesia. In particular, we had to rely on the Agricultural Census on 1983 for a number of data. As of the present date (1992) it is still the last Census available. However, the authors made a special effort to update a number of tables particularly in Chapter 2 (on the macro-economic setting) and Chapter 3 (on agricultural performance, structure and resource base) and the related text. The original report was revised and edited for this publication by the authors, although a large part of the analysis is based on the work of the individual Mission members. Ms. Theresa Panuccio (Economist, IFAD) provided invaluable assistance in seeing this book through to its completion.

Since the time the Mission visited Indonesia and completed the research for this volume, there has been much further work on Indonesia, in particular, the recent World Bank report on poverty. Having kept up very closely with this research and the recent developments of the Indonesian economy, it is comforting to note that most of the findings, conclusions and recommendations of this volume remain highly relevant today.

Erik Thorbecke
Theodore van der Pluijm
July 1992

Glossary of Terms

Alang-alang	A coarse grass, establishing itself after the slash and burn cycle
Ani-ani	Finger knife
Arisan	Type of economic, social institution
Bakul	Local trader
Balita	Children under five years of age
Bank Unit Desa	Village Banking Units
Bapak angkat	Foster father
Bupati	Head of the kabupaten
Camat	Head of the kecamatan
Desa	Village
Dharma pertiwi	Women's group (wives of police and military personnel)
Dharma wanita	Women's group (wives of civil servants)
Dukuh	Hamlet
Dukun bayi	Traditional birth attendant
Gadai	Contractual arrangements covering loans on land
Gotong-royong	Community self-help project (Java)
Hak milik	Land titling
Ijon	Contractual arrangements covering loans on harvest
Jati	Teak
Kabupaten	District
Kamar-mandi	Bathroom
Kampung	Settlement or hamlet
Kecamatan	Subdistrict
Kecap	Sauce
Kelompok akseptor	Acceptors' group
Kelompok simpan-pinjam	Savings and loan association
Kelurahan	Official administrative term for desa
Kotamadya	Municipality
Lurah	Village Head
Mapalus	Socio-cultural association (Minahasa)
Oncom	Fermented beancakes

Palawija	Secondary food crop grown in rotation with wetland rice; also refers to those crops when grown in upland areas
Pancasila	The Five Principles of the Indonesian State
Panca usaha	Five uses (package of agricultural technology)
Penghijauan	Regreening programme
Petani biasa	Ordinary farmers reluctant to adopt new techniques
Petani maju	More progressive farmers
Prokesas	Health care promoters
PT Pusri	(Perseroan Terbatas Pupuk Sriwijaya) Sriwijaya Fertilizer Inc.
Puskesmas	Community health centre at subdistrict level (*puskesmas keliling*: mobile centres) (*puskesmas perawatan*: in-patient centres)
Rukun Kampung	Lower ranks of villages
Rukun Tetangga	Lower ranks of villages
Sawah	Lowland rice fields with bunds to collect irrigation or rainwater and maintain controlled inundation
Sewa	Contractual arrangements covering loans on land
Subak	Water management organizations (Bali)
Tahu	Soyabean curd
Talun-kebun	System where a multi-storey stand of perennials is under-cropped with annual food staples
Tasar	Type of silk
Tauco	Relish
Tebasan	Contractual arrangements covering loans on harvest
Tegalan	Home garden
Tempe	Cake of fermented soyabeans
Tusam	Sumatra pine
Usaha bersama	Savings and loan cooperative or informal cooperative
Wereng	Local name for the brown plant hopper

List of Acronyms and Abbreviations

AAETE	Agency for Agricultural Education, Training and Extension
AARD	Agency for Agriculture Research and Development
ADB	Asian Development Bank
ANP	Applied Nutrition Programme
APBN	(Anggaran Pendapatan dan Belanja Negara) State budget for revenue and expenditure
AVRDC	Asian Vegetable Research and Development Centre
BAPPEDA	(Badan Perencanaan Pembangunan Daerah) Provincial Development Planning Agency
BAPPEDA TkII	(Tingkat II) Second level, subprovince
BAPPENAS	(Badan Perencanaan Pembangunan Nasional) National Development Planning Agency
BI	(Bank Indonesia) Central Bank
BIMAS	(Bimbingan Massal) Mass Guidance Programme
BKK	(Badan Kredit Kecamatan) Kecamatan Credit Organization
BKKBN	(Badan Koordinasi Keluarga Berencana Nasional) National Family Planning Coordinating Board
BKPD	(Bank Karya Produksi Desa) Business Bank for Village Production
BKOW	Provincial Women's Council
BPD	(Bank Pembangunan Daerah) Provincial Development Bank
BPH	brown plant hopper
BPS	(Biro Pusat Statistik) Central Bureau of Statistics
BRI	(Bank Rakyat Indonesia) Indonesian People's Bank
BUKOPIN	(Bank Umum Koperasi Indonesia) Indonesian General Cooperative Bank
BULOG	(Badan Urusan Logistik) National Food Procurement and Distribution Agency
BUUD	(Badan Usaha Unit Desa) Village Unit Enterprise Organization
CRDN	Centre for Research and Development of Nutrition
DGEC	Directorate-General of Estate Crops
DGFC	Directorate-General of Food Crops

DGH	Directorate-General of Highways
DGLS	Directorate-General of Livestock Services
DGSP	Directorate-General of Settlement Programmes
DGWRD	Directorate-General of Water Resources Development
DINAS	Government services
DNIKS	(Dewan Nasional Indonesia untuk Kesejahteraan Sosial) Indonesian National Council for Social Welfare
EJIS	East Java Provincial Irrigation Service
EPI	Expanded Programme of Immunization
ESCAP-CGPRT	Economic and Social Commission for Asia and the Pacific Centre for Coarse Grains, Pulses, Roots and Tubers
FAO	Food and Agriculture Organization of the United Nations
FEW	Field Extension Worker
FPP	Family Planning Programme
FTDC	Food Technology Development Centre
GDP	Gross Domestic Product
GOI	Government of Indonesia
GOLKAR	(Golongan Karya) Functional Group
GOW	District Women's Council
GNP	Gross National Product
GTZ	German Technical Assistance
HKII	Hellen Keller International, Inc.
HYV	high yielding varieties
IBRD	International Bank for Reconstruction and Development - World Bank
ICARD	Independent Centre for Agricultural Research and Development
IDA	International Development Association
IGGI	Inter-Governmental Group on Indonesia
IKOPIN	(Institut Manajemen Koperasi Indonesia) Indonesian Institute for Cooperative Management
IMR	infant mortality rate
INKUD	(Induk KUD) KUD Core
INMAS	(Intensifikasi Massal) Mass Intensification Programme
INPRES	(Instruksi Presiden) Presidential instruction - indicating funds and schemes which have been established by presidential instruction

INSUS	(Intensifikasi Khusus) Special Intensification Programme
IPB	Institute of Agriculture in Bogor
IRRI	International Rice Research Institute
ITCZ	Inter-Tropical Convergence Zone
JICA	Japanese technical aid
KB-APSARI	Contraceptive Acceptors/Users
KCK	(Kredit Candak Kulak) Petty Trading Credit
KIK/KMKP	(Kredit Investasi Kecil)(Kredit Modal Kerja Permanen) Small-Scale Investment Credit and Permanent Working Capital Credit
KNKWI	(Komisi Nasional Kedudukan Wanita Indonesia) Indonesian National Commission on the Status of Women
KOWANI	(Kongres Wanita Indonesia) Indonesian Women's Congress
KUD	(Koperasi Unit Desa) Village-Level Cooperative
KUPEDES	(Kredit Umum Koperasi Indonesia) Indonesian General Credit Union
LCC	Leguminous Cover Crops
LECS	Land Evaluation Computer System
LFPR	Labour Force Participation Rate
LIPI	Indonesian Institute of Sciences
LKMD	(Lembaga Ketahanan Masyarakat Desa) Village Security Institution
LNG	liquid natural gas
LPK	(Lembaga Perkreditan Kecamatan) Subdistrict Credit Institution
LPN	(Lumbung Pitih Nagari) Regional Savings Institution
LPSM	(Lembaga Pengembangan Swadaya Masyarakat) Community Self-Reliance Development Organization
LSD	(Lembaga Sosial Desa) Village Social Committees
MCH	Maternal and Child Health
MMR	Maternal Mortality Rate
MOA	Ministry of Agriculture
MOC	Ministry of Cooperatives
MOH	Ministry of Health
MOI	Ministry of Industry
MOPW	Ministry of Public Works
MOT	Ministry of Transmigration

NES	Nucleus Estates and Smallholders Projects
NGO	non-governmental organization
NSS	Nutrition Surveillance System
P2AT	Groundwater Development Agency
P2W-KSS	(Peningkatan Peranan Wanita Menuju Keluarga Sehat dan Sejahtera) Programme for the Improvement of Women's Social Welfare
PEM	protein-energy malnutrition
PELITA	Planning period
PKK	(Pembinaan Kesejahteraan Keluarga) Family Welfare Movement
PKMD	Village Community Health Department
PIBD	(Proyek Irigasi Bank Dunia) agency of DGWRD created to execute World Bank-assisted projects
PIR	(Perusahaan Inti Rakyat) Domestically-financed estate projects TRANS linked to the transmigration programme
PMU	Project Management Unit
PPL	(Penyuluh Pertanian Lapangan) Field Extension Worker
PPM	(Penyuluh Pertanian Madya) Senior Extension Worker
PPS	Subject Matter Specialist
PROSIDA	(Proyek Irigasi IDA) agency of DGWRD created to execute IDA-assisted projects
PTP	(Perseroan Terbatas Perkebunan) Publicly owned estates
PUSKUD	(Pusat KUD) KUD Centre
REC	rural extension centre
REPELITA	(Rencana Pembangunan Lima Tahun) Five-Year Development Plan
SAKERNAS	(Survei Angkatan Kerja Nasional) National Labour Force Survey
SATGAS	(Satuan Petugas Lapangan) field task force comprising animal health, extension and husbandry workers
SIAP	Budgetary carryovers
SPM	Special Programming Mission
SUSENAS	(Survei Sosial Ekonomi Nasional) National Socio-Economic Survey
TBA	Traditional Birth Attendant
T&V	Training and Visit system

UNDP	United Nations Development Programme
UNICEF	United Nations Children's Fund
UPGK	(Usaha Perbaikan Gizi Keluarga) Family Nutrition Improvement Programme
USAID	United States Agency for International Development
USESE	(Unit Studi dan Evaluasi Sosial Ekonomi) Unit of Socio-Economic Evaluation Studies
VCDC	Village Contraceptive Distribution Centres
VCR	Value/Cost-Ratio
WHO	World Health Organization
WID	Women in Development
YPAC	(Yayasan Pelindung Anak Cacat) Foundation for the Protection of Disabled Children
YRDP	Yogyakarta Rural Development Project

Foreword

IFAD's experience with rural poverty in Indonesia began in 1978. In 1986, an IFAD Mission visited Indonesia to undertake an in-depth assessment of the progress being made and to formulate a revised development strategy specifically aimed at improving the conditions of IFAD's target group of beneficiaries - the rural poor. The idea was to identify not only a series of policy recommendations, but also to pinpoint opportunities for effective development interventions on behalf of Indonesian small farmers, rural landless and rural women. However, the wealth of information drawn from the experience and analysis presented in this book is also of value to scholars, development workers and any others with an interest in the socio-economic realities that characterize Indonesian rural society.

This book also raises a number of issues that go beyond the immediate Indonesian setting and address fundamental questions regarding development planning in its broadest sense. For instance, in establishing that agricultural development cannot, by itself, resolve the problem of rural unemployment in Indonesia, it reminds us that the production and trading of crops are only one aspect of rural economies. We are made aware that if problems are to be tackled effectively, they cannot be isolated from the context in which they arise. For example, to combat hunger, we must also wage war on poverty and create new productive employment opportunities. In the context of Indonesia's agricultural development, it must be noted that Indonesia's performance in rice production has been remarkable. By following enlightened policies, Indonesia has become self-sufficient in rice, after having been the largest rice importing country in the world. As this volume makes clear, the time has now come to diversify into other crops. This will require a more location-specific approach, in the sense that local soil conditions must be taken into account in making decisions as to what to plant where.

Of special value is the detailed focus of the analyses and investigations of the study. Just as a microscope is an essential tool for identifying pathogens, so is detailed analysis a prerequisite for effective development intervention. The regional and commodity diversification strategy which is proposed in this volume will necessitate some important policy and institutional changes. A strong case is made that this new agricultural strategy should contribute, in an essential way, to both economic growth and rural poverty alleviation.

Finally, for development work to be successful, it is necessary to focus on research. In this connection, I trust this book on rural Indonesia will prove of interest to Indonesian policy makers and researchers as well as be of service to the international development community at large.

Idriss Jazairy
President of IFAD
Rome, July 1992

Editor's Note

This study, Rural Indonesia: Socio-Economic Development in a Changing Environment, is the third volume in the series of IFAD Studies in Rural Poverty undertaken in collaboration with New York University Press. As in the case of the first two studies, this volume attempts to fill the gap between micro-economic analysis of poverty and national planning and policy making. The rural poor, which represent a latent productive potential, need to be provided with an appropriate policy and institutional framework, resource and technology support, and an enabling marketing environment so that they can raise their productivity on land where access to it is assured, and raise their income through off-farm income-generating activities where there is scope for generation of productive employment. This volume brings out how both these strategies could be fruitfully pursued in the context of rural Indonesia. This contribution, although based on a field work some years back, comes at an appropriate time when the policy-makers in the country are engaged in the formulation of a longer term development perspective for tackling the problem of rural poverty, building on the substantial success already achieved in reducing the relative magnitude of rural poverty. A particular contribution made by the volume relates to the attempt made to delineate policies and strategies separately for the inner islands and the outer islands and for agricultural and non-agricultural activities in rural areas. The recommendations of this study have already laid an important foundation for productive interaction between the International Fund for Agricultural Development (IFAD) and the Government of Indonesia as reflected in a number of projects targeted at the disadvantaged populations both in the inner and outer islands.

Thanks are due to Ms. Barbara Alto in assisting me in the management of the publication of this study, and to Mr. Niko Pfund of the New York University Press for his support and assistance in carrying this series forward.

Theresa Panuccio
Editor

Chapter 1

Overview

Rural Indonesia: Socio-Economic Development in a Changing Environment

Although economic growth alone is not sufficient to improve the standards of living of the rural poor, it is a necessary precondition. The productive energies of the poor can be harnessed through the creation of additional or more productive employment opportunities, a more efficient allocation of resources within agriculture and an institutional and policy setting responsive to the needs of underprivileged groups.

The formulation of a rural development strategy is a difficult task within a country as large and diversified as Indonesia. The first step, therefore, is to evaluate and analyse the present socio-economic structure as it has evolved in the recent past. At the most aggregate level, the Indonesian economy has been subjected to major changes within the world economy. These changes - particularly due to the drastically altered oil picture - have had major consequences on the government budget and thereby on the magnitude and composition of development expenditure affecting the rural areas. In addition, important structural changes have taken place during the last two decades at the macro-economic level and in terms of the sectoral and intersectoral production pattern. Chapter 2 discusses the impact of these macro-economic and structural changes on the domestic economy, particularly on the rural poor.

At the next level of aggregation, it is clear that the structure, resource base and performance of the agricultural sector largely determine the employment and income opportunities available to the rural population. Chapter 3 considers these issues. As such, it analyses the role of agriculture in providing food for a growing population, inputs for the industrial sector and employment opportunities and income to the bulk of the rural population in alleviating poverty and malnutrition and in improving the balance of

1

payments. It also explores the output and employment performance of the subsectors within agriculture, as well as the pattern of land distribution and land use. Since performance can only be evaluated in the light of the prevailing resource base and operational environment, the chapter makes an inventory of the existing situation in terms of physical geography, climate, soils, hydrology, natural vegetation, landform topology, irrigation and so-called critical areas. It examines the pattern of resource use within the agricultural sector in terms of crops and cropping and farming systems and technology; and concludes with a section on agricultural research.

Any attempt at designing a development strategy responsive to the needs of the rural poor must necessarily rely on a careful analysis of the dimensions of rural poverty and identify the main target groups. This is the subject of Chapter 4 which undertakes a thorough analysis of the distribution of income and consumption by different socio-economic groups. In particular, on the basis of a social accounting matrix of Indonesia, it derives the levels and sources of income of agricultural employees (the landless) and small farmers and other target groups. We identify to some extent the regional dimensions of poverty. We see that poverty is widely spread in a geographical sense and that it is difficult to pinpoint exclusive clusters of poverty. Notwithstanding the pervasiveness of poverty, particularly in Java, it was possible with the help of a variety of indicators to identify areas of relatively high deprivation that merit the attention of policy makers.

Chapter 4 also focuses on women as a target group. It explores women's role in the local economy, women's participation in agricultural production and nonfarm employment for women. It identifies the major socio-economic factors associated with low income and inadequate health and nutrition among women. The last part of Chapter 4 analyses the relationships between rural poverty on the one hand and the pattern of ownership of land (including land productivity) and the structure of employment and the operation of labour markets on the other.

Since the most important basic need is nutrition and since under- and malnutrition are the prime manifestations of poverty, Chapter 5 analyses the pattern of food consumption, nutrition and health. It begins by exploring the pattern of food consumption, with particular emphasis on target and vulnerable groups. The chapter highlights important food policy issues, evaluating the nutritional status and health-related issues concerning target groups, looks at the principal nutritional problems prevailing in Indonesia and reviews various nutrition programmes. The end of Chapter 5 analyses the interactions that exist between food consumption and rural water and sanitation on the one hand and nutritional status and health on the other.

Chapter 6 reviews and analyses the pattern of past and present policies and interventions in agriculture and examines the role of rural institutions. It reviews the planning process and macro-economic and agricultural policies and looks at governmental organizational instruments such as the nucleus estate smallholder system, the transmigration programme, the rural credit system, cooperatives and the agricultural extension service, particularly as they affect the target groups of poor. It ends with an evaluation of the work of non-governmental development organizations.

Chapter 7 explores opportunities for agricultural development and presents various technical options based on the prevailing physical endowment in terms of the resource base, cropping pattern and present and likely changes in technology. A realistic evaluation of the potential technical options is crucial to the formulation of a development strategy. In fact, a choice has to be made among the existing options consistent with the objectives of the rural development strategy, that is, the improvement of the standards of living of the rural poor within a growth context. The design of a rural development strategy does not consist solely of the selection of the most desirable technical alternatives open to the policy makers. It also depends upon the organizational setting and the capacity of the system to modify and adapt existing institutions and create new institutions within which the desirable technical options can be promoted. Thus, a part of Chapter 7 is devoted to an examination of the complementary organizational changes that may be called for in the future to take advantage of the technical opportunities.

Finally, Chapter 8 presents a strategy based on a reorientation of the structure of production. It focuses on how to match the projected new entrants into the labour force and transmigrants to prospective employment opportunities over the next decade, paying special attention to IFAD target groups. The analytical framework used to explore the employment prospects is an interregional and intersectoral framework distinguishing between the Inner Islands (mainly Java) and the Outer Islands and between agricultural and non-agricultural activities in the rural areas, respectively.

A key concept that captures and underlies the essence of the recommended strategy in terms of the structure of rural production is commodity and regional diversification. In Java, this should take the form of greater emphasis on encouraging the cultivation of secondary food crops combined with other agricultural activities in the rain-fed upland areas. Likewise, the pattern of public expenditures on infrastructure projects should increasingly concentrate on the rehabilitation of existing irrigation schemes, the construction of rural farm-to-market roads, and the construction of water control and erosion-reducing schemes - in each case using labour-intensive techniques.

In the Outer Islands, the selection of which crops to grow and which activities to undertake in transmigration projects should be dictated by the principle of comparative advantage, bearing in mind the local climatic and agronomic conditions. Concentration on specific individual tree crops, depending on the location, appears to be indicated in most instances.

Chapter 8 explores the organizational requirements and major policy changes needed to bring about the revised structure of production. It shows that the relative shift from paddy production to production of secondary food crops in the upland areas requires a new orientation of the agricultural service institutions. Furthermore, it indicates that a commodity or crop-specific approach has to give way to a location- or region-specific approach. The conclusion in Chapter 8 is that a centralized programme structure is not appropriate, as the problems faced are different for each area.

Among our specific recommendations are the following:

(i) Appropriate organizational coordination should be worked out between the extension services of the MOA and of the Ministry of Industry (MOI), so that vocational and non-agricultural skills be extended to the target group of marginal farmers who are being squeezed out of agriculture.

(ii) A scheme should be designed that would link the training of marginal farmers and landless for non-agricultural activities together with access to credit to help them move into these activities.

(iii) A greater focus should be made by the Government on tenurial and land title questions.

(iv) A better coordination is needed of the process of agricultural production planning with that of nutritional planning.

(v) Some modification should be made in the total family approach, such as the addition of more women among extension workers to ensure that agricultural and non-agricultural services go further in reaching rural women.

The Changing Macro-economic Setting

Aggregate Performance

The macro-economic performance of Indonesia in the 1970s was outstanding. The Gross National Product (GNP) grew at 7.4 percent a year, largely influenced by the 1973 and 1979 oil price rises. Although the share of oil exports and the total value of exports amounted to slightly less than one-fourth in 1971, this share had increased to almost three-fourths in the second half of the 1970s. Clearly, oil had become the major growth engine in the 1970s. Expressed in 1973 prices, imports increased nearly six times during that decade, that is, by about 20 percent a year.

At the macro-economic level two important features of the 1970s are noteworthy: (i) the big jump in the gross domestic investment share of the GNP from 13.6 percent in 1970 to 20.9 percent in 1980; and (ii) the relatively modest increase in public sector consumption expenditures in contrast with the experience of other oil-exporting nations.

The macro-economic performance in the first half of the 1980s reveals a very different picture. Two major phenomena dominated the macro-economic scene. The first was the decline in the volume and absolute value of oil exports after 1982-83. The second was the rapid increase of non-oil imports. These factors combined to reduce the growth rate of Gross Domestic Product (GDP) to 3.6 percent per year between 1983 and 1987 and led to a large increase in the current account deficit of the balance of payments.

The macro-economic trends prevailing in the 1970s were reflected in a corresponding major change in the sectoral composition of the GDP. The share of agriculture fell from almost one-half to about one-fourth of the GDP, whereas the mining sector - heavily dominated by oil production - found its share rising from 5.2 percent in 1970 to about 25 percent in 1980. In contrast, following the drop in oil prices, its sectoral share in the GDP fell to 18 percent in 1984, whereas the share of agriculture stabilized around one-fourth of the GDP.

The share of the total labour force engaged in agricultural activities dropped from 66 percent in 1970 to 57 percent in the mid-1980s. During the 1970s, only 28 percent of the new entrants into the national labour market were absorbed by agriculture. A final trend has been the considerable slowing of inflation compared to the 1970s.

External Trade and Balance of Payments

The balance of payments performance from 1970 on was largely affected by the oil picture. Thus, following the two price hikes of 1973 and 1979, significant improvements occurred in the current account, a negligible deficit in 1973 and a relatively large surplus in 1979-80 and in 1980-81, amounting to 5 percent and 3.6 percent of the GDP, respectively. When the oil situation deteriorated, in 1982-83 the current account deficit widened to US$ 7.1 billion or 7.5 percent of the GDP. Confronted with this problem, early in 1983 the Government undertook adjustment measures in a variety of spheres, including public finances, public investment programmes, monetary policies, deregulation and currency devaluation. These measures were quite effective.

The currency devaluation of March 1983 helped bring about a major increase in the value of non-oil exports, particularly manufactured goods, whose share in total exports grew from 5 percent to 25 percent in the first half of the eighties.

During the last decade and a half, the total long-term external debt rose markedly from about US$ 3 billion in 1970 to almost US$ 27 billion in 1984. The size of the external debt relative to GNP, however, remained approximately the same at about one-third. Presently, the total debt service burden accounts for approximately one-third of gross exports earnings.

Recent Budgetary Changes

Initially the GDP growth target for the fourth Five-Year Development Plan (REPELITA IV) had been set at 5 percent per annum. This target was to be accompanied by substantial increases in development expenditure in the government budget. The worsening balance of payments and sharply declining government revenues, however, caused major downward readjustments. Nevertheless, high priority continued to be given to the continuation of projects, with special focus on equity and employment.

The total budgetary allocation to local projects channelled through local governments (i.e., Presidential Instruction (INPRES) projects) remained the same in absolute terms despite sharply cut development expenditure. The main objective of the INPRES programme has been to expand income opportunities for and services to low-income groups and zones.

Within agriculture, irrigation schemes were heavily affected by the intended cut-backs. This was partially a consequence of the lower priority given to financing new irrigation projects in the wake of achieving self-sufficiency in rice. Presently, the Government is placing more emphasis on consolidation and rehabilitation of irrigation works.

A crucial question was the impact of the budgetary cuts on employment and incomes. The employment prospects as well as the level and distribution of labour income are basic determinants of the welfare, in particular of the landless rural population and marginal farmers. The growth of the rural labour force (i.e., new entrants into the labour force for whom jobs have to be found) was estimated at about 1.5 percent per annum for Indonesia as a whole in the 1980s. The fact that Java's agricultural sector has already reached the turning point, characterized by an absolute decline in the size of the agricultural labour force, combined with a limited capacity of the Outer Islands to absorb productively new transmigrants in agriculture, means that the burden of providing new jobs will increasingly fall on non-agricultural activities and the informal sector.

The level (and the sectoral and regional distribution) of public expenditures is a major policy instrument affecting the demand for labour. Although an employment impact analysis of the original REPELITA IV concluded that the sectoral expenditure pattern was more labour intensive than that of the preceding plan, the 1986-87 round of budgetary entrenchments (particularly the cut-backs in development expenditures) was estimated to lead to a reduction in employment opportunities of at least 1 million jobs affecting mainly informal activities. Since these activities are mainly undertaken by the urban poor and rural landless, the burden of the budgetary cut-back may well fall on them.

Agricultural Performance, Structure and Resource Base

Agricultural and Rural Performance

Since 1970 the Indonesian economy has undergone a structural transformation characteristic of countries in relatively early phases of development. The relative share of agriculture (including livestock, forestry and fisheries) in GDP (at current prices) fell from about 32 percent in the mid-1970s to about 25 percent in the mid-1980s, while the relative share of agricultural employment in the total labour force declined from about 67 percent in the early 1970s to 55 percent in the early 1980s. The aggregate performance of agricultural GDP (at constant 1973 prices) from 1974 to 1984 was good, although not spectacular. Agricultural GDP grew at an annual rate of 3.8 percent, farm food crops at 4.5 percent and estate crops at 6.1 percent. Most noteworthy, was the superlative performance of the paddy subsector, leading to virtual rice self-sufficiency by the mid-1980s. No doubt, the paddy subsector contributed most to agricultural growth.

On the whole, the capacity of agriculture to provide additional employment opportunities was limited during the 1970s: The employment elasticity was estimated at 0.27; that is, a 10 percent growth in agricultural output would lead to only a 2.7 percent increase in agricultural employment. Average food consumption improved markedly until the early 1980s, and all target groups (in particular the landless agricultural workers and the small farmers) benefitted.

Chapter 3 confirms that during the last 15 years or so, agriculture played a crucial role in contributing to the major socio-economic development objectives, (i.e., growth of the GDP, employment, improved nutrition and food security, poverty alleviation and the balance of payments). At the same time, however, it is unrealistic to assume that this sector can continue to fulfil all the above interrelated functions in the future. Nonetheless, growth in tree crop production, following an acceleration of the transmigration programme, can be expected in the Outer Islands. This would lead to additional employment.

The trend toward a larger number of small farms on Java and an increasing group of "marginal" farmers and landless workers indicate that it is impossible to solve the employment and poverty problem within agriculture per se. Small and landless farmers will increasingly have to be provided with rural off-farm jobs.

Recent performance within agriculture shows that among the food crops, maize and particularly paddy have registered significant yield increases. On the other hand, no significant upward or downward trends have been noticeable for either area or yield in the case of the major food crops (i.e., cassava, soyabeans, groundnuts and sweet potatoes).

The production of cash crops has fluctuated fairly widely from year to year since the late seventies. Only rubber, coffee and tobacco performed relatively well, growing at 4.5 percent to 5.3 percent per year. In contrast, both tea and sugar cane production remained essentially stagnant. The livestock sector grew at a moderate 3.6 percent rate in the same period, while the forestry sector underwent wide fluctuations.

Resource Base, Operational Environment and Patterns of Resource Use

The diverse environments characteristic of Indonesia permit a wide range of crops to be grown and a correspondingly wide range of farming systems and techniques to be used. Crops in Indonesia are conventionally divided into (1) rice; (2) *palawija* or secondary food crops other than rice; (3) industrial crops, which include coconut, tobacco, cotton and various spice crops; and (4) estate crops, which include rubber, oil-palm, coffee, cocoa, tea and sugar cane. This taxonomy has historical origin, and it should be realized that many estate crops are, in fact, grown by independent smallholders and that some *palawija* crops (e.g., citrus) may be grown on an estate scale.

Rubber, in terms of total area planted, rivals coconut as a smallholder crop. Although at present about 80 percent of the total rubber acreage is on smallholdings, that produces only about 30 percent of output. Yield differences between rubber produced on smallholdings and that produced on estates are very large, reflecting two totally different approaches to rubber production. Likewise, coffee has traditionally been a smallholder product, and in no province do the estates constitute more than 10 percent of the area under the crop.

Rice, as a preferred staple, is given priority whenever conditions are favourable. Thus, on farms where there is year-round access to irrigation water, rice is often continuously cropped, with two, two-and-a-half or three crops per year. Where rainfall is sufficient for reasonable yields under rain-fed conditions, rice will often take precedence over other crops. The prototype cropping system for most farmers on their wetland is either one or two rice crops. On the dryland, many, if not most, farmers include significant plantings of other crops in their rotations. The enormous diversity of conditions characteristic of the operational environment in Indonesia means, however, that a myriad of farming systems can be found, many of which are highly location and situation specific. Farm household units in Indonesia are usually comprised of a number of discrete parcels of land that are not only spatially distributed but are also located in different physical environments.

Thus, a smallholder's farming system may incorporate several different cropping patterns applied specifically to the separate land parcels. For example, rice might be double cropped on irrigated *sawah*, a single rice crop might be taken from rain-fed *sawah* and followed by fallow, tilled dryland might carry either cassava or intercropped maize and legumes, coffee might be planted with shade trees on other elevated land, and vegetables might be grown in the home garden. Such a system exists at the village level, particularly in Java. In fact, in some areas it could be considered typical in the sense that it represents the system used by most farmers. But in much of Indonesia the nature of the resource endowment and the differential access to land arising from socially determined tenurial entitlements mean that many farmers have to practice totally different systems. Thus, the Javanese stereotype can only be replicated to a limited extent in other parts of Indonesia.

Agricultural technology in Indonesia is very labour-intensive. Taking the country as a whole, the physical work input provided by human labour is probably at least five times that provided by animal labour, which in turn is probably at least ten times that provided by internal combustion engines. To a large extent, Indonesia's agriculture remains powered by food staples.

Mechanical power has been more widely used for site preparation where new plantations and transmigration settlements have been established. These operations, however, often do irremediable damage to the soil; compaction reduces drainage capability and thus encourages erosion and overworking destroys topsoil structure. Notwithstanding the higher costs, labour-intensive methods and/or biological or biochemical systems may prove, in many instances, to be the only ecologically satisfactory way of opening up new land.

In the past, as a result of heavy subsidization, fertilizer has been available at low farm-gate prices and the possible economic returns have been high. Fertilizer has been heavily concentrated on the wetland rice crop. Just how efficiently fertilizer is being used is difficult to assess. The heavy subsidization of fertilizer may have introduced a price distortion leading in some cases to a socially inefficient allocation of fertilizer. The recent abolition of fertilizer subsidies renders this question moot.

One interesting practice is that of "block farming". With block farming, groups of farmers on contiguous plots adhere to an agreed upon cropping plan (same high-yielding varieties (HYVs), same planting time, etc.) that has helped raise the efficacy of pest and disease control measures.

Long-term, sustained increase in rural population has caused overcropping on marginal land. The Government, however, has shown an increasing awareness of this problem by designating "critical areas" in a planned and well-supported effort to combat soil degradation.

Livestock Husbandry, Fisheries and Forestry

Indonesia has a relatively small livestock sector; the ratios of livestock to people and to cultivated land are probably among the lowest in Southeast Asia. The dairy cattle subsector has received substantial external support in recent years, but evidence suggests many producers find their enterprises yielding little profit. It is difficult to envisage a significant extension of this subsector without continuous subsidization except where there are opportunities to sell high-priced liquid milk into upper income bracket markets. Relatively few cattle are kept in commercial herds: Java's 5.17 million cattle (in 1983) were distributed among 2.75 million households - an average of less than two animals per household. The prevailing feeding methods have the merit of using what might otherwise be wasted resources.

The fishery sector has two distinct subsectors: marine and inland fishery. Each subsector uses upward of 1 million people, mostly in small-scale enterprises. The long-term tendency for the productivity of boats and fishermen to decline suggests some degree of overfishing. The switch from traditional non-powered boats to small powered boats then to larger powered boats essentially represents adjustment to this situation. The economic position of coastal fishermen is unquestionably tending to deteriorate, particularly where communities continue to depend upon traditional crafts and methods. Raising individual productivity is likely to prove difficult without considerable structural and organizational change within the industry; as capital intensity increases so does the need for management skills.

Inland fishery could make a significant contribution to feeding both rural and urban people and in so doing provide livelihoods to many families.

Historically, forests have been an important resource in Indonesia, and before the discovery of oil they were the principal source of foreign exchange earnings. Although detailed surveys in the forest areas have yet to be completed for the whole country, some systematic afforestation and reforestation have taken place, such as plantations of *tusam* on Sumatra and Java and *jati* on Java.

In recent years, the Government has understood the need for a conservation-oriented exploitation policy and greater control over extraction operation. In 1984, export of logs was banned, which has led to heavy investment in conversion plants, particularly for plywood manufacture. "Smallholder forests" and social forestry were scheduled to receive support during a REPELITA IV.

Agricultural Research

Clearly, the diversity of crops and of operational environments demand continuing scientific effort. And, indeed, there is increasing interest in Indonesia in undertaking research on farming systems. The development of new systems continues to be seen as the key to increasing productivity and farming incomes. It has also been realized that the misuse of land, resulting in damaging soil erosion or excessive water runoff, can often be correlated with the entire farming system rather than with the cultivation of a specific crop. Accordingly, farming system research has virtually become a mandatory component of any area-specific project that includes land conservation among its objectives. Agricultural research has a long history in Indonesia, and different administrations have allocated substantial resources to institutional infrastructure and training. Yet the fact that most, if not all, major area-specific development projects supported with external finance find they have to include provisions for *ad hoc* applied research within their project frameworks indicates how stretched the agricultural research services remain.

An attempt has been made here to evaluate the present status of farming system research in Indonesia. This inquiry focused more particularly on the rain-fed and upland areas; firstly, because farm research on rain-fed areas has been relatively neglected and, secondly, because soil erosion caused by bad farming practices is most severe and common at the higher altitudes. Because of the tremendous diversity of farming conditions prevailing in Indonesia, it is felt that results from specific projects can only to a limited extent be generalized and transferred to different settings. The design of appropriate farming systems in the rain-fed upland areas relying - as it has to - on a whole combination of secondary (*palawija*) crops and other activities and products is immensely more difficult than the design of appropriate systems in the irrigated areas based very largely on paddy production.

Dimensions of Rural Poverty and Target Groups

This section looks at the factorial sources of income accruing to different socio-economic groups, the resulting income distribution among different socio-economic household groups and the consumption patterns of these different socio-economic groups.

Distribution of Income and Consumption by Socio-economic Groups

A comparison of the 1980 data with those of 1975 reveals significantly increasing polarization among agricultural households. In 1980, labourers and small operators had lower relative incomes and swelling populations, while the medium and larger operators had rapidly improving incomes and dwindling populations. The trend among non-agricultural households can be characterized as one of dampening polarization. Relative incomes tended to improve except at the top, while populations rose. Notwithstanding its limitations, the 1975 and 1980 systems of socio-economic accounts are the most consistent estimates for income and outlays available and provide a clear indication of which rural socio-economic groups within Indonesia are relatively poor agricultural labourers, small agricultural operators and rural, lower-level households. To the extent that there is variation within the groups, some of the approximately 80 million people in them are undoubtedly not poor and, conversely, some members of other groups, even larger farmers (e.g., those owning poorer quality land) may be poor.

Socio-economic Dimensions of Nutritional Inequality

This section examines nutritional implications of food consumption for different types of households. It considers 28 socio-economic groups, including 13 categories of disaggregated agricultural operators according to the amount of land they own and economically active non-agricultural households split into components based on a combination of labour status and occupational categories.

For each of the 28 odd socio-economic groups, calorie adequacy, calculated by converting the quantity of food consumed by each sample household into calories, then by comparing the results to requirement standards adjusted for the sex and age composition of each household, shows that, not unexpectedly, among the farmers there is a clear link between land ownership and calorie adequacy. Outside of agriculture it is also generally true that higher skilled groups both in the rural and urban areas rank above manual workers and menial clerical, sales and service workers.

According to National Socio-Economic Survey data (SUSENAS), average levels of rice consumption do not vary widely over the majority of household groups, although there appears to exist substantial inequalities regarding the ways different groups acquire rice. For instance, the sharp contrast between agricultural labourers and landless operators indicates that the operators' tenancy or sharecropping arrangement permit them to be less dependent upon rice markets. On average, the landless operators consumed 0.82 kg of self-produced rice, compared with only 0.17 kg for the agricultural labourers. This is a clear indication of what A.K. Sen labels "exchange entitlements".

In addition, among farmers consumption from their own production typically increases along with land size. This relationship is a useful reminder that smaller landowners are typically not "subsistence" farmers in a literal sense. It is the larger landowners, not the smaller, who manage to meet the bulk of their staple needs from self-production. By implication, the rice consumption of smaller farmers is much less insulated from a negative impact of price increases.

Regional Dimensions of Poverty

To identify the regional dimensions of poverty, we can compare indicators based on poverty lines, including "deprivation", dependence on generally non-preferred staples, infant mortality rates, illiteracy, effective remoteness from mass media, seasonality of physical access and concentration of smallholders on rain-fed land. The comparison does not uniformly show which regions have more disadvantaged rural populations. East Nusa Tenggara, for example, appears on many lists of poverty indicators but not on all. The same is true of Central Java, Yogyakarta and East Java.

Many indicators of regional inequality have been based on provincial data. For policy purposes, however, a finer disaggregation is often desired. Therefore, we will define subprovincial areas with a high concentration of smallholders and of dryland by identifying those regencies (kabupaten) in Java and Madura that fulfil two conditions: (1.a) more than half the farmers controlled less than 0.50 ha of land or, alternatively, (1.b) more than 40 percent of the farmers control less than 0.25 ha of land and (2) more than half the agricultural land is rain-fed. Regencies that fulfil the conditions are shown in Figure 4.4.

The map shows three fairly distinct and large concentrations of smallholders and of dryland. The highest proportion of smallholders and dryland occurs in the southern portion of West Java. Outside of Java and Madura, no regencies meet the stricter set of criteria (1.b and 2), but Klungkung, Badung, Karangasem, in Bali; Tabalong in South Kalimantan; Tana Toraja in South Sulawesi; and Deli Serdang in North Sumatra meet the first set (1.a and 2). The map and data underlying it provide an ambiguous poverty indicator since there can be wide variation in the quality of rain-fed land. Moreover, we must not forget that many poor people, especially agricultural labourers, live in irrigated and non-irrigated wetland areas not marked on the map. The map does however serve as a rough guide to areas that are likely to suffer population pressure and, at the same time, be less likely to benefit directly from policies geared to promoting wetland rice production.

Attempts have been made to identify poor areas at the still lower level, namely, that of subdistrict (*kecamatan*). Following a request from BAPPENAS, the Directorate-General of Agrarian Affairs prepared lists of poor subdistricts for consideration as target recipients of "food-for-work" funds. These lists, however, are not a sufficiently reliable means for pinpointing poor regions.

In conclusion, it is difficult to pinpoint pockets of poverty without more direct observation. Part of the problem, particularly in Java, is that poverty is pervasive, with poor people often living in close proximity to non-poor people. Hence, policies for more heterogeneous areas, which are common in Java, require careful design to minimize leakages to non-target groups. Poverty itself is often multidimensional. Therefore, regional groups need not register on all indicators before allocating attention to them. It can be more useful to focus specific policies on areas suffering from specific needs rather than searching for general policies to meet the amorphous notion of "poverty".

Women as a Target Group

Rural women constitute a special target group. Thus, if women in Indonesia are to be fully integrated as equal partners into national life, certain structural, cultural and institutional constraints need to be relaxed, if not removed.

Based upon an examination of socio-economic and health indicators regarding the lives of rural women in Indonesia, we see that maternal education is inversely correlated with infant mortality rates. Although since 1961 illiteracy has gone down significantly in Indonesia for both males and females, it is still considerably higher for females (37 percent of the females were illiterate in 1980 as compared to only 20 percent of the males). The lower female literacy rates in rural Indonesia may, to some extent, reflect cultural norms, but more importantly it reflects socio-economic conditions.

Some evidence shows that underemployment is significantly greater among women. If a normal working week is defined as 35 hours, more than 35 percent of the total labour force, but 51 percent of women, were underemployed in Indonesia in 1980. A J-shaped relation can be observed between employment and education. This pattern represents a large group of lower-class women without schooling who work out of economic necessity, a middle group of women possessing low and intermediate education levels who are less likely to be economically active and a small group of highly educated women who exhibit the highest labour force participation rates, working primarily in modern skilled occupations.

Although rural women still play an important role in rice production, Green Revolution technology in paddy production increased agricultural production but reduced their employment. One estimate indicates that women's employment declined by 1 percent per annum during the census period 1971-80.

The shrinkage in female agricultural employment was somewhat offset by their increased employment in trade and services. This changing pattern is to be expected since trade and services include small informal activities that require little capital and few specialized skills and is characterized by low levels of productivity and earnings.

In the production of plantation crops, there is evidence of significantly different wage structures for females and males. Furthermore, most female-headed households are in the lower 10-20 percent of the monthly income distribution. This dismal picture is particularly true for agricultural households and less extreme for non-agricultural households.

Rural Poverty, Land Distribution and Productivity, and Employment

Rural poverty is intrinsically related to (1) the pattern of ownership of land and land productivity and (2) the structure of employment and the operation of labour markets. In simplest terms, households and individuals have different endowments of physical capital (particularly land) and human capital, which determine their standards of living.

The following conclusions are a result of a detailed analysis of these issues. Firstly, all socio-economic groups benefitted from the economic growth in the 1970s and, particularly, from the rice boom after 1976. The incidence of poverty was significantly reduced and the caloric consumption of the poorest rose. Although the target groups of landless and near-landless agricultural workers and small farmers enjoyed an improvement in their standard of living, it is likely that some increased polarization occurred among agricultural households. A comparative evaluation of the 1973 and 1983 agricultural censuses reveal a trend toward downgrading farm sizes at the lower end of the distribution and the gradual elimination of marginal farmers controlling less than 1/10 ha. Both of these forces must have occurred mainly on Java and are consistent with polarization.

Secondly, the net exodus out of agriculture on Java - amounting by some estimates to a net reduction of 850 000 in rural agricultural employment between 1976 and 1982 - happened concomitantly with a rise in labour intensity (higher average number of hours or workdays per person) among the remaining labour force in agriculture. Thus, income from agricultural sources for both landless workers and farmers rose more perhaps because of greater labour intensity than higher agricultural wage rates or higher imputed labour income per hour or workday of labour. In other words, the capacity of the agricultural sector on Java to absorb additional workers had become negative, whereas its capacity to provide additional workdays of employment was still slightly positive in that period. Future displacement of agricultural labour on Java, however, appears inevitable. Whatever the scope for additional employment generation in agriculture, it is to be found in the Outer Islands rather than on Java. Present and future transmigration projects, which will increasingly be directed toward Kalimantan and Irian Jaya, continue to offer some limited scope for productive employment absorption in agriculture.

Thirdly, there is some evidence that a process of "agricultural adjustment" toward more viable and economically sustainable farms was already underway on Java in the seventies. Many truly marginal farmers on Java must have felt the squeeze of low farm returns and rising indebtedness and must have been forced to join the ranks of the landless. Likewise, a number of small farmers had to dispose of some of their land and move down to a lower farm-size stratum. This process must, incidentally, have been reinforced by the inheritance (primogeniture) system - leading to increased land parcellization and fragmentation from one generation to another. Some pull factors were, however, present even for the poorest rural groups of landless and marginal farmers. For some of them on Java, the transmigration projects offered an opportunity to improve their conditions. A large share of them must have ended up moving, almost residually, into service and household industry activities in the informal sector.

Pattern of Food Consumption, Nutrition and Health

Food Consumption and Food Policy Issues

Although the evidence suggests that during the seventies most, if not all, socio-economic groups and segments of the population improved their calorie intake, recent trends are more ambiguous. A comparison of calorie consumption at the provincial level between 1980 and 1984 based on surveys by BPS suggests that (i) calorie consumption, on average, rose in only two provinces (East Nusa Tenggara and Maluku); (ii) calorie consumption remained constant (i.e., within 2 percent of 1980 values either upward or downward) in 12 provinces; and (iii) calorie consumption fell by at least 4 percent in 12 other provinces, mainly in the Outer Islands.

Such a trend would be cause for concern if it reflected the real situation - the more so since it occurred during a period of spectacular performance in paddy production. There is, however, a large discrepancy between the national average caloric consumption based on balance sheets (2 565 calories in 1983) and that based on SUSENAS data (1 798 in 1984). It is likely that systematic underreporting in the SUSENAS surveys may account for a large part of this discrepancy. This would not, however, explain the downward trend in many provinces indicated above. On average the great bulk of the calorie consumption came from staple foods - amounting to 68 percent of total calories consumed in 1983.

The basic diet of the Indonesian population centres on rice, except for the people in the Province of Irian Jaya who prefer sweet potatoes and bananas. When any population group is heavily dependent on a single food commodity, problems arise. In Indonesia, it appears that rice and other basic staples (i.e., cassava, maize, sweet potatoes) constitute part of a food habit pattern rigidly adhered to, in part because of tradition and in part because of economic limitations. The consistent findings of nutritional investigators are the monotony of the diets of rural poor and the irregularity of consumption of foodstuffs other than the staple foods.

Several policy issues concerning food production, distribution and consumption in Indonesia merit attention. Firstly, the rice intensification programme, which was successful in leading to rice self-sufficiency and was justified at the time, has brought about some undesirable side effects. The emphasis on rice made the Government and farmers neglect secondary crops such as maize, cassava, soyabeans, peanuts and vegetables. Agricultural policy was so geared to rice production that it indirectly discriminated against the *palawija* crops. Non-rice farmers in the dry and upland areas became even more underprivileged, limited by credit restrictions for agricultural inputs, low productivity and insecure, distant markets for their products.

Thus, from an equity as well as nutritional standpoint, food diversification ranks high among food policy issues in Indonesia. A more balanced diet would go a long way toward alleviating many of Indonesia's nutritional problems.

Nutritional Problems and Programmes

The most serious and pervasive nutritional problem is that of protein-energy malnutrition (PEM). Although PEM afflicts adults, the prolonged insufficient intake of calories and protein is known to have most serious consequences among young children and women. Specifically, it affects disease resistance, immunological resistance, physical activity and growth. According to a 1984 nutrition survey by BPS-UNICEF, mild PEM afflicted 30 percent or 9 million preschool children in Indonesia. It was also prevalent among pregnant and lactating women, with 7 percent and 3 percent, respectively, suffering from the mild form.

Infant mortality rates (IMRs) are directly related to the incidence of PEM. Although it is encouraging to note that the overall IMR for Indonesia has dropped sharply from an estimated 140/1000 live births in 1971 to about 90/1000 live births in 1984, it should be noted that wide regional variations continue to prevail among provinces, ranging from about 63 in Yogyakarta to 188 in West Nusa Tenggara, and that IMR is much lower in urban areas.

Since PEM is largely a problem of inadequate food consumption, improving the entitlement and purchasing power of those afflicted should reduce its prevalence significantly. Nutrition education, however, should not be neglected, ensuring that the additional income gets translated into real dietary improvements.

Anaemia caused by insufficient intakes of nutrients such as iron, folic acid and Vitamin B_{12} is another serious nutritional problem. Its prevalence among different groups in Indonesia is as follows: pregnant women (70 percent), lactating women (40 percent), preschool children (40 percent), school children (31 percent). Among men, high prevalence of anaemia (40 percent) has been reported among plantation workers and rural poor. The main strategy to control anaemia is iron supplementation.

Still another nutritional problem is that of Vitamin A deficiency, which is responsible for the development of xerophthalmia. It is estimated that in Indonesia more than 60 000 children per year develop the disease and about 100 000 risk becoming blind. Emphasis on dietary diversification is the lasting solution for the Vitamin A deficiency. In the interim, Vitamin A supplement programmes help.

A final serious nutritional problem is that of iodine deficiency. From 50 percent to 80 percent of children surveyed in North and West Sumatra, East Java and Bali were found to have goitre.

Nutrition improvement activities in Indonesia are basically carried out through the Family Nutrition Improvement Programme (UPGK) in the form of nutrition services to family at the *desa* (village) level. The thrust of this programme is educational, designed to enable mothers to monitor and improve the nutritional status of their families. The development plan under REPELITA IV attached a high priority to food and nutrition programmes directed at achieving an adequate, equitably distributed and diversified supply of food. A diversified diet will go a long way toward solving the nutritional problems described here.

At the present, a potentially serious obstacle to the formulation of consistent policies and programmes is the inadequate coordination between the planning unit of MOA and other units in the Ministry of Health (MOH) and BAPPENAS, which concentrate on nutritional and health issues from the consumption side.

Rural Water Supply, Sanitation and Health Facilities

Programmes to develop adequate water supplies are relatively recent in Indonesia. In 1983, at the end of REPELITA III, nearly 70 percent of the rural population and 40 percent of the urban population still lacked access to clean water and 65-75 percent were without proper waste disposal facilities. Inadequate and contaminated water and poor sanitation facilities and practices contribute substantially to the high levels of morbidity and mortality. One key question that needs to be resolved is how to improve the quality of water in the rural areas.

Indonesia relies on a variety of health programmes for rural women and their children. The Village Community Health Department (PKMD) was designed to better meet the health needs of the poor by using and building upon the traditional Indonesian system of mutual self-help and, to a large extent, by relying on local resources. Lack of supervisors and trained health staff have, unfortunately, lessened the impact of this programme. The maternal child health programme has also faced a shortage of staff and inadequate supervision of traditional birth attendants. The Expanded Programme of Immunization (EPI) concentrates on six diseases, aiming at almost universal immunization of children by the turn of the century. An evaluation of this programme carried out in 1982 noted, however, that although geographical expansion was improving, there was a disappointingly low rate of immunization.

Indonesia's population planning and control programme has been recognized as one of the most effective in the world. This success has been in part attributed to strong political will and support from a government committed to fertility reduction as an integral part of overall national economic development. Since its inception, the programme strategically has concentrated on Java and Bali, and thus its success remains limited primarily to the rural areas of these two relatively small islands with very large population density. It is only recently that recognition of the need to extend the programme to the Outer Islands has taken place. This is reflected in the ambitious targets regarding population policy in REPELITA IV. One issue needs to be flagged, however: the intent to broaden family planning objectives to include other development activities. Whereas integrating or even providing a vehicle for other programmes makes sense from a conceptual perspective, it is somewhat risky to diversify a programme that is moving ahead rapidly and successfully.

Pattern of Past and Present Policies and Programmes in Agriculture and Rural Institutions

The Planning Process, Macro-economic and Agricultural Policies and Programmes

The planning process in Indonesia is highly centralized. BAPPENAS is the apex of policy making and national planning. It is complemented at the provincial level by regional planning offices known as BAPPEDAS. In spite of the stated intention to decentralize authority, the central government continues to exercise control over lower-level administrations. That is, investment programmes and projects at almost every regional and subregional level tend to be designed and selected by central ministries. There is a growing consensus that decentralization of the agricultural planning process needs to be encouraged if food production and consumption diversification and increased tree production in the Outer Islands are to succeed.

There is much evidence that during the last decade macro-economic policies, which have provided a favourable environment within which sectoral measures such as the Mass Guidance (BIMAS) programme (described below) could be implemented, have been at the base of the successful management of agriculture. Monetary and fiscal policies were effective in combating inflation and in encouraging the structural adjustments required in the early eighties as a result of the changing oil picture. Likewise, appropriate policies in the field of trade and exchange rates have contributed to the sustained growth of agricultural exports.

As a result, the overall performance of the agricultural sector was very successful. The total area under irrigation rose from an estimated 4.7 million ha in 1973 to about 7.9 million ha in 1983. A major problem that remains, however, relates to building and rehabilitating tertiary canals and channels needed to bring water to the farmers' fields.

There is no question that the price policies followed in Indonesia so far have favoured rice. The real price of rice has stayed the same from the early 1970s to the early 1980s, but the real price of fertilizer has been halved during the same period. This has led to a tremendous increase in the use of fertilizer per hectare, which increased from 19 nutrient kg in 1960 to 127 kg in 1981. Furthermore, after 1982 the price of rice became significantly higher in Indonesia than in the rest of the world.

The BIMAS programme, which provided paddy farmers with a package of services that included HYV seeds, operating credit, guidance from extension workers, and fertilizer and pesticides at subsidized prices, was instrumental in the diffusion and dissemination of the new Green Revolution technologies and the breakthrough in production that resulted in the achievement of rice self-sufficiency by the early 1980s. Notwithstanding the success of BIMAS in accelerating paddy output, note that a large amount of the credit extended to farmers was never repaid; in 1984 the credit programme of BIMAS was abolished, but the extension activities continued. In 1979, the Government of Indonesia (GOI) introduced a Special Intensification Programme called INSUS, based on group rather than individual farming. This programme grew out of the need to coordinate rice planting around the village in order to combat rice diseases, especially the *wereng* plague. The way the programme works is that a group of contiguous farmers covering about 50 ha makes joint decisions concerning planting times, application of fertilizer, harvesting and so on.

Until recently, Indonesia's agricultural policies and programmes have largely focused on rice production in the fertile lowlands. Uplands and highlands, mainly rain-fed, received much less Government attention. Whereas the GOI implemented tree crop development through various schemes such as the Nucleus Estates and Smallholders Project (NES) and the Project Management Unit (PMU), upland food production has been relatively neglected. This neglect is reflected in the fact that production of upland secondary food crops such as maize, cassava and potatoes lags far behind paddy.

Governmental Organizational Instruments

Probably the most creative and interesting form of production organization the GOI has been promoting is based on the principle of horizontal and vertical integration by tying small-scale producers and smallholders, called the "plasma", to higher-level large-scale enterprises, called the "nucleus". A prime example of this type of system is the NES. The integration is horizontal in the sense that very different producers of the same product, such as smallholders that produce tea and an existing large-scale tea plantation or estate, are brought together in one unit. The integration is vertical in the sense that the plasma (i.e., the smallholders) can benefit from economies of scale enjoyed by the nucleus (i.e., the estate) in providing of inputs and extending services and in processing and marketing the product. Integration structures can take various institutional forms. The nucleus can be a state enterprise, a private company or a cooperative owned by the producers. Alternative arrangements are also possible between nucleus and plasma regarding the provision of inputs, credit and repayment schemes and the degree to which the producers are obliged to sell their products to the nucleus. It is essential to the success of these schemes that a truly symbiotic relationship evolves between the nucleus and the plasma to the mutual benefit of both sides.

Up to now NES and alternative schemes have been developed mainly in the field of tree crops, but they are being extended to other products. These schemes are essentially land development programmes aimed at turning new settlers, both transmigrants and local population, into efficient cash crop smallholders. A typical arrangement is for the smallholders to receive between 0.50 and 1 ha of land for food crops in addition to 2-3 ha of land for tree crops. Smallholders have difficulties in securing sufficient income, especially during the first few years. The food crop component seems to be unsatisfactory, with low yields due to poor soil conditions, the absence of extension service and the lack of a market for food crops.

The transmigration programme is a large-scale and ambitious scheme for land settlement and marginal land use in Indonesia. The term transmigration programme indicates the voluntary movement of people from overcrowded areas in the Inner Islands to less developed areas in the Outer Islands. A distinction is made between sponsored migrants, who receive support from the Government and move to selected sites, and spontaneous or unassisted migrants, who receive minimal government support. The programme has increased at an almost exponential rate. If the local families and resettled families brought into the transmigration areas are added together, a total of more than 365 000 families (or close to 1.5 million people) were settled by the mid-1980s. Under REPELITA IV the Government planned to move 400 000 families under fully sponsored programmes, and another 300 000 migrant families were expected to move spontaneously. Typically, each settler family is assigned 2 ha of land, consisting of 0.25 ha of house plot, 0.75 ha of dryland and 1 ha of *sawah*. Since prospects for food crop farming are limited, a shift to new settlement with tree crops (rubber, coconut) that are better suited to the low-fertility soils in the Outer Islands suggests itself if the land is suitable.

Several issues to consider regarding the various rural credit schemes in Indonesia follow. Firstly, there is evidence that on a national average, small farmers owning less than 1/2 ha had relatively less access to BIMAS and other credit. Furthermore, under most credit programmes the bulk of loans was for trading rather than for agricultural purposes.

A second issue is that credit programmes designed for the poor sometimes require the formation of joint liability groups. The purpose is to increase the probability of repayment in cases in which borrowers cannot submit collateral for their loan. The joint liability groups use the mechanism of mutual social control to ensure that borrowers meet their obligations. Although there is a tradition in Indonesia of savings and credit groups, it is doubtful whether it makes sense to organize groups solely on a negative basis such as the institution of mutual social control. If the credit arrangement is on a joint liability basis while the economic activities are individual, there is not much incentive to maintain the group character of the operation. Consequently, it seems that the group character of credit schemes can be reinforced if other collective activities are included such as training, education, decision making, technology transfer and mutual help.

A third issue is the extent to which credit is available to women. Most of the credit goes to traders. Although many traders are women, it is important to recognise that male traders are engaged in different activities than female traders and that the differences affect the distribution of credit. Typically, female traders undertake smaller operations, such as the sale of small amounts of agricultural produce in the market place, the sale of homemade food and small-scale informal activities. It can be assumed that most of the credit extended to female traders goes to farmers' wives who are active as local traders (*bakul*). But even these women, coming from the village elite and middle groups, are no match for the larger merchants who are mostly men.

Two important observations need to be made regarding the operation of the extension service. Firstly, extension has been mainly oriented toward the lowland rice areas, applying a commodity-specific approach and delivering a standardized package to the farmers. The extension service hardly covers the upland areas. A new focus on rain-fed land and secondary crops requires a more differentiated approach given the diversity and heterogeneity of soils. This would require drastic changes in the extension service.

Secondly, in forming farmers' groups, extension workers acknowledge the presence of an upper stratum of *petani maju*, the more progressive farmers who are responsive to the new technology, and a lower stratum of *petani biasa*, the ordinary farmers who are often more reluctant to adopt new techniques. Extension workers tend to visit and work among the better-off farmers, whereas small and poor farmers are often neglected.

The cooperative movement is an important instrument used by the Government in its rural development strategy. Presently there are some limits to the capacity of cooperatives to benefit the less-privileged farmers and landless workers. If rich and poor people are together in one cooperative, the poor people can still be dominated within the organization, as the history of the cooperative movement in many parts of the world has shown. Specifically, there is some evidence that within the village-level cooperative (KUD) it is the better-off non-farmers who run the show.

Single-purpose cooperatives would appear to be more successful than multipurpose cooperatives of the KUD type. Single-purpose cooperatives, preferably based on multistranded social ties among the members, provide the members with a clear purpose for cooperation while the group is strongly cemented by numerous overlapping social ties.

Increasingly, women's organizations under governmental and non-governmental auspices are being established in Indonesia. There are, however, some areas of concern regarding these supportive services, namely, the overintegration of activities aimed at women's development and the insufficient participation of rural women regarding programmes aimed at benefiting them.

During the past few years non-governmental development organizations (NGOs), known in Indonesia as community self-reliant development organizations, have increased and expanded their field of operations. These organizations promote development by focusing on the poor strata of the population and increasing grassroots participation. They are engaged in a wide range of projects, many of them income generating. One particularly positive feature of the NGOs is that they follow a bottom-up approach as opposed to the top-down thinking prevalent in much of the bureaucracy. A recent phenomenon in specific regional projects of government agencies is the cooperation, with a NGO, a university institute and grassroots organizations. The recent reductions in the government development budget and the relative success of NGOs have improved the Government's receptivity toward these organizations.

Based upon an evaluation and analysis of policies and programmes and rural institutions, the following conclusions can be reached. Firstly, the Government exhibits a remarkably strong focus on rural areas and agricultural production, indicating an absence of urban bias in GOI policies. Furthermore, the organizational structure is not a static one but shows dynamism and flexibility. Different programmes and institutions are increasingly modified and fused in a creative way. For instance, the NES scheme is being extended from the tree crop area to other economic activities and is presently applied in transmigration schemes, whereas the cooperative idea is to some extent merged with NES schemes.

Perhaps the major limitation of the credit, cooperatives and extension programmes is that they tend to be too strongly focused on large - and middle - level farmers and do not sufficiently reach poor farmers and landless labourers. This limitation can be better understood if we consider the functioning of governmental organizations within the context of the village social structure. The village is conceived of as a homogeneous community, where democracy rules and traditional institutions such as mutual help prevail. But perhaps a more realistic appraisal is that it consists of two social strata. An upper stratum of high-ranking officials and better off farmers dominates village affairs both politically and economically. They tend to promote the interests of the upper class and represent the village in its contacts with government agencies. A Javanese village (*desa*) consists of small hamlets (*dukuh*), some of which are inhabited by a lower stratum of non-formal leaders and lower-ranking village administrators who represent the interests of their fellow hamlet inhabitants. There appears to be a cleavage between the two social strata, with the upper and lower layers tending to function separately. There is some evidence that the upper stratum captures the development programmes reaching down from the national level, implying widespread non-participation of the lower strata.

The operational significance of the above organizational network is that the rural poor are not only difficult to locate in a geographical sense but are difficult to reach with the existing apparatus. Thus, reorientation of programmes and institutions more receptive to subvillage needs and aspirations is needed. This would require a greater degree of penetration and targeting of government programmes toward the rural poor, as well as better representation of the underprivileged groups in village-level decisions.

Opportunities for Agricultural Development

Opportunities for agricultural growth fall into four categories: (i) bringing new land into agricultural production, (ii) taking land out of direct agricultural production in "critical areas" where productivity is negative because of deleterious downstream effects attributable to upstream erosion, (iii) changing the allocation of land to different crops and (iv) increasing yields under the existing cropping or farming systems through technical or technological changes.

The opportunities to open up new land for agriculture are located almost exclusively in the Outer Islands. The reason is that although Java has 3 million ha of designated forest land, very little of it is appropriate for conversion to agriculture. On the other hand, large tracks of forest in the Outer Islands could be converted into tree crops such as oil-palm and rubber, which, in cropping terms, are closest to the ecologically stable primeval forest that constitutes the climax flora of the rain forest areas of Sumatra and Kalimantan. Clearly, on these lands continuous perennial cropping is more attractive agronomically than are annual food staples.

On Java some limited areas under forest could be converted to tea plantations. There are some higher precipitation areas in Java where the soils would be suitable for growing tea, affording higher returns than from the present montane forest cover. With adequate anti-erosion measures, runoff and erosion rates would not be significantly higher under tea than at present.

On the whole, conversion opportunities on Java are more likely to be that of taking land out of agricultural production. In some of the critical areas reafforestation is an answer, but that cannot be expected on a smallholder basis. Forestry returns would match those of exhaustive cropping and provide the desired social benefits in lower watershed areas. Some retroactive recognition of usufructural rights of the de facto occupiers of subcritical forest land may be expedient for both economic and political reasons. That is, no system of use that is both agriculturally and ecologically sound is likely to be invested in without confidence by the farmers that their positions are secure and they will be able to reap a reward from the time and effort put into their holdings. It is unlikely that erosion-minimizing systems will be voluntarily adopted in the absence of tenurial rights.

If reafforestation of critical areas is not feasible, systems of agroforestry or silvipasture are viable alternatives. Note, however, that although agroforestry offers the prospects of multiple farm income, investigatory work needs to be done before a satisfactory system can be recommended for widespread adoption. In addition, the need to address soil stability adds to the complexity of the research task and may tend to limit the economic returns.

With regard to possible changes in the output mix and cropping patterns, the GOI should, as much as possible, be guided by comparative advantage and efficiency considerations. Although national food security is a valid macro-economic and political goal, attempting to grow food crops where the land is marginal for this purpose - because of edaphic characteristics - but would be suitable for perennial tree crops, can be in the best long-term interests of neither the country nor the cultivator.

The options available to adjust cropping and farming systems to increase yields can take different forms, such as changing cultivation techniques, adopting cultivars with shorter maturity periods or phasing intercropping. These alternatives, however, tend to be location and situation specific. Perhaps an outstanding example of where significant increases in yields are possible under the existing system is in the extensive areas of Sumatra rubber plantations. Through an appropriate replanting scheme, a tenfold increase in per hectare latex yields could be expected in many instances.

There is some scope for improvements in cultivars or hybrids for non-rice crops; this has already occurred to a limited extent in places in which hybrid maize has been introduced. The different environmental conditions under which these crops have to be grown, however, makes it difficult to breed, select and test universally adaptable HYVs as was the case with rice. A more successful source of increased yields would seem to be the widespread and efficient use of chemicals such as fertilizers. The extension services' past occupation with the rice crops has, by most accounts, been at the expense of acquiring expertise relevant to the *palawija* and other non-rice crops.

It appears that a continuous flow of resources is needed to maintain appropriate levels of agricultural research such as plant breeding, agronomic trials, selection, pathogen investigations and cognate activities. In agronomic research, the main need at present is to increase the number of controlled trials of improved *palawija* cultivars.

With respect to the smallholder subsector, future development policies are likely to be more successful if they are oriented toward improving farmers' income rather than physical production targets. These were valid objectives when there was a large rice shortfall but became less meaningful when expressed in such imprecise terms as intensification and diversification. Policy makers may also have to learn to live with the fact that for rice, which tolerates wide variation in soil conditions, production technology can be treated almost as a given independent variable, however this ceases to be true for most *palawija* crops.

The change of thrust from rice to *palawija* crops and the need to focus on income-generating opportunities are key elements in the design and selection of projects IFAD might support in Indonesia at the present time. In particular, the BIMAS model integrating services, inputs and projects at the national level to boost the production of one crop (paddy) is no longer the example to follow. At the same time, concentration of production diversification provides an opportunity to identify specific locations for projects that meet IFAD's goals of helping underprivileged farmers in the upland areas.

Such a reorientation has already been initiated. Extension programmes for specific commodities in specific locations are being developed by activities under the responsibility of rural extension centres (RECs) - tailored to the prevailing ecosystem(s). In addition, location-specific efforts - for *palawija* crops - are increasingly promoted by disseminating research results and production approaches to farmers through area trials, demonstration plots and pilot projects.

Strategy and Recommendations

The starting point in the formulation of any strategy is to express the policy objectives it seeks to attain clearly. Here the main objective is to design a rural development strategy oriented toward improving the standards of living of the rural poor. Furthermore, the strategy should be as consistent as possible with economic growth and efficiency.

The main vehicle for increasing the incomes of the poor is the creation of additional and more productive employment opportunities. This requires allocating resources to rural areas and introducing interregional cropping patterns that pay particular attention to creating productive employment opportunities for the target groups of landless, marginal and small farmers - including, of course, rural women. The challenge is to match the transmigrants and new entrants into the labour force to the employment opportunities during the next decade, focusing especially on our target groups.

Since future employment prospects should, as much as possible, agree with socio-economic characteristics of the rural poor, they are reviewed briefly. Poverty is inversely related to the land and human capital (i.e., educational) of the households. Thus, the greatest incidence of poverty is among small upland (rain-fed) farmers producing secondary crops. Furthermore, the highest proportion of smallholders and incidence of dryland occurs in the southern portion of West Java.

The analytical framework used to explore the employment prospects in the light of the socio-economic characteristics of the new entrants into the labour force, including those displaced from agriculture, is an interregional and intersectoral framework distinguishing between the Inner Islands (mainly Java) and the Outer Islands and between agricultural and non-agricultural activities in the rural areas, respectively.

The attainment of rice self-sufficiency does not mean that the nutritional requirements of all households are met. Although it is clear that the GOI cannot relax its efforts in terms of rice production front, what is called for at the present time is a relative de-emphasis of rice production in favour of secondary food crops and other agricultural activities.

A key concept in the recommended strategy is commodity and regional diversification. In Java, the diversification should take the form of encouraging the cultivation of secondary food crops combined with other agricultural activities in the rain-fed upland areas. Likewise, the pattern of public expenditure on infrastructure projects should increasingly concentrate on (i) the rehabilitation of existing irrigation schemes and the spatial extension of the downstream canal network, (ii) the construction of rural farm-to-market roads that better link upland and lowland areas and (iii) conservation schemes in the critical (mainly upland) watershed areas.

In the Outer Islands, in light of the underlying climatic and agronomic conditions, the selection of which crops to grow and which activities to undertake in transmigration projects should be dictated by the principle of comparative advantage. Concentration needs to be on specific tree crops which depend on location. The land clearing and preparation stage of new transmigration projects and settlement schemes should be as labour intensive as possible. The technology chosen should be based on the appropriate shadow prices reflecting the socio-economic input costs and benefits.

Now that we described the major interregional and intersectoral features of an appropriate strategy from the standpoint of the structure of production, we can examine the organizational requirements and major policy changes needed to bring about the revised structure of production.

Organizational Requirements and Policy Recommendations

The relative shift from paddy production to secondary food crops and other agricultural products in the upland areas requires a new orientation of the agricultural service institutions. A commodity, or crop-specific, approach (which was followed during the big push for rice self-sufficiency) has to give way to a location- or region-specific approach. A centralized programme is not appropriate, since the problems faced are unique for each area.

Such a region-specific approach requires organizational adjustments. At present there is strong sectoral and departmental segmentation in the government apparatus. The new approach has to be based on interdepartmental cooperation as well as on multidisciplinary research. The Government has to reinforce its emphasis on coordination of the different government agencies. A location-specific approach requires not only greater coordination but also increased dedication of field workers to small-scale settings and a strong effort to cooperate with local farmers. The management of sustainable farming systems in upland regions requires the participation and cooperation of all villages in decision-making and implementing plans. This cannot be achieved with the top-down approach.

Regional planning and implementation require imaginative interaction between provincial and district level managers on the one hand and village and community level leaders on the other. The village unit approach, which was suitable for homogeneous rice regions, is not appropriate for upland areas. Project managers will have to decide on the basis of their practical experience and knowledge of the socio-economic structure whether their entry point should be at the *dukuh* level or at the *desa* level or via some *desa* organization or even a *supradesa* organization.

In the process of shaping a rural development strategy oriented toward production and regional diversification and organizational and policy decentralization, a key issue is that of the long-run viability of individual farms and other quasi-private institutions such as the NES and PMU.

It would be a losing battle to try to go against the observed trend entailing the gradual elimination of marginal farms. Instead, the Government needs to ensure that this process occurs gradually and that, during the transitional period, marginal farmers are trained for jobs outside of agriculture. Therefore, an organizational coordination needs to be worked out between the extension services of the MOA and of the MOI so vocational and non-agricultural skills be extended to the target group of marginal farmers and near landless who are being squeezed out of agriculture. Increasingly, extension workers will have to become more polyvalent.

Much as supervised credit links agricultural extension to agricultural credit, it might be desirable to design schemes that link the training of marginal and landless farmers in non-agricultural activities to credit to help them make a start.

In many areas of Java and the Outer Islands the tenurial question is clouded and is a serious obstacle to on-farm improvements and investments. A reorientation of agricultural development toward the upland areas will require the Government to focus on the land title question more seriously than in the past. The NES-PMU type of organization has potential merits as long as a truly symbiotic relationship could be worked out between the nucleus and the plasma.

As far as the nutritional and health situation is concerned, whereas the trend toward a varied and diversified diet could go a long way in reducing malnutrition, infant mortality and the incidence of some diseases, increased nutrition education coupled with dietary behavioural changes are also necessary. Moreover, the promotion of health education suited to a rural environment, together with the inclusion of rural young women in such training and the provision of child care training facilities for young mothers, can potentially achieve greater social and economic welfare including employment.

Programmes and policies to increase and diversify food production on the one hand and to improve nutrition on the other should be as complementary as possible. This does not appear to be the case at present. Thus, the process of agricultural production planning needs to be better coordinated with that of nutritional planning.

Rural women constitute a specific target group. Concentrating exclusively, or mainly, on the so-called "productive activities" in which women engage leads to a serious underestimation of their overall contribution to the development process. The contribution of rural women to the material welfare of rural households, when their household and farm activities are properly accounted for, looms essential in the broad development context. It is crucial to provide women displaced from agriculture with opportunities to acquire relevant skills outside of agriculture.

There is some evidence that the so-called "total family approach" followed by government agencies does not permeate or reach rural women as far as it should. The addition of more women among extension workers (both agricultural and non-agricultural) would ensure that more women would be among the initial contact farmers. They would then disseminate their skills and techniques to other female farmers, starting a desirable snowball process.

Chapter 2

Physical, Historical and Macro-economic Setting

Geophysical, Social and Historical Setting

Indonesia extends over almost the entire East Indian archipelago; it includes the Greater Sunda Islands - Sumatra, Java and Madura, Borneo (except that part constituting East Malaysia and Sabah) and the Celebes; the Lesser Sunda Islands - Bali, Lombok, Sumbawa, Sumba, Flores and Timor; the Moluccas and Irian (New Guinea) as far as 141°E (see Figure 2.1). The total land area is estimated to be about 1.92 million km², of which some 80 percent is accounted for by the larger islands: Sumatra, 24 percent; Java and Madura, 7 percent; and Sulawesi (Celebes), 9 percent; and the larger island territories: Kalimantan (Indonesian Borneo), 28 percent; and Irian Jaya (West New Guinea), 21 percent. The Lesser Sunda Islands and the Moluccas, together with some 13 000 smaller islands (of which about 6 000 are inhabited), make up the remaining 20 percent of the land area.

Indonesia straddles the equator, lying for the most part between 5°N and 10°S. This position gives Indonesia a hot climate that is moderated by the surrounding seas. The large islands and territories all receive substantial rainfall, mostly from December to March, during the winter monsoon season. Many of the smaller islands have a much drier climate.

Indonesia is a country of great distances, extending over more than one-eighth of the Earth's equatorial circumference. Between longitudinal extremes (E-W) it extends over 5 000 km, and between latitudinal extremes it measures about 1 800 km. With the exception of Kalimantan, the major territories are elongated or convoluted in shape; the shortest land distance between one end of a territory and the other are accordingly great: Sumatra, 1 750 km; Java, 1 060 km; Sulawesi, 1 150 km; Irian Jaya, 1 450 km; Kalimantan, 1 120 km.

FIGURE 2.1
Map of Indonesia

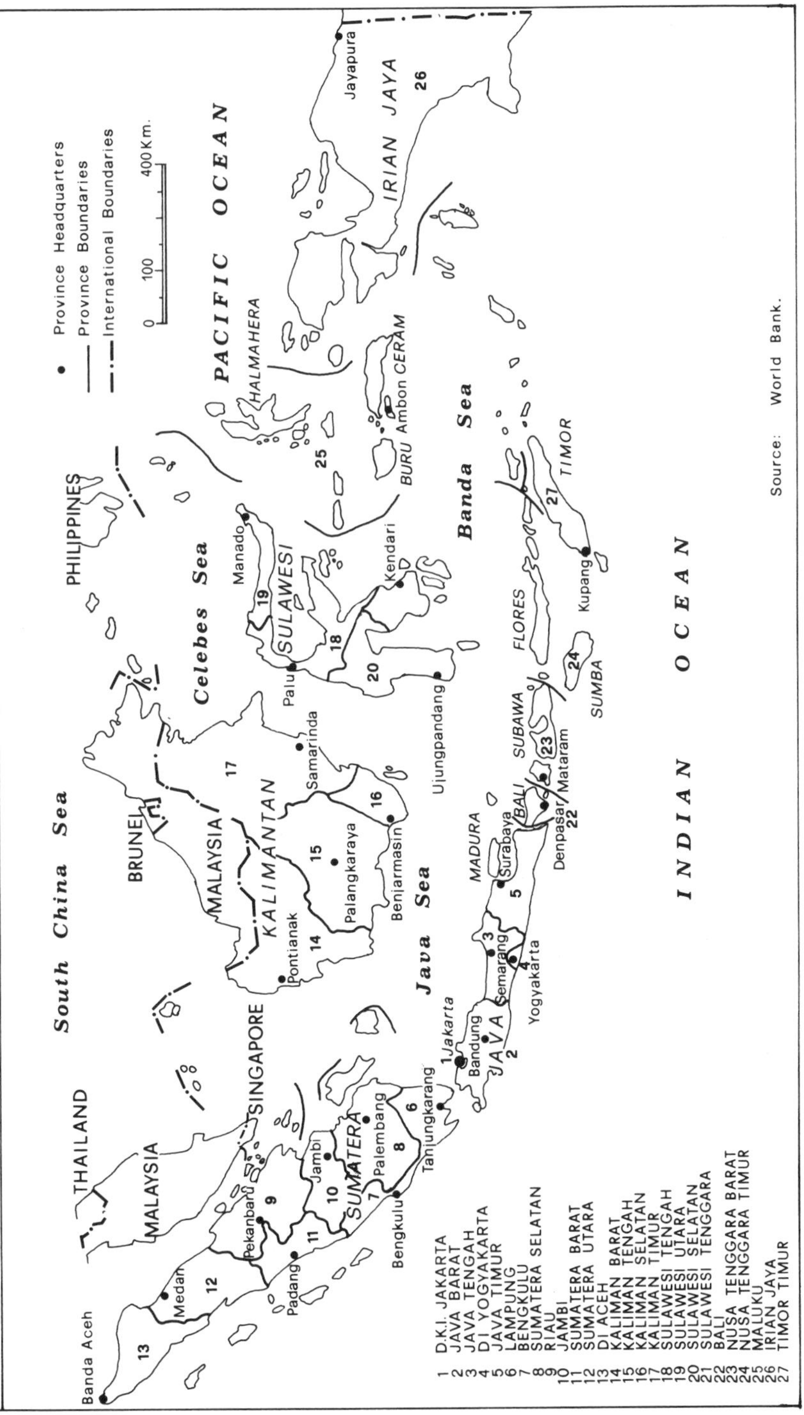
• Province Headquarters
Province Boundaries
International Boundaries
0 100 400 Km.
South China Sea
Celebes Sea
PACIFIC OCEAN
Java Sea
Banda Sea
INDIAN OCEAN
THAILAND
MALAYSIA
SINGAPORE
BRUNEI
PHILIPPINES
KALIMANTAN
SULAWESI
SUMATERA
JAVA
HALMAHERA
CERAM
BURU
IRIAN JAYA
TIMOR
FLORES
SUMBA
SUBAWA
BALI
MADURA
Banda Aceh
Medan
Padang
Pekanbaru
Jambi
Palembang
Bengkulu
Tanjungkarang
Jakarta
Bandung
Semarang
Yogyakarta
Surabaya
Denpasar
Mataram
Pontianak
Palangkaraya
Benjarmasin
Samarinda
Ujungpandang
Palu
Manado
Kendari
Ambon
Kupang
Jayapura
1 D.K.I. JAKARTA
2 JAVA BARAT
3 JAVA TENGAH
4 DI YOGYAKARTA
5 JAVA TIMUR
6 LAMPUNG
7 BENGKULU
8 SUMATERA SELATAN
9 RIAU
10 JAMBI
11 SUMATERA BARAT
12 SUMATERA UTARA
13 DI ACEH
14 KALIMAN BARAT
15 KALIMAN TENGAH
16 KALIMAN SELATAN
17 KALIMAN TIMUR
18 SULAWESI TENGAH
19 SULAWESI UTARA
20 SULAWESI SELATAN
21 SULAWESI TENGGARA
22 BALI
23 NUSA TENGGARA BARAT
24 NUSA TENGGARA TIMUR
25 MALUKU
26 IRIAN JAYA
27 TIMOR TIMUR

Source: World Bank.

With the possible exception of Canada, no major country of the world has such a long coastline in relation to its area.

Indonesia is a major part of the Sunda Mountain chain, which extends from Burma to New Guinea. The mountain chain was formed by tectonic pressure between the continental (orogenic) plates of Asia and Australasia and the volcanic activity accompanying the resultant upward buckling of the Earth's crust.

The mountains so formed have been subjected to much geological erosion, with displacement of material to areas of downward buckling. The relief of Indonesia's islands therefore includes, typically, some mountainous areas, with elevations of 1 000-3 000 m, incised foothills, and greater or lesser amounts of flatter land at, or slightly above, sea level. In the areas of volcanic activity, notably in Sumatra, Java, Northern Sulawesi, and the Lesser Sunda Islands, the most distinctive mountain features are the recently formed volcanic cones.

From the complex geophysical structure an equally complex soil pattern has evolved. Generally, the most fertile soils have developed either on deeply weathered ancient volcanic deposits, or on secondary depositions of this material; contrary to popular belief, much of the soil developed directly on more recent volcanic deposits does not display the highest agricultural potential. Where developed on material derived from granite rocks or from ancient slates, shales and metamorphosed formations, as is the case over large areas of Sumatra, Kalimantan and parts of Sulawesi, the soil tends to be less fertile.

The greatest concentrations of old volcanic material are found in Java and Bali, hence the generally higher soil fertility levels on these islands. This explains to a great extent why these two islands, together with Madura (collectively the so-called Inner Islands), have had a long history of settlement, and why some 62 percent of the population still live there, although the islands make up only slightly more than 7 percent of the total land area (Government of Indonesia 1984d, 1984e).

The total population is now estimated to be about 178 million, making Indonesia the fifth most populous country in the world. The rate of increase is now put at about 2 percent per annum.

Most Indonesians in the western and northern islands are ethnically similar to the people of the Malayan peninsula. In the other parts, however, similarities to Papuan, Melanesian and indigenous Australian people have been noted. In addition to its indigenous population, Indonesia also has a large community - possibly as large as 2 million - of people of Chinese origin.

Reflecting its geographical spread and insular fragmentation, many languages and dialects have evolved in Indonesia; some 25 distinct languages and 250 dialects have been recognised. Since gaining independence, however, official propagation of the national language, Bahasa Indonesia, has eliminated many communication difficulties.

Islam is the stated religion of some 80 percent of the Indonesians. Of the remainder, some, as in Bali, adhere to Hinduism, which spread over much of Java in earlier times, and there are also substantial numbers of Christians. In the western islands, some people, more particularly in the interior, remain animists.

During the last millennium, various external influences have affected Indonesia's history and cultural development. Before 1600, the main influence was exerted by India; Hinduism thus became the dominant religion until supplanted by Islam during the period 1400-1900. Colonial enclaves were established by the Dutch around 1600, initiating a period of European dominance that was finally eliminated only with independence in 1949.

Administrative Divisions

For administrative purposes, and also in recognition of some of the historic political entities, Indonesia is divided into 27 provincial areas. Thus, Java has its West, Central and East provinces (the latter including Madura Island) and the special provinces of Jakarta and Yogyakarta.

Sumatra has the special province of Aceh, the North, West and South provinces, and the provinces of Riau, Jambi, Bengkulu and Lampung. Bali is a province, as is Timor. Lombok and Sumbawa constitute West Nusa Tenggara, and Flores, Sumba and several smaller islands constitute East Nusa Tenggara.

Kalimantan is divided into West, Central, South and East provinces, and Sulawesi has North, Central and Southeast provinces. The two remaining provinces are Maluku, which includes all the Molucca Islands group, and Irian Jaya.

Each province is subdivided into a number of regencies (*kabupaten*); in some instances these incorporate the main conurbations, but in others such urban areas are separate municipalities (*kotamadya*). In all, there are 246 *kabupaten* and 55 *kotamadya*.

The regencies are divided into 3 529 subregencies (*kecamatan*). Each *kecamatan* comprises a number of villages (*desa*), each of which usually includes a number of hamlets or dwelling clusters. The total number of villages in 1984 was 67 534. The chief administrator of a province is the governor, who is appointed by, and reports to, the president. A *kabupaten* is headed by a *bupati*; a *kecamatan* is headed by a *camat*, and at the *desa* level a *lurah* (village head) is appointed and paid by the Government.

Macro-economic Setting

In Indonesia multiple relations exist between developments in the domestic economy - whether agricultural or non-agricultural sectors - and the nature and dimension of changes taking place in world commodity markets (including oil and gas). The results of these external economic ties are embodied, in particular, in the balance of payments and government finance accounts.

The fact that substantial segments of the agricultural and rural sectors are affected by trends in the overall economy reinforces the obvious need to reflect on the adjustments in the structure of the production system and the responses of the policy makers to the changing external environment of the Indonesian economy.

Structural Change in the Economy Since 1970

Performance of Aggregate Variables. The trend data on macro-economic performance in the 1970s and 1980s clearly shows the dominant role of oil exports - more recently joined by sales of liquid natural gas (LNG) - in influencing aggregate variables. Increased production levels, at least until 1977-78, and export volumes, as well as very favourable terms of trade effects (resulting from the 1973 and 1979 oil price rises), allowed for substantial growth in aggregate expenditure categories, in particular during the 1970s (see Table 2.1). It should be noted that, while in 1971 the share of oil exports in total value of exports amounted to 23 percent, this proportion had increased to almost 75 percent in the second half of the 1970s.

The growth rates of macro-economic variables from 1980 to 1988 indicate, however, a picture quite different from that of the preceding decade. A changing oil situation beginning in 1983 led to a substantially declining absolute value of oil exports and of its share in total exports. This was compounded by the rapid and lagged increase of non-oil imports during the period of 1979-80 to 1983-84 (from US $ 9.0 to US $ 14.8 billion). In real terms over the period 1980-84, the value of imports continued to grow at an average rate of 5 percent

Table 2.1: Aggregate Variables: Real Average Annual Growth Rates (1970-80, 1980-84, 1984-88) (Based on Rupiahs at constant 1987 prices)

	1970-80	1980-84	1984-88
GNP	7.18	6.28	5.87
GDP	7.23	5.61	4.76
Imports	17.35	5.12	-2.35
Exports	9.22	-5.20	5.32
Private consumption	6.94	7.95	2.60
General government consumption	13.11	4.99	4.40
Gross domestic investment	13.85	16.27	3.67

Source: World Bank (1991b).

per annum while exports actually experienced a negative growth of 5 percent per annum over this period. Furthermore, in contrast to the fairly rapid expansion of private consumption expenditure (8 percent per year), gross domestic investment experienced a zero growth, except for the first year of this period. This was a reflection of the slowing down of exploration activities in the oil sector and of the policy measures taken during 1983 in response to the rapidly deteriorating external and internal balances of the economy.

During 1985-88, the depreciation of the US Dollar was another source of external shocks, as a large proportion of Indonesia's debt is in currencies which appreciated against the US Dollar. The combination of lower oil prices and adverse currency fluctuations led to a rapid increase in Indonesia's debt service burden over this period.

The Government responded with two types of policy adjustments to alleviate this situation. Firstly, it adopted more austere macro-economic policies to restore financial stability. Secondly, it embarked on a major programme to restructure the economy, aimed both at reducing Indonesia's heavy dependence on oil as a source of foreign exchange and budgetary revenues, and at improving economic efficiency.

The impact of the structural changes taking place is clearly demonstrated in Tables 2.1 and 2.2. Imports decreased in the four year period 1984-88, although their share in GDP remained constant. The share of total exports of goods and non-factor services in the GDP decreased from its high level in 1980 (33 percent) to around 25 percent between 1984 and 1988. In terms of absolute change, exports recovered to an average growth of 5 percent per annum during 1984-88. Both private consumption expenditures and general government consumption saw a modest growth of 3 percent and

Table 2.2: Aggregate Variables as Percentage of the GDP (Current Rupiahs)

	1970	1975	1980	1984	1989
GNP	100.43	97.47	95.89	95.37	95.14
Factor payments to abroad (net)	-0.43	2.53	4.11	4.63	4.86
Imports of goods and n.f.s.[1]	14.98	21.03	20.21	22.08	21.95
Exports of goods and n.f.s.[1]	12.99	23.21	33.04	25.59	24.41
Private consumption	78.13	65.12	52.33	60.15	57.07
General government consumption	8.00	9.04	10.52	10.15	8.98
Gross domestic investment	15.83	23.66	24.32	26.19	31.49

[1] Non-factor services.

Source: World Bank (1991b).

4 percent, respectively, and gross domestic investment performed better than previous years, with an average growth of around 4 percent per annum.

Sectoral Composition of the GDP. During the 1970s the share of agriculture (including cash crop production, livestock, forestry and fisheries) fell from almost half to around one-quarter of the GDP. Chapter 3 gives a further elaboration of agriculture's role in the economy and the relative weight and performance of its various subsectors. In contrast to this decline was the relative expansion of the mining and quarrying sector - heavily dominated, of course, by oil production. Its share rose from 5.2 percent in 1970 to about 25 percent in 1980 - a consequence principally of the two price jumps in the world oil market in 1973 and 1979.

From 1980 to 1988, the sectoral product trends - from the point of view of public finance, employment and income generation and distribution - were very different from those of the previous decade. The price fall in oil since 1981-82 was the main determinant (reinforced by a progressive decline in oil production) of the diminishing importance of oil production in the economy, which fell to a share in the GDP of around 18 percent in 1984 and declined further to 14 percent in 1988. Oil production comprises oil and natural gas mining, oil refining and gas processing. On the other hand, at least up to 1988, the position of agriculture stabilised at slightly below 25 percent of the GDP. Favourable output trends in some major crops, in particular rice, resulted during the period 1980-88 in a 5.3 percent annual increase. Manufacturing, which had seen a modest growth during the 1960s, enjoyed high growth rates in the 1980s of around 13 percent per annum and continued this strong performance up to 1988 (see Table 2.3).

Table 2.3: Trends in Sectoral Values Added, percent 1965-90 (Annual Growth Rates at Constant Factor Cost)

	1965-73	1973-80	1980-90
GDP (at constant 1987 prices)	6.6	7.2	5.3
Agriculture	4.8	7.3	5.3
Industry	15.2	7.3	5.3
of which: Manufacturing	9.0	14.7	12.7
Services	5.0	10.1	6.6

Source: World Bank (1991a).

In concluding this section, brief mention should be made of the employment-generating role of the various sectors. Specific employment issues such as participation rates, productivity, seasonality and income levels in rural areas and in agriculture are dealt with in subsequent sections. According to the population censuses of 1971 and 1980, the share of the total labour force engaged in all agricultural activities during the 1970s dropped from 66 percent to 57 percent (see Table 2.4) and only 28 percent of the new entrants into the national labour market were absorbed by agriculture. However, some major differentiation in labour absorption took place. While employment in cash crops, livestock, forestry and fisheries, combined, increased from 6 percent to 9 percent of the total labour force, the share of employment in food crops declined from 60 percent to 48 percent. Chapter 4 gives a further analysis of these trends.

While only slightly over one-fourth of the incremental labour force found new jobs in agriculture, other sectors became relatively much more important in absorbing other new entrants. Thus, estimates are that up to 18 percent of the incremental labour force was absorbed by manufacturing, and 17 percent by the trade sector. The largest source of employment for the new entrants has been public services, where almost 30 percent found new employment (see Table 2.4).

Recent Price Developments

The hyperinflationary trends of the second half of the 1960s were followed by more moderate price increases in the early 1970s. Nevertheless, from 1973-80 the consumer price index averaged an increase of 17 percent annually. The rate of inflation levelled off further in the period 1980-90 to an average yearly rate of less than 10 percent (see Table 2.5).

Table 2.4: Employment Per Sector Percentage (1971, 1985)

	1971	1985
Agriculture, forestry, hunting and fishery	64	55
Mining and quarrying	0.2	0.7
Manufacturing	7	9
Construction	2	3
Wholesale and retail trade and restaurants	10	15
Transport, storage and communication	2	3
Public services	10	13
Other	5	2
Total labour force	100	100

Source: Government of Indonesia, Biro Pusat Statistik (1985d).

External Trade and Balance of Payments

Overall Trends in Trade and Balance of Payments. External relations play a significant role in Indonesia's economy. From 1980 to 1988 exports of goods and non-factor services accounted for 24-33 percent of the GDP. Similarly, the import ratio fluctuated around 20 percent of the GDP. Since the early 1970s, the external performance of the economy has been dependent in particular on oil production, while in the latter half of the decade LNG sales contributed to the expansion of exports. These two energy sectors typically accounted for 45-70 percent of gross export earnings from 1980-81 to 1988-89.

The sharp increases in world oil prices in 1973 and 1979 led to very significant improvements in the terms of trade, which eventually resulted in terms of trade indices of 300 or above in the period 1980-84 (1973 = 100). This remarkable rise in the import capacity fueled a similar growth of imports.

The current account of the balance of payments deteriorated gradually to create a US$ 1.2 billion gap in fiscal year 1978-79. However, the jump in the world oil price in 1979 once more improved the external payments position. The drastically improved export performance was also affected by favourable world prices of Indonesia's non-oil export commodities, such as timber, rubber and coffee. With the value of exports of these three above mentioned products rising from US$ 2.4 billion in 1978-79 to US$ 4 billion in 1979-80, total non-oil exports went up from US$ 4 billion to US$ 6.2 billion. These favourable trends led to positive outcomes. During 1979-80 and 1980-81 the surplus amounted to US $2.2 billion and US $2.1 billion, that is, 5 percent and 3.6 percent of the GDP,

Table 2.5: Selected Indicators of Prices 1980-90 (Index 1987 = 100)

	1980	1981	1985	1986	1988	1989	1990 P	Percent per Year 1873-80	1980-90
Implicit GDP deflator	55.5	..	86.2	86.3	107.6	117.4	125.0	19.8	8.3
Consumer prices	54.4	..	86.5	91.5	108.0	115.0	..	17.0	8.5
Wholesale prices	50.4	..	82.6	82.8	107.2	114.7	126.2	20.3	9.6
Export prices	..	143.5	115.4	100.0*	104.1	110.2	123.6	..	..

Note: P is provisional.
    .. Not available.
    * 1987 figure.

Source: World Bank (1991a).

respectively. Concurrently, external reserves rose by US$ 1.7 billion and US$ 2.7 billion during these two fiscal years.

The trend was reversed starting in 1981-82 when, with stagnating exports and rising imports, the current account deficit widened from US$ 2.8 billion to US$ 7.1 billion (or 7.5 percent of the GDP). Foreign reserves dropped by US$ 3.3 billion. Confronted with these phenomena and without prospects of a reversal of the unfavourable commodity demand and price developments, policy makers decided to take adjustment measures in early 1983. Projections had indicated that in the absence of such corrective policies the current account deficit for 1983-84 would have reached a level of about US$ 10 billion, or more than 10 percent of the GDP.

The adjustments taken focused on public finances, public investment programmes, monetary policies, deregulation and foreign exchange area. Austerity measures included reduction in subsidies on oil products, food and fertilizers. At the same time, efforts were made to broaden the tax base in the economy. The public investment programme was also rephased. The 125 projects affected by this decision included a total foreign exchange of US$ 21 billion. It is estimated that the cancellation or postponement of these projects implied foreign exchange savings of about US$ 10 billion. Moreover, the rephasing and the decrease in the number of infrastructure projects caused a 17 percent drop in real public capital formation in 1983-84.

After the November 1978 devaluation, the real effective rate had appreciated 41 percent in the period up to March 1983; about one-quarter was the effect of an appreciation in the nominal effective rate while the remainder originated from the rise in relative prices. It had adversely affected the export competitiveness of major commodities - the value of non-oil exports declined by almost 40 percent between 1979-80 and 1982-83. The devaluation of the rupiah by 28 percent in March 1983 nevertheless affected the various balance of payments items most significantly. Still, moderate increases in international prices of major commodities (timber, rubber, coffee and tea) also contributed to the improvement of the current account balance. Higher export receipts, combined with the fall in the value of non-oil imports, reduced the current account deficit to US$ 3.9 billion or 4.9 percent of the GDP in 1983-84. The March 1983 currency realignment and additional adjustment measures were reflected even more substantially in the 1984-85 balance of payments. For that year, the current account deficit of US$ 1.8 billion - or 2.1 percent of the GDP - stayed US$ 5.3 billion below the 1982-83 level. While one-fourth of the decline in the deficit resulted from an improvement of the oil/LNG current account, the remaining 75 percent of the narrowing of the gap was caused by the improvement in the non-oil trade balance.

In 1985-86, a sharp drop in oil prices has been the principal factor governing the changes in the balance of payments. In average terms, the 12 percent decline in the export price of crude oil and oil products, combined with a 9 percent decrease in the real price of non-oil exports and a 17 percent depreciation of the real effective exchange rate, led to a 14 percent worsening in the terms of trade. Because of weak commodity prices the proceeds of non-oil gas exports stagnated as well. However, non-oil imports decreased concomitantly by US$ 2.1 billion. Major determinants of the latter were the anticipation of reduced oil receipts, depreciation of the real effective exchange rate and quantitative restrictions. The end result of all these movements was a slight worsening in the current account deficit to US$ 2.1 billion (about 2.5 percent of the GDP, compared with 2.1 percent in 1984-85). More recently, the current account recovered from a US$ 3.9 million deficit in 1986-87 to US$ 1.4 million deficit in 1988-89. This improvement was for a large part the result of the non-oil exports which grew by 13 percent per year in real terms during the 1983-88 period. This was in response to the appropriate exchange rate policies and the series of deregulations reforms started in 1985.

Experience in Non-oil Exports. After the exchange rate adjustment of March 1983 non-oil exports - which, as mentioned earlier, had experienced a decline of some 40 percent in value between 1979-80 and 1982-83 - rose by more than half over the years 1983-84 and 1984-85 (see Table 2.6). Principal modifications in the commodity composition of exports from 1979-80 to 1984-85 were, firstly, a decline in the share of agricultural and forestry products from over 80 percent to about 60 percent of the total; secondly, an increase of manufactured goods from 5 percent to 25; and, thirdly, a virtual stabilization at around 11-12 percent of mining products (see Table 2.6).

Recent Exchange Rate Measures and Effects. In the period following the March 1983 devaluation, a flexible exchange rate policy was applied with a fully convertible currency. As noted earlier, this adjustment restored the competitiveness of the traded goods sector of non-oil exports to approximately the level prevailing immediately after the November 1978 devaluation.

Following a slightly appreciated real effective exchange rate in the period from July-August 1983 to mid-1985, in the second half of 1985 a 12 percent depreciation of the real effective exchange rate materialized. Consequently, in March 1986 the real effective exchange

Table 2.6: Trend and Composition of Non-oil Exports (as percentage of total non-oil exports)

	1979-80	1980-81	1981-82	1982-83	1983-84	1984-85	1985-86[1]	1986-87	1987-88	1988-89
Agriculture and forestry	82.9	76.5	70.2	69.3	62.8	62.0	62.1	66.8	60.7	56.9
Forestry products	35.1	29.9	22.8	22.9	21.6	19.7	19.8	23.6	25.9	23.7
Rubber	17.8	19.3	18.5	15.7	18.3	14.5	10.9	11.1	10.9	10.1
Palm oil	4.2	3.2	1.9	2.6	1.7	1.6	3.3	1.7	2.3	2.6
Coffee	11.6	10.5	8.2	9.2	9.4	9.6	11.2	11.2	5.3	4.7
Tea	1.5	1.7	2.3	3.0	2.9	3.6	2.2	1.6	1.3	1.1
Tobacco	1.0	1.2	1.2	0.9	0.9	0.7	0.9	1.1	0.5	0.4
Pepper	0.7	0.9	1.2	1.0	1.1	1.1	1.8	2.3	1.7	1.2
Animal products	4.1	4.0	5.1	6.4	5.1	3.7	4.1	5.8	5.1	6.9
Shrimp	3.5	3.0	4.0	5.2	3.8	3.1	3.6	4.4	3.7	4.4
Others	6.9	5.7	9.1	7.6	7.1	7.5	7.8	8.5	7.8	6.2
Minerals	9.9	13.8	18.1	17.2	14.9	13.1	13.0	10.7	11.7	12.8
Manufactured goods[2]	7.3	9.7	11.6	13.5	16.9	24.9	24.9	22.6	27.6	30.4
Total Non-oil Exports (in millions of US$)	6 172	5 590	4 172	3 929	5 368	5 907	5 865	6 731	9 502	12 184

1 Estimate.
2 Including unclassified.

Source: IFAD estimates based on information provided to the mission.

rate, 93.9 (December 1978 = 100), was substantially below the rate prevailing in the period immediately prior to the March 1983 devaluation (139.8), and there seemed to be no apparent urgency for a downward adjustment of the Rupiah. In addition, foreign reserves amounted to US$ 10.7 billion - of which US$ 5.8 billion was in the nature of official reserves - or the equivalent of nine months of imports of merchandise. For the next two years the Rupiah continued to depreciate.

External Resource Flows and Indebtedness. Over the last decade and a half, both the external total (including private non-guaranteed) and public debt have been increasing significantly. While total long-term external debt (disbursed and outstanding) rose from US$ 2.9 billion in 1970 to US$ 45.5 billion in 1988, external public debt alone expanded from US$ 2.5 billion to US$ 41.3 billion between 1970 and 1988. Notwithstanding this absolute growth there was no dramatic change in the relative weight of external indebtedness in the economy up to 1984. This is illustrated as follows. With total external debt increasing from 32.2 percent to 35.2 percent of the GNP over the period 1970-84, public and publicly guaranteed long-term debt rose from 27.1 percent to 30.2 percent of the GNP. Although Indonesia, compared with most other lower- middle-income economies, started off with a considerable external debt in 1970, its public indebtedness expanded much less than that of equivalent economies. This group's weighted average of the external public debt ratio (to GNP) increased from 15.2 percent to 35.0 percent during the period 1970-85. However, the four year period from 1984-88 did show a considerable increase in this ratio up to 67 percent of GDP in 1988. Almost all of this was in the form of public long-term debt.

Over the period 1980-88, debt service payments expanded considerably, both in absolute terms and relative to export earnings. Non-weighted average terms for the period 1980-88 were as follows: (i) interest rate, 7.5 percent; (ii) maturity period, 17.5 years; (iii) grace period, 5.8 years; (iv) grant element, 6.6 percent. The heavily commercial nature of borrowing terms (in 1984 more than 40 percent of disbursed and outstanding debt was provided by private creditors, especially commercial banks) as well as the sustained long-term borrowings increased total debt service from US$ 2.8 billion to US$ 8.5 billion in the period 1980-88. The public debt service ratio (i.e., interest and principal payments to total exports) reached a level of 42.7 percent in 1988, including amortization of LNG expansion credits, as compared to 13.9 percent in 1980.

These facts, combined with the uncertainties characterizing the world oil market and the not very favourable short- and medium-term outlook for Indonesia's main agricultural and mining commodities, have made for a cautious policy of debt management, capital inflows and close monitoring of the external balance imperative.

Management and Impact of Public Finances

Principal Developments in Revenues and Expenditures (1979-80 to 1985-86). During the second half of the 1970s, public finances were greatly affected by the rapid increase in oil revenue. A steep rise in tax receipts was followed by a sharp expansion in routine expenditure. (The difference with current expenditures is that the latter excludes amortization payments and includes fertilizer subsidies as well as the recurrent component of development expenditures.) All in all, the current budgetary surplus stabilized at around 9 percent of the GDP over the period 1979-80 to 1981-82. However, in 1982-83, that is, just before the squeeze implemented in the second quarter of 1983, the current account surplus fell to 7.2 percent of the GDP (see Table 2.7). That the stabilization policy implied concrete results is evidenced by the increased government current account surplus from fiscal year 1983-84 up to 1988-89.

The public sector in Indonesia is composed of the Central Government, 27 provincial governments (including Jakarta and two special regions - Aceh and Yogyakarta), 289 municipal and local governments and about 220 public enterprises.

In the period following the 1983 policy measures, three major changes in the relative priority of the expenditures programmes dominated: firstly, the decline in the share of the central departments; secondly, the growing importance of transfers to lower level government; and, thirdly, the doubling of development expenditures through the channel of project aid. Throughout the period 1979-80 to 1988-89 the allocation for the key social service sectors was kept at approximately the same percentage. In contrast, development expenditures for agriculture and irrigation, and transportation fluctuated rather significantly. Regarding agriculture and irrigation, while experiencing a substantial rise in these outlays from 1979-80 to 1980-81 - from 12.7 percent to 15.7 percent - during the remaining part of REPELITA III their share dropped gradually to only 5.8 percent in 1984-85 but increased again to 12.3 percent in 1988-89. This is in sharp contrast with the 24 percent contribution of agriculture to the total GDP.

Table 2.7: Selected Government Finance Indicators (Percent GDP)

	1979-80	1980-81	1981-82	1982-83	1983-84	1984-85	1985-86	1986-87	1987-88	1988-89
Current budgetary surplus	8.6	9.7	8.5	7.2	9.4	10.7	7.7	3.3	5.7	5.7
Overall surplus or deficit (-)	1.2	2.1	-2.3	-4.8	-2.6	0.6	-7.9	-4.5	-1.9	-3.3
Borrowing from banking sector	-3.6	-3.8	-0.2	1.4	-2.4	-3.2	0.8	0.3	0.1	0.2
Foreign borrowing (net)	2.3	1.8	2.5	3.5	5.0	2.6	2.1	4.4	1.9	3.0
Net domestic expenditures[1]	8.1	10.3	13.3	11.6	9.8	9.3	10.7	8.4	10.2	8.3

[1] Domestic content of current and investment expenditures less non-oil revenues; it measures the excess of Government Rupiah expenditures to its Rupiah revenue and is an indicator of the net, first-round effect of the budgetary operations of the economy through domestic demand.

Source: IMF (1990).

Apparently higher priority was assigned to the transportation (and tourism) sector. In 1988-89, these sectors obtained about 17 percent of development expenditures compared to relatively modest shares in the beginning of this decade.

Budgetary Developments and Adjustments in the Mid-1980s

For REPELITA IV the GDP growth target was set at 5 percent per annum. The significant GDP growth rate foreseen in the plan was to be accompanied by substantial increases in routine and development expenditures in the government budget.

The adverse developments in the external sector (i.e., the worsening balance of payments and sharply declining government revenues), however, have caused major readjustments in the two expenditure categories. For example, the total expenditures for 1985-86 approved in the budget were 7.4 percent below the level originally planned in the REPELITA IV document. Although the final budget for routine outlays was 3 percent higher than the REPELITA IV figure, the development budget had been set at 17 percent below the plan figure (see Table 2.8).

The fall in oil revenues, the depressed commodity prices and, more specifically, the prudent fiscal policies of the Government ultimately made strong cutbacks in 1986-87 inevitable. Total expenditures and net government lending in 1986-87 were projected to fall by 9 percent - reflecting the desire of policy makers to pursue austerity measures. Whereas most expenditures categories were cut, the amount allocated to subsidies was 13 percent above the 1985-86 budget.

This included a new subsidy to the National Food Procurement and Distribution Agency (BULOG) to cover the costs for the storage of rice in view of the new supply-and-demand conditions. The fertilizer subsidy, although 19 percent under the estimated actual allocation for 1985-86 of Rp 825 billion, still accounted for 8 percent of the total development expenditures.

The tightening revenue position also affected the financing of development expenditure. Compared with the actual 1985-86 figures, in line with expectations, Rupiah-financed development expenditures (*inter alia*, outlays for defence, fertilizer subsidies and the recently defunct export certificates scheme) fell by about one-third, whereas foreign contributions were kept unchanged, at least in nominal terms. As a consequence, the external contribution to development expenditures rose from 32 percent to 42 percent. Considering the sombre outlook for oil export earnings (for fiscal years 1986 and

Table 2.8: Expenditures Planned in Repelita IV and Approved Expenditure Budgets (APBN)

Budget Component/Year	REPELITA IV (Rp Billion)	APBN	Percent Difference APBN Compared to REPELITA IV
Routine budget			
1984-85	10 101.1	10 101.1	0.0
1985-86	12 042.8	12 399.0	3.0
1986-87	14 582.5	13 125.6	-10.0
Development budget			
1984-85	10 459.3	10 459.3	0.0
1985-86	12 849.0	10 647.0	-17.1
1986-87	15 415.2	8 296.0	-46.2
Total expenditures			
1984-85	20 560.4	20 560.4	0.0
1985-86	24 891.8	23 046.0	-7.4
1986-87	29 997.7	21 421.6	-28.6

Source: Paauw and Stavenuiter (1986).

1987), the very tight balance of payments position and the likely overall government deficits, requirements for a substantial contribution of foreign capital to the financing of government development outlays remained unaltered. This is despite further cut-backs in imports and in public sector expenditures.

For the purpose of reducing development expenditures for the 1986-87 budget, a number of decisions were made by the end of 1985. In the first place, no new exclusively Rupiah-financed projects would be started in 1986-87. Furthermore, in the selection of investment projects high priority ratings were given to:

(i) The completion of ongoing projects and the allocation of funds to such projects was to be governed by the absorptive capacity criteria. Furthermore, the decision was made that for the new budget year, carried-over expenditures from SIAPs (i.e., unspent balances) would not be allowed to materialize, except for INPRES programmes.

(ii) Foreign-financed projects with ensured provision of Rupiah counterpart funds.

(iii) The continuation of projects with special focus on equity and employment.

(iv) The provision of resources for the operation and maintenance of projects already completed. This is demonstrated in the shift in expenditures toward the routine budgets for personnel and materials that were not reduced and the continued emphasis laid on operation and maintenance funding in development budgets of infrastructure sectors such as roads and irrigation.

With regard to foreign-financed projects with ensured provision of rupiah counterpart funds, external loan disbursements were projected to attain a level similar to the 1985-86 actual figures. There were two main causes for this rising share of foreign resources - the shortage of counterpart funds and a more critical look at implementation capacity. Nevertheless, externally cofinanced projects have easier access to domestic resources. Examples are the increased counterpart funds for smallholder tree crops and a number of irrigation projects.

Concerning the continuation of projects with special focus on equity and employment, budgetary data indicate that the lower government-oriented INPRES programmes have maintained their allocations in absolute terms despite sharply cut overall development expenditures. Moreover, regional development outlays were the only category in which funds were significantly increased, from Rp 850 billion to 939 billion - or from 7.8 percent to 11.3 percent of total development expenditures. In fact, the main objective of the INPRES programmes is to expand income opportunities for and services to low-income groups and zones, within the context, however, of adhering to a rough regional balance in development expenditures.

With regard to total allocations to agriculture, budgetary resources for this sector in the 1986-87 budget dropped by 22 percent, in line with the curtailment in total development expenditures. On the other hand, compared with the actual figures for 1985-86, the proposed allocation remained essentially at the same level.

Under the 1986-87 budget, agriculture received 13.3 percent of total development expenditures against 10.5 percent in fiscal year 1985-86. It is evident, however, that this relative increase was caused solely by the rise in fertilizer subsidies. Heavily affected by the intended cut-backs were irrigation schemes, partly because of the lower priority given to financing new irrigation projects after achieving self-sufficiency in rice. Presently the Government is placing more emphasis on consolidation and rehabilitation of irrigation works. This reorientation may not be too undesirable to the extent that it leads to concentration on tertiary systems that are very labour intensive, an issue that is discussed later.

For the first time in almost 20 years, the budget of 1986-87, as announced by the President on 7 January 1986, included a drop in total expenditures. As indicated earlier, development expenditures were heavily affected by this curtailment. An oil price of US$ 25 per barrel had been the basic underlying assumption for determining the magnitude of total Government outlays. However, as early as mid-January it became clear that this price level was much too optimistic in relation to the price adjustments occurring in the world oil market. (Each US$ 1 decrease in the price of oil (exported) negatively affects Indonesian trade balance by around US$ 400 million with tax revenues falling by Rp 300 billion.) Assuming an average oil price of US$ 15 per barrel, the estimated additional reduction in revenues was assessed at Rp 3 trillion, about 15 percent lower than the original level of receipts. These extremely adverse events made it urgent to review and compare the nature and potential effects of a number of different policy instruments, particularly on the rural poor.

A crucial question is that of the impact of budgetary cuts on employment and incomes. The creation of sufficient job opportunities is a key to the alleviation of poverty on the one hand, and a continuation of economic growth on the other. Indonesian policy makers - as reflected, for instance, by the REPELITA IV document - emphasize the fundamental importance of providing employment opportunities to help the urban and rural poor.

The number of employment opportunities and the level and distribution of labour income are basic determinants of the welfare of the landless rural population and marginal farmers, which accounted for some 70 percent of the country's population and work force and roughly 75 percent of the households living in poverty in 1980. It must be kept in mind that the growth of the rural labour force (supply side) - estimated at some 1.5 percent per annum for the entire country in the 1980s - is likely to be about 3 percent in the Outer Islands and roughly 1 percent in Java and Bali.

The fact that Java's agricultural sector has already reached the turning point, characterized by an absolute decline in the size of the agricultural labour force combined with the limited capacity of the Outer Islands to absorb productively new transmigrants in agriculture, means that the burden of providing new jobs will fall increasingly on non-agriculture activities and the informal sector (see Chapter 4). The level (and the sectoral and regional distribution) of public expenditures is a major policy instrument and should be regarded as an important source of autonomous income growth. Government outlays affect demand for labour: firstly, by way of the direct employment created by the investment projects; secondly, by employment expansion in sectors wherein production increase is a result of public investment demand; and, thirdly, through demand side multiplier effects from household income created by public expenditure, including current outlays.

An employment impact analysis of the original REPELITA IV document concluded that the sectoral expenditure pattern as put forward was more labour intensive than that of the preceding plan. It was estimated that the envisaged public expenditure programme would enable an expansion of direct and indirect employment roughly similar to the growth of the total labour force. In addition, by stressing expenditures in agriculture, local infrastructure and other programmes (e.g., transmigration) with a relatively low import content, employment absorption capacity would have been higher than under REPELITA III.

It has been mentioned earlier that the overall economic impact of the 1986-87 budget - that is, net domestic expenditures amounting to 5.6 percent of the GDP - was the lowest of the period elapsed since the start of REPELITA I (1969). Consequently, the employment and income-generating capacity of rural development programmes were likely to fall.

In order to reduce to the maximum possible extent, the adverse impact of the necessary budgetary adjustment measures taken on employment and incomes of the asset-poor or assetless rural households during the remaining years of REPELITA IV and beyond, public expenditures should be focused on smaller-scale, less capital-intensive projects.

Chapter 3

Agricultural Performance, Structure and Resource Base

Role of Agriculture in the Economy

In a country at Indonesia's stage of development, agriculture has to make a number of major and interrelated contributions to the process of socio-economic development. Firstly and foremost, it has to contribute to the GDP and provide food for a growing population and raw materials for the industrial sector. Secondly, it must provide productive employment opportunities and income for the bulk of the population residing in the rural areas. Thirdly, it must play a crucial role in alleviating poverty and malnutrition through a structure and pattern of production that allows small farmers and landless agricultural workers to share in the benefits of agricultural growth. Finally, agriculture must contribute to improving the balance of payments situation - through increased exports (foreign exchange earnings), import substitution (saving foreign exchange) and reduced dependence of the economy on foreign sources of (food) supply.

Since 1970, the Indonesian economy has undergone a structural transformation characteristic of countries in the relatively early phases of development. The relative share of agriculture (including livestock, forestry and fishery) in the GDP (at current prices) fell from about 32 percent in 1974-75 to about 26 percent in 1986-87, while the relative share of agricultural employment in the total labour force declined from about 67 percent in the early 1970s to 55 percent throughout the mid-eighties. There are however different estimates of sectoral employment; on the basis of the Input-Output Tables, the share of agricultural employment fell from 67.2 percent in 1971 to 58.3 percent in 1980, while according to 1976 National Labour Force Survey (SAKERNAS) and 1982 SUSENAS data this share declined from 61.6 percent in 1976 to 54.7 percent in 1982.

The aggregate performance of the agricultural GDP (at constant 1973 prices) over the period 1974-80 was good - although not spectacular. The agricultural GDP grew at an annual rate of 3.3 percent, farm food crops at 3.6 percent and estate crops at 5.0 percent (see Table 3.1). Essentially, the same growth pattern continued in the eighties (see Table 3.2), expressed at constant 1983 prices) with agricultural GDP growing at 3.0 percent per year between 1980 and 1987. A significant slowdown in the growth rate of estate crops can be noticed. The performance in the paddy subsector was superlative, as discussed later in this chapter, leading to virtual rice self-sufficiency by the mid-1980s. There is no doubt that it is the sector that contributed most to agricultural growth.

Agriculture continued to absorb employment and productivity at an annual growth rate of 1.4 percent between 1971 and 1980. As can be seen from Table 3.3, the employment picture differed significantly from one subsector to another. Food crops (mainly paddy) displayed the lowest growth rate of employment and the highest labour productivity rate. Although the labour productivity estimates presented in Table 3.3 have to be taken as highly speculative, there is no doubt that the employment elasticity in food crops was very low (estimated at 0.13) in contrast to the other agricultural subsectors. This means, for example, that a 10 percent increase in food crops' production would only give rise to a 1.3 percent increase in food crops' employment. On the whole, the capacity of agriculture to provide additional employment opportunities was quite limited during the 1970s (the overall employment elasticity was estimated at 0.27). It will be shown in Chapter 4 that Indonesia is nearing the so-called turning point, at which the size of the absolute labour force in agriculture can no longer increase, and will gradually begin to decline. This broad picture hides some important regional differences and recent trends (which will also be discussed in Chapter 4).

Evidence regarding trends in food consumption and caloric intake (see Chapter 5) show that average food consumption improved markedly until the early 1980s. Likewise, evidence that will be presented in Chapter 4 suggests that all target groups (in particular the landless agricultural workers and the small farmers) benefited from the growth pattern prevailing throughout the 1970s. The proportion of rural poor (based on a poverty line estimated on the basis of calorie requirements and household budgets; see Rao 1984) appears to have declined significantly as well. In brief, agriculture continued to improve food consumption and nutrition, and to alleviate poverty to some extent.

Table 3.1: Gross Domestic Product by Industrial Origin at Constant 1973 Market Prices (Old Series), 1974-80 (Rp. billion)

	1974	1975	1976	1977	1978	1979	1980	Annual Growth Rate 1974-80
Agriculture	2 811	2 811	2 944	2 992	3 135	3 256	3 425	3.1
Farm food crops	1 681	1 696	1 755	1 735	1 835	1 909	2 073	3.3
Farm non-food crops	307	312	325	385	388	402	417	5.1
Estate crops	174	183	188	201	210	231	233	4.8
Livestock products	186	202	216	177	184	202	212	2.0
Forestry	325	274	310	335	352	338	308	-0.8
Fishery	138	144	150	159	166	174	182	4.6
Mining and quarrying	859	828	952	1 070	1 049	1 047	1 035	2.9
Oil	755	718	814	916	902	861	836	1.5
Natural gas	5	6	17	15	2		27	62.8
Other	99	104	121	140	125	159	171	10.4
Manufacturing	755	848	930	1 058	1 236	1 395	1 705	18.0
Refinery oil	66	58	56	76	71	79	87	4.5
LNG		-	-	12	59	100	136	-
Other	689	790	874	970	1 106	1 216	1 483	16.5
Electricity, gas and water	37	41	46	49	57	69	78	15.8
Construction	320	365	385	464	529	563	639	14.2
Commerce, hotels, etc.	1 224	1 294	1 351	1 438	1 530	1 681	1 852	7.3
Transport and communications	288	303	343	439	514	560	609	15.9
Banking, etc.	88	102	117	151	165	180	208	19.5
Ownership of dwellings	174	198	209	252	288	306	336	13.3
Public administration and defence	443	564	596	689	768	805	972	17.1
Other services	270	277	283	280	296	303	310	2.1
Gross domestic product	7 269	7 631	8 156	8 882	9 567	10 165	11 169	7.6

Source: Government of Indonesia, Biro Pisat Statistik, various years.

Table 3.2: Gross Domestic Product by Industrial Origin at Constant 1983 Market Prices, 1980-1987 (Rp. billion)

	1980	1981	1982	1983	1984	1985	1986	1987[1]	Annual Growth Rate 1980-87
Agriculture	16 399.2	17 187.0	17 370.9	17 696.2	18 431.1	19 209.0	19 707.4	20 230.4	2.9
Farm food crops	9 661.1	10 639.1	10 736.0	11 057.4	11 598.7	11 894.6	12 187.2	12 419.4	3.6
Farm non-food crops	1 837.1	2 010.0	2 033.3	2 294.9	2 349.3	2 575.7	2 590.4	2 702.7	5.9
Estate crops	497.9	517.6	592.4	375.3	445.5	510.8	561.8	534.0	1.0
Livestock products	1 585.9	1 620.6	1 695.8	1 754.3	1 890.1	2 036.5	2 062.1	2 102.7	4.1
Forestry	1 700.9	1 260.6	1 146.4	994.2	894.4	850.7	888.7	987.6	-5.2
Fishery	1 116.3	1 139.1	1 167.0	1 220.1	1 253.1	1 340.7	1 417.2	1 484.0	4.1
Mining and quarrying	16 077.8	16 340.1	13 876.2	13 967.9	14 788.7	13 980.5	14 629.7	14 090.6	-1.5
Oil and natural gas	15 524.7	15 767.2	13 249.0	13 346.2	14 203.4	13 368.7	13 974.1	13 392.8	-1.7
Other	553.1	572.9	627.2	621.7	585.3	611.8	655.6	697.8	3.3
Manufacturing	7 304.4	7 878.4	793.1	8 211.3	9 770.3	10 678.2	11 181.5	12 053.6	8.1
Refinery oil	185.8	169.8	142.3	129.4	386.5	759.0	917.9	926.5	49.8
LNG	1 671.9	1 711.6	1 781.7	2 790.2	2 918.5	2 922.8	3 268.4		13.6[2]
Other	5 446.7	5 997.0	6 049.1	6 210.7	6 593.6	7 000.7	7 340.8	7 858.7	5.5
Electricity, gas and water	312.1	360.8	421.6	524.3	550.3	594.9	645.9	715.2	16.1
Construction	3 849.8	4 367.9	4 408.5	4 597.2	4 393.8	4 508.0	4 609.0	4 802.9	3.1
Commerce, hotels, etc.	10 112.4	10 949.5	11 756.5	12 009.4	12 159.7	12 456.1	12 996.0	13 773.8	4.5
Transport and communications	2 910.5	3 309.3	3 539.6	3 978.0	4 442.4	4 481.8	4 630.6	4 848.1	8.3

Table 3.2: Gross Domestic Product by Industrial Origin at Constant 1983 Market Prices, 1980-1987 (Rp. billion) (Cont'd)

	1980	1981	1982	1983	1984	1985	1986	1987[1]	Annual Growth Rate 1980-87
Banking, etc.	1 234.0	1 940.7	2 034.9	2 039.2	2 422.3	2 430.6	2 565.0	2 678.6	14.6
Ownership of dwellings	1 683.0	1 822.7	1 878.9	1 961.8	2 072.3	2 145.2	2 220.8	2 298.9	4.6
Public administration and defence	4 128.3	4 664.6	5 266.0	5 711.5	5 996.7	6 455.1	6 862.1	7 366.1	9.8
Other services	2 663.3	2 792.1	2 851.0	3 000.8	3 116.8	3 180.2	3 270.2	3 448.9	3.7
Gross Domestic Product	66 674.8	71 613.1	71 377.2	73 697.6	78 144.4	80 119.6	83 318.2	86 307.1	3.7

[1] Preliminary figures.

[2] Figure refers to annual growth rate 1980-86.

Source: Government of Indonesia, Biro Pusat Statistik, various years.

Table 3.3: Sectoral Employment and Productivity, 1971 and 1980

	Employment Levels[1] (Thousand workers)		Employment Annual Growth Rate	Productivity Levels (Rp per thousand workers)		Productivity Annual Growth Rate	Growth in value-added (percent p.a.)	Elasticity of Employment
	1971	1980	1971-80	1971	1980	1971-80	1971-80	1971-80
Agriculture								
Food crops	26 121	27 500	0.6	163	230	3.9	4.5	0.13
Cash crops	1 206	1 134	6.6	1 149	1 027	-1.2	5.2	1.25
Livestock	348	1 200	14.7	2 194	992	-8.4	5.1	2.90
Forestry	135	502	15.6	4 008	2 815	-3.9	11.2	1.39
Fishery	602	827	3.6	1 139	958	-1.9	1.6	2.22
Subtotal	28 413	32 164	1.4	268	370	3.6	5.1	0.27
Mining								
Petroleum[2]	46	28	-5.4	119 776	421 115	15.0	8.8	-0.62
Other	46	333	24.7	4 500	1 883	-9.2	13.2	1.86
Subtotal	92	361	16.4	62 471	34 401	-6.4	8.9	1.84
Manufacturing								
Food processing	615	1 187	7.6	1 050	1 474	3.8	11.7	0.65
Textiles	933	1 235	3.2	230	467	8.2	11.6	0.27
Wood and products	455	1 071	10.0	80	312	16.3	28.9	0.36
Paper and products	54	81	4.6	1 408	1 550	1.1	5.7	0.81
Chemicals	150	185	2.4	2 428	3 343	3.6	6.1	0.39
Non-metallic	244	411	6.0	445	593	3.2	9.4	0.64
Iron and steel	14	52	15.5	4 082	4 223	0.4	15.9	0.97

Table 3.3: Sectoral Employment and Productivity, 1971 and 1980 (Cont'd)

	Employment Levels[1] (Thousand workers)		Employment Annual Growth Rate	Productivity Levels (Rp per thousand workers)		Productivity Annual Growth Rate	Growth in value-added (percent p.a.)	Elasticity of Employment
	1971	1980	1971-80	1971	1980	1971-80	1971-80	1971-80
Engineering	328	777	10.1	1 212	1 337	1.1	11.3	0.89
Other	86	288	14.4	141	216	4.9	19.9	0.72
Subtotal	2 879	5 289	7.0	664	940	3.9	11.2	0.63
Electricity, gas and water	40	62	4.9	402	373	-0.8	4.1	1.21
Construction	728	1 547	8.7	1 418	1 669	1.8	10.7	0.82
Services								
Trade	4 574	6 793	4.5	970	992	0.3	4.8	0.94
Transport	1 021	1 972	7.6	1 346	1 121	-2.0	5.4	1.40
Financial and business	100	282	12.2	8 339	8 341	0.0	12.2	1.00
Public administration	1 423	1 982	3.8	643	1 245	7.6	11.7	0.32
Other	2 998	4 688	5.1	314	518	5.7	11.1	0.46
Subtotal	10 116	15 717	5.0	840	1 031	2.3	7.4	0.68
Total	42 268	55 140	3.0	591	877	4.5	7.6	0.40

[1] Sectoral employment levels were obtained by a proportionate adjustment in the estimates in the Input-Output Tables to reflect a revised aggregate employment level. The latter was calculated on the basis of an adjusted labour force participation rate for 1980 and an estimated employment rate.

[2] Includes LNG.

Source: Thorbecke (1992).

It is difficult to measure exactly agriculture's net contribution to the balance of payments. In principle, it would consist of the value of all agricultural exports minus the value of all agricultural products and inputs (such as fertilizer) used in agricultural production.

Table 3.4 reveals that the performance of the agriculture sector as a foreign exchange earner has fluctuated fairly widely, largely because of export price movements. The share of agricultural exports as part of total non-oil exports remained around 80 percent during the early 1970s before dropping rather sharply to about 30 percent in the mid to late 1980s. However, perhaps the most useful indicator of agriculture's contribution to the balance of payments is given in the last row of Table 3.4, which shows that the net export surplus of the food, beverages, tobacco and edible oils and seeds category (including processed and manufactured goods) increased sharply since the early 1980s. This suggests that the sector is improving its capacity to generate foreign exchange on a net basis.

Although this brief overview shows that in the last 15 years agriculture has played a crucial role in contributing to the major socio-economic development objectives, it would be quite unrealistic to expect this sector to continue to fulfil all these interrelated functions in the future. In particular, Java has pretty much exhausted its capacity to generate additional employment opportunities in agriculture on a net basis. There is some room for food diversification toward secondary crops in the rain-fed upland areas, which is likely to create new sources of employment but, in all likelihood, further gradual mechanization in paddy production will result in a continuing decline of the agricultural labour force there.

On the other hand, growth in tree crop production following an acceleration of the transmigration programme can be expected in the Outer Islands (particularly in Kalimantan). This would lead to some additional employment, counteracting at least partially the fall in the agricultural labour force in Java.

The trend toward a larger number of smaller farms on Java and an increasing group of "marginal" farmers and landless workers is a symptom and reminder of the impossibility in the future of solving the employment and poverty problem within agriculture *per se*. The target groups of small farmers and landless will increasingly have to be provided with rural off-farm jobs. These issues will be discussed in some detail in Chapter 4 and in Chapter 8.

Table 3.4: Agricultural Exports and Imports and Estimated Net Contribution of Agriculture to Balance of Payments, 1970-89 (US$ millions and percent)

	1970	1975	1980	1985	1986	1988	1989
Total agriculture and forestry exports	574	1 455	4 754	2 974	3 153	4 593	4 638
Above as percentage of total non-oil exports	81.0	8.10	52.5	30.1	33.1	32.1	29.5
Total exports of food, beverages, tobacco, and edible oils and seeds	207	577	1 665	1 859	2 013	2 614	2 613
Total imports of food, beverages, tobacco, and edible oils and seeds	104	596	1 376	708	866	1 020	1 243
Net exports of food, beverages, tobacco, and edible oils and seeds	103	-19	289	1 151	1 147	1 594	1 370

Source: UNCTAD (1991).

Performance Within Agriculture

As we have discussed, the overall performance of agriculture in the recent past has been remarkable. Table 3.5 presents, for the major food crops, data on total production, harvested area and yield, respectively, annually for the period 1979-89. In particular, it can be seen that (average) paddy production between 1979 and 1984 grew at an annual rate of about 7.9 percent, and maize production at 8.1 percent. In contrast, cassava and soyabeans grew only marginally. There was a marked slowdown in the growth rates of paddy (3.2 percent annually) and most other crops in the most recent period (1984-89) - the main exception being soyabeans output which increased by 11.9 percent annually. Clearly, the process of crop diversification had not progressed much as of the end of the eighties. Since production is equal to the product of the harvested area and the yield, the two lower panels of Table 3.5 can be used to assess the relative impact of these last two variables on production. Thus, one can see that, in the period under consideration, higher yields were mainly responsible for the excellent paddy production performance up to the mid-eighties; while both area planted and yield contributed about equally to the growth in maize production. Generally speaking, the yields of cassava, soyabeans, maize and sweet potatoes continued to increase throughout the period.

Table 3.6 provides data on annual production and yield for the major cash crops between 1979 and 1987. It can be seen that each of these cash crops fluctuated fairly widely from year to year during that time. Again, if we concentrate on the last few years, the annual (average) growth rate of rubber for the period 1979-87 was 2.8 percent, and for coffee, 6.6 percent. In contrast, both tea and tobacco production remained essentially stagnant. All the crops depicted in Table 3.6, except for tea, are predominantly in the hands of smallholders, as is discussed in detail later in this chapter. In general, yields went up except for sugar cane and largeholder production (i.e., in private and government estates); these cash crops grew much more rapidly than those of smallholders over the recent past.

The livestock sector, which is discussed in some detail later in this chapter, grew at a moderate 3.6 percent rate during the period 1979-84 while the forestry sector - also discussed later in the chapter - experienced a sharp drop in 1981 and only a slight increase afterward.

Table 3.5: Food Crops Production, Harvested Area and Yield, 1979-89

	1979	1980	1981	1982	1983	1984	1985	1986	1987	1988	1989[1]	Average Annual Growth Rate 1979-84	1984-89
Production (Million Tonnes)													
Wetland paddy	24.58	28.15	31.12	31.48	33.35	36.21	37.03	37.74	37.97	39.32	42.42	8.1	3.2
Dryland paddy	1.58	1.65	1.68	1.79	1.97	2.07	2.00	1.98	2.11	2.36	2.36	5.6	2.7
Total paddy	26.16	29.80	32.80	33.27	35.32	38.28	39.03	39.72	40.08	41.68	44.78	7.9	3.2
Maize	3.63	3.99	4.51	3.24	5.10	5.36	4.33	5.92	5.15	6.65	6.21	8.1	3.0
Cassava	13.82	13.77	13.30	12.99	12.10	14.21	14.06	13.31	14.36	15.47	17.09	0.6	3.8
Soyabeans	0.68	0.65	0.70	0.52	0.54	0.74	0.87	1.22	1.16	1.27	1.30	1.7	11.9
Peanuts	0.42	0.47	0.47	0.44	0.47	0.52	0.52	0.64	0.53	0.58	0.61	4.4	3.2
Sweet potatoes	2.05	2.10	2.05	1.67	2.03	2.30	2.16	2.09	2.01	2.16	2.12	2.3	-1.5
Harvested Food Crop Areas (Million Hectares)													
Wetland paddy	7.68	7.82	8.19	7.87	7.94	8.42	8.75	8.88	8.79	8.92	9.31		
Dryland paddy	1.13	1.18	1.19	1.12	1.16	1.22	1.15	1.10	1.13	1.21	1.14		
Maize	2.59	2.73	2.96	2.06	3.00	3.02	2.44	3.14	2.62	3.40	2.91		
Cassava	1.44	1.41	1.39	1.32	1.22	1.34	1.24	1.17	1.22	1.30	1.40		
Soyabeans	0.78	0.73	0.81	0.61	0.64	0.84	0.90	1.25	1.10	1.17	1.18		
Peanuts	0.47	0.51	0.51	0.46	0.48	0.53	0.51	0.60	0.55	0.60	0.61		
Sweet potatoes	0.27	0.28	0.27	0.22	0.26	0.28	0.25	0.25	0.23	0.25	0.23		

Table 3.5: Food Crops Production, Harvested Area and Yield, 1979-89 (Cont'd)

	1979	1980	1981	1982	1983	1984	1985	1986	1987	1988	1989[1]	Average Annual Growth Rate 1979-84	1984-89
	Average Food Crop Yields (Tonnes per Hectare)												
Wetland paddy	3.2	3.6	3.8	4.0	4.2	4.3	4.2	4.2	4.3	4.4	4.6		
Dryland paddy	1.4	1.4	1.5	1.6	1.7	1.7	1.7	1.8	1.9	1.9	2.1		
Maize	1.4	1.5	1.5	1.6	1.7	1.8	1.8	1.9	2.0	2.0	2.1		
Cassava	9.6	9.8	9.6	9.8	9.9	10.6	10.9	11.4	11.7	11.9	12.2		
Soyabeans	0.87	0.89	0.87	0.86	0.84	0.89	0.97	0.98	1.05	1.07	1.10		
Peanuts	0.90	0.93	0.93	0.95	0.98	0.99	1.03	1.06	1.05	1.07	1.10		
Sweet potatoes	7.6	7.5	7.6	7.6	7.8	8.2	8.4	8.3	8.8	8.7	9.3		

[1] Provisional estimates

Source: Government of Indonesia, Biro Pusat Statistik (1984q and 1989).

Table 3.6: Major Cash Crops, Production and Yields, 1979-87

	1979	1980	1981	1982	1983	1984	1985	1986	1987	Average Annual Growth 1979-87
	Production (Thousands of Tonnes)									
Rubber	898	1 002	1 046	900	1 231	1 107	1 054	1 095	1 123	2.8
Coffee	228	285	295	281	302	309	913	356	379	6.6
Tea	125	106	110	94	113	116	132	129	126	0.0
Sugar cane	1 601	1 831	1 700	1 627	1 587	1 769	1 766	2 013	2 176	3.9
Tobacco	87	116	118	106	120	121	163	103	81	-0.1

	1979	1980	1981	1982	1983
	Average Yields (Tonnes per Hectare)				
Rubber (kg dry rubber/ha)					
Smallholders	519	523	503	458	506
State estates	1 103	1 213	1 239	1 214	1 290
Coffee (kg/ha)					
smallholders	623	591	588	524	562
State estates	636	750	858	657	486
Tea (kg/ha)					
Smallholders	641	668	758	544	745
State estates	1 602	1 834	1 909	1 580	1 743
Sugar cane (tons cane/ha)					
Smallholders	84	75	86	73	58
State estates	92	83	69	49	68
Tobacco (kg/ha)					
Smallholders	552	546	526	505	527

Source: Government of Indonesia, Biro Pusat Statistik (1984q and 1989).

Land Distribution and Land Use

The total land area of Indonesia is about 181 million ha, of which 120 million ha is forest. The cropped area consists of 22 million ha, with 6 million ha devoted to perennial crops, 7 million ha to wetland crops and 9 million ha to dryland crops.

Table 3.7 gives the distribution of farmland by farm size and province. It can be seen that, in particular, Javanese provinces display a high proportion of farms of smaller size. Other provinces, such as on Kalimantan, have a much higher proportion of larger farms. Table 3.8 in turn, presents the distribution of households by farm size and province. Here again, it can be seen that the four provinces on Java have a very high proportion of households controlling small farms, that is, at least 60 percent in each of these four provinces. At the national level, about 47 percent of farm households controlled farms of less than 0.5 ha. Strikingly, the Agricultural Census of 1983 revealed that about 1.14 million households operated marginal farms of less than 0.1 ha.

A comparison of the number of food crop households, land controlled and average size of land controlled between the two agricultural censuses of 1973 and 1983 yields the following main trends (see also Table 3.9). Firstly, average farm size for Indonesia as a whole increased only slightly from 0.99 ha to 1.05 ha. Secondly, even in densely populated Java, total area farmed increased slightly, yet average size of land controlled remained virtually unchanged in Central and East Java and rose only marginally in West Java and Yogyakarta. Thirdly, in most other provinces, farm households, acreages, and average farm size tended to increase, with some notable exceptions, such as in Lampung, West and East Nusa Tenggara, Central Kalimantan and North Sulawesi.

Resource Base

Indonesia's present wealth derives mainly from its natural resource endowment which provides its agriculture, commercial forestry, fisheries and petroleum and other mineral resources. Of particular relevance to agriculture and rural development, the main focus of this volume, are the main features of the physical geography, the climate, the soils, the hydrology and the vegetation. These are very briefly discussed in the sections that follow.

Physical Geography

Sumatra, Java and the Lesser Sunda Islands are relics of the inner ring of the Sunda Mountain chain; typically they have axial montane or elevated areas. Coasts abutting the shallow Java Sea have extensive flattish areas, but elsewhere such areas only occur to a limited extent.

Table 3.7: Distribution of Farmland by Farm Size and Province, 1983
(Percentage of Total Provincial Farmed Land)

Province	Estimated Share of Total Operated Land Farm Size (Land Controlled in Hectares)						
	-0.25	+0.25 to -0.50	+0.50 to -1.00	+1.00 to -2.00	+2.00 to -3.00	+3.00	Total
D.I. Aceh	2	6	16	33	23	20	100
North Sumatra	3	7	19	37	21	14	100
West Sumatra	3	9	26	42	17	3	100
Riau	0	1	4	15	17	63	100
Jambi	0	1	4	13	17	65	100
South Sumatra	0	2	8	26	25	40	100
Bengkulu	0	2	9	31	32	26	100
Lampung	1	4	15	36	27	17	100
West Java	9	16	25	29	13	9	100
Central Java	8	17	30	31	11	3	100
D.I. Yogyakarta	9	14	25	35	17	0	100
East Java	8	17	29	30	12	3	100
Bali	3	11	24	33	18	11	100
West Nusa Tenggara	4	9	20	32	19	16	100
East Nusa Tenggara	1	2	10	32	26	29	100
West Kalimantan	0	1	2	8	9	81	100
Central Kalimantan	0	0	2	13	16	68	100
South Kalimantan	2	7	15	31	26	19	100
East Kalimantan	1	1	6	24	28	39	100
North Sulawesi	1	4	12	29	21	34	100
East Sulawesi	0	1	5	16	16	62	100
Southeast Sulawesi	2	5	17	35	22	19	100
Central Sulawesi	1	2	11	40	45	0	100
Maluku	0	1	5	17	18	58	100
Irian Jaya	3	6	15	25	25	26	100
East Timor	1	1	4	19	22	53	100
All Indonesia	4	8	16	27	18	28	100

Source: Government of Indonesia, Biro Pusat Statistik (1983a).

Table 3.8:   Distribution of Households by Farm Size and Province, 1983 (Total Provincial Farm Households, percent)

Province	Estimated Share of Total Number of Households Farm Size (Land Controlled in Hectares)						
	-0.25	+0.25 to -0.50	+0.50 to -1.00	+1.00 to -2.00	+2.00 to -3.00	+3.00	Total
D.I. Aceh	15	18	25	25	10	7	100
North Sumatra	22	17	25	23	8	5	100
West Sumatra	16	21	31	23	6	3	100
Riau	11	7	12	26	17	27	100
Jambi	9	8	15	24	20	25	100
South Sumatra	6	8	19	32	19	16	100
Bengkulu	5	7	20	33	21	14	100
Lampung	6	14	27	31	14	8	100
West Java	42	23	19	11	3	2	100
Central Java	34	26	24	12	3	1	100
D.I. Yogyakarta	40	21	20	13	4	1	100
East Java	35	26	23	11	3	2	100
Bali	22	23	27	18	6	4	100
West Nusa Tenggara	26	21	24	18	6	5	100
East Nusa Tenggara	7	9	22	33	16	13	100
West Kalimantan	4	6	11	22	15	42	100
Central Kalimantan	4	3	10	29	21	32	100
South Kalimantan	16	21	23	22	11	7	100
East Kalimantan	10	7	16	29	20	19	100
North Sulawesi	14	13	23	26	11	12	100
East Sulawesi	10	10	21	30	18	12	100
Southeast Sulawesi	15	15	27	26	10	6	100
Central Sulawesi	6	7	17	29	20	21	100
Maluku	9	6	15	27	17	25	100
Irian Jaya	30	15	20	17	10	7	100
East Timor	13	6	13	26	19	24	100
All Indonesia	27	20	22	17	7	6	100

Source: Government of Indonesia, Biro Pusat Statistik (1983a).

Table 3.9: Number of Food Crop Households, Land Controlled and Average Size of Land Controlled in 1973 Agricultural Census and in 1983 Agricultural Census by Province

Province	1973			1983		
	No. of Food Crop Households (In Thousands)	Land Controlled (In Thousands of Hectares)	Average Size of Land Controlled (Hectares)	No. of Food Crop Households (In Thousands)	Land Controlled (In Thousands of Hectares)	Average Size of Land Controlled (Hectares)
D.I. Aceh	353	374	1.06	334	394	1.18
North Sumatra	816	805	0.99	839	872	1.04
West Sumatra	426	344	0.81	421	385	0.91
Riau	199	507	2.55	191	497	2.60
Jambi	143	241	1.69	191	441	2.31
South Sumatra	377	703	1.86	447	901	2.01
Bengkulu	85	154	1.82	115	211	1.83
Lampung	447	673	1.51	678	877	1.38
D.K.I. Jakarta	21	19	0.94	-	-	-
West Java	2 468	1 525	0.62	2 872	1 917	0.67
Central Java	2 766	1 753	0.63	2 940	1 928	0.66
D.I. Yogyakarta	344	181	0.53	354	236	0.67
East Java	3 066	2 026	0.66	3 200	2 103	0.66
Bali	305	267	0.87	293	258	0.88
West Nusa Tenggara	281	289	1.03	336	331	0.99
East Nusa Tenggara	365	653	1.79	434	710	1.63
West Kalimantan	274	982	3.59	334	1 367	4.09
Central Kalimantan	100	524	5.23	131	433	3.32
South Kalimantan	258	270	1.05	279	325	1.16

Table 3.9: Number of Food Crop Households, Land Controlled and Average Size of Land Controlled in 1973 Agricultural Census and in 1983 Agricultural Census by Province (Cont'd)

Province	1973			1983		
	No. of Food Crop Households (In Thousands)	Land Controlled (In Thousands of Hectares)	Average Size of Land Controlled (Hectares)	No. of Food Crop Households (In Thousands)	Land Controlled (In Thousands of Hectares)	Average Size of Land Controlled (Hectares)
East Kalimantan	58	93	1.61	73	152	2.07
North Sulawesi	218	352	1.62	245	368	1.50
Central Sulawesi	132	283	2.14	172	384	2.23
South Sulawesi	648	737	1.14	685	827	1.21
Southeast Sulawesi	103	151	1.47	124	206	1.66
Maluku	120	260	2.17	150	397	2.64
Irian Jaya	-	-	-	127	169	1.32
All Indonesia	14 374	14 168	0.99	15 927	16 689	1.05

Source: Government of Indonesia, Biro Pusat Statistik (1983a).

Kalimantan is mostly flattish, though a mountainous area is present in the north. Sulawesi has a number of isolated massifs. Irian Jaya resembles Kalimantan, except that the mountains are more central to the territory.

Climate

Although on the equator, Indonesia's climate is influenced by the proximity of seas and by the area's altitude; temperatures therefore seldom reach the extremes experienced on large continental land masses. Most islands receive moderate to heavy rainfall; some of the eastern islands are, however, semi-arid. Rainfall varies considerably with location and season.

Soils

Indonesia has a complex soil pattern. Some soils are of excellent quality for agriculture, and many are of limited value. The largest areas of poorer soils occur in the Outer Islands. Many of the 15 major soil types represented in the area are markedly acidic, which means that while they may be satisfactory for acid-tolerant crops, for example, rice, rubber and oil-palm, some of the preferred rain-fed food staples grow less well.

Hydrology

The shapes of Indonesia's islands, except in the case of Kalimantan and Irian Jaya, do not provide large catchment areas. Rivers tend, therefore, to be short, and the macro-relief has generally permitted well-developed drainage systems. Water runoff from the higher areas is usually rapid. Ground water resources have not been extensively explored, but in some instances are proving to be capable of providing water in sufficient quantity for irrigation.

Natural Vegetation

Indonesia has many areas where tropical rain forests are the natural climax, and in the Outer Islands large areas of such forest remain and provide the timber or timber products that are an important proportion of the country's exports. The rain forests, however, constitute only one element in the vegetation pattern; in the dry eastern islands a savannah type vegetation is more common. Often the transition between these two extremes occurs over a relatively short distance, as in South Sulawesi, reflecting climatic discontinuities.

The Operational Environment

The natural resource endowment provides the basic physical environment within which land-based economic activities must necessarily operate. The manner in which these activities, particularly agriculture, can be practised is largely determined by the combinations of physical variables present at the locale of operations - making up what may conveniently be termed the operational environment. The following sections briefly describe some typical natural - and contrived - agricultural environments, and discuss some of the factors that influence their use.

Landform Typology

Various landforms relevant to agriculture and the rural economy are distinguishable. They are: (i) beaches, (ii) mangrove swamps, (iii) tidal swamps, (iv) flood plains, (v) dissected peneplains, (vi) littoral massifs, (vii) valley floors, (viii) valley walls, (ix) ridges, (x) hillsides.

Agriculture and other rural activities thus have to be conducted in a wide range of geophysical environments, and many adaptive systems have evolved, from the exploitation of wetland *sawahs* for rice production to the cultivation of rain-fed crops on steep hillsides.

Irrigation

The macro-geomorphology does not provide many opportunities for water storage and most irrigation is, therefore, based on run-of-the-river diversion schemes. The larger schemes, in which the water distribution is measured, are described as technical. When distribution is controlled but not measured, the schemes are denoted as semi-technical. If no formal system of water control exists, then schemes are classified as non-technical - the category into which most traditional systems fall.

Critical Areas

A mandatory requirement for all land capability assessments is that they should particularly focus on the dangers of land degradation and soil erosion - two risks to which Indonesia's planners are having to pay increasing attention. Evidence has long been accumulating that, in many areas, any form of tillage exacts a high price in terms of soil loss and fertility depletion. This is a price that Indonesia, with increasing numbers of people dependent on the land, can less and less afford to pay.

Large tracts of *Imperata cylindrica* in many of the Outer Islands bear witness of the land degradation which occurs when shifting cultivation is practised on soils once capable of supporting dense forest. It is now being increasingly realized that sedentary rain fed food crop production in some transmigration sites may be having the same effect, notwithstanding the use of fertilizers. Heavier cropping, thus induced, may in fact be permanently degrading land at a faster rate that would have occurred under a shifting cultivation regime. Although we are disinclined to accept some of the more alarmist views expressed by some sections of the environmentalist movement, we do not doubt the need for very cautious estimation when the sustainability of tillage cropping on potential transmigration sites is being evaluated.

Avoiding or minimising land degradation risks in new settlements is possible, provided adequate preliminary survey and planning tasks are competently performed. Dealing with the more intractable problem of the extensive degradation of land presently farmed is much more difficult; few farmers - least of all those with small, virtually subsistence, holdings - willingly accept either that their practises are mining their land or that they should desist from doing so, when they have no other place to go to.

Overcropping is an almost inevitable sequel when population pressures on land limit the opportunities for shifting cultivation - the traditional way of cropping with declining fertility. Understandably, the worst affected areas are in Java, where population pressure has been greatest. Reliable quantitative data are exiguous, but a GOI/USAID team supported opinions that over a million hectares of land had deteriorated to the extent that it could no longer sustain even subsistence farming, and that the area of such land was increasing at the rate of 200 000 ha per year. The livelihoods of some 12 million people were estimated to be at risk from land degradation. (USAID 1983.) (A sequel of this report was the formulation of the Upland Development and Conservation Project now being co-financed by USAID and IBRD.)

The severity of the land degradation problem has prompted GOI to designate and gazette "critical areas", with the intention that these should be accorded priority in the application of appropriate measures.

It should be noted that these areas include land where soil erosion, often a distinct problem, is deemed to be excessive. Areas considered critical are concentrated in the higher parts of watersheds, and usually the worst-affected places are the hillside slopes. ("Watersheds" in Indonesia, as often elsewhere, connote river basins as defined by geographical watersheds.)

While it would be incorrect to categorize all high steep slopes as marginal in an agricultural sense - some, for example, can be satisfactorily terraced for tea cultivation - the great many, and probably a majority, have this status. They have been increasingly utilized for cultivation in recent years, as population growth has intensified the need for land - any land - on which to farm. Thus there has been a progressive elimination of the natural forest cover, and incursions into the gazetted national montane forest lands have occurred on a wide scale notwithstanding vigorous action by the authorities to check such movements. In many areas, the administrations have had to become reconciled to this de facto occupation in the face of local leaders' reluctance to strictly enforce relevant regulations. The problem thus has political and social, as well as agricultural dimensions.

We had several opportunities to observe the agricultural dimension. Poor crops of cassava growing on slopes where the soil was clearly eroding fast were everywhere to be seen in some areas. The scale of degradation was readily apparent; re-establishment of *pinus* forest, such as was seen nearby, would clearly have been difficult on the badly eroded soils.

Soil erosion can afflict damage not only at the place where it occurs, but also at a distance. Tillage on any slope invariably creates conditions where the soil is less stable; the sediment and bed loads of all Java's rivers have measurably increased throughout this century as the area under cultivation has increased, and excessive siltation of irrigation works in lower areas has been a pervasive impediment to effective operation. Losses due to suboptimal use of command areas, and the increased cost of canal maintenance are thus measures of the social costs imposed by soil erosion.

Steps to combat soil erosion are thus predicated not only where, as noted above, this is a prime cause of land degradation. In other areas the rate of soil loss, while significant, may yet be below the rate of pedogenesis. Agronomically this loss can, therefore, be discounted. But even these small losses contribute to the damage downstream, and thus also need to be addressed.

An associated problem of increasing severity is that of rapid runoff of the precipitation received in the upper parts of watersheds; this can lead to much flood damage in the lower-lying flood plain areas. This, again, correlates with extension of cultivation into previously forested areas; when denuded of tree cover the absorption capacity is lowered and the proportion of rainfall immediately entering the drainage system is correspondingly increased.

The "critical areas" are thus an important dimension of an operating environment that has, indeed, very many dimensions, as the discussion above will have made clear. The overall picture is one of immense complexity, the intricacies of which defy simple explanation. Understanding it, however, is essential if efficient and effective agricultural interventions are to be planned.

Patterns of Resource Use

Indonesia's diverse operational environment permits the growth of a very wide range of crops, and the use of a correspondingly wide range of farming systems and techniques. These topics are discussed in the next three sections. Descriptions of livestock, fisheries and forestry subsectors are then presented.

Crops

Four types of crops are grown in Indonesia: (i) rice; (ii) *palawija* crops; (iii) "industrial" crops, which include coconut, tobacco, cotton and various spice crops; and (iv) "estate" crops, which include rubber, oil-palms, coffee, cocoa, tea, sugar cane, cinchona and hemp. This taxonomy has historical origin, and many estate crops are, in fact, grown by independent smallholders, and some *palawija* crops, for example, citrus, may be grown on an estate scale. Classification of crops under this system provides the basis for the distribution of administrative responsibility within the various departments of MOA and accounts for some seemingly anomalous division of responsibilities. It should also be noted that in Indonesia, an "estate" is any land operated by a parastatal or private corporate body under the Right of Exploitation Law.

Both wetland and dryland types of *rice* are grown. Wetland rice grown in *sawahs* may be fully irrigated, semi-irrigated or wholly rain-fed, and constitutes the bulk of production. HYVs are used on about 80 percent of the total wetland rice-production area. The first HYV introductions were IR5, IR8 and IR20; these were soon largely superseded by the locally bred PELITA I-1 and PELITA I-2, which had more acceptable taste. These cultivars were, however, widely devastated in 1976 by the brown plant hopper (BPH), requiring the emergency introduction of IR26, followed by the release of IR28, IR29, IR30 and IR32. The insect, *Nilaparvata lugens* locally known as *wereng*, directly attacks the rice plants, causing "hopperburn", and also transmits the grassy stunt, ragged stunt and wilted stunt virus diseases. Evolution of a new strain of BPH, Biotype 2, required in turn that these cultivars be replaced by IR36, IR38 and IR42. Locally bred replacements for the PELITA cultivars, such as Serayu, Asahan, Brantas and Citarum, also failed to resist BPH (Biotype 2), but proved resistant to a third biotype (Biotype 3). Cisadene, released with Cimandiri, Ayung and Semeru (high elevation type) in 1980, has been widely used. The International Rice Research Institute (IRRI) is continuing its efforts to supply genotypes that combine good yield potential with disease and pest resistance, and have better taste than the earlier IRRI varieties. Tungro virus, transmitted by several green leafhopper species (*Nephotettix spp.*), is often a cause of poorly filled grain; suboptimal growing conditions can have the same effect.

Yields of wetland rice vary considerably. Paddy (unhusked rice) yields of 4-7 tonnes could be expected from many fields, but on some rain-fed plots 2 tonnes is an optimistic estimate. Average dryland rice yields have been consistently recorded at less than half those of wetland rice.

Overall rice yields are thus not high by the standards set by some other countries, for example, Japan. As will be discussed in Chapter 6, greater quality discrimination is likely to be applied in future by the bulk-buying agency BULOG, and many farmers may experience some previously unencountered difficulties in realizing the standard price for all their crop.

Although nationally wetland rice areas account for some seven-eighths of the total, and in 1983 contributed more than 94 percent to total production, dryland rice has comparatively greater importance in some provinces, as is shown in Table 3.10.

Maize is the second most important grain staple, and is becoming more widely cultivated both as a non-irrigated crop on *sawah* land under rain-fed conditions, and also as a dryland crop. It is more important in the drier areas, for example, the eastern half of Java. Total national production, however, is only about 20 percent that of rice. Both white and yellow types are grown.

Where grown without appropriate fertilizer applications, the yields from this somewhat demanding crop tend to be low. National average

Table 3.10: Dryland Rice Areas, 1983, 1986 and 1989

Islands/Provinces	Percentage of Total Rice Area		
	1983	1986	1989[1]
Java	6	6.3	6.4
West Java	7	6.9	7.6
Sumatra	21	16.0	16.6
Riau	37	33.1	29.7
Lampung	41	30.7	31.0
Bali	2	1.7	1.4
Nusa Tenggara Timur	49	47.5	44.6
Sulawesi	12	7.6	5.8
Southeast Sulawesi	62	40.9	22.0
Kalimantan	27	28.8	26.9
West Kalimantan	40	40.6	33.1
Maluku	97	57.4	84.1
Indonesia	-	11.0	10.9

[1] Provisional

Source: Government of Indonesia, Biro Pusat Statistik (1989).

yields have consistently been approximately those achieved by a dryland paddy. There are a few good crops, but the majority are poor and many exhibit symptoms of nutrient deficiency. Downy mildew (*Sclerospora maydis*) is probably the most serious disease affecting maize, and in the selection of open-pollinated varieties for release, such as Harapan Baru, Arjuno and Bromo, resistance to this diease has been an important criterion. Production from hybrid seed does not yet figure widely in smallholder production, but some farmers are using the released Hybrid C-1.

Sorghum is grown for use as poultry food in some of the drier parts of East Java, but the amount is statistically unimportant.

Cassava has been an important crop during the present century, and Indonesia was for a time one of the world's largest exporters of the dried products. Internal demand now absorbs the bulk of the crop. Production of cassava is widely distributed, as it is popular as a subsistence root, and the leaves are also consumed; many small plantings are found in *tegalans* (home gardens) in most of the densely settled areas. Nonetheless, the officially estimated total harvested area in 1983 was less than 1.25 million ha, about 14 percent of the total rice hectarage. Short-duration cultivars are generally used, therefore annual planted and harvested areas are likely to be approximately the same. Production was estimated to be about 12.25 million tonnes, suggesting an average yield of just below 10 tonnes per hectare, low by international standards.

As a significant cash crop, distribution is less widespread. There are extensive areas of dense plantings in Lampung Province in Southern Sumatra, where several processing factories have been established, and also in Central Java, where it was virtually the only crop to be seen on some large expanses of eroding hillsides. By virtue of its ability to withstand moisture stress, it is a major feature of the cropping systems of some of the drier areas, such as Madura and the *kabupaten* of Gunung Kidul (special province of Yogyakarta) located on the south Java limestone massif.

Of the total production in 1983, 68 percent came from Java. East Java (which includes Madura) contributed some 25 percent of the national total. Of the provinces of the Outer Islands, Lampung Province was the largest producer, followed by Southeast Sulawesi, indicating a strong correlation with rainfall.

As is well known, cassava is one of the more exhausting crops, and this characteristic cannot always be moderated by the use of fertilizers (for reasons that are beyond the scope of this volume). Based on the available evidence, it would seem that, in practice, very little fertilizer is applied to the crop. There can be little doubt that overcropping with cassava has been a potent factor in the process of land degradation.

Sweet potatoes (*Ipomaea batatas*) are the next most important root crop, but total production was only about a sixth that of cassava in 1983. It exhibits some tolerance to drought, but not as great as that of cassava. Yields obtained are similar. The national per capita annual consumption in 1983 was estimated at about 12 kg - compared with 145 kg of paddy and 57 kg of cassava - which suggests relatively modest production for the market. In Maluku and Irian Jaya, sweet potatoes are much more important than cassava; in 1983 the tonnage produced there was more than three times as much.

Yams (*Dioscona spp.*) and *cocoyams* (*Colocasia spp.*) are also grown, but are statistically unimportant.

Potatoes (*Solanum tuberosum*), or white potatoes or Irish potatoes, are intensively produced in some of the higher parts of Indonesia. They are, for instance, of considerable local importance in the Malang area of East Java. There is also a production area in the Karo *kabupaten* of North Sumatra, where the crop goes mainly to the Singapore market. Reported yields were of the order of 6-10 tonnes per hectare, making it a remunerative crop for smallholders. Control of late blight (*Phytophthora infestans*), and other diseases associated with humid conditions, has proved difficult. Total national production is, and is likely to remain, limited due to the lack of favourable crop-growing areas.

Soyabeans have a long history of cultivation in Indonesia as a food crop, and are used in a number of traditional ways: for example, to produce the curd *tahu*, fermented beancakes *tempe* and *oncom*, the relish *tauco* and the sauce *kecap*. Production specifically for soyabean oil is negligible. In the 1980s, Java accounted for about 80 percent of the total production; East Java produced two-thirds of the island's total. Total national production in 1989 was 1.39 million tonnes, from 1.25 million ha. The growth in production in the last few years has been remarkable.

In recent years, vigorous governmental efforts have been made to stimulate production. The plant, however, is unresponsive to policy measures. To produce well it prefers a richer soil, well aerated but with plenty of soil moisture, although not too much rain. Strains are season-length specific and the symbiotic *rhizobia* species needed for good nitrogen-fixation are usually strain-specific. Soil acidity often limits plant productivity. The seeds tend to lose viability quickly in the humid tropics. An effective response to the often-cited farmers' complaint - "We don't have improved seed" - does not, therefore, lie within the domain of simple administrative action; much agronomic research may need to be performed before the logistics of seed supply can be properly organized, and this inevitably takes time. By international standards, Indonesia's yields, averaging less than 1.1 tonnes/ha in recent years, are somewhat on the low side.

Peanuts (groundnuts) yield significantly better than soyabeans in some of the wetter parts of the country; in West Java during 1979-83, for example, average peanut yields were consistently one-third greater than soyabean yields. In the Outer Islands, South Sulawesi has consistently been the largest provincial producer. Java contributed nearly 70 percent, and Sumatra nearly 12 percent, of the total national production of 0.46 million tonnes in 1983.

Mungbeans, chickpeas, cowpeas, hyacinth beans and other pulses are widely grown on a small scale, and are often used as a binder on the lips of terraces. Data on the production of these pulses are not routinely generated at the provincial and national levels.

Bananas are a widely established homestead crop, and make a significant contribution toward meeting dietary needs. They will yield, albeit often poorly, in a wide range of soil and climatic conditions. For profitable commercial production, however, the requirements are more stringent, which probably explains the absence of any extensive plantations.

Citrus of a variety of species have been extensively planted in Indonesia in the past, but production has more recently suffered severe setbacks due to widespread infection by citrus vein phloem disease - the so-called "citrus greening" - attributable to a complex of viruses. Control of this disease has necessitated statutory regulations requiring wholesale removal of trees and prohibition of planting in some areas and the imposition of strict quarantine measures in the unaffected areas.

Trees of other fruit species are also widely planted on smallholdings and are used to meet both consumption and market needs. These include the celebrated *durian* (soursop) and *mango*, *rambutan* (lychee), *sapodilla, rose apple, langsat* (duku), *avocado* and *papaya*. *Pineapples* are also widely cultivated. *Apples* are commercially produced on a limited scale where suitable climatic conditions prevail, as at higher altitudes in some areas of East Java.

The *sugar palm* (Arenga pinnata) is still used at the village level for making a type of *gur*, but the scale of production is not recorded.

Agro-industries exploiting the output of the various fruits are mostly small scale and are oriented toward meeting the demands of local higher-income groups. Quantitative uptake of fruit is therefore relatively small, and opportunities for farms to supply large-scale export-oriented processing factories, such as in Malaysia and The Philippines for example, do not yet exist.

The balance of the *palawija* crops is made up of miscellaneous minor horticultural and vegetable crops, such as *tomatoes, cabbages, beans, sweet peppers (capsicum spp.), onions, carrots, radishes* and various curcubits. Apart from a limited amount of commercial production in peri-urban areas, most of these crops are produced for household consumption. Usually they are grown in the home garden.

Rubber (Figure 3.1), in terms of total area planted, rivals coconut as a smallholder crop. In 1983, the total area of rubber was estimated to be 2.46 million ha, of which slightly more than 80 percent was on smallholdings. Production by the smallholder component of the subsector was, however, disproportionately small, at only 31 percent of the estimated total of 1 million tonnes. The estimated average dry rubber yield on the estates, at about 700 kg per hectare, is low compared with the 2 000 kg per hectare achievable under optimal conditions; the smallholdings, at about 340 kg per hectare, achieved barely one-sixth of that amount.

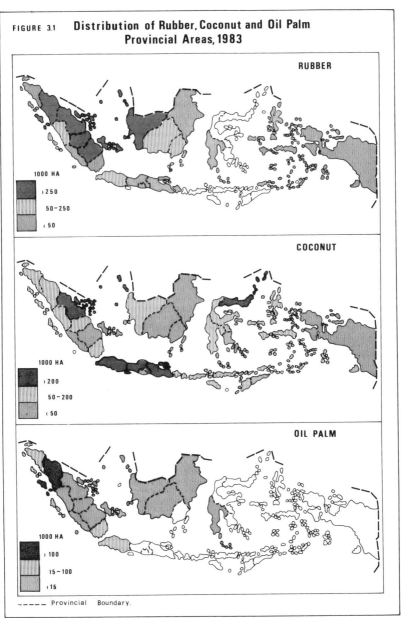

FIGURE 3.1   **Distribution of Rubber, Coconut and Oil Palm Provincial Areas, 1983**

RUBBER

1000 HA
) 250
50 – 250
(50

COCONUT

1000 HA
) 200
50 – 200
(50

OIL PALM

1000 HA
) 100
15 – 100
(15

– – – – Provincial   Boundary.

Source: Adapted from figures supplied by Directorate–General of Estate Crops.

The yield difference reflects two totally different approaches to rubber production. The estates are planted and managed in accordance with conventional practice: regularly spaced trees, uniform genetic material (e.g., budgrafts of selected clones), fertilisers, cover crops, standard tapping procedures, and block replacement of trees when production declines. Smallholdings typically have sparse stands of over-aged inferior trees many of which have been mutilated by poor tapping methods. Apart from some clearance of tapping routes, no weeding is practised. Because of the usually great distance from an owner's dwelling, tapping often tends to be sporadic, done only when cash is required. Adulteration and poor processing of the latex result in minimal farm-gate prices, which in turn discourage better management.

Most of this neglected smallholder rubber is in Sumatra, where the majority of the rubber estates are located. Visits to some smallholdings, where rubber established under the aegis of replanting and transmigration schemes was coming into bearing, provided ample evidence that much higher levels of productivity can be achieved under smallholder systems; in fact, in many areas there appeared to be no reason to suppose that the economic returns on smallholders would be less than on estates. The NES is a promising vehicle. (See Chapter 6 for a discussion of this programme.)

Although in national terms these very large areas of senile rubber represent an underutilization of the resource endowment, it is easy to see why many farmers are not interested in switching to a more intensive system of production. Investment costs for their holdings have been low, maintenance costs are low, and the trees constitute a resource that can quite literally be tapped as and when circumstance permits, and returns appear attractive. Memories of low producer prices are undoubtedly another factor determining investment at the micro-level.

Coconuts (see Figure 3.1) are classified as an industrial crop, as they are the main domestic source of the consumed vegetable oils. A significant proportion of the crop, however, is consumed as fresh fruit, that is, the "meat" is used directly as food, for home-produced oil (klentic oil, which is boiled out), and for the preparation of culinary products.

Coconuts are almost exclusively a smallholder crop; estates were estimated to account for about 2 percent of the total area in 1981, and their production does not feature in the published national statistics. Total area under smallholder coconuts was estimated to be 2.9 million ha in 1983, with a production of copra (or copra equivalent) of 1.6 million tonnes. The indicated yield of about 0.55 tonnes per hectare is extremely low compared with the 2-4 tonnes per hectare that could be expected from well-adapted cultivars or hybrids, under good field management conditions. Under optimal conditions, Dwarf x Tall hybrids may yield 6 tonnes/ha.

Evidence serves to confirm the reported condition of the majority of coconut plantings: a generally senescent tree population, many trees not producing, few trees likely to produce more than 50 nuts per year and a lack of replacement plantings. This picture prevailed even in the proximity of the Coconut Research Institute in North Sulawesi. Most copra is sun dried.

Efforts to improve this subsector have included extensive aided replanting schemes, serviced by large-scale production, by the MOA, of improved seedlings for distribution to farmers. Depending on the location, distributed seedlings are either improved varieties or Dwarf x Tall hybrids resulting from controlled pollination; currently pollen is being imported from the Ivory Coast but plans are being made to meet needs from local sources.

During a recent visit to a demonstration farm in southern Sumatra where hybrid seedlings had been used, we were very favourably impressed by the vigour and bearing capacity of the trees. Sustained maturity yields of 80-90 nuts per tree per annum could be expected, provided fertilizers were applied as required, the leguminous cover crop maintained and appropriate measures taken to minimize the incidence of pest damage, for example, by the rhinoceros beetle (*Oryetes rhinoceros*).

Castor (*Ricinus communis*) was formerly a smallholder crop of some significance, more particularly in the Lesser Sunda Islands, but production has lessened considerably in recent years, probably because of lack of competition in world markets.

Oil-palms (Figure 3.1), in contrast with rubber, have until comparatively recently been solely an estate crop, notwithstanding their introduction over a century ago, and large-scale plantings since 1911. Significant smallholdings of oil-palm date only from their establishment as units within the so-called "plasma" areas of NES/PIR developments. The institutional structure and operational aspects of the NES/PIR scheme are discussed in Chapter 6.

A visit to oil-palm NES sites in West Sumatra and in West Java showed that the palms in West Sumatra were beginning to bear well, and yields approaching 20 tonnes per hectare of bunch fruit could be expected at maturity. Oil-palm plantations have also been established as part of transmigration projects on acrisols in Kalimantan and reportedly have survived prolonged water stress and fire damage exceptionally well during a drought period.

Substantial resources have been devoted to improving the quality of plant material, and capacity now exists to supply large quantities of improved Dura Dumpy x Pisifera hybrid seed. Total oil-palm area increased from 0.23 million ha in 1979 to 0.33 million ha in 1983. Total palm oil production now exceeds 1 million tonnes per annum, with Sumatra still contributing over 95 percent.

Tobacco (Figure 3.2), like coconuts, is an almost wholly smallholder crop, although in a number of instances production is vertically linked with major tobacco companies, which supply plant material and support services. The only significant estate production is in North Sumatra which concentrates on the production of cigar wrapper leaf.

The principal concentrations of smallholder production occur in central and eastern Java and on Madura. Sulawesi is also a significant producer. Several different types of tobacco are produced - barn-dried and flue-dried Virginia and sun-dried native tobaccos - depending on local conditions.

Pepper (*Piper nigrum*; Figure 3.2) has long been an important export commodity produced mainly by smallholders. Sumatra's southern mainland and its offshore islands were the most important centre of production, but the crop is now more dispersed. Total estimated area in 1983 was 77 000 ha. The crop has been the subject of an aided replanting programme, and in Lampung there is tangible evidence of success.

Sugar cane (Figure 3.2) production is concentrated on Java, with lesser amounts grown on the other larger islands. Total sugar production in 1983 was estimated at about 1.55 million tonnes, produced from about 130 000 ha of smallholder cane and about half this quantity of estate cane.

Unavailability of irrigation water, especially in the lower rainfall areas, can greatly affect the levels of cane production. At a site near Malang in East Java, smallholders depending solely on rainfall were achieving only half the 120-140 tonnes per hectare cane yields of adjacent farmers with irrigation. Clearly, this situation represents different levels of operating profitability, and one in which different levels of risk attach to use of land.

Cotton (Figure 3.3), as a commercial crop, is a relatively recent development. Cultivation started in Lombok, but declined after 1973; since then the main producers have been smallholders in the drier parts of Java and on Sulawesi. The production area of smallholders

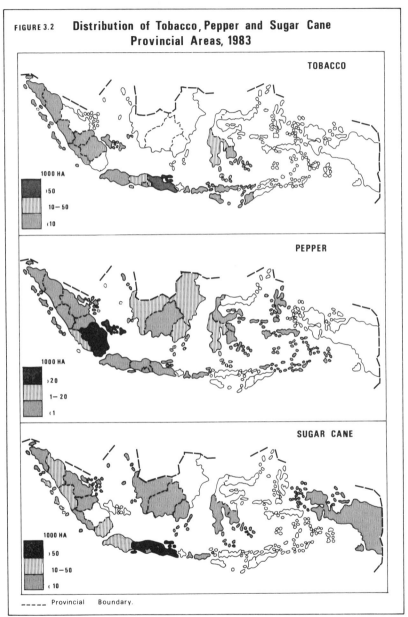

FIGURE 3.2 **Distribution of Tobacco, Pepper and Sugar Cane Provincial Areas, 1983**

TOBACCO

1000 HA
> 50
10 – 50
< 10

PEPPER

1000 HA
> 20
1 – 20
< 1

SUGAR CANE

1000 HA
> 50
10 – 50
< 10

_____ Provincial   Boundary.

Source: Adapted from figures supplied by Directorate–General of Estate Crops.

FIGURE 3.3   **Distribution of Cotton, Rosella Hemp and Kapok
Provincial Areas, 1983**

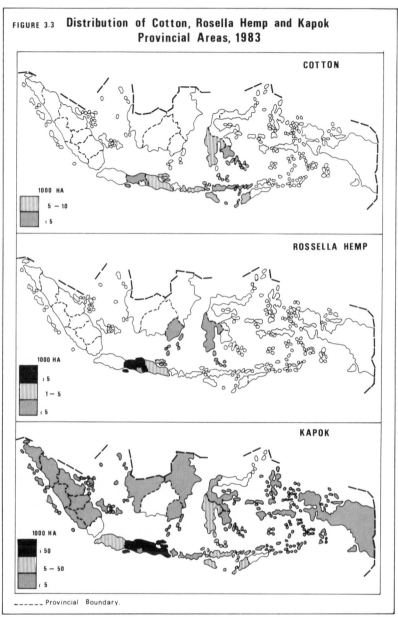

Source: Adapted from figures supplied by Directorate-General of Estate Crops.

increased rapidly during the period 1979-83, rising steadily from about 4 000 ha to about 33 000 ha, with average yields in the range of 375-500 kg lint per hectare. In 1980, about 3 000 ha of cotton were grown on state estates, with a reported average yield of about 900 kg per hectare; this suggests that proper management and pest control are needed.

Rosella hemp (Figure 3.3) and, to a lesser extent, *Manilla hemp* (Abaca, *Musa textilis*) are also sources of fiber grown on a minor scale. In 1979, smallholder production of rosella hemp accounted for about two-thirds of total output, but by 1983 the rapidly increasing estate hectarage contributed more than half, notwithstanding some growth in the smallholder component. Total production area in 1983 was about 15 000 ha.

Kapok (Figure 3.3) is a traditional smallholder product, and remains a significant contributor to income in some of the drier areas. As in the case of other tree crops having a sparse stand - for example, coconuts - attributions of area may be somewhat arbitrary, and are likely to include land on which dryland food crops are also grown. But even when allowance is made for this fact, the estimated 1983 total of just over 0.4 million ha suggests that the production potential is substantial. There is evidence, however, that declining demand has reduced interest in the crop, and that tree replacement is on the wane.

Vanilla (Figure 3.4) is produced commercially by some specialist smallholders, and the high standard of management evident at small plantations in Central Java is impressive. National production area is thought to be about 1 000 ha, and there is interest in expansion.

Cloves (Figure 3.4) are an important smallholder crop in Indonesia, and are widely distributed. Plantings are mainly in intermediate- and higher-elevation areas. Although often established in stands of a few trees, small plantations of 0.5-1 ha and larger are frequently seen. Total smallholder area was estimated to be 0.59 million ha in 1983; estate plantings were then estimated at less than 20 000 ha.

In the 1970s, clove production was badly affected by the spread of a bacterial infection - the so-called "Sumatra Disease". In 1980 it was estimated that in West Sumatra 10 percent of the trees planted before 1970 had succumbed. This gave stimulus to new plantings, which increased the estimated total area by an average of over 10 percent per annum over the period 1978-83. Internal demand is high for use as a flavouring for Indonesian cigarettes.

Nutmeg (Figure 3.4) is likewise a predominantly smallholder crop. Traditionally a product of the "Spice Islands", now constituting the

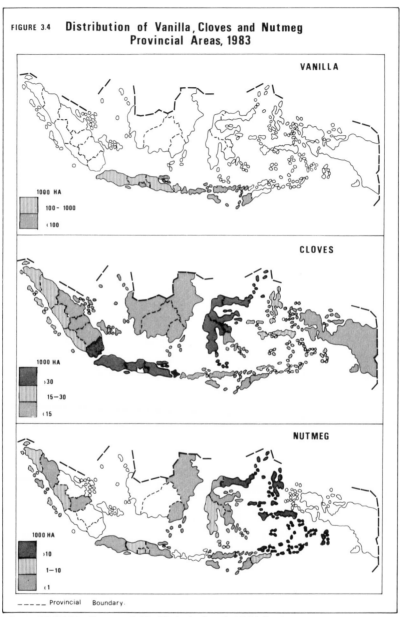

FIGURE 3.4 **Distribution of Vanilla, Cloves and Nutmeg
Provincial Areas, 1983**

VANILLA

1000 HA
100 - 1000
‹ 100

CLOVES

1000 HA
›30
15 — 30
‹15

NUTMEG

1000 HA
›10
1 — 10
‹1

_ _ _ _ _ Provincial Boundary.

Source: Adapted from figures supplied by Directorate–General of Estate Crops.

province of Maluku, the reported total area has remained at about 57 000 ha throughout 1979-80.

Cardamom is another spice increasingly grown for the commercial market. Smallholders in West Sumatra are finding the crop remunerative and many are members of a cooperative handling it. Production data are not yet consolidated nationally. The same is true for ginger, which is widely grown as a homestead crop.

Citronella (lemon grass) (Figure 3.5) has been a crop of local importance in some areas, but cultivation for essential oil extraction has declined very sharply in recent years. Total area was estimated to be about 4 500 ha in 1983.

Cashew (Figure 3.5) is almost exclusively a smallholder crop, with an estimated 180 000 ha total area in 1983, up sharply from about 80 000 kg per hectare in 1978. Estimated average production was about 100 kg/ha, suggesting that serious production was limited to only a few areas. Some attempts to establish cashew estates have encountered severe difficulties: One set up in Central Java in the 1970s failed to bear adequately and production output was switched to cashew wine, made from the green fruit receptacle.

Cinnamon (cassia) (Figure 3.5) on smallholdings was estimated to cover some 77 000 ha in 1983, yielding about 16 000 tonnes of dried bark. Sumatra is the main production area. While *cinchona* (quinine tree) is grown on a small scale by some estates, *sago palms* constitute a sparse stand in many areas; at maturity the trees provide the input to small-scale rural enterprises producing food starch.

Tea (Figure 3.6) cultivation has been less dominated by estates than has been the case with oil-palms, but they still accounted for about 55 percent of the total area of 110 000 ha in 1983, and produced over 75 percent of the output. Suitable conditions occur mainly at higher elevations in the heavier rainfall areas, and for black tea production, plantations need to be concentrated around processing facilities. Bandung in West Java is a major producing area, and smaller concentrations have appeared in Central Java, where smallholdings constitute about three-quarters of the total crop area, as is true in West Sumatra. Many smallholders process their tea themselves, producing green tea. Considerable support is now being given to the expansion of smallholder tea areas, and several new processing facilities are either under construction or in the planning stages.

In one area in Central Java, the extension of smallholder tea areas is being promoted under a NES-type project, with investment credits being advanced for land development. It is clear that this extension will prove intrinsically more expensive than many of the earlier estate

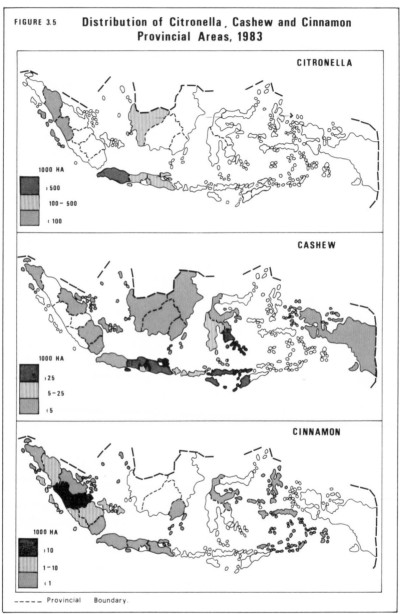

FIGURE 3.5 **Distribution of Citronella, Cashew and Cinnamon Provincial Areas, 1983**

CITRONELLA

1000 HA
> 500
100 – 500
< 100

CASHEW

1000 HA
> 25
5 – 25
< 5

CINNAMON

1000 HA
> 10
1 – 10
< 1

– – – – – Provincial Boundary.

Source: Adapted from figures supplied by Directorate-General of Estate Crops.

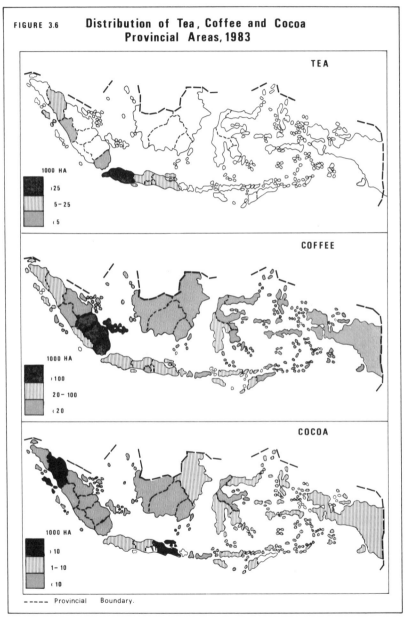

FIGURE 3.6   Distribution of Tea, Coffee and Cocoa
Provincial Areas, 1983

Source: Adapted from figures supplied by Directorate-General of Estate Crops.

developments, since the latter were able to take advantage of easier terrain.

Coffee (Figure 3.6) is traditionally a smallholder crop; in no province do the estates constitute more than 10 percent of the area under the crop.   The name Robusta was coined in Java for *C. canephora* when it was introduced in the 1880s to replace *C. arabica*, which had become unfruitful because of Hemilia rust, and Robusta remains the main type grown.

The crop is widely grown, with northern and southern Sumatra, West and Central Java and Bali and West Sulawesi being the principal producers.   The total area of smallholder coffee crop was estimated to be 0.74 million ha in 1983, with a production of 282 000 tonnes.   An estate area of 42 000 ha was credited with a production of about 17 000 tonnes.   Thus, even on the estates it would appear that yields are well below the 800-1 400 kg per hectare achieved on representative trial sites with improved Robusta clones.

The area planted with coffee has increased sharply in recent years in response to improving international prices; the smallholder area grew by 14 percent per annum between 1978 and 1981.   Production is now nearly double that of 1969-71.   Considerable scope would appear to exist, however, for improvement in quality; possibly the installation of more cooperatively operated processing and/or drying plants could contribute to the realization of this objective.

Cocoa (Figure 3.6) has grown in importance in recent years, with smallholders farming some 40 percent of the total area, which in 1983 was put at 43 000 ha. However, the bulk of cocoa is produced by large estate companies.   Production data suggest that yields from much smallholder cocoa must be minimal; total smallholder output is estimated at 10 percent or less than that from the estates.

Notwithstanding the excellent condition and bearing potential exhibited by some cocoa produced in North Sumatra, it is generally a difficult crop for smallholders to grow in the absence of strong extension support and reliable plant protection.   Concentrations around large-scale processing plants, such as that seen in North Sumatra, may well be the most effective mode of production.

This brief review of the more important crops grown in Indonesia is by no means comprehensive. *Wheat* cultivation, for example, is being tried in North Sulawesi, and *asparagus* and *mushrooms* are being promoted as potential export products.   *Mulberry* is grown for silkworm raising.   Efforts are being made to revive the trade of *orchids*, once a major export.

But even when these and other peripheral crops are discounted, the crop flora of Indonesia is one of exceptional diversity. This testifies to the skill of the Indonesian people in exploiting, at the micro-level, the options offered by their land resources; it also provides an indication of the complexity of the rural economic situation confronting planners.

Cropping Systems

Cropping systems - and cropping systems research as a discipline - pertain to the proportional allocation of parcels of land to different crops, to the short- and medium-term alternation of crops, to the combinations of crops that may be grown either simultaneously or sequentially on the same piece of land and to the timing and phasing of these cropping activities. Our interest in cropping systems focuses primarily on the annual food crops.

A distinction can and should be made between cropping systems and cropping patterns. There is a tendency in Indonesia to use the terms interchangeably, which is often a source of misunderstanding.

In simple terms, patterns are what emerge when systems are followed. The pattern is the visible product of the system or systems. A study of patterns often permits inferences to be made about the system or systems of which they are a product; the patterns, however, may neither define nor elucidate the systems. By the same token, a study of relevant systems will often allow useful predictions to be made as to the nature of the cropping patterns that will emerge but, similarly, the systems do not necessarily serve to define the patterns.

Identified cropping patterns at times are used as models that can be imitated with advantage. But the circumstances of agriculture more often dictate that improvement is a consequence of some adjustment of the systems, which in turn affects the cropping pattern. The subtleties of this argument can be seen by likening systems to substance and patterns to form.

Other than where there is a specialization in livestock or long-cycle perennial crops, production of the basic food staples is the fundamental purpose of cultivation throughout the smallholder subsector, and the systems that seek to maximise the output of these crops are the core of agricultural practice. Systems for the production of other crops, for either consumption or sale, constitute peripheral components that are opportunistically integrated when needs demand and circumstances permit.

Rice, as the preferred staple, is the crop that will be given priority in the cropping system, whenever conditions are favourable for its production. Thus, on farms where there is year-round access to irrigation water, rice is often continuously cropped, with two, two-and-a-half or three crops per year. Where rainfall is sufficient to allow reasonable yields under rain-fed conditions, the production of rice will often take precedence over other crops. Thus in some areas, land that can only receive irrigation water seasonally may still be double-cropped with rice, that is, an irrigated crop followed by a rain-fed one relying on retained moisture and growing-period rainfall. In those places where irrigation cannot be practiced, rice remains the preferred crop wherever satisfactory yields can be obtained under rain-fed conditions. Depending on the amount and monthly distribution of the rainfall, either one, two or in some cases more, rice crops will be grown annually.

The characteristics of the practised rice cropping systems - that is, the choice of cultivars, establishment techniques (e.g., dry seeding, transplanting), tillage methods, management practices, and so on - are determined by an array of factors, many of which are location- or site-specific. It should be noted, however, that the availability of an increasingly broad range of rice HYVs - differing in maturity periods, water requirements, disease resistance, suitability for specific soil conditions, and so forth - may significantly increase the number of system options open to the farmer; the possibility of increasing annual cropping intensity by the use of quick-maturing cultivars is an obvious example.

The behavioural response of farmers to the broadening of rice cultivation system options may have important macro-policy implications. Some farmers may use a change to quicker maturing cultivars to open up opportunities (time windows) for the insertion of additional crops in their rotations. Other farmers, possibly a majority in some areas, may seize the opportunity to change to another system (or modify their existing one) to intensify rice production on their land at the expense of other crops. There may be no *a priori* reasons to suppose that one of these courses offers advantage compared to the other. (This topic is returned to in Chapter 7, where some of the preconditions for change are discussed.)

Table 3.11 presents the results of an analysis carried out on data for the monthly distributions of the planting and harvesting of the aggregate areas of food crops in East Java Province in 1983. Line 1 indicates in percentage terms the relative areas planted to the listed crops. Rice, and the other main staples - maize and cassava - together occupied 88 percent of the total area planted that year. This province is one of the more important contributors to national soyabean

Table 3.11: Monthly Distribution of the Planting and Harvesting of Food Crops in East Java, 1983

Month	Crops (Percentage x 10 of Total Food Crop Planted Area)							Totals
	Wetland Rice	Dryland Rice	Maize	Cassava	Soyabeans	Peanuts	Sweet Potatoes	
	(a) Planting (Total Planted Area: 3 961 million ha)^f							
January	95	5	34	16	2	3	1	156
February	71	0.6	8	8	5	1	0.6	94
March	27	0.1	26	7	10	4	1	75
April	23	0.1	17	4	14	7	0.8	66
May	30	0.1	11	3	10	2	1	57
June	29	0.1	10	2	3	3	1	48
July	17	-	11	1	10	2	0.9	42
August	8	-	10	1	11	2	0.8	33
September	5	-	8	1	4	1	0.5	19
October	5	5	71	19	2	2	0.5	104
November	35	13	94	35	4	5	1	187
December	83	2	22	13	0.6	2	0.6	123
Totals	428	26	323	103	75	35	10	1 000
1. Crop proportion of total food crop planted area, percent	43	3	32	10	7	3	1	100
2. No. of months when more than 10 percent of crop planted	3	3	3	4	5	3	5	
3. No. of months when 5-10 percent of crop planted	5	1	3	2	3	7	7	
4. No. of months when more than 5 percent of crop planted	8	4	6	6	8	10	12	

Table 3.11: Monthly Distribution of the Planting and Harvesting of Food Crops in East Java, 1983 (Cont'd)

Month	Wetland Rice	Dryland Rice	Maize	Cassava	Soyabeans	Peanuts	Sweet Potatoes	Totals
			Crops (Percentage x 10 of Total Food Crop Planted Area)					
			(b) Harvesting (Total Harvested Area: 3 439 million ha)[1]					
January	3	0.3	14	2	0.1	0.2	0.3	26
February	7	7	77	3	2	0.8	0.2	97
March	34	12	90	2	3	6	0.5	147
April	98	2	26	2	3	3	0.8	135
May	94	0.4	13	4	7	2	0.8	121
June	43	0.1	26	4	14	6	0.9	94
July	32	-	17	10	15	8	1	83
August	32	0.1	13	25	7	3	2	82
September	26	-	14	21	5	3	1	70
October	21	-	13	14	14	3	1	66
November	13	-	10	8	11	3	1	46
December	8	-	24	3	2	1	0.7	39
Total	409	22	337	100	83	38	10	1 000
1. Crop proportion of total food crops harvested area, percent	41	2	34	10	8	4	1	100
2. No. of months when more than 10 percent of crop harvested	3	2	2	4	4	3	5	
3. No. of months when 5-10 percent of crop harvested	5	1	4	1	2	6	5	
4. No. of months when more than 5 percent of crop harvested	8	3	6	5	6	9	10	

[1] Planted and harvested areas do not correspond because (1) harvested areas include some planted in 1982, and exclude those planted in 1983 for harvest in 1984; and (2) crop loss areas are discounted.

Note: Row and column figures may not total correctly because of rounding.

Source: Calculated from data from Government of Indonesia, Biro Pusat Statistik.

production, but in planted area terms this crop occupied less than one-fifth that occupied by rice. The timing of the plantings of maize and cassava suggests that, for the most part, they were not follow-on crops after wetland rice, but were in dryland areas. The timing for the plantings of soyabeans suggests that they, too, were mainly a dryland crop, possibly interplanted in maize or cassava. There is no obvious reason to suppose that the seasonally well-distributed plantings of peanuts and sweet potatoes were biased toward wetland, but in any case these crops were statistically unimportant. It is difficult to avoid the conclusion that, for most farmers, the cropping system on their wetland was either one or two rice crops, with very little attempt to grow anything else. On the dryland areas many, if not most, farmers did not include significant plantings of other crops in their rotations.

Inspection of the corresponding data for the other provinces of Java reveal, as expected, some regional variations in the proportionalities of the different crops. But the general symmetry of the planting patterns persists, and cursory analysis serves to confirm the observed general concentration on the main staples in the practised systems, and the much lesser importance of the other crops. That this is also generally true in the Outer Islands is substantiated by the data presented in Table 3.12, which show the percentages of individual food crop areas in the total food crop planted areas in several of the provinces in 1988. Significant inclusions of non-main staples in cropping system can only have been at all widespread in D.I. Aceh and West Nusa Tenggara. In D.I. Aceh, soyabeans have become more important since a zero-tillage technique for cropping following rice has been adopted; in West Nusa Tenggara, soyabeans would appear to rank as a staple.

The general finding underscores the need to quantify the actual employment of different cropping systems when they are presented in order to portray farming practices in a given area. W.R. Falcon et al. (1984) describes observed cropping systems in three locations in Java. Collateral evidence indicates that the crop calendars shown accurately represent what some farmers practise. The inclusion of rainfall and relevant data is helpful, as it has considerable explanatory value. But for the purposes of intervention planning, unless there is quantification of the extent to which, for example, follow-on crops after rice actually occur, the value of these system identifications is limited. An analysis of the data presented in Figure 3.7 suggests, for instance, that all the cropping systems shown for irrigated soils in Kediri, West Java, are atypical as regards the province as a whole.

Why farmers do not actively practise the more diversified system often purported as typical remains a question. Field observations,

Table 3.12: Crop Proportions of Total Provincial Food Crop Planted Areas, 1988

Province	Percentage of Total Provincial Food Crop Planted Area							
	Wetland Rice	Dryland Rice	Maize	Cassava	Soya-beans	Peanuts	Sweet Potato	Total
D.I. Aceh	64.0	1.7	3.1	1.3	25.4	3.9	0.6	100.0
North Sumatra	69.7	9.4	9.6	3.2	3.5	2.9	1.8	100.0
West Sumatra	84.0	3.7	2.9	2.0	4.2	2.3	0.9	100.0
Jambi	64.2	18.4	2.3	7.9	4.3	1.7	1.2	100.0
Riau	52.9	28.5	7.1	4.5	3.5	2.4	1.1	100.0
South Sumatra	61.9	18.1	5.4	6.3	3.6	3.1	1.6	100.0
Bengkulu	55.1	21.4	8.2	4.9	1.8	5.1	3.6	100.0
Lampung	29.8	14.4	23.7	18.4	12.2	1.2	0.3	100.0
Bali	58.0	0.8	19.7	6.1	7.9	4.1	3.3	100.0
West Nusa Tenggara	57.3	4.0	5.6	2.7	24.2	4.0	2.3	100.0
East Nusa Tenggara	14.5	13.3	48.5	18.3	0.4	1.8	3.1	100.0
South Kalimantan	81.1	8.8	2.7	2.6	1.0	3.3	0.5	100.0
North Sulawesi	29.7	6.0	45.0	3.0	12.2	2.4	1.7	100.0
South Sulawesi	58.7	1.3	27.7	3.5	3.3	4.7	0.7	100.0
S.E. Sulawesi	21.9	14.7	37.1	16.1	3.1	4.2	2.8	100.0

Notes: Figures may not total correctly due to rounding. Corresponding data for the remaining provinces were not included in the source used.

Source: Calculated from data from Government of Indonesia, Biro Pusat Statistik (1989).

however, suggest some possible reasons for reluctance to lengthen yearly cropping time. The shorter time periods actually used may reflect a balance between dry season soil water amounts and crop transpiration needs that is more precarious than is commonly thought. Destruction of the structure of soils by puddling for rice may make dry season fallowing the only option. Tillage by manual methods is exhausting work, particularly in the heavier soil, and the expectable returns to catch-cropping may not warrant the effort involved. Use of quicker maturing cultivars to create "time windows" may be at the expense of lower yields and greater risks, so that net aggregate advantage is small - a zero-sum gain situation. Socio-technical factors may be relevant: Freely roaming cattle grazing stubbles may deter any departures from the established local cropping practices, and attempting non-rice crops in the midst of late-irrigated rice may be

a) Garut West Java

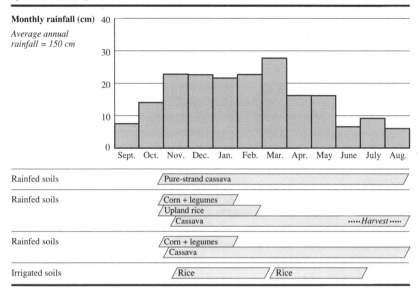

b) Gunung Kidul D.I. Yogyakarta

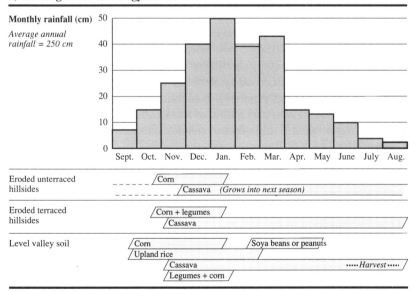

Figure 3.7: Cropping Systems and Rainfall Patterns in Three Locations in Java

Source: Falcon, et al. (1984).

Note: See text for discussion of representativeness of these cropping systems.

c) **Kediri East Java**

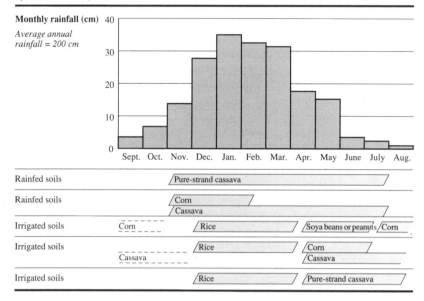

Figure 3.7: Cropping Systems and Rainfall Patterns in Three Locations in Java (Cont'd)

impracticable. These may all be factors accounting for the agricultural rather than horticultural intensity of so many Indonesian smallholdings, despite their small size.

Quantitative data of good quality, in terms of representativeness, on the cropping systems practised in Indonesia are still largely lacking, notwithstanding the extensive field studies carried out by the cropping systems agronomists and other specialists based at the Central Research Institutes at Bogor.

It should be obvious, but regrettably does not always appear to be so, that a quantification of existing cropping systems is a necessary input when serious attempts are made to devise intervention policy instruments oriented specifically toward inducing changes in those systems. Not only must the relative use of systems be quantified, but the spatial distributions must also be determined.

Table 3.11 serves also to explain the uselessness of aggregate data for the performance of this task. Lines 2-4 show the number of months when significant percentages of the various crops are planted and harvested. These data show the wide spread of planting and harvesting times, and the absence of any sharp timing discontinuities that would assist in a decomposition of the data, so as to reveal more clearly the prevalence of systems with specific characteristics. It is clear that the lack of comprehensive knowledge in this field will only be remedied by *ad hoc* investigations, which will inevitably be costly in regard to both time and resources. In the context of planning area-specific projects, it may be necessary to include subcomponents undertaking this type of investigation effort.

Farming Systems and Technology

A "farming system" connotes the aggregate of the assortment of agricultural activity systems practised by an individual farmer; it may include, for instance, arable cropping, plantation operation, horticulture, livestock husbandry, aquaculture, on-farm processing, farm-level forestry, custom work for other farmers and so on. Often, the activity patterns of a number of farmers will be sufficiently similar to allow their farming system to be attributed type status.

An identification of types of farming systems has become the methodological cornerstone of studies - now almost a discipline - that seek better understanding of the *modi operandi* of farms and that explore ways in which their net productivity can be increased. The approach seeks to overcome one of the frequent shortcomings of activity-specific studies at the farm level: disregard of the influence of activities' interaction.

As is discussed later in this chapter, systematic farming systems research has increasingly been a part of the general research effort in Indonesia and has been a feature of several agricultural development projects. High hopes are often entertained that research of this sort will yield clearer perceptions of the opportunities for agricultural advancement and thus be of value in the orientation of research station effort and the design of appropriate interventions.

Farming systems research is a much needed and worthwhile activity, which, in Indonesia particularly, deserves every encouragement and support. However, a sense of realism should prevail about the applicability of research findings. Circumstances dictate that myriad farming systems can be found in Indonesia, and many are location- and situation-specific. Their classification poses many intractable problems, which is why no systematic review is attempted here.

Since the size of the holding is an important general determinant of the farming system practised or feasible, it is relevant to first examine how the total farmed area of Indonesia is divided into operating units.

Enumerations of farm units were made in the course of the nationwide 1983 Agricultural Census carried out under the aegis of the BPS. An analysis of the published reports of the census has enabled the calculation of Tables 3.7 and 3.8, which were presented and discussed earlier in this chapter.

These data show that Indonesia is, indeed, a country of many sub-half-hectare farms. They also show that if an area of about 1 ha or more is taken as the criterion for defining a "large farm", then in most provinces a major portion of the land is, in fact, taken up by much larger units - an aspect of much significance when, for instance, the likely production effects of extension and other supportive measures are being considered, and research priorities are being set. In a situation like that in North Sulawesi Province, where 84 percent of the land is operated by the 49 percent of the farmers, who have holdings greater than 1 ha, it is easy to see that if research focuses solely on the systems used by the larger farmers, and effective extension reaches down only to this level, progress toward overall production goals may nevertheless be quite substantial.

As is well known, farm units in Indonesia are usually made up of a number of discrete parcels of land that are not only spatially distributed but are also located in different physical environments. Thus, an individual holding may include parcels of land that can be used for different agricultural or horticultural purposes. Thus, in addition to the home garden located close to the dwelling, there may be some adjacent dryland, some additional dryland elsewhere, some rain-fed *sawah* and some irrigable *sawah*. In most instances, the separate plots will be within reasonable travelling distance, but in some areas plots may be more remote and alternative accommodation must be used when they are worked.

In this context, a smallholder's farming system may incorporate several different cropping systems. Thus, rice might be double-cropped on irrigated *sawah*; a single rice crop might be taken from rain-fed *sawah* and followed by fallow; tilled dryland might carry either cassava or intercropped maize and legumes; coffee might be planted with shade trees on other elevated land; and vegetables might be grown in the home garden.

Such a system has frequently been found in the course of field studies at the village level, particularly in Java, and it is probable that in a number of areas it could be considered as typical in the sense that it represents the system used by most farmers. But it is clear that over much of Indonesia many farmers have to use totally different systems. The extent to which the system described above may be quite atypical is shown by the data presented in Table 3.13, which reveals the proportions of irrigated wetland, rain-fed wetland and dryland in the provincial totals of cultivated land, as recorded in the reports of the Agricultural Census of 1983. It has been difficult to duplicate the conditions and outcome to any significant extent.

Corresponding data for the *kabupatens* of Central Java, presented in Table 3.14, show that the aggregate provincial data probably fail to convey the full extent to which the irregularities of the resources distribution at the local level imposes on farmers the need to adopt differing systems of farming. Quite obviously the typical systems of Wonogiri *kabupaten* will not adequately represent the typical systems of Kudus *kabupaten*.

The corresponding data for West Java and East Java reveals similar inequalities in the resource availability, as shown by the data presented in Table 3.15.

If the land defined by the census categories could be considered homogeneous, then conceivably farming system homologues could be based on general topological symmetries. But, as the discussion on the resource base and operational environment has shown, the physical qualities of land show great variation, as does its economic potential.

The series of data presented do not lessen the belief that at a local level - within, say, a *kecamatan* or possibly a *kabupaten* area - the categorization of farming systems may be possible and can prove useful. But the data strongly suggest that reliable results cannot be expected if use is made of supposedly "representative" farming systems to make quantitative forecasts of the impact of developmental interventions applied over whole provinces or regions.

Traditionally, power on Indonesian farms has been provided by human muscle or by draught animals. Recently, however, tractors have been introduced. This development has been the cause of much controversy: On the one hand it has been argued that tractors can improve farm efficiency, but on the other hand it is alleged that because of labour displacement the social costs of such increased efficiency are too high.

If social costs are discounted, and operational arrangements permit full use, then there can be no doubt that tractors can be a cheaper source of farm power than either human or animal muscle - fossil fuels are still much cheaper than grown fuels. Recognition of this fact and confirmatory use help explain the 19 percent average annual growth in the numbers of tractors in the 11 years following 1973, when the total inventory of two- and four-wheel machines climbed from 1 914 to 13 003. The government should, however, investigate the social costs

Table 3.13: Distribution of Cultivated Land by Province, 1983[1]

Province	Percentage of Provincial Total		
	Irrigated Wetland	Rainfed Wetland	Dryland
D.I. Aceh	16	19	65
North Sumatra	14	20	67
West Sumatra	26	15	59
Riau	0.5	9	91
Jambi	4	16	81
South Sumatra	4	21	75
Bengkulu	12	13	76
Lampung	8	9	82
West Java	30	19	50
Central Java	25	21	54
D.I. Yogyakarta	15	7	78
East Java	30	16	54
Bali	28	0.7	72
West Nusa Tenggara	35	18	47
East Nusa Tenggara	6	5	90
West Kalimantan	3	16	81
Central Kalimantan	0.3	19	81
South Kalimantan	1	51	48
East Kalimantan	1	20	79
North Sulawesi	7	4	89
Central Sulawesi	11	4	86
South Sulawesi	15	26	59
Southeast Sulawesi	6	7	87
Maluku	0.2	0.02	99
Irian Jaya	0.2	4	96
All Indonesia	4.78 m ha[2]	2.10 m ha[2]	12.63 m ha

[1] "Controlled" land, that is, land owned, plus land rented in, less land rented out.

[2] The 4.78 m ha of irrigated wetland include areas served by village irrigation.

Sources: Provincial percentage calculated from data from Government of Indonesia, Biro Pusat Statistik (1983a) except for all Indonesia which is from Government of Indonesia, Directorate-General of Water Resources Development.

of increased tractor use in terms of foregone employment and if the costs appear too high as the analysis that follows indicates, slow down this process. The 1984 inventory of tractors, subdivided into categories, is given in Table 3.16.

Table 3.14: Distribution of Cultivated Land: Central Java, 1983[1]

Kabupaten	Percentage of Provincial Total		
	Irrigated Wetland	Rainfed Wetland	Dryland
Cilacap	14	36	50
Banyumas	28	12	60
Purbolinggo	31	8	61
Banjarnegara	13	10	77
Kebumen	22	20	58
Purworejo	25	11	64
Wonosobo	19	9	71
Magelang	34	10	56
Boyolali	13	19	68
Klaten	59	4	37
Sukoharjo	44	19	37
Wonogiri	13	12	75
Karanganyar	40	6	54
Sragen	23	30	48
Grobogan	11	43	46
Blora	5	44	51
Rembang	6	39	55
Pati	21	34	45
Kudus	33	42	25
Jepara	37	12	51
Demak	28	36	35
Semarang	22	13	65
Temanggung	24	8	68
Kendal	37	7	56
Batang	42	8	51
Pekalongan	40	20	40
Pemalang	40	15	44
Tegal	52	17	30
Brebes	44	22	34
Central Java	25	21	54
	(0.49 m ha)	(0.41 m ha)	(1.08 m ha)

[1] "Controlled" land, that is, land owned, plus land rented in, less land rented out.

Source: Calculated from data from Government of Indonesia, Biro Pusat Statistik (1983a).

The actual amounts of draught animal power available and used for tillage purposes are not easily quantified. Total numbers of cattle and buffalo are reported, but of these some will belong to farmers who do

Table 3.15: Distribution of Cultivated Land in Selected Kabupatens in West Java and East Java

	Irrigated Sawah Percent	Rainfed Sawah Percent	Dryland Percent
West Java			
Cirebon	67	13	20
Indramayu	63	22	15
Garut	25	14	80
Lebak	6	24	70
East Java			
Jember	60	5	36
Sidoarjo	60	3	37
Sampang	2	21	76
Pacitan	3	10	87

Source: Calculated from data from Government of Indonesia, Biro Pusat Statistik (1983a).

Table 3.16: National Farm Tractor Inventory, 1984

	No. of Tractors	Assumed Mean Horsepower[1]	Total Horsepower[1]
Two-wheel tractors	8 881	(10)	88 810
Four-wheel tractors:			
Mini	2 470	(12)	29 640
Small	642	(20)	12 840
Medium	146	(35)	5 110
Large	864	(50)	43 200
Total	13 003		179 600

[1] 1 hp + 0.753 kW.

Source: Government of Indonesia, Biro Pusat Statistik (1984a).

not practice animal-draught tillage, and other animals will be either too immature, untrained or otherwise not available for work. These reductions in the working strengths have been allowed for in our calculations by attributing cattle with 0.25 hp per head and buffaloes with 0.33 hp per head. When applied to the 1983 reported cattle and buffalo population, the total animal horsepower amounted to just short of 3 million.

To arrive at power availabilities at the provincial level, the relevant power coefficients were applied to the reported cattle, buffalo, and tractor-type inventories, and the aggregate contribution to national totals calculated. The results are presented in Table 3.17. With respect to tractor horsepower, it should be noted that West Java claims almost 30 percent of the total, and that Aceh, North Sumatra, Central Java, East Java and South Sulawesi together account for another 46 percent. Distribution of animal power is similarly non-uniform, with East Java accounting (by the method used) for over 30 percent, Central Java for nearly 15 percent, and South Sulawesi for over 10 percent.

To obtain a measure of the contributions possible from tractor and animal power to the total tillage power requirements at the provincial level, calculations were made of the percentages of the 1983 wetland rice harvested area that could be cultivated by, respectively, tractors and draught bovines, assuming a uniform input power requirement of 1 hp per hectare. It should be noted that horsepower (hp) is a measure of the *rate* of work performance, not the *amount* of work performed. The results of these calculations, and the residual hectarages of wetland rice, are presented in Table 3.18.

The degree to which the residual wetland rice areas - Column 3 of Table 3.18 - accurately represent the extent of reliance on manual tillage methods is, of course, sensitive to the assumptions made respecting mechanical and animal power inputs, and inspection of data on *kabupaten* level distributions of tractors and bovines suggest high levels of intraprovincial variability will also occur.

The spread of the generated provincial data relative to the corresponding national aggregate figures, as shown in Table 3.18, agrees with our own observations and with information gleaned from relevant reports. The aggregate figures are of a plausible magnitude, given the total power capabilities of limited numbers of tractors and draught animals. When allowances are made for the fact that the power requirements for dryland tillage have been wholly discounted, and the high proportion of dryland in some areas, then the extent to which manual labour is the only utilized power source becomes very apparent. Taking the country as a whole, the physical work input provided by people for the performance of all agricultural tasks is probably at least five times that provided by animals, which in turn is probably at least ten times that provided by internal combustion engines. To a very large extent Indonesia's agriculture remains powered by food staples.

Table 3.17: Distribution of National Tractor and Animal Power by Province, 1983-84

	Percentage of Total Tractor Horsepower[1]	Percentage of Total Animal Horsepower[2]
D.I. Aceh	7.4	3.6
North Sumatra	10.7	2.9
West Sumatra	2.2	2.9
Riau	0.8	0.6
Jambi	0.5	0.9
South Sumatra	1.8	1.7
Bengkulu	0.3	0.6
Lampung	3.4	1.8
West Java	29.5	6.4
Central Java	8.6	14.9
D.I. Yogyakarta	0.6	2.2
East Java	11.6	30.7
Bali	2.1	3.6
West Nusa Tenggara	0.6	4.6
East Nusa Tenggara	2.6	5.8
West Kalimantan	0.6	0.7
Central Kalimantan	0.3	0.2
South Kalimantan	1.3	0.6
East Kalimantan	0.4	0.2
North Sulawesi	2.3	1.8
Central Sulawesi	2.7	1.6
South Sulawesi	8.3	10.8
Southeast Sulawesi	1.1	0.6
Maluku	-	0.3
Irian Jaya	-	0.1
All Indonesia	100.0	100.0
	(0.18 m hp)	(2.99 m hp)

[1] Aggregate provincial tractor horsepower, attributing mean values to types per 1984 provincial inventories.

[2] Aggregate provincial animal horsepower, attributing 0.25 hp to each cattle head, and 0.33 hp to each buffalo head recorded in 1983 provincial inventories.

Source: Calculated from data from Government of Indonesia, Biro Pusat Statistik.

Mechanical power has been more widely deployed for site preparation where new plantations and transmigration settlements have been established. Much evidence is now accumulating that indicates high costs often attach to these operations in terms of irremediable damage to the soil: Compaction reduces drainage capability and thus

Table 3.18: Power Availability for Wetland Rice Cultivation by Province, 1983-84

	Percentage of Wetland Rice Cultivable by Tractors[1]	Percentage of Wetland Rice Cultivable by Animals[2]	Percentage of Wetland Rice for Which Neither Tractor nor Animal Power Available[3]
D.I. Aceh	5.5	44.6	49.9
North Sumatra	4.1	18.8	77.1
West Sumatra	1.4	28.8	69.8
Riau	1.6	21.0	77.4
Jambi	0.7	20.0	79.3
South Sumatra	1.1	16.6	82.3
Bengkulu	1.0	29.5	69.5
Lampung	3.3	29.0	67.7
West Java	3.1	11.2	85.7
Central Java	1.2	35.1	63.7
D.I. Yogyakarta	1.1	63.0	35.9
East Java	1.5	65.2	33.3
Bali	2.3	66.0	31.7
West Nusa Tenggara	0.5	64.3	35.2
East Nusa Tenggara	6.3	100.0[4]	-
West Kalimantan	0.6	13.1	86.3
Central Kalimantan	0.7	6.8	92.5
South Kalimantan	0.9	6.9	92.2
East Kalimantan	2.6	16.7	80.7
North Sulawesi	7.4	95.1	-
Central Sulawesi	6.9	66.6	26.5
South Sulawesi	2.7	58.8	38.5
Southeast Sulawesi	12.8	100.0[4]	-
Maluku	-	100.0[4]	-
Irian Jaya	-	100.0[4]	-
All Indonesia	2.3	37.7	60.0
	(0.18 m ha)	(2.99 m ha)	(4.77 m ha)

[1] Assuming one tractor horsepower per hectare wetland rice harvested, 1983.

[2] Assuming one animal horsepower per hectare of wetland rice harvested, 1983.

[3] Calculation residual.

[4] Animal strength exceeds requirement for wetland rice cultivation.

Source: Calculated from data from Government of Indonesia, Biro Pusat Statistik data.

encourages erosion, and overworking destroys topsoil structure. Notwithstanding the higher costs, labour-intensive methods and/or biological or biochemical systems may prove, in many instances, to be the only ecologically satisfactory way of opening up new land.

The attractiveness of cheap fossil fuel has sometimes proved irresistible, notwithstanding the social costs. In 1984, there were reportedly nearly 45 000 small rice mills, with capacity of up to 300 kg per hour, and nearly 4 000 rice mills with greater capacity. This constitutes a rural capacity - if operated at full stretch - to process the entire rice crop. It is therefore not surprising that the opportunities have greatly diminished for women to earn their livelihoods by custom hand-pounding (husk removal) of paddy.

Farm equipment inventories generally remain small. Where no animal or tractor power is used tillage will be accomplished with a hand hoe costing less than US$ 3. For animal-draught cultivation in rice paddies, simple ard-type ploughs and locally made "ladders" or floats are used.

Most rice is threshed by hand; overall about half is normally threshed in the field and about half at the homestead. Farmers have been quick to see the labour-saving potential of pedal- and engine-powered threshers. About 36 000 were in use in 1984, up sharply from a reported 309 in 1978.

Hand sprayers are the most popular means of applying plant protectants. The total number in use in 1984 was estimated at 0.57 million, the result of a 20 percent average annual growth since 1973. Power sprayers, many of which were probably used on larger plantations, only totalled 5 750 units in 1984. Little use is made of water-lifting devices for irrigation; in 1985 the number of pumps was recorded as 6 516. Despite many endeavours by interested agencies - such as the Dutch-assisted Appropriate Technology Unit at the Institute of Technology, Bandung, the Indonesian Institute of Sciences (LIPI) and Dian Desa (a Yogyakarta-based NGO) - there has been little success in efforts to design a satisfactory low-cost crop dryer suitable for smallholders. Most farmers still rely on direct sun drying of grain and cassava; in 1983 only 1 120 dryers were listed in the machinery inventory. In some areas where lack of labour is an obvious constraint - for example, some parts of West Sumatra - hand-powered winnowers were clearly popular, but elsewhere they appear to be less used.

The replacement of the the *ani-ani* (finger knife) by the sickle is a cause célèbre that ranks with the displacement of rice hand-pounding. Many traditional grain varieties have been self-selected for a tendency to shatter, so care in harvesting is needed. But HYV's can be more roughly treated, so introduction of rice HYVs has permitted much greater use of sickles, and womens' involvement using the *ani-ani* has dramatically declined.

Fertilizer has been available at low farm-gate prices in recent years, as a result of heavy subsidization, and the economic returns possible have been high. In 1985, farmers paid Rp 100 000 per ton for urea, sulphate of ammonia, diammonium phosphate, triple superphosphate and muriate of potash, which was below even the per ton price for maize. Not surprisingly, demand matched supply and year-end carryover stocks were reported as minimal. Consumption data, as calculated by deducting exports from production and imports for the years 1981-85 are shown in Table 3.19. Table 3.20 shows how, in 1983, available fertilizer was applied to the main staples under cultivation. The percentage use column of this table was computed by applying the per hectare use rate (Agricultural Indication, 1983) to harvested crop areas (Statistik Indonesia 1984). These data indicate the heavy concentration of fertilizer use on the wetland rice crop.

Just how efficiently fertilizer is being used is difficult to assess; some well-placed observers have suggested that large amounts are misapplied, in the sense that crop responses are small, possibly because of limiting factors other than nutrient supply. If farm-gate fertilizer prices are below cost, what appears to be a positive value/cost ratio (VCR) may, in real terms, be negative. Although the national interest might, in the broadest sense, be best served by maintaining VCRs above 2 (FAO's recommended minimum), the interests of an individual farmer - and, of course, any specific crop-intensification programme - will still be served even if an accounting VCR of only 1.1 is achieved.

As Table 3.19 shows, nitrogen has greatly exceeded the growth of other nutrients. Taking urea and ammonium sulphate together, elemental nitrogen usage increased by an average 21 percent annually between 1981 and 1985. This increase probably contributed very significantly to the achievement of rice self-sufficiency. Available data are not adequate, unfortunately, to permit this contribution to be quantified, or the overall VCR to be calculated.

Obtaining the best possible returns to fertilizer must be a priority for Indonesia; failure to do so will simply mean that a resource is being underused. There is not much scope to improve the soil using animal manure - there are simply not enough animals in relation to the amount of cultivated land. In the densely settled areas, fertilizers are the only practicable means of fertility replenishment.

Table 3.19: Fertilizer, Product Basis, 1981-85 (million tonnes)[1]

	1981	1982	1983	1984	1985
Urea	1.16	2.40	1.92	2.91	3.26
Ammonium sulphate	0.40	0.35	0.35	0.45	0.56
Triple superphosphate	0.68	1.01	0.77	0.86	1.00
Miscellaneous	0.12	0.01	0.01	0.01	0.01
Totals	2.25	3.85	3.12	4.33	4.83

[1] Production plus imports minus exports.

Source: Calculated from information provided by Government of Indonesia, Ministry of Agriculture.

Table 3.20: Fertilizer Use, 1983

	Kilograms per Hectare	Percentage of Total Fertilizers Usage
Wetland rice	273	79.6
Dryland rice	59	2.5
Maize	111	12.3
Cassava	39	1.8
Soyabeans	69	1.6
Peanuts	76	1.3
Sweet potatoes	98	0.9
Total		100.0

Source: Calculated from data from Government of Indonesia, Biro Pusat Statistik (1984q).

Plant protectant distribution through crop intensification programmes grew from about 6 500 tonnes in 1980 to about 14 250 tonnes in 1985. Table 3.21 indicates that wetland rice was the main crop beneficiary of these materials. On a per hectare basis, however, applications to soyabeans approximated those of wetland rice.

Herbicides have yet to feature prominently in local practice. On well-managed oil-palm and rubber plantation, leguminous cover crops (LCCs) are used very successfully for weed control. Hopes had been entertained that LCCs could be used to suppress *Imperata cylindrica* when land is opened for food cropping, and early trials were promising. Subsequent work has, however, indicated that high phosphate expropriation may prejudice yields of interplanted crops.

The practice of "block farming", with groups of farmers on contingent plots adhering to an agreed cropping plan - same HYV, same planting time, and so on - has helped to improve the pest- and

Table 3.21: Plant Protectants Use, 1987

	Insecticides Percentage of Total Used	Fungicides, Rodenticides, etc., Percentage of Total Used
Wetland rice	88.8	89.5
Dryland rice	1.4	2.1
Maize	1.8	1.3
Cassava	0.3	0.2
Soyabeans	6.9	3.4
Peanuts	0.6	3.5
Sweet potatoes	0.1	0.1
Total	100.0	100.0

Source: Government of Indonesia, Biro Pusat Statistik (1987).

disease-control measures taken by the farmers. Such benefits are the main reason for promoting the formation of farmer groups.

Livestock Husbandry

Indonesia has a relatively small livestock sector; the ratios of livestock to people, and to cultivated land, are probably among the lowest in Southeast Asia. Estimates of the actual livestock population vary. Enumeration may not be very reliable, and distributional data should be treated as indicative only.

Table 3.22 presents the BPS estimates for the numbers of livestock in each province in 1983, and Table 3.23 presents the percentages of the total provincial rural households keeping ruminant livestock.

Dairy cattle in Indonesia are almost exclusively Holstein-Friesians. Significant numbers are kept only in North Sumatra and the Java provinces, but even there the percentage of households producing milk with these animals does not exceed 0.6 percent on a provincial basis.

Most milk-producing households operate on a small scale, with an average of about two milk cows. With followers, the larger herds may extend to 10-15 head. Total production in 1983 was estimated at about 145 000 tonnes of fresh milk, from 180 000 cattle. All commercial milk producers are required to be members of a KUD, which channels their milk to processors, that either retail it fresh or use it for milk powder production.

The subsector has received very substantial external support in recent years; 179 000 cows were imported in the period 1978-83, largely from Australia and New Zealand. Artificial insemination

Table 3.22: Livestock Populations by Province, 1983 (in Thousands)

	Dairy Cattle	Other Cattle	Buffaloes	Goats	Sheep	Pigs	Horses	Indigenous Hens	Improved Layers[1]	Improved Broilers[1]	Ducks
D.I. Aceh	0.8	207	169	270	38	5	5	2 775	60	18	841
North Sumatra	12	158	144	475	41	567	7	5 019	1 131	384	726
West Sumatra	2	191	134	113	2	33	5	2 402	636	90	524
Riau	-	32	30	121	2	24	-	1 944	340	77	159
Jambi	0.8	35	55	95	22	4	1	2 086	189	13	207
South Sumatra	1	143	43	170	16	46	1	3 153	583	172	612
Bengkulu	0.3	27	29	66	3	-	1	648	38	13	118
Lampung	0.4	177	33	435	33	20	-	3 904	690	14	358
West Java	40	170	443	1 609	3 010	14	14				
Central Java	43	1 343	327	3 057	842	92	22	21 163	3 226	372	2 462
D.I. Yogyakarta	3	236	17	397	54	10	1	2 818	1 557	307	220
East Java	66	3 422	187	2 634	551	47	35	20 066	4 405	1 050	2 764
Bali	-	426	7	50	3	539	4	2 989	697	222	516
West Nusa Tenggara	0.2	277	203	245	44	17	67	2 093	97	5	409
East Nusa Tenggara	0.6	485	156	306	84	928	160	2 621	55	11	81
West Kalimantan	0.7	87	1	47	1	454	-	2 320	258	88	235
Central Kalimantan	0.1	15	4	11	-	83	-	918	25	38	104
South Kalimantan	0.1	55	14	39	2	2	1	1 514	193	122	771

Table 3.22: Livestock Populations by Province, 1983 (in Thousands) (Cont'd)

	Dairy Cattle	Other Cattle	Buffaloes	Goats	Sheep	Pigs	Horses	Indigenous Hens	Improved Layers[1]	Improved Broilers[1]	Ducks
East Kalimantan	0.1	10	6	24	1	70	-	750	429	454	83
North Sulawesi	0.2	202	-	74	-	189	12	1 311	229	33	73
Central Sulawesi	0.1	172	11	123	4	71	5	948	63	5	99
South Sulawesi	0.7	836	340	345	8	158	151	5 154	427	72	1 837
Southeast Sulawesi	0.1	65	8	46	-	4	4	901	7	1	67
Maluku	0.2	32	7	94	4	41	4	628	55	17	29
Irian Jaya	0.3	14	-	17	2	425	1	485	133	30	21
All Indonesia (million)	0.18	8.86	2.39	11	4.79	4.07	0.53	106	18.8	8.16	17.1

[1] Poultry on large establishments excluded.

Source: Government of Indonesia, Biro Pusat Statistik (1984q).

Table 3.23: Percentages of Rural Households Keeping Livestock, 1983

	Dairy Cattle	Other Cattle	Buffaloes	Goats	Sheep
D.I. Aceh	-	19	17	17	1
North Sumatra	0.2	6	6	11	0.6
West Sumatra	0.1	23	13	9	0.1
Riau	-	4	4	10	0.1
Jambi	-	8	8	12	2
South Sumatra	-	8	2	7	0.5
Bengkulu	0.1	8	8	20	1
Lampung	-	13	2	19	0.9
West Java	0.3	2	6	14	24
Central Java	0.6	22	4	28	6
D.I. Yogyakarta	0.3	35	2	35	4
East Java	0.6	47	2	24	5
Bali	-	61	1	4	0.1
West Nusa Tenggara	-	32	13	18	2
East Nusa Tenggara	-	14	9	19	2
West Kalimantan	-	8	0.1	4	-
Central Kalimantan	-	4	0.4	2	-
South Kalimantan	-	7	1	3	0.1
East Kalimantan	-	4	2	5	0.1
North Sulawesi	-	28	0.1	7	-
Central Sulawesi	-	29	2	14	0.3
South Sulawesi	-	29	16	15	0.3
Southeast Sulawesi	-	14	2	10	-
Maluku	-	5	1	10	0.2
Irian Jaya	-	2	0.1	2	0.1
All Indonesia	0.3	21	5	18	7
(Total Households in Million)	0.065	3.97	0.916	3.36	1.29

Source: Calculated from data from Government of Indonesia, Biro Pusat Statistik.

programmes have been established, using imported and locally produced semen. But it seems that many producers find their enterprises yielding little profit. Although the Holstein-Friesian may have thrived under the skilled management applied to large herds in preindependence days, it would seem they pose a management task that is beyond many smallholders. It is difficult to envisage significant expansion of this subsector without continuous subsidization, except where there are opportunities to sell high-price liquid milk in upper-income bracket markets.

Cattle, which in the Indonesian context connotes all cattle other than "dairy" cattle, include the Sumba Ongole (purebred *Bos indicus*), the Penanakan Ongole (*Bos indicus cross*), the Madura cattle (mixed blood), the Bali cattle (*Bibus sundaicus*), the Aceh cattle, Brahman (*Bos indicus*) and Brahman crosses and Grati cattle (Friesian crosses). None of these cattle are good milk producers; they are kept either as draught animals or for meat production. More than half of the cattle population is kept on Java, and most of these are Penanakan Ongole. They are usually somewhat smaller than the Sumba Ongole, and do not fatten well. They are well adapted, however, to the climatic conditions of Java, and are useful draught animals. Slaughter weights are about 350 kg - 400 kg for males and 300 kg - 350 kg for females. Madura and Aceh cattle are much smaller, with mature weights of about 250 kg - 300 kg for males and about 150 kg for females. Despite the low bodyweights they have some use for field cultivation purposes.

Bali cattle are descended from the wild Banteng. They can be crossed with *Bos indicus* but male offspring are infertile. The breed has a reputation for good reproductive performance, but this has not always been achieved under ranching conditions. They fatten well, and are capable of draught work on lighter soils. They respond well to skilled smallholder management, and have been used for the Smallholder Cattle Projects supported by IFAD.

Brahman and Brahman crosses have been used for ranching projects in the Outer Islands, but to date few projects have been wholly successful. A major constraint appears to have been the difficulty of upgrading and maintaining pastures. Grati cattle are used for beef-lot operations, more particularly in semi-urban areas. Statistically the numbers are not very important.

Relatively few cattle are kept in commercial herds: Java's 5.17 million cattle (in 1983) were distributed among 2.75 million cattle-keeping households - an average of less than two animals per household. Purposive production of feed for cattle is rare. Direct grazing of roadsides, waste ground, fallow croplands and forest areas usually provides a large proportion of the feed consumed. Crop residues are also fed, and where animal movement is restricted farmers may use cut-and-carry systems. Although these feeding methods have merit in that they use what might otherwise be wasted resources, it is clear that animal productivity is low.

Buffalo are preferred as draught animals on the heavier soils, where their 450 kg - 550 kg maturity weight provides greater pulling power than cattle. They also thrive somewhat better in wet and humid conditions. In West Java they outnumber cattle substantially, but nowhere else. As with cattle, herd sizes are small, averaging just over two animals per buffalo-keeper on Java, and just under three for the rest of Indonesia. Feeding systems for buffalo are much the same as those for cattle. They are kept mainly for traction purposes, with some cost recovery through the disposal for meat of unwanted young stock and adults by culling. Use for milk production is important only in North Sumatra, where the Murrah type is bred.

Goats are mainly of two types: the more popular Kacang (peanut) goat, which is relatively small, and the larger grade Ettawah (which is a Jamnapari cross). The Ettawah milks well, and is kept mainly for this purpose in some areas. Herd sizes average just over three head on Java, and below four elsewhere. The data in Table 3.23 suggest that in many areas goats and cattle are alternatives rather than complementary at the household level. Of the 25 provinces listed, in 19 instances the percentage of households keeping goats is either less than three-quarters or more than four-thirds of the percentage of households keeping cattle. Goats are frequently kept by landless rural people, and housed in pens or stables close to their dwellings. As household enterprises, these can be quite remunerative, but the viability of commercial goat-keeping appears to be more questionable.

Sheep are classified as Javanese thin-tailed, Priangan and the East Java fat-tailed. Some authorities regard the Priangan as a strain of the Javanese thin-tailed. In 1983, Java accounted for over 90 percent of the total sheep population. Over 60 percent - just over 3 million sheep - were in West Java, where they were shared among 0.84 million households, not all of which may have had agriculture land holdings. Standards of management and levels of productivity are generally acknowledged to be very low; many sheep appeared unthrifty, and heavy parasite burdens were suspected. Sheep are thought to be carriers of malignant catarrhal fever, attacks of which are often fatal to Bali cattle.

Pigs are kept only by members of non-Muslim minority groups. Important areas of production are North Sumatra, Bali, East Nusa Tenggara, West Kalimantan and Irian Jaya. When Jakarta is excluded, Java had a pig population of about 150 000 in 1983, kept by about 22 000 households.

Chickens are widely distributed as household stock, with over 100 million *Kampung* hens kept by 15 million households. Although these birds have the potential to contribute to meeting domestic consumption needs, they are insufficiently productive for the commercial markets. Such markets are largely catered to by producers using exotic layer and broiler strains. Vertical integration is increasingly a feature of the subsector and, as a measure to protect the interests of smaller producers, statutory limits to the size of commercial flocks have been introduced. There are indications that there are efficiency costs to these limits because of the existence of strong scale economies in these activities. Broiler units are limited to marketing 750 birds per week per person, and layer flocks are limited to 5 000 birds per person. Ducks are kept in many households in a similar way to the *Kampung* hens; they are also kept by specialist duck herders who systematically scavenge rice stubbles. Under Indonesian conditions and with skillful management, good yields of duck eggs and table ducks are possible under this system.

Apiculture is encouraged by the MOA, which distributes frame hives. Production data are not available.

There is some evidence of *sericulture* in Indonesia. There are mulberry plantings in Central Java, but there is no available data on the size of the subsector. Total silk production is not believed, however, to exceed 10 tonnes per annum. There are plans to develop *tasar* silk in South Sulawesi.

Although the distribution of *livestock* ownership differs from that of land occupation, there is essentially very little difference between the livestock and cropping subsector in terms of structural fragmentation, and at the micro-level the cropping and livestock-keeping systems are often to various degrees interdependent. Fragmentation clearly poses severe problems in the provision of husbandry extension and veterinary services. There have been numerous schemes by which cattle and small ruminants have been introduced into rural communities with meagre results, due to lack of follow-up support. It is also clear that to many livestock-keepers an "inefficient" animal that can sustain itself on rough grazing and minimal attention may be a more attractive proposition than a supposedly more "efficient" animal requiring more time, land and resources. The conventional wisdom that livestock act as banks for savings does not ring entirely true; they are, to be sure, stores of wealth, but most Indonesian farmers probably prefer to see the animals generate that wealth themselves.

While livestock expansion in the less densely settled areas of the Outer Islands can be a defensible development policy, the approach on Java is inevitably more problematic. The food requirements of the

1.5 million tons of ruminants on the hoof in Java probably equals the basic food requirements - in protein and caloric terms - of 30 million people. Most of that feed now comes from sources people could not use. This would not remain true, however, if all these animals were to be placed on the nutritional planes necessary for high output levels; producing the feed to ensure this would inevitably mean that the capability to produce food for people would need to be relinquished on a massive scale.

Realizing greater livestock productivity will require increased attention to animal health. There is a high incidence of liver flukes among cattle, buffalo, goats and sheep. Haemorrhagic septicaemia is similarly widespread, particularly during the wet seasons. Outbreaks of bovine malignant catarrh are common, particularly in Java and the Eastern Islands. Eradication campaigns and quarantine measures have eliminated foot-and-mouth disease from some islands, but serious outbreaks still occur on Java. Brucellosis, bovine tuberculosis and bovine trypanosomiasis are common in some areas. Endoparasite burdens of goats and sheep are often high, and the latter also suffer from foot rot. Newcastle disease and coccidiosis are prevalent among poultry. A measure of the economic cost of livestock diseases is provided by the estimates presented in Table 3.24.

Institutional efforts in the animal health field include vaccination services, general health monitoring, quarantine measures and disease containment. Vaccines are produced at the Vaccine Production Institute at Surabaya. It is clear, however, that the encouragement of higher levels of disease prophylaxis in the livestock sector generally remains an important task of the Directorate-General of Livestock Services.

Artificial insemination has been more successful in Indonesia than in many other developing countries. The Lembang Artificial Insemination Centre was established in 1977, and now handles semen of Brahman, Ongole, Murrah buffalo and Friesian-Holstein breeds. Production in 1983 was 366 360 doses, of which 83 percent were distributed. Reportedly, 93 percent of the dairy farmers make use of the artificial insemination programme; conception rates typically run at about 40 percent.

During the last 20 years, the Government of Indonesia has recognized the importance of livestock and stressed the multipurpose characteristics of the sector investment and support programmes. In addition to the nutritional objectives, the sector provides raw materials for industry. Furthermore, livestock has the potential to generate more employment opportunities - in particular for the landless, marginal

Table 3.24: Estimated Annual Loss in Animal Production Caused by Livestock Diseases

Disease	Production Loss US$ Million (1984)
Newcastle Disease	40.32
Fascioliasis (Liver Flukes)	32.00
Trypanosomiasis	22.40
Foot and Mouth Disease	14.72
Haemorrhagic Septicaemia	8.64
Ascariasis (Endoparasites)	6.72
Brucellosis	3.52
Anthrax	3.20

Source: Calculated from data from Government of Indonesia, Biro Pusat Statistik.

farmers and women - increase rural incomes and use land resources more productively, especially through the use of draught power and manure.

For REPELITA IV, the primary aims for livestock development were the following:

- to increase farm incomes and employment opportunity through enhanced production and productivity of livestock;
- to import substitution of livestock products;
- to meet the demand for draught animals and supply of manure needed for crop production;
- to conserve indigenous breeds such as Bali cattle; and
- to improve grassland productivity through establishment of better quality forages, thus improving total natural resources and the environment.

Within the context of the overall livestock development strategy, the principal policies of the Government of Indonesia stress animal distribution programmes using local and imported stock, animal disease control and dairy development programmes. Efforts with a more limited coverage are focusing on improving use and numbers of draught animals through intensification schemes, stimulating formation of groups of village poultry producers and improving extension services for cattleholders.

Based upon these resource and resource-use analysis in policy design and implementation, main emphasis should be on (see also Chapter 7):

(i)   increased animal productivity
(ii) using existing resources more efficiently, in particular through the development of more productive systems of fodder supply
(iii) improved delivery of veterinary and livestock extension services
(iv) poultry production that has substantial feed conversion capabilities in order to decrease dependence on vegetable protein

Fisheries

The fishery sector in Indonesia has two distinct subsectors: marine fishery and inland fishery. Each subsector provides employment for upward of 1 million people, mostly in small-scale enterprises.

With 5.8 million km² of territorial waters within the declared Exclusive Economic Zone, and with 61 000 km of coastline from which to operate, *marine fishery* possibly has the greatest overall potential for expansion. The sustainable total catch has been estimated at 4.7 million tonnes per annum, distributed as shown in Table 3.25. Total marine catch in 1983 was estimated at 1.49 million tonnes, that is, 32 percent of the potential. Average annual growth rate between 1969 and 1983 was almost 6 percent. Currently, shrimp - caught mainly in coastal waters - contribute about US$ 250 million to annual export earnings.

There are indications, however, that the potential of some inshore waters is already being realized. Diminishing catches by small-scale fishermen led, in 1980, to a decree restricting the operation of trawlers. This measure notwithstanding, over-exploitation remains a danger, and an official document (Government of Indonesia, Directorate-General of Fisheries 1986) states that the waters of the north coast of Java, Bali, the Malacca Straight and the east coast of South Sumatra are nearing a critical situation due to overfishing. Provincial production data for 1981 indicate marine catches totalling 0.7 million tonnes from Java and the eastward-facing provinces of Sumatra. Even when allowance is made for the proportion caught offshore and off the south coast of Java, these data certainly indicate that in the named areas the pressure on stocks must be heavy.

The long-term tendency for the productivity of boats and fishermen to decline - reportedly from 4.0 - 2.8 tonnes per boat per year, and 1.0 - 0.8 tonnes per fisherman per year, over the period 1940-67 - suggests that some degree of overfishing has been a long-standing phenomenon and that the switching from traditional non-powered

Table 3.25: Potential Yearly Marine Fishery Production (in thousands of tonnes)

	Inshore (0-12 Miles)	Offshore (12 miles EE2 boundary)	Totals
Malacca Straits	82	115	197
West Sumatra	155	176	331
West Kalimantan	480	652	1 132
North Java	825	-	825
South Java and Nusa Tenggara	390	418	808
East Kalimantan and Sulawesi	425	105	530
Maluku and Irian Jaya	580	307	887

Source: Government of Indonesia, Directorate-General of Fisheries (1986).

boats to small powered boats, and then to larger powered boats, essentially represents adjustment to this fact. Data pertaining to East Kalimantan, presented in Table 3.26, suggest that motorization, with an ability to reach distant waters, may become increasingly necessary in order to maintain production levels.

Marine fishery was reportedly the principal economic activity of 0.278 million households in 1981; currently, 1.23 million people are said to depend on the subsector for their employment (Directorate-General of Fisheries 1986). Recent detailed data are not available, but those relating to Java for 1980-81 show increasing numbers of households depending on marine fishing, with consistently diminishing yearly productivity (see Table 3.27).

The economic position of coastal fishermen is unquestionably tending to deteriorate, particularly in communities that continue to depend upon traditional craft and methods. On the evidence available, however, raising individual productivity is likely to prove difficult without considerable structural and organizational change within the industry. The technical equipment needed for more modern and more productive marine fishing will inevitably be more expensive and require more elaborate support facilities. Experience has shown that finding the optimal technological solutions can be costly and that as capital-intensity increases so does the need for management skills.

Inland fishery includes openwater fishing and various forms of fish culture (aquaculture). Open-water fishing was reportedly practiced by nearly 300 000 households in 1981. Using 140 000 boats, 5 000 of which were motorized, their production was put at about 265 000 tons. Some doubts must attach, however, to the reliability of these statistics:

Table 3.26: Fishing Boats and Production East Kalimantan, 1980-84

	1980	1981	1982	1983	1984
Marine fishery					
Non-powered boats	4 736	3 131	NA	NA	NA
Powered boats	2 787	3 040	NA	NA	NA
Inland fishery					
Non-powered boats	4 091	8 236	NA	NA	NA
Powered boats	2 572	3 419	NA	NA	NA
Registered boats					
Motor longboats	416	NA	NA	4 598	4 631
Speedboats	227	NA	NA	2 103	2 118
Canoes with outboard motors	123	NA	NA	2 082	2 098
Production					
Marine fishery					
(production tonnes)	38 948	40 717	41 511	42 960	43 080
Inland fishery (openwater) (production tonnes)	20 216	23 869	23 014	19 952	22 950

Source: Government of Indonesia, Biro Pusat Statistik (1984q).

Table 3.27: Marine Fishery, Households and Production - Java, 1980-81

	1980			1981		
	Households Thousands	Tonnes Thousands	Tonnes/ HH	Households Thousands	Tonnes Thousands	Tonnes/ HH
D.K.I. Jakarta	0.6	25.5	44.4	1.2	18.5	15.3
West Java	8.0	90.1	11.2	10.8	95.5	8.9
Central Java	12.5	123.8	9.8	12.9	99.1	7.7
D.I. Yogyakartana	NA	0.4	NA	3.0	0.5	0.2
East Java	26.1	140.4	5.4	33.1	141.4	4.3
All Java	47.2	380.3	8.1	61.0	355.1	5.8

Source: Government of Indonesia, Biro Pusat Statistik (1984q).

West Java was said to have 18 percent of these households but employed less than 1 percent of the boats and contributed only 1.5 percent to the total catch.

Aquaculture methods include brackish water ponds used for fish and shrimp production, freshwater ponds, penning of fish in irrigation channels, fixed and floating cages, and confinement in flooded rice paddy fields. Non-intensive systems rely on natural food, low-grade agricultural by-products (e.g., rice husks and unseparated bean) and household wastes. Intensive systems use more nutritious feeds - often with 20-25 percent crude protein, fed at 3 percent of fish or shrimp bodyweight per day.

Estimations of the facilities available for aquaculture were made in the course of the 1983 agricultural census. Table 3.28 shows the total area in each province of freshwater ponds-plus-cages and brackish water ponds, whose yields are estimated to be 127 000 and 93 000 tons, respectively, suggesting a relatively low productivity per hectare in the case of the brackish water ponds, which are used mainly for the production of milkfish (*Chanos chanos*). Production from paddy fields was approximately 62 000 tons in 1983, with three-quarters coming from West and East Java.

Inland fishing is clearly capable of making a significant contribution to meeting the dietary needs of both rural and urban people, and in so doing providing a livelihood to many families.

Forestry

Historically, forests have always been an important resource in Indonesia, and prior to the discovery of oil, were the principal source of foreign exchange earnings. Although rarely matching the quality of that provided by Burma and Indochina, Indonesia has been a volume exporter of teak (*Teckona grandis*), known locally as *jati*, since the early days of international commerce. With increased settlement reducing the forest areas, Java has become less important as a source of teak, but extraction of this species from forests in the Outer Islands continues on a significant scale.

Other traditional forest wood products have included *keruing* (*Dipterocarpus spp.*), *meranti* and *damar* (*Shorea spp.*), *Merbau* (*Intsia spp.*), ironwood, sandalwood, ebony and amboina. Other products that are still important include bamboo, rattan cane, copal resin from *Agathis spp.*, and seeds of *Tengkawang* (*Shorea stenopteka*). Resin and turpentine are yielded by the indigenous Sumatra pine (*Pinus merkusii*), known locally as *tusam*.

The flora of most Indonesian forests, other than at higher elevations, are generally dominated by the evergreen *dipterocorpaceae*, and the term "dipterocarp forest" has gained currency to describe them, though species of other botanical families

Table 3.28: Distribution of Fish Production Ponds and Cages by Province, 1983

	Fresh Water Ponds/Cages[1] Hectares	Brackish Water Ponds Hectares
D.I. Aceh	353	17 297
North Sumatra	2 131	680
West Sumatra	733	-
Riau	74	44
Jambi	113	2
South Sumatra	412	11
Bengkulu	305	51
Lampung	511	321
West Java	10 880	30 197
Central Java	1 083	20 087
D.I. Yogyakarta	61	-
East Java	15 467	19 578
Bali	90	117
West Nusa Tenggara	318	3 348
East Nusa Tenggara	28	53
West Kalimantan	214	na
Central Kalimantan	156	na
South Kalimantan	58	1 074
East Kalimantan	103	1 402
North Sulawesi	935	225
Central Sulawesi	164	924
South Sulawesi	800	41 599
Southeast Sulawesi	121	1 802
Maluku	2	55
Irian Jaya	54	28
All Indonesia	35 211	153 039

[1] Census summations were based on m^2 estimations.

Source: Government of Indonesia, Biro Pusat Statistik (1983a).

may account for as much as 75 percent of the total stand, and include many other useful species.

Detailed surveys in the forest areas have yet to be completed for the whole country. Reconnaissance has however indicated that altogether forests cover over 60 percent of the total land surface, and can be categorized as of 1980 as shown below:

	Millions of Hectares
Dipterocarpus forest	
Upland	48.0
Lowland	54.2
Swamp forest	
Freshwater	11.8
Saltwater	3.8
Pine forests	0.2
Forestry plantations	1.7
Total	119.7
Distribution	
Java	3
Outer Islands	116

Somewhat less than half the forest area is considered to be commercially exploitable, and use designation under the REPELITA IV is as follows:

- Permanent production forests - 33.6 million ha
- Limited production and protected forests - 30.4 million ha
- Natural conservation zone forests - 18.7 million ha
- Reserve forests - 30.1 million ha

Although some systematic afforestation and reforestation has taken place, the exploitation system has been one of a selective extraction from large concession areas followed by natural regeneration. Research has shown that regeneration often fails to reproduce the original stands, and further ecological degradation accompanies shifting cultivation where this tracks forest exploitation. Much of the forest areas are therefore "secondary" forest by sylvicultural definition.

It is now realized that in the past forest resources were sometimes over-estimated, through not allowing for the differences in density of riverain and interfluve stands. Recent years have seen a greater governmental awareness of a need for a conservative exploitation policy and greater control over extraction operations. Export of logs was banned effective from the end of 1984. This has led to heavy investment in conversion plants - particularly for plywood manufacture - by timber companies anxious to maintain access to their concessions. This resulted in substantial conversion overcapacity. Operating margins were eroded by low plywood demand and prices in 1984-85, but have now improved following reductions in the plywood import tariff imposed by Japan, the principal customer for this material.

Export of rattan has increased dramatically in recent years - to US$ 80 million worth in 1984. Efforts are being made, with technical assistance from the Philippines, to convert more rattan to finished goods before export, thus increasing value. A proposal for banning raw rattan exports has been put forward.

Total timber production is now approximately 30 million m^3 per year, with up to a one-third being absorbed by plywood production and the remainder used as saw timber. Total exports were projected to take about 40-45 percent of total production during REPELITA IV. "Smallholder forests" and social forestry were scheduled to receive support during REPELITA IV.

Agricultural Research

Indonesia's ability to maintain the momentum of its agricultural advance depends to a great extent on the flow of relevant research information to farmers and policy makers.

Agricultural research has a long history in Indonesia and successive administrations have allocated substantial resources to the development of an appropriate institutional infrastructure and to the training of the required personnel. Substantial external support has been received, notably from the World Bank, USAID and the Dutch and Australian governments.

The effectiveness of the agricultural research system in terms of extending the relevant knowledge boundaries and of feeding information to other agencies supporting the agricutural sector depends on the continuation of adequate budgetary allocations and purposive efforts to maintain two-way communications between the generators and users of new information. There was no opportunity to assess the technical quality of the research effort or to determine whether or not the present and foreseen financial allocations will suffice for effective operations in the future. It can be noted, however, that most, if not all, major area-specific development projects supported with external finance are finding it necessary to include provisions for *ad hoc* applied research within their project frameworks. That this should be proving necessary can perhaps best be seen as an indication of how stretched the agriculture research services remain despite the expansion that has taken place and is being continued with external support. For example, IBRD's US$ 65 million loan for the ongoing Agricultural Research Project II. The diversity of crops and the operational environment and the difficulties so often encountered in maintaining plant and animal health in the humid tropics demand a continuing input of scientific effort. Notwithstanding the valuable results of international research linkages, such as those with IRRI - to whom Indonesia has generously acknowledged its debt - and with the regional crop development centres, (e.g. ESCAP-CGPRT and AVRDC) there is no substitution for the extensive in-country applied or adaptive research before innovative techniques can be either recommended or relied upon to produce desired results at the farm or sectoral levels.

Research Institutions

Overall responsibility for the centrally financed agricultural research institutions is vested in the Agency for Agriculture Research and Development (AARD), which was given its own budget and operational autonomy within the MOA in 1976. It now has direct managerial responsibilities for the commodity-specific or subsector-specific research institutions that were formerly controlled by individual directorates-general. In the case of the Research Institutes for Estate Crops and the Sugar Research Institute, the legal autonomy previously granted was preserved, but the head of AARD took over chairmanship of the respective management boards.

Within the AARD structure, functional responsibilities are assigned to sectoral central research institutes covering, respectively, food crops, industrial crops, horticultural crops, livestock, fisheries and estate crops. Other centres have responsibility for soil research, agro-economic research, and agricultural data processing. Service functions performed by AARD include the operation of the National Library for Agriculture Sciences.

Each central research institute supervises the work of subsidiary institutes - 24 in total - which specialize in specific research subjects or implement research programmes oriented toward the needs of specific regions. Five agricultural quarantine service subcentres are operated. The regional distribution of the principal AARD research units is shown in Table 3.29. In addition to the locations shown, many AARD staff are posted to out-stations and trial farms established in appropriate field locations on the various islands. The total number of graduate staff employed by AARD now exceeds 2 000.

In addition to the economic evaluations of technical research results undertaken by the Agro-economic Research Centre of AARD, similar studies are conducted by a number of other institutions

Table 3.29: AARD Research Units

Food Crops (Under Research Coordinating Centre for Food Crops, Bogor, West Java)
West Java
  Bogor Research Institute for Food Crops
  Sukamandi Research Institute for Food Crops
East Java
  Malang Research Institute for Food Crops
Sumatra
  Sukarami Research Institute for Food Crops
South Kalimantan
  Banjarbaru Research Institute for Food Crops
South Sulawesi
  Maros Research Institute for Food Crops

Industrial Crops (Under Research Coordinating Centre for Industrial Crops, Bogor, West Java)
West Java
  Research Institute for Species and Medicinal Crops
East Java
  Research Institute for Tobacco and Fiber Crops
North Sulawesi
  Research Institute for Coconut

Horticultural Crops (Under Research Coordinating Centre for Horticultural Crops, Jakarta)
West Java
  Lembang Research Institute for Horticultural Crops
West Sumatra
  Solok Research Institute for Horticultural Crops

Livestock (Under Research Coordinating Centre for Animal Husbandry, Bogor, West Java)
West Java
  Research Institute for Animal Production
  Research Institute for Veterinary Science
  Animal Husbandry Research Unit, Bogor
  Animal Health Research Institute, Bogor

Fisheries (Under Research Coordinating Centre for Fisheries, Jakarta)
Jakarta
  Research Institute for Marine Fisheries
West Java
  Research Institute for Fresh Water Fisheries

South Sulawesi
   Research Institute for Coastal Aquaculture

Estate Crops
West Java
   Bogor Research Institute for Estate Crops
   Gambung Research Institute for Estate Crops
Central Java
   Research Centre Getas
East Java
   Jember Research Institute for Estate Crops
   Pasuruan Research Institute for Estate Crops
North Sumatra
   Medan Research Institute for Estate Crops
   Sungei Putih Research Institute for Estate Crops
   Coconut Research Centre
   Marihat Centre Institute for Estate Crops
   Tanjung Morawa Centre Institute for Estate Crops
South Sumatra
   Sembawa Research Institute for Estate Crops

Soils
   Research Centre for Soil Sciences, Bogor, West Java

Agro-economics
   Centre for Agro-economic Research

National Library for Agricultural Sciences
Centre for Agricultural Data Processing
Secretariat, Agency for Agricultural Research and Development

Source: Government of Indonesia.

operating either independently, or under the aegis of university faculties of agriculture and rural development. Notable among these are the Independent Centre for Agricultural Research and Development (ICARD) and the Unit of Socio-Economic Evaluation Studies (USESE).

Farming System Research

With regard to the development of improved cropping systems, AARD has no illusions as to the time needed to advance from initial trials to firm recommendations. Table 3.30 sets out, with slight truncation and amendment in the interests of clarity, the perceived timetable for cropping systems research and development for selected areas. Although we have certain technical reservations about the methodology set out, we nevertheless believe that the time scheduling exhibits an appropriate sense of realism in the face of the unforeseeable but predictable difficulties to be expected.

Because cropping systems can be regarded - for reasons explained earlier - as subsystems of more comprehensive farm systems, research into the latter is the next step up the investigatory ladder. More particularly in the context of specific projects or programmes, there has often been a purposive allocation of resources, aimed at the evolution and diffusion of innovative farming systems. The term "farming systems approach" generously encapsulates what are seen as relevant study methodologies.

In view of the high level of interest in this field, we have attempted to evaluate on the basis of field evidence and relevant research and project documentation the progress that has been made, and to see what successes have been achieved or setbacks experienced, and what lessons there are to be learned from them. This enquiry into the status of farming system research has focused more particularly on the rain-fed and higher areas; firstly, because more generally farm research pertaining to rain-fed areas has been relatively neglected in the quest for rice self-sufficiency and, secondly, because deleterious soil erosion, engendered by bad farming practices, is most severe and most common at the higher altitudes.

Among the efforts studied, we have included those described in documentation on the Citanduy Project, those conducted within the UNDP/FAO project entitled "The Improvement of Rain-fed and Mixed Farming in Selected Provinces" (West Java and South Sumatra) and those made under the aegis of the Kali Konto Project in East Java carried out in the framework of the Dutch assistance programme. The project plan for the Upland Development and Conservation Project, now under implementation with USAID and IBRD funding, has also been studied.

One of the first things to emerge from this review was that while there can be a general subscription to the idea of a "farming systems approach", in practice different agencies quite obviously interpret the concept in different ways. For instance, the Citanduy Project has established a series of "model farms", in which bench terracing is carried out with the explicit intent of reducing downstream damage from precipitation. Collaterally, a "technology package" is applied on the improved land to demonstrate that an economic return on the investment can also be earned. This is expected to induce other

Table 3.30: Cropping System Research and Development for Selected Areas

Phase and Time Period	Activities
Phase I Preliminary	Research site selection and categorization: Soil taxonomy Rainfall distribution Other climatic variables Irrigation potentials Agro-economic profile of area
Phase II Years 1-2	Agronomic testing on small plots: Crop varieties Fertilizer responses Crop combinations Trials of other relevant technologies Area farm performance recordings: Incomes Labour inputs Product prices Problem-focussed surveys
Phase III Years 1-3	Identification of target subareas according to: Water availability Soil capability Market accessibility Identification of existing cropping systems: Low input systems Optimal management systems Identification of potential "improved cropping systems": Low input systems Optimal management systems Observation of existing systems Testing of potential improved cropping systems (0.1 ha plots)
Phase IV Years 3-5	Pre-recommendation testing: Research-managed plots (3-4 ha) Local constraints identification: Local biological constraints Local institutional constraints

Table 3.30: Cropping System Research and Development for Selected Areas (Cont'd)

Phase and Time Period	Activities
Phase V	Introduction of improved cropping systems: Cropping system-oriented support, not specific crop-oriented support Multi-agency involvement

Source: Effendi, et al. (1982).

farmers to carry out conservation works and thus help meet the social objectives.

The impact of these efforts at the Citanduy Project has been the subject of an independent study conducted collaboratively by USESE and ICARD. The investigatory method, however, veers toward treating the "model farm" holistically, and while able to analyse the differences in the sources and amounts of income earned, respectively, by "model farm" operators, spontaneous adopters of the collateral "technology package" and non-adopters, does not attempt to analyse the technical pros and cons of any particular mix of the ingredients of the improved technologies or the interdependency of the relevant variables. If, in fact (as has been suggested by one well-placed observer), the terracing effectively facilitated irrigation, then it might be more correct to attribute the income increments to "terracing plus irrigation" rather than to "terracing" per se. In general, this study has problems in penetrating the intricacies of the differential adoption of elements, casting doubt on its evaluation of what the "technology package" - or elements thereof - might achieve elsewhere. Notwithstanding these limitations, strong claims continue to be made that the "model farms" variant of the "farming systems approach" can form the basis of an extension system, and belief in this concept is clearly discernible in the project plan prepared for the USAID/IBRD-funded project mentioned earlier. Because of the tremendous diversity of farming conditions prevailing in Indonesia, there are questions about generalizable and transferable results forthcoming from this project. The project design implicitly recognizes that much more research and investigation is needed before the components of a series of optimal "model farm" systems, appropriate to varying climatic, edaphic, social and economic environments, can be positively identified. Accordingly, in many ways the USAID/IBRD project can, perhaps, more correctly be regarded as a "research" project, of which the scale of funding (US$ 50 million) provides a measure of the levels of expenditure that may prove necessary before the use of the "farming system approach" actually begins to pay off.

The case for more cognate research and detailed investigations is supported by the results of the UNDP/FAO project implemented during the period 1980-85 in West Java and South Sumatra. The project's approach was founded on the belief that a systematic synthesis of research station findings would allow the formulation of indicative "farming systems" that farmers would find more rewarding than their traditional ones.

In the case of its West Java sites, the project had great difficulty classifying farms into types and groups as a basis for an improvement programme; although in some sites income improvements were achieved as a result of the technological innovations, and some experience was gained by farmers working together in organized groups, it had to be admitted that "the tentative efforts by this project to whole farm development have proved difficult in the field". The prime cause of this difficulty was identified as the commodity or crop-specific orientation of the components of the extension services. A secondary cause identified was simply the shortage of skilled workers.

The difficulty experienced in West Java in even classifying existing farm systems on the ground tended to frustrate, from the start, the objective of carrying out detailed studies of whether and how farmers actually absorbed or adopted technological innovations.

The heterogeneity of farm conditions in a given area militates against any preidentification of a supposedly superior system, as became very obvious at the South Sumatra sites. It provided further evidence that farmers as a class rarely actually adopt "packages" or "recommended systems" as such, but that they adopt selectively (and often experimentally) the "tryable" discrete elements of such packages that they judge may help realize their perceived goals.

The South Sumatra site was a low-and-declining fertility area settled by transmigrants, who were attempting to sustain themselves by food crop production. The field research here indicated marked responses to phosphorus, to organic manure when placed in planting holes and to lime (attributed in the latter case simply to the replacement of bases - mainly Ca and Mg - from the topsoil and clay exchange complex, rather than to pH adjustment). Deep tillage was found detrimental, contraindicating the use of the inverting mouldboard plough. Terracing was found to be ineffective in combatting soil erosion.

The use of fertilizers, farmyard manure and improved seeds could be given most of the credit for improved crop output and for the reintroduction of crops that had ceased to be grown in the area due to soil fertility depletion. As in West Java, it was found that the innovative "systems" sought simply were not identifiable. (Also, and of interest in the context of this volume generally, the conclusion was reached that "contrary to what had previously been suggested commercial food crop production in the South Sumatra sites was not a viable proposition and, at best, only a subsistence or semi-commercial type of farming was attainable".)

Work being undertaken under the aegis of the Kali Konto Project in East Java, supported by the Netherlands, exhibits a more thorough understanding of the need for meticulous initial groundwork if the "farming systems approach" is to be fruitful. Commendable baseline studies of some specific areas have already been completed, and through seminars and systematic training, staffers are learning the techniques for coordinating, at the field level, studies covering land capability, cropping, livestock husbandry and forestry. Some attempts have been made to use the data thus acquired to formulate recommendable farming or agroforestry systems. But here, again, experience has revealed a gap that so often persists between what scientists think farmers should be doing, and what the farmers actually want to do. This is evidenced by the fact that farmers requested that "demonstration" plots should be adjusted to more closely conform with their perceptions of needs, which will often reflect their actual experiences when attempting to dispose of produce through the available market channels.

Overall, these experiences in the field of farming systems research provide a salutory warning that a long lead time must be expected between the establishment of institutions or project components specifically to undertake this task and the production of operationally useful results. Notwithstanding the excellent pioneering efforts in East Java, it would be unrealistic - given the likely personnel constraints - for Indonesia to expect significant progress in this field for some years.

Chapter 4

Dimensions of Rural Poverty and Target Groups

Chapter 4 discusses contours of rural poverty and stratification within Indonesia. It begins by focusing upon the distribution of income over different types of factors and households. It then discusses the nutritional implications of Indonesia's national consumption surveys and the regional inequalities. Next, the chapter analyses the socio-economic characteristics that make women a target group for poverty alleviation. Finally, it examines dynamic relationships among rural poverty, land distribution, productivity and employment.

Distribution of Income and Consumption by Socio-economic Groups

Indonesian System of Socio-Economic Accounts, 1980, published in 1986 by the Biro Pusat Statistik, provides a convenient starting point for viewing issues of rural poverty and stratification within the context of Indonesia's economy. This System of Accounts brings together information from several sources regarding production, trade, consumption, government revenue and expenditures, investment, savings, and so on. It then attempts to reconcile these frequently conflicting data within a consistent framework. Such reconciliation is particularly important since data obtained from individual, isolated sources are often misleading. For instance, what appears as poverty in some consumption surveys is often merely a reflection of underreporting. Household income data are also underreported, typically more so than consumption data. The System's accounting constraints permit such data deficiencies to be rectified to some extent; but it should also be stressed that the reconciled estimates now available for 1980 are still explicitly "provisional," and we shall have occasion to point out some of their weaknesses.

Factor Income Generation

Table 4.1 presents the System of Accounts estimated distribution of 1980 GDP by production sector and factor type in billions of current Rupiahs. The last row of Table 4.1 shows that 1980 value added was divided into five portions of roughly equal size, namely,

(i) *paid labour income* (19.4 percent, or 9.3 percent for rural and 10.1 percent for urban), which comprises all payments, including those in kind, to people with the status of employee

(ii) *unpaid labour income* (18.4 percent), which is an imputed valuation of the labour compensation accruing to self-employed and "unpaid" family workers

(iii) *unincorporated capital income* (20.3 percent), which includes remuneration to agricultural land, owner-occupied housing and the like

(iv) *private domestic and government corporate capital income* (20.7 percent), which reflects the revenues of these agents, both as sole owners of enterprises and as participants in various joint ventures

(v) *foreign corporate capital income* (20.2 percent), which is especially prominent in the petroleum sector

When interpreting the income distribution shown in Table 4.1, keep in mind that it pertains to factor incomes before direct taxes. For instance, some of the large foreign corporate income is redistributed to the GOI in the form of taxes. Table 4.1 does, however, include indirect taxes minus subsidies. In sector 12, subsidies outweigh indirect taxes so much so that the result is a huge negative Rp 607 billion. A large portion of this negative amount is caused by fertilizer subsidies. With declining oil revenues, such subsidies will become more difficult to sustain.

Table 4.1 also shows that wages (i.e., paid labour incomes) are a relatively small portion of total income. In fact, they represent only a little more than half of all labour income. It also shows that a large proportion of paid labour income, particularly in urban areas, derives from sector 21: public administration, defense, social services like education and so on. Since wages in these sectors are determined largely through bureaucratic processes, even paid labour incomes often do not reflect competitive labour-market forces. This is also true to a large extent in those sectors, indicated in Table 4.1 by the size of government capital revenue, where government enterprise constitutes a

Table 4.1: Distribution of Value Added by Sector of Production and Factor Type, 1980 (Billions of Rupiahs)

Sector of Production	Labour				Capital				Ind. Tax Minus Subs.	Total Sectoral Value Added
	Paid		Unpaid			Corporate				
	Rural	Urban	Rural	Urban	Unicorp-orated	Private Domain	Govern-ment	Foreign		
1. Farm food crops	627	45	3 111	75	2 198	3	-	-	44	6 102
2. Other crops	379	53	372	11	1 209	62	241	52	31	2 411
3. Livestock and products	54	14	205	16	856	30	4	2	9	1 191
4. Forestry and hunting	63	13	161	6	568	414	43	131	14	1 412
5. Fishery, drying and salting of fish	82	25	162	19	420	54	3	20	7	793
6. Coal and metal ore, petroleum and natural gas mining	69	115	-	-	-	-	3 026	8 899	6	12 115
7. Other mining and quarrying	54	34	55	8	150	2	7	-	12	322
8. Food, beverages and tobacco manufacturing industries	158	127	120	43	577	169	170	102	284	1 750
9. Wood and wood products indust. and construct.	737	505	297	128	266	665	155	19	147	2 917
10. Spinnings, textile, leather and apparel manufact. ind.	65	114	39	26	156	85	24	52	14	576
11. Paper and print. indust., manuf. of transport equip., metal prod. and other manufact. ind.	79	253	37	33	163	342	97	149	74	1 228
12. Chemical, fertilizer, clay products, cement and basic metal manufact. industries	91	174	57	20	86	261	842	159	-607	1 083

Table 4.1: Distribution of Value Added by Sector of Production and Factor Type, 1980 (Billions of Rupiahs) (Cont'd)

Sector of Production	Labour				Unincorp-orated	Capital			Ind. Tax Minus Subs.	Total Sectoral Value Added
	Paid		Unpaid			Private Domain	Corporate			
	Rural	Urban	Rural	Urban			Govern-ment	Foreign		
13. Electricity, gas and water supply	27	59	-	1	2	15	115	11	1	231
14. Wholesale and retail trade, services allied to transport, storage, warehousing	120	427	1 510	1 387	1 077	1 201	479	286	207	6 693
15. Restaurants and other eating places	17	47	87	124	455	21	-	2	63	821
16. Hotel and lodging	8	46	-	2	54	16	32	7	21	188
17. Road transport and railways	149	229	165	172	367	164	18	-	29	1 292
18. Air and water transport and communic.	59	180	4	3	18	15	333	-	6	618
19. Banking and insurance	43	194	-	1	17	43	434	29	3	765
20. Real estate and business services	36	91	6	12	1 136	251	23	-	37	1 589
21. Public admin. and defense, social and related community serv. and recreational serv.	1 508	2 007	11	12	113	122	156	-	50	3 980
22. Personal, household and other serv.	130	183	280	265	29	-	-	-	29	915
Total	4 556	4 935	6 679	2 365	9 913	3 941	6 202	9 920	481	48 992
Percentage of Total	9.3	10.1	13.6	4.8	20.3	8.0	12.7	20.2	1.0	100.0

Source: Government of Indonesia, Biro Pusak Statistik (1980a, 1986b and 1986c).

significant portion of sectoral production (estate crops, petroleum, fertilizer and banking etc.).

Table 4.1 also indicates that private domestic corporate capital receives a relatively small share of GDP when compared with the other categories of capital income. Most capital income accruing to private individuals derives from unincorporated, or informal, enterprises. To the extent that most such enterprises are typically small, the Indonesian economy as a whole cannot reap the advantages of scale.

To highlight the income-generating scope of agriculture within Indonesia's economy, Table 4.2 computes proportions of factor incomes arising from various sectors, combining some of the production categories found in Table 4.1. Table 4.2 shows that the five agricultural sectors plus food, beverage and tobacco processing account for only 27.9 percent of total value added. They provided, however, slightly less than half (47.4 percent) of unpaid labour income and slightly more than half (58.7 percent) of unincorporated capital income. In contrast, mining (which includes labour-intensive quarrying but is dominated by oil production) generated almost a quarter (25.4 percent) of total value added and 59.5 percent of corporate capital income but only a small fraction of labour income. After agriculture and public services, trade provides the largest share of labour income. On the whole, the various manufacturing sectors contribute a very minor part of total GDP and of total labour incomes. (Later in this chapter, we show, however, that the manufacturing sectors did absorb at least one-fourth of incremental employment during 1971-80.)

To refine our view of labour absorption in the Indonesian economy, Table 4.3 displays the distribution of worker equivalents by sector of production and occupational categories. Worker equivalents account for the fact that many people often work in several sectors and occupations during the course of a single year. A person working part of the time in one sector and part in another is recorded as partial worker equivalents in the respective sectors. This is more meaningful than a mere head count of workers in each sector, which leads to double counting.

The interested reader is invited to examine Table 4.3. Here we note that in the last line approximately two-thirds (65.3 percent) of the worker equivalents are unpaid, and almost one-half (47.5 percent) are agricultural. Slightly more than one-fourth (25.3 percent) of all worker equivalents are clerical, sales and service workers; more than the number engaged in the production, transport and manual-work occupations. Also note that although agricultural workers are, by

Table 4.2: Percentage of Factor Income by Sector of Production, 1980

Sector of Production	Labour		Capital		Total
	Paid	Unpaid	Unincorporated	Corporate	Value Added
Food crops	7.1	35.2	22.2	0.0	12.5
Estate crops	4.6	4.2	12.2	1.8	4.9
Livestock and products	0.7	2.4	8.6	0.2	2.4
Forestry and hunting	0.8	1.8	5.7	2.9	2.9
Fishery, drying and salting of fish	1.1	2.0	4.2	0.4	1.6
Food, beverages and tobacco manufacturing industries	3.0	1.8	5.8	2.2	3.6
Subtotal	17.3	47.4	58.7	7.5	27.9
Mining and quarrying	2.9	0.7	1.5	59.5	25.4
Wood prod. and construct.	13.1	4.7	2.7	4.2	6.0
Other manufacturing	8.2	2.3	4.1	10.0	5.9
Trade	5.8	32.0	10.9	9.8	13.7
Public Services	37.1	0.3	1.1	1.4	8.1
Transport	6.5	3.8	3.9	2.6	3.9
Real estate	1.3	0.2	11.5	1.4	3.2
Other	8.0	8.4	5.6	3.6	6.0
Total	100.0	100.0	100.0	100.0	100.0

Source: Government of Indonesia, Biro Pusat Statistik (1980a, 1986b, and 1986c).

definition, confined to the agricultural sectors, other occupational categories also appear in those sectors. There are, for instance, professionals, technicians, managers, and supervisors (e.g., veterinarians, agronomists and plantation foremen) in the agricultural sector.

Table 4.4 is perhaps more useful for beginning to identify target groups because it displays relative wage rates or, more precisely, annual average labour incomes computed as a percentage of the national average in each sector and occupational category. For example, annual average income in the food crops sector is only 54 percent of the national average (which was Rp 327 700 per labour equivalent in 1980).

Unlike Tables 4.1 to 4.3, Table 4.4 emphasizes a distinction between rural and urban paid and unpaid workers. With the exception of the last column, which combines both paid and unpaid workers, the percentages in Table 4.4 refer to paid workers only. It was on the

Table 4.3: Distribution of Worker Equivalents by Sector of Production and Occupation (Thousands)

Sector of Production	Agriculture		Production, Transportation Manual		Clerical, Sales, Services		Professionals, Managers, etc.		Total	
	Paid	Unpaid	Paid	Unpaid	Paid	Unpaid	Paid	Unpaid	Paid	Unpaid
Farm food crops	3 420	18 327	29	49	11	24	2	12	3 463	18 312
Other crops	1 311	1 434	77	17	58	8	8	3	1 454	1 461
Livestock and products	219	892	3	3	4	6	1	1	226	901
Forestry and hunting	111	341	35	36	17	7	2	1	164	385
Fishery, drying and salting of fish	304	520	3	3	4	6	1	0	312	529
Coal and metal ore, petroleum and natural gas mining	-	-	54	-	24	-	9	-	-	87
Other mining and quarrying	-	-	126	207	13	4	3	0	143	211
Food, beverages and tobacco manufacturing industries	-	-	924	617	71	29	8	3	1 003	649
Wood and wood products indust. and construction	-	-	2 266	1 088	83	19	30	10	2 379	1 117
Spinnings, textile, leather and apparel manufact. ind.	-	-	812	391	46	9	13	2	870	420
Paper and print. indust. manuf. of transport equip., metal prod. and other manufact. ind.	-	-	484	126	81	7	31	4	596	137
Chemical, fertilizer, clay prod., cement and basic metal manufact. industries	-	-	515	316	66	8	17	4	598	328
Electricity, gas and water supply	-	-	52	1	19	0	8	0	78	1

Table 4.3: Distribution of Worker Equivalents by Sector of Production and Occupation (Thousands) (Cont'd)

Sector of Production	Agriculture		Production, Transporation Manual		Clerical, Sales, Services		Professionals, Managers, etc.		Total	
	Paid	Unpaid	Paid	Unpaid	Paid	Unpaid	Paid	Unpaid	Paid	Unpaid
Wholesale and retail trade, Serv. allied to transport storage, warehousing	-	-	175	171	798	7 638	16	8	990	7 817
Restaurants and other eating places			6	7	163	922	4	1	172	930
Hotel and lodging			3	0	56	2	2	0	61	3
Road transport and railways			871	883	156	45	5	3	1 032	931
Air and water transp. and communic.			203	10	111	2	39	1	352	12
Banking and insurance			3	0	99	0	6	0	108	0
Real estate and business services			64	11	100	12	13	2	177	25
Public admin. and defense, social and related community serv. and recreational services			223	5	1 611	10	1 992	17	3 826	32
Personal, household and other serv.	-	-	609	1 549	895	1 059	20	55	1 524	2 664
Total	5 366	21 514	7 537	5 489	4 484	9 815	2 228	128	19 615	36 946
Percentage of Total	9.5	38.0	13.3	9.7	7.9	17.4	3.9	.2	34.7	65.3

Source: Government of Indonesia, Biro Pusak Statistik (1980a, 1986b and 1986c).

Table 4.4: Annual Average Labour Income per Worker Equivalent by Sector of Production, Occupation and Location, as a Percentage of National Average

Sector of Production	Agriculture		Production, Transporation		Clerical, Sales, Services		Professionals, Managers, etc.		Average Paid and Unpaid
	Rural	Urban	Rural	Urban	Rural	Urban	Rural	Urban	
Farm food crops	58	72	65	79	63	146	99	255	54
Other crops	87	131	66	143	81	172	164	405	85
Livestock and products	78	193	117	149	180	399	398	490	78
Forestry and hunting	142	165	108	132	153	212	178	222	135
Fishery, drying and salting of fish	107	99	58	98	85	103	130	177	105
Coal and metal ore, petroleum and natural gas mining	-	-	466	667	703	879	439	931	646
Other mining and quarrying	-	-	151	203	291	381	490	614	130
Food, beverages and tobacco manufacturing industries	-	-	69	105	142	173	99	191	83
Wood and wood products indust. and construct.	-	-	141	181	147	255	200	624	145
Spinnings, textile, leather and apparel manufact. ind.	-	-	48	69	57	118	161	216	59
Paper and print. indust. manufact. of transport equip., metal prod. and other manufact. ind.	-	-	123	147	150	217	336	617	168
Chemical, fertilizer, clay prod., cement and basic metal manufact. industries	-	-	82	145	156	244	252	719	113

Table 4.4: Annual Average Labour Income per Worker Equivalent by Sector of Production, Occupation and Location, as a Percentage of National Average (Cont'd)

Sector of Production	Agriculture		Production, Transporation		Clerical, Sales, Services		Professionals, Managers, etc.		Average Paid and Unpaid
	Rural	Urban	Rural	Urban	Rural	Urban	Rural	Urban	
Electricity, gas and water supply	-	-	239	261	342	347	876	856	533
Wholesale and retail trade, serv. allied to transport, storage, warehousing	-	-	71	157	119	199	210	513	119
Restaurants and other eating places	-	-	57	57	85	128	126	242	76
Hotel and lodging	-	-	187	226	178	273	447	1 132	276
Road transport and railways	-	-	98	130	75	111	94	140	111
Air and water transp. and communic.	-	-	149	177	189	271	221	300	206
Banking and insurance	-	-	560	447	690	629	696	1 268	671
Real estate and business services	-	-	215	173	151	235	292	439	219
Public admin. and defense, social and related community serv. and recreational serv.	-	-	204	217	185	290	266	385	280
Personal, household and other serv.	-	-	69	80	48	57	97	134	62
Averages	70	100	108	141	144	216	269	408	100
Total paid income (Rp 10^9)	1 148	121	1 540	1 476	813	1 957	1 055	1 381	4 935
Total unpaid income (Rp 10^9)	3 966	121	993	558	1 689	1 621	31	66	2 365

Source: Government of Indonesia, Biro Pusat Statistik (1986).

basis of such wage rates for paid workers that the incomes of unpaid workers were computed. The two sets of percentages are virtually, but not exactly, the same since the calculations were based on more disaggregated categories than those published, including a distinction between males and females. For instance, a large proportion of lower paid females among unpaid workers in the food crops sector accounts for the fact that the overall average for both paid and unpaid workers in that sector (54 percent) is below any of the percentages for that sector's paid workers.

Recall that average incomes in the food crop sector were only 54 percent of the national average. This is the lowest of all sectoral returns to labour. Elsewhere within agriculture, only the forestry sector displays incomes significantly above the national average regardless of occupation. Outside of agriculture and food processing, the textile sector, the personal services sector, and the eating places sector (which has more sidewalk stalls than restaurants) are characterized by low average incomes. The lowest paid labour incomes, only 48 percent of the national average, are found among rural production workers in the textile sector and rural service workers in the personal services sector. Both these sectors employ large numbers of females.

Comparison of the final columns of Tables 4.3 and 4.4 shows only four sectors that absorb more than a million worker equivalents and also provide incomes above the national average, namely, wood processing and construction (which are combined because it is often impossible to distinguish which of the two sectors carpenters belong to); trade; road and rail transport; and public administration, defense and the like. With the exception of the last sector, which is less likely to hire part-time employees, the sectors are the likeliest to provide off-farm employment.

To quantify more precisely the income farmers derive from non-agricultural pursuits, we will look at how the 1980 factor incomes discussed above were distributed across socio-economic groups of households.

Household Income Distribution

Table 4.5 shows the household distribution of three basic forms of income, namely, those deriving from labour (disaggregated by occupational type), from unincorporated capital, and from various transfers. These transfers, which reflect a form of income redistribution, originate from households (e.g., rural households

Table 4.5: Distribution of Labour Income by Household Type, Occupation (Billions of Rupiahs)[1]

Household Type	Agriculture		Production Transportation		Clerical Sales		Professional Management		Total Labour	Unincorporated Capital	Transfers from				Total
	Paid	Unpaid	Paid	Unpaid	Paid	Unpaid	Paid	Unpaid			Hh	Comp.	Govt.	RoW	
Agric. labourers	1 008	44	131	21	65	58	40	1	1 367	163	25		59	9	1 623
Agric. operators															
Small	114	2 492	166	142	56	244	47	5	3 266	818	78		93	28	4 282
Medium	22	675	37	29	14	52	17	1	846	1 541	18		28	24	2 457
Larger	21	677	21	21	13	36	19	1	810	3598	50		54	25	4 538
Rural: Lower	69	133	1 173	689	254	1 218	86	5	3 627	713	60		77	19	4 496
Inactive	7	18	17	12	10	23	69	3	159	386	12	93	18	5	874
Higher	11	35	36	94	436	101	797	16	1 526	271	11	129	27	6	1 971
Urban: Lower	13	8	1 330	444	684	1 380	142	13	4 013	864	90		211	20	5 197
Inactive	1	1	14	9	26	23	88	2	165	657	39	197	75	8	1 140
Higher	4	2	92	90	1 213	175	1 132	49	2 758	701	25	936	151	23	4 594
Total	1 269	4 087	3 017	1 551	2 770	3 310	2 435	97	18 535	9 913	408	1 355	794	167	31 172

[1] Hh, Households; Comp., companies; RoW, Rest of the World.

Source: Government of Indonesia, Biro Pusak Statistik (1980a, 1986b and 1986c).

supporting students in urban areas or urban workers sending remittances to retired parents in rural areas), from companies (e.g., dividends), from Government (the imputed value of subsidized education and health services consumed by households) and from the rest of the world (e.g., remittances from Indonesians working in the Middle East).

The household categories in Table 4.5 are defined in terms of major income source. The three main sets of categories are agricultural (including a few *urban* farmers, fishermen and so on), rural non-agricultural and urban non-agricultural. The agricultural households are further subdivided into labourers (most, but not all, of whom are landless), small operators owning less than 1/2 ha (including landless tenants), medium operators owning between 0.5 and 1.0 ha and larger operators owning more than 1 ha (most of whom, by international standards, would also be called small farmers since less than 1 percent of the agricultural population live in households owning more than 5 ha). Both rural and urban non-agricultural households are subdivided into three categories:

(i) lower households, headed mainly by the self-employed; menial clerical, sales and services workers; and manual workers

(ii) inactive households, which include young students and aged retirees, as well as the unemployed

(iii) higher households, which consist primarily of employers and employed elites such as bureaucrats, professionals, managers and the military

It is clear from Table 4.5 that all household types have several sources of income. Some non-agricultural households derive part of their income from agriculture; conversely, agricultural households also receive non-agricultural incomes.

Table 4.6 quantifies this latter relationship by computing the percentage of income accruing to agricultural households from agricultural labour and capital (e.g., land, cattle, fishing boats) and from non-agricultural labour and capital. The proportion of agricultural income is virtually the same for labourers and small operators (72 percent and 74 percent) but drops to 64 percent for medium operators, then rises sharply to 85 percent for larger operators. An examination of the labour/capital disaggregation indicates that proportions of agricultural capital incomes increase over the four household categories. This is not surprising since the agricultural

Table 4.6: Agricultural and Non-agricultural Incomes of Agricultural Households, 1980

Agricultural Households	Agricultural			Non-agricultural		Transfers	Total
	Labour	Capital	Total	Labour	Capital		
Billions of Rupiahs							
Labourers	1 052	112	1 164	315	51	93	1 623
Small operators	2 606	549	3 155	660	269	199	4 282
Medium operators	697	873	1 570	149	668	70	2 457
Larger operators	698	3 151	3 849	112	447	129	4 538
Percentages							
Labourers	65	7	72	19	3	6	100
Small operators	61	13	74	15	6	5	100
Medium operators	28	36	64	6	27	3	100
Larger operators	15	69	85	2	10	3	100

Source: Government of Indonesia, Biro Pusak Statistik (1980a, 1986b and 1986c).

households are defined in terms of the main agricultural asset - land. It is perhaps more interesting to note that the pattern for non-agricultural capital is less clear, being largest among the medium agricultural operators, then falling among the larger operators. Perhaps medium operators have limited opportunities for acquiring more land as opposed to non-agricultural assets such as vehicles, or, if they do acquire land, they are likely to move into the larger operator category.

Returning to Table 4.5, we can calculate that the first household group, agricultural labourers, receives about 80 percent of the *paid* agricultural labourers income (Rp 1 008 billion out of Rp 1 269 billion). Such a concentration of paid agricultural income among the agricultural labourers is not surprising but is nonetheless important from a policy perspective. It indicates that one way to raise the incomes of these households, which are among the poorest, is through policies aiding *paid* agricultural workers.

Outside of agriculture we can calculate that labour incomes constitute more than three-fourths of the household income of the rural lower (81 percent), rural higher (77 percent) and urban lower (77 percent) non-agricultural households. In contrast, the urban higher households derive about 40 percent of their income from non-labour sources. As we would expect, non-labour income is an even larger portion of income among the inactive (82 percent for rural and 86 percent for urban).

To obtain a clearer idea of inequality among household groups, we will examine the data in Table 4.5 on a per capita basis. But first we will briefly look at what households do with the incomes they receive.

Household Outlays

Table 4.7 presents estimates, consistent with those of the previous tables, for household outlays on food and non-food consumption, household transfers, taxes and savings. The lower panel of percentages shows that proportions of income spent on food range from 61 percent to 51 percent among the four categories of agricultural households and from 57 percent to 29 percent among the remaining categories of non-agricultural households. Taxes appear to be slightly more burdensome to the rural inactive. The inactive in both urban and rural areas have the lowest savings rates, in contrast to the larger agricultural operators (20 percent) and the higher non-agricultural households in both rural and urban areas (17 percent and 22 percent, respectively).

Table 4.7: Outlays by Socio-economic Group, 1980

Socio-economic Group		Food	Non-food	Total consumption	Transfers to households	Taxes	Savings	Total Outlays
				Billions of Rupiahs				
Agricultural labourers		984	412	1 396	23	35	169	1 623
Agricultural operators:	Small	2 427	1 397	3 824	76	68	315	4 282
	Medium	1 373	706	2 079	18	55	305	2 457
	Larger	2 320	1 154	3 475	53	104	906	4 538
Rural:	Lower level	2 570	1 562	4 131	53	61	251	4 496
	Inactive	485	297	782	12	38	42	874
	Higher level	923	653	1 576	19	37	339	1 971
Urban:	Lower level	2 014	2 606	4 619	72	145	360	5 197
	Inactive	414	643	1 056	23	13	48	1 140
	Higher level	1 314	2 056	3 370	60	155	1 009	4 594
Total		14 823	11 485	26 308	409	710	3 745	31 172
				Percentages				
Agricultural labourer		61	25	86	1	2	10	100
Agricultural operators:	Small	57	33	89	2	2	7	100
	Medium	56	29	85	1	2	12	100
	Larger	51	25	77	1	2	20	100
Rural:	Lower level	57	35	92	1	1	6	100
	Inactive	55	34	89	1	4	5	100
	Higher level	47	33	80	1	2	17	100
Urban:	Lower level	39	50	89	1	3	7	100
	Inactive	36	56	93	2	1	4	100
	Higher level	29	45	73	1	3	22	100
Total		48	37	84	1	2	12	100

Source: Government of Indonesia, Biro Pusak Statistik (1980a, 1986b and 1986c).

Figures 4.1 and 4.2 summarize household incomes and outlays on a per capita basis. Each household group is represented by a bar whose width is proportional to the group's population size and whose height reflects its per capita income and outlays. Dotted lines reflect the national average. Areas protruding over the dotted lines indicate the size and origin of transfers that would be required to elevate to the national average all groups falling below it. Table 4.8 provides the underlying numerical details.

For agricultural households, annual income and outlay averages range from Rp 104 000 among the agricultural labourers to Rp 324 000 among the larger operators. Per capita labour incomes actually fall over the four agricultural categories, whereas capital incomes rise sharply. Other sources of income (interhousehold transfers, the imputed value of government subsidies on health and education, remittances from abroad etc.) do not contribute significantly.

Regarding the *outlays* of agricultural households, note that per capita food expenses more than double as we progress from labourers to larger operators, ranging from Rp 63 000 to Rp 166 000. It is possible to lose sight of this steep increase if we focus on *proportions* of outlays devoted to food, which we have seen in Table 4.7 *drop* from 61 percent to 51 percent.

Outside agriculture, average incomes and outlays range from Rp 199 000 among the rural lower households to Rp 484 000 among the urban higher households. Both the rural lower and inactive households have averages below those of the medium and large agricultural operators but noticeably above the agricultural labourers and small operators. The urban lower households have per capita incomes and outlays that also fall below larger agricultural operators but that surpass all other rural household categories. The urban inactive, dominated by students and retired people rather than unemployed job seekers, seem relatively well off. (Unemployed individuals, especially in urban areas, typically reside in households whose head is active.) In making such comparisons between urban and rural groups, however, recall that urban prices tend to be higher. Hence, higher per capita urban incomes and outlays do not necessarily imply higher living standards.

Trends and Evaluation

So far this section has examined data from Indonesia's 1980 System of Socio-Economic Accounts, which follow the 1975 System published in 1983. It is useful to compare data from these two systems.

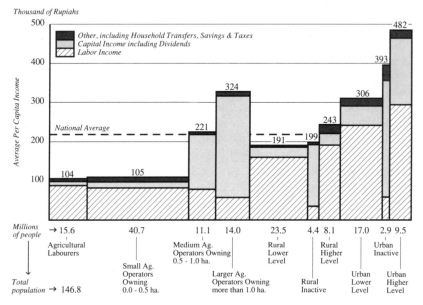

Figure 4.1: Per Capita Income Distribution By Household Group and Source, 1980
Source: Downey (1984).

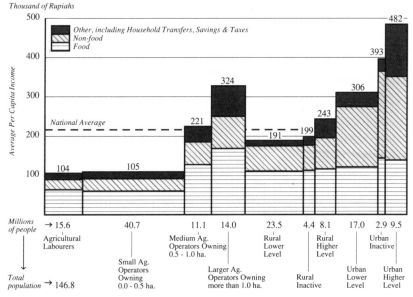

Figure 4.2: Per Capita Outlay Distribution By Household Group and Expenditure Type, 1980
Source: Downey (1984).

Table 4.8: Per Capita Incomes and Annual Outlays by Socio-economic Group, 1980 (Thousands of Rupiahs)

Socio-Economic Group		Per Capita Incomes 1980				Per Capita Annual Outlays			
		Labour	Capital[1]	Other	Total	Food	Non-food	Other[2]	Total
Agricultural labourers		88	10	6	104	63	26	15	104
Agricultural operators:	Small	80	20	5	105	60	34	11	105
	Medium	76	139	6	221	124	64	34	221
	Larger	58	257	9	324	166	82	76	324
Rural:	Lower level	154	30	7	191	109	66	15	191
	Inactive	36	154	8	199	110	67	21	199
	Higher level	188	49	6	243	114	81	49	243
Urban:	Lower level	236	50	20	306	118	153	34	306
	Inactive	57	294	42	393	143	222	29	393
	Higher level	290	172	21	484	138	216	129	484
Indonesia		126	77	9	212	101	78	33	212

[1] Capital includes dividends.

[2] Other includes household transfers, savings and taxes.

Source: Government of Indonesia, Biro Pusak Statistik (1980a, 1986b and 1986c).

Table 4.9 compares per capita incomes and populations across socio-economic groups. The first two columns present per capita income data in current prices. Since group-specific deflators appropriate for computing incomes in constant prices do not exist, Table 4.9 facilitates comparisons by also showing each group's per capita average income as a percentage of the national average. Thus, the per capita income (and outlays) of agricultural labourers appears to have dropped from 56 percent of the average in 1975 to 51 percent in 1980. Small agricultural operators exhibit a similar drop. It is possible that the *absolute* position of poorer agricultural households improved over the period of 1975-80, but their *relative* status appears to have fallen. A World Bank study (Rao 1984) claims that the incidence of poverty declined from 57 percent of the population to 40 percent during the 1970s. In contrast, medium and larger operators show a marked improvement in relative position. They move, respectively, from 77 percent and 115 percent of the national average to 109 percent and 160 percent.

With regard to population changes among agricultural households, Table 4.9 indicates a slight increase of 0.9 million among labourers and a substantial increase of 11.6 million among small operators. The populations of medium and larger operators appear to have fallen by 4.6 and 4.0 million, respectively. The total population whose primary source of income is agricultural appears to have increased from 77.5 million in 1975 to 81.4 million in 1980. These trends indicate significantly increasing polarization among agricultural households. The labourers and small operators have lower relative incomes and swelling populations, whereas the medium and larger operators have rapidly improving incomes and dwindling populations.

Outside of agriculture, Table 4.9 shows that urban higher-level households, while maintaining their position as the highest ranking group, seem to have slipped from 279 percent of the national average to 228 percent. The relative incomes of all other non-agricultural groups seems to have increased except among the urban lower households, which remained virtually the same. The population of all non-agricultural groups display increases, but by far the largest increments are among the lower groups: 4.2 million in rural areas and 4.9 in urban areas. The trend among non-agricultural households can be characterised as one of dampening polarization: Relative incomes tended to improve except at the top, whereas populations rose.

Given the implications of the above trends, it is necessary to examine limitations of the estimates presented in Table 4.9. To some extent, the trends may stem from discontinuities in the methods used

Table 4.9: Comparison of Per Capita Household Incomes and Populations by Socio-economic Group, 1975-80

Socio-Economic Group		Per Capita Income (current prices) (Rp 000)		Per Capita Incomes as Percentage of National Average		Populations (millions)	
		1975	1980	1975	1980	1975	1980
Agricultural labourers		42	104	56	51	14.7	15.6
Agricultural operators:	Small	43	105	57	52	29.1	40.7
	Medium	58	221	77	109	15.7	11.1
	Larger	86	324	115	160	18.0	14.0
Rural:	Lower level	60	191	80	95	19.3	23.5
	Inactive	65	199	87	99	3.8	4.4
	Higher level	83	243	111	120	7.7	8.1
Urban:	Lower level	117	306	156	151	12.1	17.0
	Inactive	130	393	173	189	2.0	2.9
	Higher level	209	482	279	228	8.0	9.5
Indonesia		75	212	100	100	130.6	146.8

Source: Government of Indonesia, Biro Pusak Statistik (1980a, 1986b and 1986c).

to reconcile conflicting data. For instance, Table 4.9 suggests that government policies to increase rice production favoured larger landowners disproportionately. Undoubtedly such was the case for owners of wetlands, but in fact larger operators are more likely to possess dryland and farm estate crops. The 1975 set of accounts imputed agricultural land income on the basis of detailed information about land quality (dryland, irrigated wetland, non-irrigated wetland etc.), cropping intensities, land tenure relationships, and so on (Keuning 1984).

Similarly, the apparent drop in the position of the urban higher-level households appears suspect during a period when mounting oil revenues stimulated sectors of the economy that employed members of urban higher-level households. This drop may be due in part to procedures used to estimate household incomes and expenditures. Among non-agricultural households in 1975, the distribution of capital incomes was imputed after calculating total expenditures. These expenditures, in turn, were based on imputations for certain sets of commodities. For example, purchases of durable goods such as televisions and, more importantly, vehicles are grossly underreported in Indonesia's national consumption surveys. Precisely because durables are long lasting, they are purchased infrequently by individual households. We cannot expect many sample households to have acquired, say, an automobile during the previous three months, the surveys' reference period for durables. For this reason, the 1975 System of Socio-Economic Accounts imputed expenditures on durables by using data about household *possession* of these items not reported *purchases* (Downey 1984). For 1980 no comparable data are available to make a similar imputation. As a consequence, both the consumption and the income of the urban elites may be significantly underestimated in 1980.

Regarding population estimates, other sources provide a different picture. Unadjusted 1980 Census data indicate that agricultural labourers *decreased* from 14.7 million in 1975 to 12.0 million in 1980. More significantly, the Census shows that landless tenants, a component of small agricultural operators, increased dramatically from 2.4 to 9.0 million. It is difficult to discern trends among the other size categories of agricultural operators because the classification categories were not equivalent, but the total agricultural population in the Census appears to have dropped from 77.6 million in 1975 to 75.2 million in 1980.

Compensating for this drop in total agricultural population, the Census data display a marked increase in the rural non-agricultural population (totalling 41.5 million instead of the 36.0 million in Table 4.9). A detailed examination of the Census data reveals that the bulk of the increase occurred among the less-skilled rural non-agricultural self-employed.

According to the statisticians who constructed the 1980 System of Socio-Economic Accounts, the estimates of the agricultural population in the 1980 Population Census were difficult to accept primarily because of the huge reported increase in landless tenants. The increase from 2.4 to 9 million was a spurious result due to insufficiently probing inquiries about land ownership in the Population Census. Hence the estimates were adjusted on the basis of information taken from the 1983 Agricultural Census, which was more thorough in its questions about land ownership. According to these latter data, landless tenant households increased by 81 percent from 1975 to 1983. This is still a substantial increase but much more credible than the nearly fourfold increase implied by the 1980 Population Census.

An inconsistency, however, still remains. The 1983 Agricultural Census (Series B, Table 25) suggests that both the medium and larger operator households *increased* in number by 6 percent and 55 percent, respectively, from 1975 to 1983. Table 4.9, as we have seen, has populations in both these categories *decreasing*. In the case of the medium operators, the increase is, indeed, small and we should note that the Agricultural Census pertains to *all* households who have any agricultural activities, not simply to those whose *main* source of income is from agriculture. Adjusting for this difference in definition reduces the number of total rural agricultural households from 17.1 to 15.7 million. Data on the distribution of these more narrowly defined households over size of land owned have not been published, but larger landowners are likely to have agricultural activities as their main income source. Even if the number of medium operators, defined in terms of main income source, decreased somewhat, the data from the Agricultural Census suggest a significant increase in the number of larger operators.

In summary, the distribution of agricultural households by size of land owned probably widened at both extremes and flattened somewhat in the 0.5-1.0 ha range (this issue is discussed in more detail later in this chapter).

The 1983 Agricultural Census estimate of 15.7 million rural households with their main income source from agriculture compares with 15.8 million in the 1975 System of Socio-Economic Accounts. In other words, both the 1980 Population Census and the 1983 Agricultural Census indicate that the absolute number of households deriving income primarily from agriculture has *fallen* or nearly *remained the same*, not risen as the 1980 System of Socio-Economic Accounts implies.

This observation indicates some limitations of the System of Socio-Economic Accounts. Even given the reservations, however, estimates from both the 1975 and 1980 System of Socio-Economic Accounts are the most consistent estimates for income and outlays available and provide a sufficiently clear indication of which rural socio-economic groups within Indonesia are relatively poor, namely, agricultural labourers, the small agricultural operators and the rural lower-level households. To the extent that there is variation within the household groups defined, some of the approximately 80 million people in these groups are undoubtedly not poor, and, conversely, some members of other groups, even larger farmers (e.g., those owning poorer-quality land), are likely to be poor.

Socio-economic Dimensions of Nutritional Inequality

Despite its paramount importance, nutritional adequacy is difficult to measure accurately. Indonesia's BPS attempts to be thorough in the surveys it conducts. Its 1976 SUSENAS, the basis of this discussion, collected information about approximately 100 different types of food, seeking as many as 14 pieces of information about each one. The three most common questions about a particular type of food pertained to the *value* consumed in the categories of purchase, self-production and other (gifts, wages in kind, government allotment etc.). For many foods, SUSENAS asked additional questions about the corresponding quantities consumed. Quantities were recorded in both local measurement units (which vary widely throughout Indonesia) and their standardized equivalents. SUSENAS also inquired about prices paid or, in the event of non-purchased foods, prices prevailing in the nearest market. Underlying this extensive set of questions was an operationally complex definition of consumption. Food acquired but not consumed was excluded, and food eaten by *non-household* workers in a household enterprise and food prepared for subsequent sale were considered part of production outlays not consumption. (Presumably food eaten by guests was part of household consumption.) The reference period was either the previous seven days or the previous calendar week, whichever respondents found more convenient to recall. The respondent was the household member most versed in the intricacies of the household's consumption. To the extent possible, all other members were asked about their consumption of snacks and meals away from home. As we shall see, the SUSENAS food data are instructive, but not accurate enough. To enable us to examine nutritional implications of the food consumption reported in Indonesia's 1976 SUSENAS data, Table 4.10 provides a detailed socio-economic classification of households. It disaggregates agricultural operators into 13 categories according to the amount of land they own and economically active non-agricultural households into components based on a combination of labour status and occupational categories. A footnote marks the subgroups that, along with employers, were treated as higher level earlier in this chapter. Subgroups earlier characterized as lower level are 420, 632, and 640. Table 4.10 divides the economically inactive into three groups (SG 701-703), depending on the age of the household head.

For each of the groups in Table 4.10, Table 4.11 records the total population (adjusted to agree with the 1975 System of Socio-Economic Accounts) and the percentage of that population that falls into four categories of calorie adequacy. Calorie adequacy was calculated by converting each sample household's quantity of food consumed into calories, then contrasting the results with requirement standards adjusted for the sex and age composition of each household's members (cf. Downey 1984 for details).

The bottom line of Table 4.11 indicates that about one-fifth of all Indonesians (19.5 percent, or roughly 25 million people) attain less than 60 percent of their required calories. Approximately another one-third (31.3 percent) appear to attain less than 85 percent of their requirements.

To a large extent underreporting is responsible for what appears as undernutrition. Underreporting is also a serious problem in that it is biased. To understand this problem more clearly, we will scrutinize Table 4.11 with the aid of Figure 4.3.

Figure 4.3 distributes subgroups' populations over the four categories of calorie adequacy. The detached bars on the right and left reflect national expected values. The contiguous bars represent the socio-economic subgroups. The widths of the bars vary in proportion to populations. The less populous employee elites, marked with a footnote in Table 4.11, have been gathered into the HL R and HL U bars, and the inactive have been gathered into the 7 R and 7 U bars. Areas above and below the central horizontal line represent, respectively, people whose SUSENAS consumption exceeds or fails to reach 85 percent of their required calories. This split at 85 percent does not mark a calorie-poverty line in any technical sense. It

Table 4.10: Detailed Socio-economic Household Classification

Subgroup Codes	Definitions
	Agricultural Operators
	Land Owned (L in hectares)
100	L = 0.00
101	0.00 < L ≤ 0.10
102	0.10 < L ≤ 0.20
103	0.20 < L ≤ 0.30
104	0.30 < L ≤ 0.40
105	0.40 < L ≤ 0.50
107	0.50 < L ≤ 0.75
110	0.75 < L ≤ 1.00
115	1.00 < L ≤ 1.50
120	1.50 < L ≤ 2.00
130	2.00 < L ≤ 3.00
150	3.00 < L ≤ 5.00
151	5.00 < L
310 R/U	*Non-agricultural Employers*
	Non-agricultural Own-Account Workers
410 R/U[1]	Professionals and technicians (ISCO 0/1) and self-employed in wholesale trade, inns, finance, insurance and real estate (ISIC 61, 64, 81, 82, 83)
420 R/U	Other non-agricultural own-account workers
510	*Agricultural Labourers*
	Non-agricultural Employees
610 R/U[1]	Managers, supervisors (ISCO 20, 21, 30, 31, 40, 41, 50, 51, 70)
621 R/U[1]	Non-teacher professionals and technicians (ISCO 0/1 except 13)
622 R/U[1]	Teachers (ISCO 13)
631 R/U[1]	Higher clerical and sales workers (ISCO 32, 33, 34, 38, 39, 42, 43, 44)
632 R/U	Other clerical, sales and service workers (ISCO 36, 37, 45, 49, 52 to 59)
640 R/U	Manual workers (ISCO 7, 8, 9 except 70)
650 R/U[1]	Military
	Economically Inactive
701 R/U	With heads less than 25 years old
702 R/U	With heads between 25 and 50 years old
703 R/U	With heads more than 50 years old
900 R/U	*Unclassified*

[1] "Higher level" employee subgroups.

R = rural, U = urban.

Source: Downey (1984).

Table 4.11: Distribution of Persons by Estimated Percentage of Required Calories Available and by Non-agricultural Subgroup

		Row percent of People by percent of Required Calories Available:				Population (10^6)
		-60	61-84	85-109	110	
Agricultural Subgroup						
100:		30.5	26.5	22.7	20.3	2.42
101:		23.9	29.3	24.3	22.6	5.31
102:		25.3	30.1	24.7	20.0	4.90
103:		21.8	31.3	28.9	18.0	6.14
104: Agricultural		18.8	36.0	24.0	21.3	4.56
105: operators		26.0	27.4	27.4	19.1	5.77
107:		21.5	29.7	27.3	21.6	8.28
110:		19.5	26.6	25.1	28.9	7.44
115:		14.1	25.6	31.4	29.0	7.57
120:		13.8	23.4	26.8	36.1	4.16
130:		5.5	23.5	28.6	42.4	3.46
150:		6.1	25.1	25.7	43.1	2.08
151:		1.5	20.7	22.3	55.5	0.73
510: Agricultural labourers		25.2	35.8	23.3	15.6	14.74
Rural agriculture		20.2	29.5	26.1	24.2	75.40
Urban agriculture		18.3	27.5	29.5	24.8	2.16
All agriculture		20.2	29.4	26.1	24.2	77.57
Non-agricultural Subgroup						
310: Employers	R	16.9	39.4	23.2	20.5	3.34
	U	17.9	35.0	19.7	27.5	1.82
410:[1] Self-employed	R	23.8	41.2	28.4	6.7	0.16
Professionals	U	13.8	42.9	10.3	33.0	0.15
420: Other self-	R	19.7	31.3	29.5	19.5	10.35
employed	U	17.5	36.6	26.2	19.7	4.90
610:[1] Managers and	R	14.8	37.6	24.6	13.0	1.34
supervisors	U	16.5	26.9	33.0	23.6	2.19
621:[1] Professional	R	3.2	12.5	25.2	59.2	0.44
non-teachers	U	9.1	45.0	20.1	25.8	0.58
622:[1] Teachers	R	13.8	32.3	24.4	29.5	1.42
	U	10.7	24.3	41.5	23.5	0.72
631:[1] Higher clerical	R		33.5	27.5	24.5	0.61
and sales	U	14.5	35.6	31.3	18.7	1.80
632: Other clerical	R	26.3	34.3	20.0	19.4	2.96
sales and service	U	24.5	34.9	21.8	19.0	2.56
640: Manual workers	R	19.6	35.7	28.4	16.4	5.96

Table 4.11: Distribution of Persons by Estimated Percentage of Required Calories Available and by Non-agricultural Subgroup (Cont'd)

		Row percent of People by percent of Required Calories Available:				Population (10⁶)
		-60	61-84	85-109	110	
	U	23.5	38.6	20.1	17.9	4.70
650:[1] Military	R	4.4	16.6	49.5	29.5	0.41
	U	8.2	33.7	34.9	23.2	0.78
701: Inactive -25	R	14.4	39.2	33.2	13.2	0.44
	U	25.5	34.3	10.6	29.7	0.14
702: Inactive 25-50	R	14.6	29.6	35.6	20.3	1.82
	U	24.9	39.5	25.8	9.8	0.89
703: Inactive 50+	R	14.6	19.1	34.9	31.4	1.45
	U	21.8	37.9	20.4	19.9	0.92
900: Unclassified	R	22.5	24.9	43.2	9.4	0.16
	U	11.4	14.9	44.4	29.4	0.01
All rural non-agriculture		18.4	32.7	28.1	20.9	30.86
All urban non-agriculture		18.8	35.6	25.1	20.5	22.17
All non-agriculture		18.5	33.9	26.9	20.7	53.03
All Indonesia		19.5	31.3	26.4	22.8	130.60

[1] See Table 4.10.

Source: Downey (1984).

provides a convenient watershed for emphasizing reported food-consumption inequality within and among subgroups.

Compared with a national expected value of 49.2 percent for people above the 85 percent line, only 38.9 percent of the agricultural labourers (SG 510) report food consumption sufficient to attain this level. Among the agricultural operators, there is a clear association between land ownership and calorie adequacy. The proportions of these operators, with at least 85 percent of their required calories, range from a low of 43.0 percent among the landless (SG 100) to a high of 77.8 percent among the landowners with 5 ha or more (SG 151). In a similar vein, indicators of severe calorie deficiencies - the population shares reporting less than 60 percent of their requirements - are most concentrated among the landless (SG 100: 30.5 percent) and least concentrated among the largest landowners (SG 151: 1.5 percent).

This association between land ownership and calorie adequacy is not surprising, since a high-priority use for land is food production. It

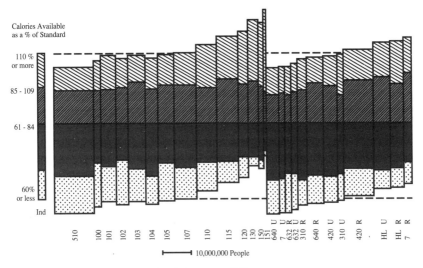

Figure 4.3: Calorie Adequacy by Subgroup, 1975
Source: Downey (1984).
Note: For definition of groups see Tables 4.10, 4.11 and 4.12.

is also generally true that higher-level groups (HL R, HL U) rank above the manual workers (SG 640) and more menial clerical, sales and service workers (SG 632). Again, this is not surprising since the higher-level groups are defined in terms of status and occupational categories, which reflects superior endowments of skills and other forms of human capital.

What is surprising is that several of the lowest-ranking subgroups are urban. As a particularly unusual example, Table 4.11 suggests that 41.9 percent of the urban military population (SG 650 U), almost double the proportion of the rural military, achieve less than 85 percent of its calorie requirements.

The oddity of these rankings appears in sharp focus when they are contrasted with subgroup rankings based on other dimensions of well being. For instance, Table 4.12 ranks subgroups according to the average number of years spent in school. Once again there is a clear association between land ownership and educational attainment, but the relative position of agricultural and non-agricultural subgroups and of rural and urban subgroups is quite different. The educational endowment of the agricultural subgroups falls below the national average, with the sole exception of the largest landowners (SG 151); and rural non-agricultural subgroups fall below their urban

Table 4.12: Estimated Years of School Per Potential Labour-Force Participant Not in School, by Sex and Subgroup (Ranked), 1975

Subgroups			M	F	M + F
Rural	Urban				
	622 U:*	Teachers	11.50	7.71	9.44
	621 U:*	Professional non-teachers	9.83	6.91	8.30
	610 U:*	Managers and supervisors	9.68	6.74	8.17
	650 U:*	Military	8.98	6.91	7.94
	631 U:*	Higher clerical and sales	9.32	6.60	7.90
	900 U:	Unclassified	9.70	6.08	7.70
622 R:*		Teachers	9.22	6.02	7.55
650 R:*		Military	7.62	5.65	6.62
	410 U:*	Own-account professionals	7.56	5.36	6.38
631 R:*		Higher clerical and sales	7.13	4.72	5.91
610 R:*		Managers and supervisors	7.03	4.73	5.88
	310 U:	Employers	6.10	4.53	5.29
	702 U:	Inactive 25-50	6.37	4.53	5.29
621 R:*		Professional non-teachers	6.37	4.16	5.20
	701 U:	Inactive -25	5.49	4.68	5.07
	703 U:	Inactive 50+	6.18	3.87	4.87
	640 U:	Manual workers	5.47	3.78	4.63
	632 U:	Other clerical, sales, service	5.59	3.71	4.61
900 R:		Unclassified	4.92	3.70	4.38
	420 U:	Other own-account workers	5.08	3.61	4.31
702 R:		Unclassified	4.89	2.96	3.72
410 R:*		Own-account professionals	4.29	2.79	3.54
151:		Agricultural operators owning 5.0+ ha	4.15	2.82	3.50
701 R:		Inactive -25	4.27	2.85	3.49
310 R:		Employers	4.16	2.79	3.43
		Indonesian average	4.01	2.73	3.44
150:		Agricultural operators owning 3.0-5.0 ha	3.77	2.69	3.24
640 R:		Manual workers	3.81	2.62	3.21
420 R:		Other own-account workers	3.87	2.57	3.16
130:		Agricultural operators owning 2.0-3.0 ha	3.64	2.60	3.13
632 R:		Other clerical, sales, service	3.74	2.38	3.02
120:		Agricultural operators owning 1.5-2.0 ha	3.45	2.49	2.97
115:		Agricultural operators owning 1.0-1.5 ha	3.43	2.41	2.92

Table 4.12: Estimated Years of School Per Potential Labour-Force Participant Not in School, by Sex and Subgroup (Ranked), 1975 (Cont'd)

Subgroups			M	F	M + F
Rural	Urban				
110:		Agricultural operators owning .75-1.0 ha	3.25	2.27	2.75
107:		Agricultural operators owning 0.5-.75 ha	3.22	2.21	2.71
105:		Agricultural operators owning 0.4-0.5 ha	3.08	2.08	2.56
104:		Agricultural operators owning 0.3-0.4 ha	3.07	2.08	2.56
103:		Agricultural operators owning 0.2-0.3 ha	3.02	2.05	2.51
101:		Agricultural operators owning 0.0-0.1 ha	2.94	2.10	2.51
510:		Agricultural labourers	3.02	1.98	2.46
102:		Agricultural operators owning 0.1-0.2 ha	2.96	2.00	2.45
100:		Agricultural operators owning no land	2.83	2.04	2.43
703 R:		Inactive 50+	3.46	1.61	2.27

* For codes see Table 4.10.
Source: Downey (1984).

counterparts. In principle, there is no reason why patterns of stratification regarding nutrition should be the same as those for educational attainment, but the pattern for education is generally repeated for other dimensions of well-being such as housing quality and possession of durables (Downey 1984), making the nutritional pattern all the more suspect.

Food eaten outside the home probably accounts for many of the oddities in Table 4.11. Of the more than 100 food categories SUSENAS distinguishes, only *one* refers to prepared foods consumed outside the household. Since the SUSENAS rationale for making detailed inquiries about different types of grains, fruits, vegetables and so on, is to jog respondents' memories, we must consider whether a single question is sufficient to stimulate complete recall of all the various foods respondents (and *a fortiori* other household members) obtain during a week from itinerant vendors, wayside stalls, cafeterias, mess halls, restaurants and so on. Many such meals and snacks consumed by office workers, students and the like may well be overlooked by all but the most assiduous SUSENAS enumerators and respondents.

To the extent that food outside the home is more available in urban areas and more frequently consumed by people in certain status or occupational categories (such as the military), those areas and people are more likely to display spurious calorie deficiencies.

Although the SUSENAS data do not seem adequate to cover foods consumed outside the home, they do provide useful information about the way food consumed in the home is acquired. Therefore, we will next examine the different ways food, specifically rice, is acquired.

Different Modes of Food Acquisition

SUSENAS recorded whether rice and most other food commodities were acquired by purchase, self-production or other (gift, wages in kind, etc.) means. Table 4.13 presents the rice data (adjusted to conform with the 1975 System of Socio-Economic Accounts). The bottom of the left-hand panel shows that, nationally, final household consumption of rice averaged 2.22 kg per person per week (rice consumed as prepared foods is not included). In agriculture, the subgroup means dip in irregular fashion from 2.09 kg for labourers (SG 510) to a low of 1.83 kg for operators (SG 105), then increase to a high of 3.07 kg for the largest landowners (SG 151). Outside agriculture, the subgroup means display less variation. The urban manual workers (SG 640 U) have the lowest mean (2.13 kg), and the rural non-teacher professionals have the highest (3.07 kg).

Although average levels of rice consumption do not vary widely over the majority of subgroups, Table 4.13 shows substantial inequalities regarding the ways different subgroups acquire rice. For example, the sharp contrast between agricultural labourers (SG 510) and landless operators (SG 100) indicates that the latters' tenancy or sharecropping arrangements permit them to be less dependent upon rice markets. On average, the landless operators consume 0.82 kg of self-produced rice, compared with only 0.17 kg for the agricultural labourers. This is a clear indication of what A. K. Sen (1982, p. 5) labels "exchange entitlements".

Besides displaying differences between agricultural labourers and landless operators, Table 4.13 shows that among the landed operators consumption for own production typically increases along with land size. This relationship is a useful reminder that smaller landowners are typically not "subsistence" farmers in a literal sense. It is the

Table 4.13: Rice:: Weekly Per Capita Quantity Consumed (Grams) and Prices Per Kilogram, 1975

Socio-Economic Subgroup	Bought	Self-produced	Other	Total	Price per kg (Rp)	Socio-Economic Subgroup	Bought	Self-Produced	Other	Total	Price per kg (Rp)
In agriculture						*Outside Agriculture*					
100:	1 125	818	40	1 982	120	310: Employers	R 2 038	236	38	2 312	128
101:	1 244	848	29	2 121	121		U 2 199	40	43	2 282	135
102:	1 226	577	69	1 871	120	410: Self-employed	R 2 151	0	9	2 160	135
103:	1 185	737	10	1 932	122	Professionals	U 2 357	87	4	2 447	139
104: Agricultural	959	1 023	35	2 016	121	420: Other self-	R 2 053	207	60	2 321	125
105:	984	823	26	1 834	126	employed	U 2 298	21	23	2 342	132
107: Operators	848	1 232	8	2 088	121	610: Managers and	R 1 855	193	336	2 385	127
110:	845	1 387	8	2 240	124	supervisors	U 1 883	13	456	2 352	135
115:	883	1 425	14	2 322	123	621: Professional	R 2 479	448	141	3 069	123
120:	973	1 565	13	2 551	125	non-teachers	U 1 904	85	398	2 388	137
130:	1 087	1 605	5	2 697	130	622: Teachers	R 1 889	380	121	2 390	126
150:	954	1 750	-	2 704	131		U 1 923	134	419	2 476	133
151:	1 766	1 307	-	3 072	130	631: Higher clerical	R 1 838	341	344	2 523	122
510: Agricultural labourers	1 790	165	136	2 091	124	and sales	U 1 872	6	364	2 243	135
						632: Other clerical	R 1 943	146	83	2 172	126
						sales and service	U 2 063	9	177	2 249	132
						640: Manual workers	R 2 017	163	58	2 238	126

Table 4.13: Rice: Weekly Per Capita Quantity Consumed (Grams) and Prices Per Kilogram, 1975 (Cont'd)

In agriculture

Socio-Economic Subgroup	Bought	Self-produced	Other	Total	Price per kg (Rp)
Rural agriculture	1 151	950	42	2 143	124
Rural non-agriculture	1 973	243	126	2 341	125
All rural	1 390	744	66	2 200	124
Urban agriculture	1 530	947	52	2 530	123
Urban non-agriculture	2 053	30	195	2 278	133
All urban	2 007	111	182	2 300	132
All agriculture	1 162	950	42	2 154	124
All non-agriculture	2 006	154	154	2 315	129
All Indonesia	1 505	626	88	2 219	126

Outside Agriculture

Socio-Economic Subgroup	Bought	Self-Produced	Other	Total	Price per kg (Rp)
650:Military	U 2 040	19	72	2 130	133
	R 1 642	135	866	2 643	128
701: Inactive -25	U 1 289	53	1038	2 380	131
	R 1 297	1249	47	2 593	112
702: Inactive 25-50	U 1 930	178	212	2 319	135
	R 1 569	640	232	2 441	119
703: Inactive 50+	U 1 930	63	171	2 164	133
	R 2 038	124	509	2 671	125
900: Unclassified	U 2 192	56	165	2 413	132
	R 1 744	30	616	2 390	121
	U 1 978	0	168	2 146	126

Source: Downey (1984).

larger landowners who manage to meet the bulk of their staple needs from self-production. By implication, the rice consumption of smaller farmers is less insulated from the negative impact of price increases.

In this context of differential market dependency, note that purchased rice noted in Table 4.13 makes up slightly more than two-thirds of all rice consumption nationally. Such a huge proportion implies much more extensive rice markets than the 30-40 percent estimated by Mears (1981).

Although non-agricultural subgroups purchase most of their rice, their non-purchases are worth attention in certain cases, in particular, a great deal of other rice among the elites, especially the military (SG 650). Here, "other" reflects wages in kind paid to what BULOG, the Indonesian agency officially charged with controlling the price and supply of rice and other basic foods, designates literally as "target groups". The purpose of paying part of the salaries of government employees and the military in kind is to protect them from inflationary pressures (Arifin 1975). These subgroups have little claim to such privileged treatment on the basis of greater need when compared with, say, agricultural labourers and small farmers. Government-employee recipients of this rice allotment are reportedly selling or otherwise disposing of it in order to obtain a more expensive but tasty variety in the market.

Another aspect of rice inequality is the disparate array of prices different socio-economic groups face. Table 4.13 prices reflect not only purchases but also the imputed prices for consumption from own production and other. These prices per kilogramme range from Rp 139 among the urban self-employed professionals (SG 410 U) to Rp 112 among the rural inactive with household heads under 25 years of age. As we might expect, urban subgroups generally face higher prices. In part, this is due to their consuming less from own production, which tends to be cheaper (at least by the amount of trade and transport margins). In part, however, the higher prices reflect a premium paid for better-quality rice.

Patterns of price variation among the rural subgroups are unclear. Higher-level subgroups and the larger landowners appear to pay higher prices, but the agricultural labourers (SG 510) face about the same prices as professional non-teachers (SG 621 R). Perhaps rice-price variation does not appear to follow a clearer social pattern because of the variability of transportation costs, particularly in rural areas.

Summary

The primary aim of the above discussion has been to underscore limitations of Indonesia's SUSENAS data as a basis for estimating food adequacy. Food consumed outside the home, particularly by household members other than the survey respondents, probably accounts for the extremely low ranking of many urban non-agricultural subgroups when compared with rural ones. Among the agricultural subgroups, however, there seems to be a distinct positive correlation between land owned and calorie adequacy. Outside of agriculture, there is corresponding correlation between the occupation and status categories of various subgroups and their calorie adequacy: Within the separate categories of rural and urban subgroups, those defined in terms of higher levels of human capital also tend to have better diets. Because there is wide variation within subgroups as well as among them, however, it is possible that even some larger landowners (perhaps those on poorer land) and some higher-level households are also undernourished. But here again we cannot be sure whether what appears as undernutrition might not simply be underreporting.

Although SUSENAS data appear to record food consumed outside the home inadequately, they do provide interesting insights into how food consumed within the home is acquired. In the example for rice presented here, SUSENAS data indicate that agricultural labourers are much more dependent on markets than the landless tenants and that larger farmers tend to be more self-sufficient in rice than smaller ones. The SUSENAS data on rice prices indicate that urban subgroups typically pay more than rural subgroups.

Regional Dimensions of Poverty

Various attempts have been made to identify pockets of poverty in Indonesia. One such attempt has been reported in a World Bank Study, *Indonesia: Strategy for a Sustained Reduction in Poverty* which uses official estimates of poverty line to calculate the incidence of poverty by area within Indonesia. The official poverty line is estimated on the basis of a minimum daily caloric intake (2 100 calories per capita per day) and an allowance for other non-food basic necessities (derived from percentage of the expenditures by households on non-food items). On this basis the estimated official poverty line for rural areas is Rp 7 746 per capita per month in 1984 and Rp 10 294 per capita per month in 1987. Applying these poverty lines, it is estimated that 21.2 percent of the rural population were in poverty in

1984, but this percentage came down to 16.4 percent in 1987 (Table 4.14). The corresponding percentages were 40.4 percent in 1976 and 28.4 percent in 1980 (World Bank 1990).

As for the incidence of rural poverty by area, while the differential between Java and Bali on the one hand, and the Outer Islands on the other, has decreased between 1984 and 1987, the incidence of rural poverty in the Eastern Outer Islands remained significantly higher than other regions.

Table 4.15 compares 1981 per capita (urban plus rural) production and consumption of rice, maize, cassava and yams. Its data on maize and cassava consumption (the fourth and sixth columns) illustrate the importance of non-rice staples in the diets of Lampung, Central and Eastern Java, Yogyakarta, East Nusa Tenggara, North and Southeast Sulawesi, Maluku and Irian Jaya. Perhaps more importantly, it shows that some of these areas reportedly produce much more rice than they consume. The consumption data are once again from SUSENAS sources and are therefore probably underestimates (particularly in Jakarta where meals outside the home are common). Even if we scale up all the rice-consumption averages by 8.3 percent so national consumption at least equals national production, we find that Central Java, Eastern Java and Yogyakarta are among the net exporters of rice. Hence food poverty and deprivation for these areas as a whole is more likely to stem from insufficient purchasing power rather than from insufficient production capability. On the other hand, areas like Lampung, East Nusa Tenggara, and Southeast Sulawesi may be dependent on non-rice staples because they cannot produce enough rice locally. It would appear that Maluku has special problems in producing not only rice but also maize and cassava.

To some extent dependency on non-rice staples may be a matter of taste, but it is also likely to be a fairly reliable indicator of poverty. To the extent that it is, poorer areas have the most diversified diets in terms of basic staples. On nutritional grounds, Chapter 5 shows that Indonesians should move in the direction of more diversified and balanced diets (less dependent on rice) that not only prevent protein-energy malnutrition but also provide the other nutrients crucial to the alleviation of diseases such as Vitamin A deficiency and anaemia. Attempts to diversify diets simply by increasing non-rice staples, especially cassava, must confront the fact that many poorer areas already depend heavily on non-rice staples.

Given the limitations of SUSENAS consumption data, it is useful to investigate other indicators of poverty. One such indicator is infant mortality, which is discussed in Chapter 5 (Table 5.10). Here it is

Table 4.14: Incidence of Poverty by Area, 1984-1987[1]

	1984			1987		
	Urban	Rural	Total	Urban	Rural	Total
Java and Bali	25.0	23.6	24.0	21.0	17.8	18.8
Outer Islands	<u>18.4</u>	<u>16.6</u>	<u>16.9</u>	<u>17.6</u>	<u>14.0</u>	<u>14.8</u>
Western[2]	14.0	9.6	10.5	13.7	8.3	9.5
Eastern[3]	30.3	29.7	29.8	28.4	24.2	24.9
Total	<u>23.1</u>	<u>21.2</u>	<u>21.6</u>	<u>20.1</u>	<u>16.4</u>	<u>17.4</u>

[1] Estimates based on the Official Poverty Line, see text.

[2] Includes provinces in Sumatra and Kilimantan.

[3] Includes the island of Sulawesi, and East Nusa Tenggara, West Nusa Tenggara, East Timor, Maluku, and Irian Jaya.

Source: World Bank (1990).

sufficient to point out that the 1984 infant mortality rates in the Eastern Islands are very high, especially in West and East Nusa Tenggara (129 and 106, respectively), Maluku (105) and Irian Jaya (108). On the other hand, the infant mortality rate in rural West Java is high (94) compared with the national value (90) and with the estimates of 81 and 84 for Central and East Java, respectively.

Table 4.16 presents indicators that reflect perhaps less basic but nonetheless important aspects of poverty. It shows illiteracy rates among the rural population aged ten years or older (the potential labour force). By this criterion, the most deprived areas are Irian Jaya (58 percent), West Nusa Tenggara (49 percent), West Kalimantan (46 percent), South Sulawesi (43 percent), East Java (41 percent) and Bali (41 percent). Levels of illiteracy in Central Java (37 percent), Yogyakarta (35 percent) and East Nusa Tenggara (37 percent) are also above the national expected value (33 percent).

The Census question that generates these illiteracy rates simply inquires whether the respondent can read and write a simple letter. Since no actual test of literacy is made, the answers tend to be subjective. Hence it is useful to examine the second column in Table 4.16 to see the proportion of the rural population ten years or older who actually read a magazine or newspaper during the week previous to the survey (conducted in 1984). Whereas the first column implies that two-thirds of the rural potential labour force can read and write, the second column indicates that only 8 percent actually used these skills to read magazine or newspaper articles. Rates of readers are especially low in rural Central Sulawesi (2 percent), East Nusa

Table 4.15: Annual Per Capita Production and Consumption of Basic Staples by Province, 1981 (kilograms)

	Rice		Maize		Cassava		Yams	
	Prod.	Cons.	Prod.	Cons.	Prod.	Cons.	Prod.	Cons.
D.I. Aceh	188	155	1	0	10	5	4	1
North Sumatra	117	141	5	1	25	10	18	8
West Sumatra	179	153	2	1	13	2	5	1
Riau	72	125	4	0	27	10	5	1
Jambi	160	140	1	0	9	8	3	3
South Sumatra	120	126	1	1	29	22	8	3
Bengkulu	128	155	4	1	13	4	17	2
Lampung	98	121	15	4	141	85	3	2
D.K.I. Jakarta	5	110	0	1	0	3	0	1
West Java	156	146	3	1	57	9	11	3
Central Java	135	105	34	18	96	36	7	5
D.I. Yogyakarta	119	89	40	7	193	75	4	4
East Java	140	98	54	22	112	39	8	3
W. Nusa Tenggara	180	145	9	4	28	8	16	4
E. Nusa Tenggara	53	89	76	86	244	55	56	9
East Timur	-	-	-	-	-	-	-	-
West Kalimantan	145	133	3	3	49	17	6	2
South Kalimantan	225	135	2	2	20	11	3	2
East Kalimantan	86	124	2	2	30	12	8	3
North Sulawesi	53	125	26	31	34	17	18	6
Central Sulawesi	107	135	21	7	35	14	17	3
South Sulawesi	197	130	57	15	31	12	7	2
S.E. Sulawesi	40	84	57	49	172	64	32	2
Maluku	12	65	8	11	63	93	39	14
Irian Jaya	2	108	2	1	20	11	252	7
Indonesia	131	121	24	11	73	26	12	4

Source: Government of Indonesia, Biro Pusat Statistik (1981b and 1984d).

Tenggara (3 percent), Riau (4 percent) and West Kalimantan (4 percent). In view of its high level of illiteracy, rural Irian Jaya records a surprisingly high percent (19 percent) of its population reading printed media. In general, the large discrepancy between estimates of literacy and evidence of actual reading suggests either that greater efforts are needed to promote literacy or that the literate population is grossly in need of more printed materials.

Table 4.16 also indicates remoteness by showing the more rural access to radio and television programmes than to printed media. During the reference period, nationally almost half of the potential

Table 4.16: Rural Illiteracy and Access to Mass Media Among People Aged Ten Years or Older

	Rural Illiterate (percent)	Rural Access to Mass Media During Week Previous to Survey		
		Read Newspaper (percent)	Listen to Radio (percent)	Watch Television (percent)
D.I. Aceh	27	11	42	39
North Sumatra	19	13	27	45
West Sumatra	20	18	28	43
Riau	27	4	49	37
Jambi	26	6	35	33
South Sumatra	22	11	39	45
Bengkulu	27	11	43	31
Lampung	24	6	44	27
West Java	29	10	61	30
Central Java	37	7	56	34
D.I. Yogyakarta	35	18	80	50
East Java	41	6	47	38
Bali	41	9	65	51
West Nusa Tenggara	49	5	34	20
East Nusa Tenggara	37	3	13	2
East Timor	-	-	18	19
West Kalimantan	46	4	31	39
Central Kalimantan	22	5	28	17
South Kalimantan	26	14	57	48
East Kalimantan	33	8	28	34
North Sulawesi	10	17	24	38
Central Sulawesi	19	2	21	14
South Sulawesi	43	7	42	23
Southeast Sulawesi	34	9	32	17
Maluku	19	7	29	6
Irian Jaya	58	19	29	37
Indonesia	33	8	48	34

Sources: Government of Indonesia, Biro Pusat Statistik (1984s) except for Rural Illiterate which is from Government of Indonesia, Biro Pusat Statistik (1980b).

labour force (48 percent) listened to the radio, and about one-third (34 percent) watched television. Once again, however, the rates for listening to the radio and watching television are particularly low in East Nusa Tenggara (13 percent and 2 percent, respectively). They are also very low in East Timor, which supplies insufficient data to appear on other lists of poverty indicators. Typically, access to radio and television tends to be above the national expected values in Java.

Table 4.17 provides a different measure of remoteness by using data regarding the principal means of physical access to the villages (*desa* and *kelurahan*) in each province. The second column from the right shows the percentage of villages whose principal means of access are roads that can be travelled by four-wheel vehicles during only part of the year. Nationally, about one-fourth (26 percent) of all villages fall into this category. In West Kalimantan and Irian Jaya, the percentages are almost double. They are also very high in East Nusa Tenggara (45 percent), Maluku (41 percent) and Riau (39 percent). By comparison, Java appears relatively better off: Smaller percentages of villages (which does not imply *fewer* villages) in Java must rely mainly on roads that are passable only part of the year. In Kalimantan and other areas heavily dependent upon water transportation, particularly inland waterways, access may also be very seasonal.

The above indicators of regional inequality are based on provincial data but often a finer disaggregation is desired. Although that is usually not possible for consumption data because comprehensive coverage of smaller geographical units requires extremely large and expensive samples, other types of data do permit us to examine smaller regions.

Figure 4.4 defines subprovincial areas with high concentrations of smallholders and of dryland. The lightly shaded areas display regencies (*kabupaten*) in Java and Madura that fulfil two conditions: (1) more than half the farmers control less than 0.50 ha of land and (2) more than half the agricultural land is rain-fed (dry). The darker areas are regencies in which the second condition remains unchanged, but the first condition (now 1a) becomes that more than 40 percent of the farmers control less than 0.25 ha of land.

Figure 4.4 shows three fairly distinct and large concentrations of smallholders and dryland. The highest proportion of very small holders (criteria 1a) and dryland occurs in the southern portion of West Java. Outside of Java and Madura no regencies meet the second, stricter set of criteria (1a and 2), but a few meet the first set (1 and 2) (Klungkung, Badung, Karangasem in Bali; Tabalong in South Kalimantan; Tana Toraja in South Sulawesi; and Deli Serdang in North Sumatra).

This map does not provide an unambiguous poverty indicator since there can be wide variation in the quality of rain-fed land. Moreover, it should not be forgotten that many poor people, especially landless agricultural labourers, live in areas unmarked in Figure 4.4. However,

Table 4.17: Percentage of Villages in Each Province by Principal Means of Physical Access, 1983

	Water Ways	Asphalted Roads	Gravelled/Metalled Roads		Dirt Roads		Subtotal Roads Only Seasonally Passable		No. of Villages ('000)
			A1	B1	A2	B2	B1	B2	
D.I. Aceh	2	10	43	14	11	20	33		5.6
North Sumatra	3	28	24	6	15	25	31		5.6
West Sumatra	3	31	31	6	7	22	28		3.6
Riau	19	15	13	2	14	36	39		1.1
Jambi	20	14	26	3	17	20	23		1.2
South Sumatra	9	30	25	4	18	14	18		2.4
Bengkulu	3	34	29	4	12	18	22		1.2
Lampung	2	31	19	1	31	15	16		1.5
D.K.I. Jakarta	2	93	3	-	2	-	-		0.2
West Java	0	27	42	3	16	12	16		6.6
Central Java	0	19	52	6	12	10	16		8.5
D.I. Yogyakarta	-	31	41	4	19	4	8		0.6
East Java	0	23	41	4	23	9	13		8.4
West Kalimantan	25	5	4	1	8	57	58		4.7
Central Kalimantan	58	4	2	1	7	29	30		1.1
South Kalimantan	14	20	30	4	10	23	27		2.4
East Kalimantan	43	10	3	1	9	33	34		1.1
North Sulawesi	5	46	17	2	12	18	21		1.3
Central Sulawesi	8	20	31	3	14	24	27		1.3
South Sulawesi	4	29	33	1	15	17	18		1.2
Southeast Sulawesi	12	23	34	4	14	12	16		0.7

Table 4.17: Percentage of Villages in Each Province by Principal Means of Physical Access, 1983 (Cont'd)

	Water Ways	Asphalted Roads	Gravelled/Metalled Roads		Dirt Roads		Subtotal Roads Only Seasonally Passable		No. of Villages ('000)
			A1	B1	A2	B2	B1	B2	
Bali	1	56	15	0	24	4		4	0.6
West Nusa Tenggara	1	40	28	1	22	9		10	0.6
East Nusa Tenggara	3	8	17	3	28	42		45	1.7
East Timor	-	8	26	2	34	31		32	1.8
Maluku	31	15	3	4	10	37		41	1.8
Irian Jaya	33	9	5	2	3	48		50	0.9
Indonesia	8	22	31	5	15	21		26	67.5

A1 and A2 Passable by four-wheel vehicles year round.
B1 and B2 Passable by four-wheel vehicles only part of the year.

Source: Government of Indonesia, Biro Pusat Statistik (1983v).

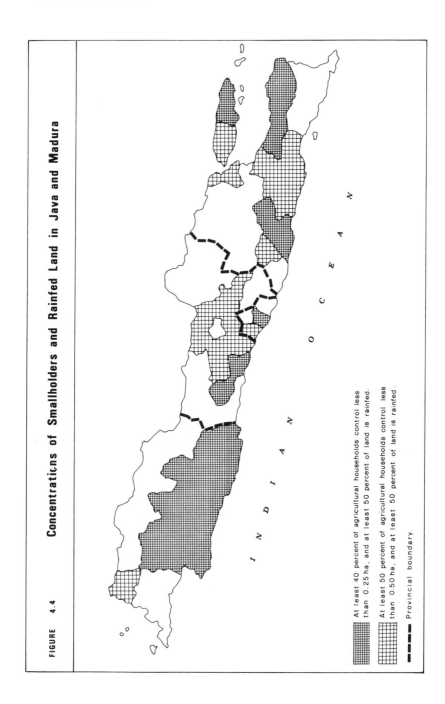

FIGURE 4.4   Concentrations of Smallholders and Rainfed Land in Java and Madura

Figure 4.4 does serve as a rough guide to those areas likely to suffer greater population pressure and, at the same time, less likely to benefit directly from policies geared to promoting wetland rice production.

Summary

The above indicators based on poverty lines, deprivation, dependence on generally non-preferred staples, infant mortality rates, illiteracy, effective remoteness from mass media, seasonality of physical access and concentrations of smallholders and rain-fed land do not paint a uniform picture of which regions have more disadvantaged rural populations. East Nusa Tenggara appears on many lists of poverty indicators but not all. The same is true of Central Java, Yogyakarta and East Java. West Java has "insignificant deprivation" but the highest infant mortality rates and the highest concentration of smallholders and rain-fed land.

From the disparity in the indicators we can conclude that it is difficult to pinpoint pockets of poverty without more direct observation. Part of the problem, particularly in Java, is that poverty is pervasive and poor people often live in close proximity to non-poor people. Given this pervasiveness of poverty in Java, pinpointing micropockets may not be too important. Poor people can be found in abundance almost everywhere. On the other hand, because poor people often live juxtaposed to non-poor, programmes directed more to regions than to socio-economic groups may end up benefiting many people other than the target groups. Hence, policies for more heterogeneous areas, which are common in Java, require careful design to minimize leakages to non-target groups.

Women as Target Group

One important focus of any study on Indonesia should be on the position of women and children among the landless and rural poor. In principle, the 1945 Indonesian Constitution makes no distinction between men and women in Indonesia. Under Articles 21 and 17, equal rights and obligations are guaranteed in labour, health, politics and law.

The problem is how women can use their rights. As an example, consider labour laws. Working mothers have the right to take time off to breast-feed their infants. But many women remain ignorant of such rights, and relevant laws and regulations are not consistently enforced (Government of Indonesia, Biro Pusat Statistik/UNICEF 1984). GOI's present cabinet (total: 31 members) includes two women: the Minister of State for the Role of Women and the Minister of Social Affairs. At the higher levels of policy making and management, however, women are markedly underrepresented. Although they account for almost 25 percent of all civil service employment, they occupy only 52 out of 1 377 senior civil service posts.

This imbalance between principles and practice becomes even clearer if we examine male/female scores on various socio-economic indicators. For example, the male/female ratios in secondary and higher education (1.6:1), government service employment (3:1), literacy (1.3:1), labour force participation (2:1) and participation at the policy-making levels of the legislative and executive branches of government (more than 10:1).

The struggle for women's rights (ability to move freely outside the home, to get an education and to think and act independently) was pioneered by R. A. Kartini in Indonesia at the beginning of the twentieth century. For encouraging an appreciation of the importance of female equality among her people, Kartini's birthday has been designated a national holiday.

To understand the position of women in Indonesia, we need to understand their role within the cultural context under which they live. An often-mentioned, strongly held opinion in Indonesia is that issues widely discussed by Western women are not considered relevant or applicable to most women in Indonesia. Many aspects of Indonesian women's life today reflect cultural traditions, where prevailing social norms tend to emphasize submissiveness and obedience as ideal feminine qualities. Also note, however, that when compared with their Muslim sisters in other Third World countries, Indonesia women overall enjoy high status.

Professor Pudjiwati Sajogyo, an authority on Women in Development (WID) issues, noted in an interview that the real benefits of economic growth have still not been achieved by rural Indonesian women, mostly because their real contribution to the production and distribution of goods and services is yet to be recognized. Their role tends to be viewed mostly in the context of their family. But this is to ignore the fact that they are responsible for inordinate cost savings as unpaid family workers, producing goods and services for household consumptions and trade, casual wage earnings and some seasonal agricultural and off-farm economic activities to increase their family's welfare.

The following sections present socio-economic and health indicators relevant to rural women in Indonesia. They show that rural women constitute a special target group for economic and, in particular, rural development. Structural, cultural and institutional constraints need to be removed if women in Indonesia are to integrate fully, as equal partners into national life.

Women and Education

Female literacy and educational attainment are central for sustaining social welfare objectives in a developing country. Education can contribute substantially to minimizing rural poverty. Moreover, its relevance to health cannot be over-emphasized.

For example, a considerable body of evidence shows that maternal education is highly inversely correlated with IMRs. A study done in Indonesia in 1976 reported that the IMRs for children born to women who completed primary school education was 25 percent less than for those born to women who had only some primary schooling or none. IMRs for children born to women with at least a junior high school education were 50 percent lower again.

Gender Variations. Table 4.18 shows the changing trends over a 20-year period. The declining rates of females unable to read and write (55 percent) was somewhat greater than among males (46 percent).

Rural/Urban Variation. Table 4.19 presents the urban/rural differentials where it is noted that about one-half of all urban villages had junior secondary schools and one-third had senior secondary schools. In rural villages these facilities were minimal. The implications are that rural children find it difficult to continue their education (boarding is seldom an option for a rural child), both for cultural and economic reasons.

Female Literacy and Education. Data from the BPS population census reveal that women and girls have clearly been major beneficiaries of the growth in education and literacy programmes. Interestingly, although the percentage of females never attending school declined by 29 percent between 1971 and 1980 (males declined by 33 percent), the percentage of females completing primary school rose by 12 percent. At the same time, that of males apparently declined by about 4 percent.

The educational gap between the sexes is greatest at both ends of the spectrum. In percentage terms, in 1980 almost twice as many women as men never attended school (19.1 million females opposed to 9.7 million males). The statistics given in 1984 by the Ministry of Education and Culture report almost identical proportions of

Table 4.18: Illiteracy Rates for Population Aged Ten Years or Older by Gender (percent)

Indonesia	1961	1971	1980
Males	44	28	20
Females	69	50	37
Indonesia	57	39	29

Source: Government of Indonesia, Biro Pusat Statistik (1984q).

Table 4.19: Villages with Schools by Type and Location, 1980 (percent)

Level of School	Urban	Rural
Primary	87	74
Junior secondary	47	11
Senior secondary	33	3

Source: Government of Indonesia, Biro Pusat Statistik (1980a).

enrollment at the primary level (95 percent). At the secondary level, however, the male/female ratio for completion was 1.6:1 in 1980; the gap is even wider at the university level.

The lower female than male literacy rates in rural Indonesia, to some extent probably reflect cultural norms, but they more importantly have socio-economic causes as well. Poor rural households are highly dependent on family labour, particularly in food preparation, small animal-raising activities and responsibility for the care of younger siblings. This situation makes it harder for families to spare them for secondary schooling.

Formal and informal education can provide women with simple tools to improve the quality of rural life. Direct knowledge about health and nutrition, consumer purchasing ability, analytical skills will make them better informed producers and consumers. But as a form of human capital, education probably has its greatest impact on income. Improving the economic lot of the rural women will subsequently improve their purchasing power. Rural poverty alleviation is almost a prerequisite for improving the lot of women and children. Overall, increased education will make women more receptive to social, economic and cultural change.

Role of Women in the Local Economy

Female Labour Force Participation. A number of socio-demographic and cultural factors affects the participation of women in the labour force, which is measured in terms of female labour force participation rate (LFPR). In Indonesia, the female LFPR is defined as the proportion of the female population aged ten or older who worked for pay or profit at least one hour during the previous week.

Urban/Rural Differentials. In general, women in rural areas in Indonesia are more economically active than those in urban areas; rural working women outnumber their urban counterparts by nearly five to one.

In general, the Indonesian labour force registers very wide seasonal fluctuations, a large amount of temporary part-time and unpaid employment and frequent multiple occupations by the same individuals. These features are often more pronounced for women.

Participation by Age Group. According to the 1985 BPS, the LFPRs have not changed from 1960 to 1980. Although participation in absolute numbers grew, this was mainly due to absolute increases in the number of women in the working-age population rather than in participation rates. Table 4.20 shows female labour participation rates (aged ten years or older) by economically and not economically active groups. In 1980 the economically active groups consisted of 17.3 million females, or 32.7 percent of all women. Of these, 16.9 million (31.9 percent) were defined as employed during the week before enumeration. The rest, about 400 000 or 0.7 percent, were looking for work. In 1982 the number of females in the labour force and their participation rate rose as compared to 1980. The number of employed women and the LFPR increased to 20.7 million and 36.9 percent, respectively, whereas the number of women looking for work rose to 800 000, or more than 1 percent.

In 1980 the number of women outside the labour force was 35.7 million (67.3 percent). In 1982 that number fell both relatively and absolutely. Among the women, the number and percentage attending school rose, whereas the number engaged solely in housekeeping decreased significantly.

LFPR figures for Indonesia in 1982 show that although about 62 percent of the men were employed, only about one-third of the women were.

Underemployment and Longer Working Hours. If 35 hours represents the normal working week, more than 35 percent of the total Indonesian labour force was underused in 1980. Among females, the

Table 4.20: Female Participation Rates in Age Groups Ten Years or Older by Type of Activity (thousands)

	1980		1982	
	No.	Percent	No.	Percent
Economically active	17.3	32.7	21.5	38.3
Employed	16.9	31.9	20.7	36.9
Looking for work	0.4	0.7	0.8	1.4
Not economically active	35.7	67.3	34.7	61.7
Attending school	8.4	15.9	10.4	18.5
Housekeeping	21.6	40.8	20.2	35.9
Others	5.7	10.7	4.1	7.3
Not stated	-	-	0.0	0.0
Total	53.0	100.0	56.2	100.0

Sources: For 1980, Government of Indonesia, Biro Pusat Statistik (1980a). For 1982, Government of Indonesia, Biro Pusat Statistik (1982d).

rate was 51 percent, 66 percent more than for males. In the 25-44 age group, which includes more than 40 percent of the female labour force, 65 percent worked less than 35 hours a week. Underemployment in the 25-44 age group may be partially explained by the combination of agricultural labour and household work performed by women.

Economic conditions tend to be worse in rural areas, and rural women work out of need. Women generally work longer hours than men, adding income-earning activities to their normal housekeeping chores. According to a study in West Java by P. Sajogyo (1986b), in 1980 women worked an average of 7.5 to 10.5 hours per day; from 20 percent to 45 percent of this time was spent on income-earning activities. A similar study in Central Java by White and Hastuti (1983) found that women worked an average of 11.1 hours per day throughout the year of which 5.9 hours were spent in market activities.

Regional Variations in Female Labour Force Participation. Table 4.21 shows wide regional variations in LFPR for women, with high participation rates for Yogyakarta (51 percent), West Kalimantan (44 percent) and Bali (40 percent) and a lower participation rate for South Sulawesi (17 percent). Interestingly, the third smallest LFPR is reported by women in the urban areas of D.K.I. Jakarta (23 percent).

Relationship Between Education and Employment for Women

Theoretically, education influences economic status, abilities and skills. Competition and demand in the labour market presumably will

Table 4.21: Female Labour Force and Female LFPR by Province, 1980

Province	Female Labour Force			Female
	Working	Looking for Work	Total	LFPR
D.I. Aceh	242 839	5 395	248 234	27.5
North Sumatra	1 135 061	15 284	1 150 345	40.2
West Sumatra	372 777	4 917	377 694	30.4
Riau	172 940	5 042	177 982	24.4
Jambi	145 114	3 295	148 409	31.1
South Sumatra	539 731	7 003	546 734	34.7
Bengkulu	104 798	2 042	106 840	42.1
Lampung	379 904	6 570	386 474	26.1
D.K.I. Jakarta	501 671	22 527	524 198	22.6
West Java	2 323 457	70 460	2 393 917	24.7
Central Java	3 687 822	67 853	3 755 675	39.7
D.I. Yogyakarta	551 039	5 298	556 337	51.0
East Java	3 945 812	78 852	4 024 664	35.6
Bali	352 329	10 848	363 177	39.6
West Nusa Tenggara	274 817	11 178	285 995	31.0
East Nusa Tenggara	400 518	3 434	403 952	41.2
East Timor	-	-	-	-
West Kalimantan	368 801	4 611	373 412	44.2
Central Kalimantan	130 446	998	131 444	44.2
South Kalimantan	255 019	7 613	262 632	35.6
East Kalimantan	82 571	1 471	84 042	21.1
North Sulawesi	176 604	11 085	187 689	25.0
Central Sulawesi	111 625	8 231	119 856	28.3
South Sulawesi	354 404	26 620	381 024	17.2
Southeast Sulawesi	85 736	2 910	88 646	27.4
Maluku	123 564	2 613	126 177	26.6
Irian Jaya	115 191	1 703	116 894	32.4
Indonesia	16 934 590	387 853	17 322 443	32.7

Source: Government of Indonesia, Biro Pusat Statistik (1980a).

favour those with more education and better skills. Furthermore, education helps raise the level of aspirations and expectations for a better standard of living and income, which in turn serves as an incentive to enter the labour force. Thus, we would expect people with higher levels of education to exhibit a higher LFPR. In Indonesia, however, inconsistent trends appear.

Table 4.22 shows that in 1982 women who never attended school exhibited very high LFPRs (49.9 percent in the rural areas). If these figures are examined with a third variable, such as type of activity, superimposed we find that in 1982 the majority of women with no or little education were engaged primarily in agriculture. Conversely, women with higher LFPRs and higher educational attainment were in the services category. But the dynamics of LFPRs and educational attainment basically reflect the fact that among women with very little education, economic rather than educational factors may determine entry into the labour force, whereas the reverse is more likely for women who are highly educated.

Raharjo and Hull (1984) in their analysis of labour force participation by educational level contend that Indonesia, like many other developing countries, display a J-shaped relationship between employment and education (Figure 4.5). This pattern represents a large group of lower-class women without schooling who work out of economic necessity, a middle-sized group with low and intermediate education levels who are less likely to be economically active, and a small group of highly educated women who exhibit the highest LFPRs, working primarily in modern skilled occupations. This finding recurs over all Indonesian censuses, despite varying definitions of economic activity, and pertains to both rural and urban areas and all age groups.

Women in Agricultural Production

Rice. Rice paddy cultivation, largely in Java, is characterized by hired labour despite the existence of both peasant farms and rental or sharecropping features. Although the proportion of wage labour figures for male/female tend to show large variations in paddy production, they still suggest the high levels of hired labour in which the main tasks are performed by women (declining rates for women are discussed later in this book).

A division of labour within rice production shows that ploughing, harrowing, hoeing and constructing or repairing dykes are virtually always men's work. Preparing the seed-bed, pulling seedlings and adjusting water supply are also mainly men's tasks. Women's chores

Table 4.22: Female LFPR by Educational Attainment and Urban/Rural, 1980 and 1982.

	Urban		Rural		Urban + Rural	
	1980	1982	1980	1982	1980	1982
Never attended school	33.0	39.3	41.0	49.9	39.9	48.5
Not yet completed primary school	20.3	22.6	30.2	34.8	28.3	32.4
Primary school	19.0	22.9	32.5	39.6	28.2	35.0
Junior high school (general)	15.0	17.1	23.1	27.7	18.1	21.7
Junior high school (vocational)	23.1	29.4	31.5	41.6	27.2	35.5
Senior high school (general)	29.0	33.4	38.2	41.2	31.2	35.1
Senior high school (vocational)	54.3	58.7	66.7	74.8	59.7	65.5
Academy	58.8	64.0	60.7	89.7	59.2	68.7
University	69.3	78.6	56.0	76.7	66.8	78.3
Not stated	18.9	27.0	28.8	44.1	26.5	41.5
Total	24.2	27.8	35.2	41.5	32.6	38.3

Source: Government of Indonesia, Biro Pusat Statistik (1982d).

are mainly transplanting, weeding and harvesting. Weeding, particularly, shifts from women to men and back to women in some villages. Foot threshing harvested stalk paddy (a new task appearing with high-yielding varieties, local varieties are stored in bundled form) also seems to be mainly a women's task. This division of labour is not necessarily mutually exclusive.

A discussion of the division of labour within agricultural production must acknowledge the fact that occupational multiplicity is a significant feature of the agrarian structure of Java. Both men and women obtain large proportions of their income outside paddy cultivation and from off-farm jobs (Sajogyo 1983). Perhaps because of this pattern of multiple occupations, Sajogyo notes, the sexual division of labour within the household is in practice not as clear cut as has been suggested. Men, for example, are sometimes at home babysitting and cooking while women and girls are harvesting or trading at the market. In addition, studies of household decision-making patterns have found that wives are neither so excluded from decisions in the extradomestic domain nor so wholly in charge of the domestic domain as is implied by the normative segregation of roles. Nonetheless, official rural extension still focuses on agriculture for men and home

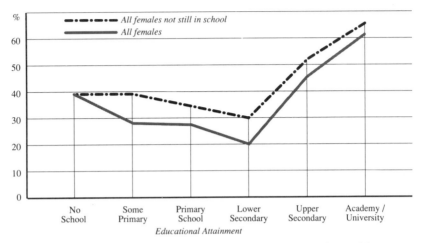

Figure 4.5: Labour Force Participation* Rates by Educational Attainment**
Females Aged Ten Years or Older (Indonesia, 1980)

* Percentage of women "economically active", including those working (at least one hour
during the reference week) and looking for work.
** Highest level attained (graduated).
Source: Government of Indonesia, Biro Pusat Statistik (1982b).

economics, health and family planning activities for women (White
and Hastuti 1983; Wigna 1982).

*The Declining Female LFPR in Agriculture: Implications for Work
and Incomes.* As in many other low-income countries, the largest
share of the female labour force in Indonesia is in the agricultural
sector, although the percentage has declined from 68 percent in 1971
to less than 54 percent in 1980. As shown in Table 4.23 this
decreasing trend has occurred in both urban and rural areas. The
shrinkage was offset by increased employment in the trade and service
sectors, which together provided most of the new jobs in urban and
rural areas. Trade and services include many small, informal
economic activities that require relatively little capital and few
specialized skills. Such activities are also characterized by low levels
of productivity and earnings.

Mubyarto and others (Mubyarto 1986) note that the "green
revolution has increased agricultural production, but reduced
employment especially for the landless and for rural women".
Employment elasticity of agriculture declined from 0.44 to only 0.28,
the lowest figure of all the economic sectors. Agriculture's declining
role in absorbing labour has most seriously affected rural women in
Java, and their employment has declined by 1 percent per year during

Table 4.23: Employed Female Population by Main Industry and Urban/Rural Location, 1976 and 1980

Field of Employment	1976(1)			1980(2)		
	Urban	Rural	Urban + Rural	Urban	Rural	Urban + Rural
Agriculture	10.83	66.61	59.63	7.23	63.19	53.78
Mining and quarrying	0.06	0.11	0.10	0.40	0.35	0.35
Manufacturing	14.18	11.31	11.67	16.00	11.64	12.38
Electricity, gas and water	0.03	-	0.00	0.12	0.02	0.04
Construction	0.15	0.07	0.08	0.41	0.20	0.24
Hotel/trade, restaurant and hotels	40.08	16.63	19.57	34.50	15.75	18.90
Transport, storage and communication	0.58	0.03	0.10	0.53	0.05	0.13
Finance	0.54	0.04	0.10	1.26	0.11	0.30
Services	33.42	5.18	8.72	38.46	7.93	13.06
Unknown	0.13	0.02	0.03	0.07	0.02	0.03
Not stated	-	-	-	1.04	0.74	0.79
Total	100.00	100.00	100.00	100.00	100.00	100.00
	(2 038 419)	(14 260 336)	(16 289 755)	(2 847 940)	(14 086 650)	(16 934 590)

Source: For 1976, Government of Indonesia, Biro Pusat Statistik, (1976).
For 1980, Government of Indonesia, Biro Pusat Statistik, (1980b).

the census period 1971-80. The reasons include reduction in harvesting hours, in part due to a shift from men to women tasks and part to a replacement of the *ani-ani* (finger knife) with sickles; an increase in male ground preparation inputs; and a reduction in transplanting hours.

Sajogyo (1983) further contends that older women (especially those doing harvesting chores) have been most severely affected with subsequent detrimental effects on women's incomes.

Women's Participation in Animal Production. In rural areas, the primary source of labour for livestock holders is still the family. Husbands, wives, daughters and sons are all involved in animal husbandry. Recent data show that in West Java women did 15 percent of that work. In the case of small ruminant production, 47 percent of the women from Garut and 46 percent of the women from Ciburuy, both located in upland areas, and 43 percent of the women from Cirebon in the lowland areas, participated significantly.

In Cirebon, farmers' wives were more involved in activities such as herding, feeding, watering and controlling animals' health. In Garut the men performed the bulk of activities such as tending the animals, collecting feed, feeding, bathing and watering. Cutting grass, however, seemed to be the responsibility of women and children. Interestingly, the older the women, the more they were involved in working with animals while their husbands concentrated on marketing and selling the livestock.

Women's Participation in Plantation Crops Production. Plantation agriculture (rubber, tobacco) in Sumatra, from its beginning in the latter part of the nineteenth century was based on the importation of labour - initially from China, Singapore and Malaysia, and in the latter years from Java. In the earliest period of estate crops expansion, the number of women was severely limited, as were the jobs which they were allowed to perform (Stohler 1979).

Sajogyo (1983) quotes reports by *Koelie Budget Commissie, 1940* showing data concerning living standards among labourers in different plantations in Java from 1929 to 1949. From these data, we see that women did participate in various kinds of plantation work, including that involving tea, coffee, rubber, tobacco and sugar cane.

In the tobacco industry - the primary estate crop through the first decade of the twentieth century - women were confined to sorting and bundling of leaves on a piecework basis. At that time, the involvement of women in plantation agriculture was either as labourers in the field or as foremen in the factories. However, male and female workers' wages were significantly different, with female workers getting lower wages than their male counterparts. Unfortunately, even after an 80-year period, the females wage situation in plantation crop production has not changed substantially. A study in a rubber plantation in West Java reported significant wage differentials between male and female labourers (Sajogyo 1983).

Non-farm Employment Status of Women in Java

B. White (1986a) in Rural Non-Farm Employment in Java draws attention to the fact that the great majority of non-farm employment in Java is still found at the single person or household enterprise level (Table 4.24, rows 1-3) or in enterprises employing a small number of workers. He also notes that although more women than men classify themselves as unpaid family workers, roughly the same number of women as men describe themselves as "in charge" both in and outside of farming. Thus, the non-farm sector has a relatively higher proportion of women entrepreneurs than the agriculture sector.

White further notes that although the proportion of women in agriculture with self-employed or employer status is much lower than that of men, they still constitute 34 percent of all women in agriculture or about 20 percent of all self-employed/employer farmers. Interestingly, this figure, suggesting that one-fifth of Java's farms are run by women, coincides with estimates of rural female-headed households in Java (White 1986a).

Female-headed Households and Economic Implications

Single-parent households, especially those headed by women, may have deleterious economic implications for the welfare of those households, particularly for women and children. In surveys and population polls conducted by the BPS, head of household is defined as "that person within the household who is responsible for the daily needs of the family". Normally, the husband or father is reported as the household head. If the husband is absent or if a woman is divorced, widowed or a single parent, however, the woman is recorded as the household head. Official figures for the number of female heads of households are believed substantially to understate their actual number (Government of Indonesia, Biro Pusat Statistik/UNICEF 1984).

Comparative economic status analysis of male- and female-headed households usually show that a substantial segment of all female-headed households are in the lowest 10-20 percent of the monthly income distribution (see Table 4.25). This is particularly true for

Table 4.24: Employment Status of Women in Various Sectors, Java 1980 (Excluding D.K.I. Jakarta)

	Agric. (1)	Mfg. (2)	Const. (3)	Trade (4)	Transp. (5)	Serv. (6)	Total R/U (7)	R (8)
Self-employed								
Without paid or unpaid help	12	17	13	49	18	19	22	21
With help of family members or temporary paid worker(s)	22	10	13	40	6	6	21	22
Unpaid family worker	39	19	9	15	4	14	27	31
Employer with permanent worker(s)	1	2	2	1	5	3	1	2
Employee	26	42	61	4	66	57	27	23
Not stated	1	1	1	1	2	1	1	2
Total	100	100	100	100	100	100	100	100

Note: Tables disaggregating sectors for rural and urban areas separately are not available for Java; and totals in columns 7-8 include minor sectors not included in columns 1-6 (Mining, electricity/gas/water, finance).

Source: Government of Indonesia, Biro Pusat Statistik (1980b).

agricultural households and is less extreme for non-agricultural households. Conversely, male-headed households usually rank in the top 20-30 percent of the monthly income distribution, both in agricultural and non-agricultural groups.

Combined with lower education, fewer skills and less work experience, these factors severely limit women's earning capacity and place households headed by women at a serious economic disadvantage.

An analysis by UNICEF (1984) provides some clues to the causes of low income among households headed by females. The average household headed by males 1.2 income-earning members, whereas the corresponding figure for households headed by females is 0.6. This fractional average means that many female heads do not work and depend on family members or others outside the household for support. Moreover, those women who are employed work fewer hours per week, at every income level, than their male counterparts in the same

Table 4.25: Household Size and Average Monthly Income in Agricultural and Non-agricultural Households by Income Decile and Male or Female Household Head, 1976

House-hold Income Decile	House-hold Size	House-hold Income RP/oo	Male Head (percent)	Female Head (percent)	House-hold Size	House-hold Income Rp/oo	Male Head (percent)	Female Head (percent)
First	4.3	1 557	14	24	2.6	1 534	2	11
Second	4.4	3 981	12	16	2.6	3 836	4	18
Third	4.6	5 955	11	13	3.1	5 790	7	15
Fourth	4.8	7 948	10	9	3.6	7 739	7	10
Fifth	5.0	10 180	11	10	3.9	9 936	12	11
Sixth	5.1	13 007	10	8	4.3	12 842	11	18
Seventh	5.3	16 213	8	5	4.6	15 721	13	8
Eighth	5.6	20 629	6	4	5.1	20 251	13	7
Ninth	6.1	28 421	8	4	5.6	28 090	14	6
Tenth	6.5	71 990	6	4	6.7	61 146	16	5
Total or average	5.0	14 093	100	100	4.6	20 461	100	100
Total house-holds ('000)			12 132	1 483			10 310	2 597

Source: Government of Indonesia, Biro Pusat Statistik (1984q).

income decile - an average of less than 24 hours a week for women as compared with nearly 64 hours a week for men.

Maternal Mortality Rate

Estimates of maternal mortality due to inadequate prenatal care or to complications of pregnancy and childbirth run as high as 2.5 percent of all deaths of women. Factors contributing to maternal mortality include poor nutritional status, iron-deficiency anaemia, close pregnancy intervals and poor hygiene. Various studies have reported 40 maternal deaths per 10 000 pregnancies, with rural levels reaching 80 per 10 000. Table 4.26 presents data from 12 hospital-based studies concerning 36 062 women between 1977 and 1980. It shows an overall maternal mortality rate (MMR) of about 37 in 10 000 cases. This rate is eight times higher than rates reported from developed countries in the early 1970s.

Table 4.26 Maternal Mortality Rates in 12 Teaching Hospitals in Indonesia, 1977-80 (per 10 000 Maternity Cases)

Site	No. of Cases	No. of Deaths	MMR
Semarany	2 897	2	7
Palenbany	2 588	2	8
Padany	3 351	3	9
Denpasar	2 650	4	15
Surabaya	2 062	5	24
Menado	2 557	6	24
Yung Pandang	989	3	30
Jakarta	4 451	15	34
Malang	3 140	12	38
Badung	5 617	23	41
Yogyakarta	1 549	11	71
Medan	4 211	49	116
Total	36 062	135	37

Source: International Journal of Gynaecology and Obstetrics 19, 1981.

Among the nutritional factors associated with maternal mortality is iron-deficiency anaemia, which affects an estimated 70 percent (or 3.3 million) pregnant women nationwide. Data from the 12-hospital study showed a threefold difference in MMRs between anaemic (70) and non-anaemic (19) women for urban and rural areas combined. Similarly, the MMRs for pregnant women who made no antenatal visits was more than five times as high (59.9) as for those who made one or more visits (11.4). Rural poor women clearly have less access to *puskesmas* (health community centres) and other health facilities than their urban counterparts.

Rural Poverty, Land Distribution and Productivity, and Employment

Rural poverty is intrinsically related to (1) the pattern of ownership of land and land productivity, (2) the structure of employment and (3) the operation of labour markets. In its simplest form, it can be stated that individuals and households have different endowments of physical (particularly land) and human capital. There is a high correlation between a household standard of living and the amount and quality of land that it owns (or controls) as well as the level of education and possession of skills of the household members. Earlier it was shown that the amount of calories consumed per capita was significantly related to the amount of land owned and cultivated by the different socio-economic groups in agriculture. Similarly, among the rural non-agricultural socio-economic household groups, a major determinant of food consumption was the level of education and skills of household members as reflected by their occupational status.

If a household is nearly landless and enjoys little human capital, then unless it benefits from private or governmental transfers, its entitlement of food and other basic necessities will be limited - resulting in poverty.

This section looks at the relationship between rural poverty and land distribution and employment. Specifically, it explains the effects of the changing pattern of agricultural production and employment since 1970 on the magnitude and composition of rural poverty.

It begins by reviewing briefly the evidence regarding poverty and income distribution trends between 1970 and the 1980s on the basis of macro- and micro-sources and analyses. (This evidence is derived from a poverty line estimated on the basis of calorie requirements and observed household budgets; see Socio-Economic Dimensions of Nutritional Inequality.) There appears little doubt that some alleviation of poverty occurred during that period. Thus it was estimated that the poorest 40 percent of the rural population in Indonesia enjoyed an increase in consumption of about 2.4 percent per year between 1970 and 1980 and that the incidence of poverty declined significantly during that same decade; that is, from 67 percent in 1970 to 53 percent in 1980 for rural Java and from 44 percent to 30 percent in the rural areas of the Outer Islands (Rao 1984). This trend is confirmed by evidence on calorie intake per capita per day from cereals and tubers among the poorest quintile of the population in rural Java, which indicates that it rose from 1 059 calories in 1969-70 to 1 224 in 1981 (Sajogyo and Wiradi 1985 p. 30).

Given the weight of Java in the total population of Indonesia, it is hardly surprising that the bulk of the rural poor are estimated to be located there. As Table 4.27 shows, in 1980 35 million out of a total 48 million rural poor were in Java. Also note that Rao estimated that there were 4.8 million nutritionally deprived people, half of whom lived in the Eastern Islands. (These figures convey at best a general order of magnitude since they are based on assumptions and survey data subject to observation errors.)

The trend towards poverty alleviation continued during the difficult stabilisation and adjustment phase from 1983 on. The best evidence available regarding the changing poverty and nutritional picture is contained in two recent studies based on a comparison of the Susenas

Table 4.27: Poverty Magnitudes by Major Regions, February 1980

Item	Major Regions					
	Java	Sumatra	Kalimantan	Sulawesi	Eastern Islands	Indonesia
Population (million)						
Rural	67.1	22.1	5.2	8.6	8.6	111.6
Urban	23.0	5.4	1.4	1.6	1.2	32.6
Total	90.1	27.5	6.6	10.2	9.8	144.2
Population in poverty (million)						
Rural	35.1	4.7	0.6	3.7	4.1	48.2
Urban	6.8	0.9	0.1	0.3	0.3	8.4
Total	41.9	5.6	0.7	4.0	4.4	56.6
Population in deprivation (mln.)						
Rural	0.3	0.9	0.2	0.3	2.4	4.2
Urban	0.3	0.1	*	0.1	*	0.6
Total	0.6	1.0	0.3	0.4	2.5	4.8
Incidence of poverty (percent)						
Rural	52.3	21.5	12.4	42.7	47.7	43.3
Urban	29.6	15.8	8.1	21.1	24.3	25.8
Total	46.5	20.4	11.5	39.3	46.7	39.3
Incidence of deprivation (percent)						
Rural	0.5	4.2	4.5	3.6	27.9	3.8
Urban	1.2	1.5	1.2	3.6	4.8	1.5
Total	0.7	3.7	2.6	3.6	26.1	3.3

* Less than 0.1 million.
Source: Rao (1984).

tapes on household consumption for 50,000 randomly sampled households in 1984 and 1987. (See Ravallion and Huppin (1989) and Huppi and Ravallion (1990).) It was found that the proportion of the population below the lower selected poverty line fell from 1 in 3, in 1984, to slightly over 1 in 5 by 1987.

It is likely that while poverty was being alleviated on the one hand, household income distribution was becoming more uneven on the other. A comparison of income distribution by major socio-economic groups between 1975 and 1980 shows an increased income polarization between the target groups of agricultural workers (landless) and small farmers and some of the better-off rural and urban groups was likely to have taken place. Likewise, Rao concludes that the share of the poorest 40 percent in total consumption probably declined over the 1970s (Rao 1984, p. ix).

Now that we described the likely past trends regarding poverty and income (consumption) distribution, the next step consists of identifying the changes in the structure of production (particularly within the rice economy), land distribution and employment that might have contributed to the above trends. Firstly, at the aggregate level, Table 4.28 indicates that the number of farm households continued to grow markedly on Java and the Outer Islands. The most noteworthy statistic in Table 4.28 is the continuing decline of the average-size farm on Java from 0.67 ha in 1963 to 0.63 ha in 1983. These data contrast with some increase in the average farm size outside Java from 0.99 ha in 1973 to 1.08 ha in 1983. At the national level, the total number of food crop households increased from 14.3 million in 1973 to 17.6 million in 1983, whereas the number controlling farms of less than 0.5 ha dropped from 6.56 million to 6.50 million in the same period. The only significant change appears in the 1 ha to 3 ha category, where the number of households increases from 3.45 million to 4.37 million, and in the marginal size group (less than 0.1 ha), where a sharp drop from 490 000 to 180 000 households is reported (Government of Indonesia, Biro Pusat Statistik 1983k). Although the Agricultural Census states that "the definition has been made uniform" in the comparison of the 1973 and 1983 Census, some systematic biases may be present, which would account for the surprisingly sharp fall in the number of holdings in the smallest group (i.e., less than 0.1 ha). Careful reading of the definitions suggests that, in fact, the comparison applies only to households controlling *sawah* land of between 0.5 and 0.1 ha - the households below the 0.5 ha category having been excluded. Available data only permit us to infer what happened to farm stratification on Java between 1973 and 1983. The fact that the average land size controlled by food crop household remained approximately equal for the three main Java provinces (West Java 0.62-0.67 ha, Central Java 0.63-0.66 ha and East Java 0.66 in both census years), combined with the sharp drop in farms smaller than 0.1 ha at the national level (most of which are likely to be on Java), suggests that the number and proportion of small farms (say between 0.1 and 0.5 ha) are likely to have risen considerably. Otherwise, with

Table 4.28: Number of Farm Households and Average Size Holding on Java and Outer Islands, 1963, 1973 and 1983

	1963	1973	1983
Java			
Number of farm households (in millions)	7.9	8.6	10.1
Average land ownership (ha/farm)	0.67	0.64	0.63
Outer Islands			
Number of farm households (in millions)	4.2	5.7	7.5
Average land ownership (ha/farm)	1.72	1.57	1.69
Indonesia			
Number of farm households (in millions)	12.1	14.3	17.6
Average land ownership (ha/farm)	1.03	0.99	1.08

Source: Based on data from the Government of Indonesia, Agricultural Censuses (1963, 1973 and 1983).

the large decline in the smallest category farms - as reported in the 1983 Census - the provincial averages would have increased much more sharply had the farm size distribution remained the same above 0.1 ha.

Assuming that the two censuses are in fact consistent and comparable, we can speculate that within the lower tail of the farm size distribution on Java a gradual downgrading of the size of farms took place except for the most marginal farmers (those controlling between 0 and 0.1 ha), who joined the landless. It is also likely that a process of land concentration might have taken place in the farm size of 1 ha-3 ha.

It was observed that at the national level the number of households in this class rose markedly. Even though much of this increase could be accounted for by the transmigration programme in the Outer Islands, it is reasonable to expect that some movement may be taking place on Java at both ends of the distribution toward a larger number of increasingly smaller farms and increasingly larger farms, respectively.

Further evidence in support of the above is provided by Mubyarto et al. (1986) who stated that "the relative speed of the increase in farmers especially on the island of Java with its limited agricultural area, has vastly increased the number of small or minute farms owning less than 0.5 ha" (p. 3). Likewise, Sajogyo and Wiradi (1985) reported that, on the basis of 12 village studies in Java, "the degree of landlessness rose from 30 percent to 50 percent during the period 1970 to 1980". If the preceding interpretation is correct, it would suggest that a process of agricultural adjustment toward more viable and economically sustainable farms was already underway on Java in the 1970s. A key question at this stage is whether the smaller farmers are gradually being forced out because of the marginal returns on own-farm production or being pulled into off-farm work - either as agricultural workers for large farmers or into jobs outside agriculture. This question is addressed next on the basis of evidence regarding the changing employment pattern, the operation of labour markets and estimates of labour productivity prevailing in, and incomes accruing to, different economic sectors and activities.

Table 4.29 shows the changing employment pattern between 1976 and 1982 on Java and Outer Islands by sector. The most noteworthy trend is the reduction in rural employment in agriculture from 18.4 million in 1976 to 17.5 million in 1982. The fall in agricultural employment in Java affected women particularly. It was estimated that Green Revolution technology displaced female agricultural workers in Java at 1 percent per year from 1970 to 1980.

In contrast, during the same period rural agricultural employment rose sharply in the Outer Islands, from 9.9 million to 13.3 million over the same period. The transmigration programme is largely responsible. During REPELITA III (1979-80 to 1983-84), 320 000 households were relocated under sponsored programmes and about 150 000 families moved spontaneously. Transmigration provided one safety valve for some of the rural and urban landless on Java.

Major differences prevailed in labour productivity among the agricultural subsectors, as was shown in Table 3.1. The lowest labour productivity, by far, is in the food crops subsector (Rp 230 000 per worker in 1980 as compared to about Rp 1 million per worker in the other three subsectors - cash crops, livestock and fishery). Also significant is the fact that between 1970 and 1980 labour productivity per worker was reported to have increased only in food crops at a rate of 3.9 percent per year, while declining in all other agricultural subsectors. This information needs to be clarified.

Table 4.30 shows that the structure of employment changed drastically both on Java and the Outer Islands during the 1970s. Not only was the contribution of agriculture to incremental employment absorption between 1971 and 1980 negative on Java, but no less than 74 percent of the incremental labour force was absorbed by the service sector (trade, transport, public administration, and utilities). Manufacturing only attracted one-fourth of the additional labour force. The pattern of employment diversification can also be noticed in the Outer Islands, but to a lesser extent, as agriculture continued to

Table 4.29: Total Employment by Sector, Java and the Outer Islands, 1976 and 1982

	1976			1982		
	Java	Outer	Indonesia	Java	Outer	Indonesia
Urban: Male and female						
Agriculture	197	539	736	503	291	794
Mining	9	13	22	24	33	56
Manufacturing	670	204	874	1 341	267	1 698
Electricity/gas/water	14	6	20	26	8	34
Construction	239	86	325	439	237	676
Trade	1 341	672	2 014	2 340	858	3 198
Transport	415	180	594	612	235	847
Finance/insurance/etc.	50	14	64	64	16	80
Other services	1 550	680	2 237	2 521	886	3 318
Subtotal	4 485	2 400	6 886	7 870	2 831	10 701
Rural: Male and female						
Agriculture	18 395	9 986	28 381	17 545	13 255	30 799
Mining	71	20	91	211	123	334
Manufacturing	2 287	807	3 094	3 194	1 220	4 414
Electricity/gas/water	6	1	7	16	12	28
Construction	393	98	491	1 099	371	1 471
Trade	3 711	1 090	4 800	4 078	1 278	5 356
Transport	498	192	690	679	270	949
Finance/insurance/etc.	17	13	30	25	8	33
Other services	1 992	818	2 809	2 553	1 164	3 717
Subtotal	27 370	13 025	40 393	29 400	17 701	47 101
Urban and Rural:						
Male and female						
Agriculture	18 593	10 525	29 117	18 048	13 546	31 593
Mining	81	33	113	235	155	391
Manufacturing	2 957	1 011	3 968	4 535	1 487	6 022
Electricity/gas/water	20	7	27	42	20	62
Construction	631	184	815	1 538	608	2 146
Trade	5 052	1 762	6 814	6 418	2 136	8 554
Transport	913	371	1 284	1 291	505	1 796
Finance/insurance/etc.	68	27	94	89	24	113
Other services	3 541	1 505	5 047	5 074	2 051	7 125
Total	31 856	15 425	47 279	37 270	20 532	57 802

Source: Government of Indonesia, Biro Pusat Statistik (1976 and 1982d).

Table 4.30 Java and the Outer Islands: Patterns of Employment and Productivity, 1971-80

	Java			Outer Islands		
	Employment		Labour	Employment		Labour
	Composition 1980 (percent)	Share of Increment 1971-80 (percent)	Product Level 1980 (Rp 000/ Worker)	Composition 1980 (percent)	Share of Increment 1971-80 (percent)	Product Level 1980 (Rp 000/ Worker)
Agriculture	51	-8	324	68	29	433
Manufacturing	11	24	889	6	12	1 102
Construction	4	12	1 880	2	8	1 193
Trade	15	26	893	8	18	1 290
Transport	3	6	773	3	4	1 906
Public administration	4	34	1 193	4	24	1 225
Other services	11		413	6		833
Miscellaneous[1]	1	6	2 100	1	6	2 065
Total[2]	100	100	628	100	100	724

[1] Non-oil mining, electricity, gas and water, and finance.

[2] Excluding oil and LNG.

Source: Government of Indonesia, Biro Pusat Statistik (1980a and 1980b).

provide employment to 29 percent of the new entrants into the labour force.

The structural changes in the employment pattern displayed by Java (and even more so by Indonesia as a whole) differ significantly from the trends characterizing two other successful rice economies during similar stages of development. The ratio of incremental employment into the tertiary sector to that into the manufacturing sector was 1:1 in Japan and 2:1 in Korea, compared to 4:1 in Indonesia (between 1971 and 1980) and 3:1 on Java. Similarly, Japan and Korea displayed relatively larger outflows of labour out of agriculture than Indonesia and rates of growth of agricultural output at least as high (World Bank, Indonesia, Wages and Employment, 1985b, p. xxi). The large relative flow of labour into service activities in Indonesia, combined with other evidence discussed subsequently, suggest that a number of marginal farmers, as well as many new entrants into the labour forces appeared to have been pushed into the informal service sector more so than being pulled into it.

Micro-economic data from West Java villages indicate that agricultural households appeared to allocate more hours of work to agricultural activities on a per-household basis in 1982 as compared to 1976. There is some evidence that this trend was associated with agricultural diversification into non-paddy crops, fish-ponds and livestock. Thus, if the village case studies are representative, an increase in labour intensity in Java (in terms of work hours per farm family) took place at the same time as a reduction in the size of the agricultural labour force. This might to some extent be explained by a more even distribution of labour requirements throughout the year caused by an increase in the multiple cropping index for paddy and some diversification into other foodcrops and livestock. These same West Java households spent about half their family labour time on non-agricultural tasks (mainly construction, transport and trade). Whereas the number of hours allocated to these activities rose between 1976 and 1983, significantly less time was spent on manufacturing activities.

Evidence regarding agricultural and non-agricultural labour income on a per-hour basis is somewhat ambiguous. B. White (1986a, pp. 39-41) argues on the basis of micro-village evidence in both low and upland areas of Java that the "majority of nonfarm activities available to poorer households yield (sic) lower labour incomes than agricultural wage labour" (including imputed labour income from work on own land). Likewise, the World Bank study on Wages and Employment (1985b) states that returns to labour (per work hour) are substantially lower in activities outside the rice labour market (of the order of 30 percent less based on field studies) (p. xvii). This might mean that in rural Java a labour surplus exists in the sense that there is a pool of labour units (rather than labourers) in marginal activities with earnings per hour significantly less than the rice wage rate. The existence of this differential is explained by the fact that landowners are willing to pay a higher wage as an incentive to labourers to work harder and more productively (i.e., the wage-efficiency relationship). In fact, although the direction of causality is from higher wages to greater labour intensity and productivity, it is likely that a higher wage permits landowners to screen and select the more productive workers as well.

In contrast, a more recent study argues on the basis of village wage data from 1976 to 1983. Whereas real wages for both agricultural and non-agricultural labour increased from 1976 to 1983 (particularly in 1980-81 coinciding with the superlative performance of the rice sector), non-agricultural wages are above agricultural wages with a slight widening of differentials (World Bank, 1985b, pp. 129-130). Likewise, Rietveld (1986) concludes on the basis of a quantitative study of villages in rural Java that the returns to labour are on average found to be larger outside agriculture than inside it.

One way of reconciling these two sets of potentially conflicting findings is to hypothesize that the wage distribution of non-agricultural activities is bimodal with some activities, such as trade and construction, yielding high wage rates and more truly marginal activities, such as household industry and other selective informal activities, generating low wage rates. Table 4.31 provides some support for this view. In particular, it shows that in 1983 the wage rate for farm labour (i.e., Rp 173 per hour) fell somewhere in between labour-income per hour worked in household industry (Rp 78) at one extreme and trade (Rp 354) and non-agricultural labour (Rp 244) at the other. Also note that the high household income reported from working on one's own farm includes imputed land rent in addition to imputed labour income.

One final piece of evidence should be examined before reaching some tentative conclusions regarding the relative strength of the forces that tended to push people out of agriculture as opposed to those tending to pull them into non-agricultural activities. The ratio of household income received by small farmers (less than 0.25 ha) to that earned by farm labourers fell from 1.79 in 1976 to 1.61 in 1983. It is extremely likely that this ratio fell even more sharply for marginal farmers (in the 0-0.1 ha category) compared to farm labourers. Interestingly, the income position of small farmers relative to medium farmers (0.25-0.50 ha) also worsened in the same period, the corresponding ratio falling from 0.95 in 1976 to 0.82 in 1983. Here again an even more pronounced drop is likely to have taken place when marginal farmers are compared to medium farmers.

At this stage we can draw some inferences and suggest some answers to the questions raised earlier. Firstly, all socio-economic groups benefited from the economic growth that occurred in the 1970s and, particularly, during the rice boom after 1976. The incidence of poverty was significantly reduced and the caloric consumption of the poorest people rose at least until 1981. Although the target groups of landless and near-landless agricultural workers and small farmers enjoyed an improvement in their standard of living, it is likely that some increased polarization occurred among agricultural households. Some additional evidence was presented in support of the contention made earlier that labourers and small farm operators underwent a reduction in their relative incomes and swelling populations while medium and large farmers enjoyed an increase in their relative incomes. A comparative evaluation of the 1973 and 1983 Agricultural

Table 4.31: Average Returns to Household Labour in Alternative Activities, West Java Villages, 1976 and 1983

	Labour Income Per Hour Worked[1]	
	Level 1983 (Rp/hour)	Real Increase 1976-83 (percent p.a.)
Agriculture[2]	386	-0.9
Farm labour	173	-0.4
Non-agriculture		
Household industry	78	8.9
Trade	354	-0.4
Non-agricultural labour	244	2.4
Average	225	3.6

[1] Average for households participating in the sector in question.

[2] Calculated as net household cash returns per hour of family labour input; the reason it is higher than for farm and non-agricultural labour is because of the inclusion of returns to land and management in this figure.

Sources: World Bank (1985).

Censuses revealed a trend toward downgrading farm sizes at the lower end of the distribution and gradually eliminating marginal farmers controlling less than 0.1 ha. Both of these forces must have occurred mainly on Java and are consistent with the above polarization hypothesis.

Secondly, the net exodus out of agriculture on Java - amounting to a net reduction of 850 000 in rural agricultural employment between 1976 and 1982 - happened concomitantly with a rise in labour intensity (higher average number of hours or workdays of labour per person) among the remaining labour force in agriculture. Thus, income from agricultural sources for both landless workers and farmers rose perhaps more because of greater labour intensity (reduction in the degree of underemployment) than higher agricultural wage rates or higher imputed labour income per hour or workday of labour. In other words, the capacity of the agricultural sector on Java to absorb additional workers had become negative, whereas its capacity to provide additional workdays of employment, although still slightly positive between 1976 and 1982, is likely to approach zero presently. Future displacement of agricultural labour on Java is inevitable.

Thirdly, the agricultural adjustment described previously is likely to have been influenced by a combination of push and pull factors. There is little doubt that many truly marginal farmers on Java must have felt the squeeze of very low farm returns and rising indebtedness and must have been, more or less, forced to join the ranks of the landless.

Likewise, it is likely that a number of small farmers had to dispose of some of their land and move down the stairs of land stratification to a lower stratum. This process, incidentally, must have been reinforced by the inheritance (primogeniture) system leading to increased land parcellization and fragmentation from one generation to another. Some pull factors were, however, present even for the poorest rural groups of landless and marginal farmers. For some of them on Java, the transmigration projects offered an opportunity to improve their condition. It is unlikely that the more remunerative off-farm activities in the rural areas (manufacturing, construction and public administration) provided more than minimal opportunities to the poorer rural target groups so that a large share of them must have ended up moving, almost residually, into service and household industries activities in the informal sector.

It appears that the more remunerative off-farm employment tended to go to the medium and large farmers more than to the landless and near landless. White (1986a) has argued that the pattern of development on Java, characterized by large farmers receiving a significantly higher proportion of their income from off-farm activities than small farmers, contrasts with the more typical East Asian pattern (Korea, Taiwan, China), where a negative correlation exists between farm size and the proportion of income derived from non-agriculture. If this were the case, the Javanese pattern would be a cause for concern and, at least potentially, a factor that could reinforce the polarization trend. Here again, the evidence is ambiguous. Rietveld (1986) concludes on the basis of a 12-village study in Java that the proportion of non-agricultural income in total income decreases almost monotonously with increasing farm size. He argues that non-agricultural activities are especially important for the poor - yet that involvement in these activities is not a sign of poverty since all size farmers are engaged in them with average returns to labour apparently higher than in agriculture.

In Chapter 8, some implications of the above trends on the capacity of the Indonesian economy to absorb the increasing labour force are discussed further.

Chapter 5

Pattern of Food Consumption, Nutrition and Health

The Government of Indonesia (GOI) is fully aware that food supply is one of its most important national problems and a prerequisite for national development. This awareness implies that planning the supply of food should be directed toward solving the nutritional problems of the country and enhancing the health and well-being of the people. From the supply side, the food problem is generally associated with increased food production and employment generation. From the consumption side, the problem is related to the prices of food commodities, the purchasing power of consumers, and the taste and preferences of consumers.

Concern for the nutritional problems among the rural poor has prompted the GOI to mandate the improvement of diet diversification (Presidential Decrees 14, 1974, and 20, 1979). On a national basis, the food and nutritional problem is not only linked to a monotonous diet but also to the expansion of agricultural and agrobusiness job opportunities and to issues of equity, such as a fair share of the income distribution, particularly among the lower socio-economic strata of the population.

Food Consumption Pattern

Indonesia is not, in aggregate terms, a food-deficit country. According to the Food Balance Sheet for 1983, estimated per capita availability of energy, protein and fat is 2 565 kilocalories, 53 gm of protein and 40 gm of fat, respectively, more than sufficient to meet the needs of the population. The Food and Agriculture Organization's recommendations are 2 100 kilocalories and 46 gm of protein. Of these, 98 percent of the kilocalories, 89 percent of the proteins and 92 percent of the fat come from vegetable sources.

Keep in mind that the figures of adequate food supply are meant to be used for monitoring and surveying food consumption as well as for planning and evaluating food supply at the national or provincial level. In practice, adequate aggregate food availability does not necessarily ensure adequate household or individual food consumption. Income distribution or household purchasing power is a fundamental mediating factor in ensuring adequate caloric intake. Given low levels of per capita income and high levels of inequality, a large proportion of the rural population will probably not consume adequate food, even if national requirements are met. Other variables, such as inadequate intrahousehold food distribution, adherence to traditional monotonous diet and scant nutrition knowledge, complicate this issue even further.

Conversely, increases in household income are usually followed by diversification of the food basket (both in quantity and quality of food supply), necessary for a nutritionally balanced diet.

Commodities Providing the Food Supply

Table 5.1 shows the overall food consumption picture for Indonesia for 1982 and the different commodities providing that food supply. Tables 5.2 and 5.3 show the average protein and caloric intake per capita by food categories, respectively. Observe that in 1980 the average caloric intake for the rural population was 1 794 and in 1984 it was 1 796, while the protein intake went up from 42.7 to 43.3 gm per capita.

Interesting observations can be made by taking a look at Table 5.4, which shows the per capita consumption, per day, per province, for calories and protein for 1980 and 1984. Although wide provincial variations are evident, a downward trend in consumption is noticeable for North, West and South Sumatra, West Nusa Tenggara and West and Central Kalimantan. Downward trends were particularly severe in West Kalimantan, where kilocalorie consumption went from 2 160 in 1980 to 1 850 in 1984. Similar downward trends in protein consumption are noticeable, that is, from 51.6 gm in 1980 to 45.8 gm in 1984. Upward trends took place in Maluku, where kilocaloric consumption rose from 1 810 in 1980 to 2 078 in 1984. Similar upward trends are also observed for protein consumption, which went from 38.9 gm in 1980 to 47.0 gm in 1984. On the whole, Table 5.4 suggests that (1) caloric consumption rose in only two provinces (East Nusa Tenggara and Maluku); (2) caloric consumption remained constant (i.e., within 2 percent of 1980 either up or down) in 12 provinces; and (3) caloric consumption fell by at least 4 percent

Table 5.1: Food Consumption and Commodities Providing Food Supply, 1982

Commodity	Total Use[1] (tonnes)	Per Capita Consumption[2] (kg/yr)
Cereals		
Wheat flour	1 091 000	7.13
Rice	21 774 000	138.77
Corn	3 562 000	19.01
Starchy foods		
Sweet potatoes	1 676 000	9.63
Cassava/tapioca/sago	12 595 000	65.86
Sugar	2 548 000	16.66
Pulses, nuts and oil seeds		
Groundnuts (shelled)	5 000 000	3.05
Soyabeans/green peas	675 000	3.89
Coconuts	3 564 000	10.48
Fruits	4 252 000[3]	25.01
Vegetables	2 033 000	11.55
Meat	482 000	3.02
Eggs	267 000	1.44
Milk	653 000	4.17
Fish	1 829 000[4]	10.15
Oils and fats		
Coconut	419 000	2.74
Palm oil	407 000	2.66
Palm kernel oil	69 000	0.45
Animal oils and fats	17 000	0.11

Note: Total per capita consumption was		Of vegetal origin (percent)
Energy	2 438 kcal/day	98
Protein	45.61 g/day	88
Fats	40.36 g/day	92

[1] Production and/or - stock changes and imports-exports.
[2] Mid-year population in 1982 was 152 988 000.
[3] About 48 percent are bananas.
[4] Of this amount 72 percent were sea fish.

Source: Government of Indonesia, Biro Pusat Statistik (1984b).

Table 5.2: Average Protein Intake Per Capita (in Grams) by Food Categories (Based on Expenditure Items)

Food	Rural	
	1980	1984
Cereal	24.4	23.6
Tubers	1.0	0.9
Fish	6.1	7.4
Meat	0.9	1.2
Eggs and milk	0.7	1.1
Vegetables	2.0	2.6
Nuts	5.0	3.5
Fruits	0.4	0.5
Miscellaneous food items	2.1	2.3
Prepared food	-	0.2
Alcoholic beverages	-	-
Total of Food	42.7	43.3

Source: Government of Indonesia, Biro Pusat Statistik (1984b).

Table 5.3: Average Caloric Intake Per Capita (in Grams) by Food Categories (Based on Expenditure Items)

Food	Rural	
	1980	1984
Cereal	1 239	1 200
Tubers	122	99
Fish	33	37
Meat	12	18
Eggs and milk	16	20
Vegetables	28	36
Nuts	52	40
Fruits	34	38
Miscellaneous food items	257	281
Prepared food	0.9	7
Alcoholic beverages	0.1	0.3
Tobacco, betelnut	-	-
Total of Food	1 794	1 796

Source: Government of Indonesia, Biro Pusat Statistik (1984b).

Table 5.4: Average Caloric and Protein Intake, Per Capita, Per Day, Per Province, 1980 and 1984

	Kilocalories		Protein	
	1980	1984	1980	1984
D.I. Aceh	2 188	2 202	54.8	53.9
North Sumatra	2 043	1 778	49.0	43.3
West Sumatra	2 056	1 854	44.3	40.8
Riau	1 923	1 949	46.1	45.7
Jambi	2 018	1 936	47.3	45.7
South Sumatra	2 027	1 787	47.2	42.6
Bengkulu	2 065	2 108	44.1	48.1
Lampung	1 948	1 847	42.1	39.5
D.K.I. Jakarta	1 544	1 521	39.2	37.8
West Java	1 850	1 825	44.9	45.2
Central Java	1 610	1 580	37.8	38.1
D.I. Yogyakarta	1 474	1 490	32.7	34.7
East Java	1 626	1 602	39.2	39.4
Bali	1 824	1 815	40.7	42.2
West Nusa Tenggara	1 774	1 638	41.1	41.4
East Nusa Tenggara	1 783	1 899	45.8	48.8
West Kalimantan	2 160	1 850	51.6	45.8
Central Kalimantan	2 001	1 814	48.2	44.8
South Kalimantan	1 940	1 868	47.0	46.5
East Kalimantan	1 882	1 803	49.3	46.3
North Sulawesi	2 007	1 898	47.8	47.0
Central Sulawesi	2 208	2 041	46.4	40.8
South Sulawesi	1 955	1 961	47.7	49.4
Southeast Sulawesi	2 231	2 191	53.0	51.8
Maluku	1 810	2 078	38.9	47.0
Irian Jaya	1 629	1 657	38.5	38.5
East Timor	NA	NA	NA	NA
Indonesia	1 794	1 798	42.7	43.3

NA   Not available

Source: Government of Indonesia, Biro Pusat Statistik (1984b).

in 12 other provinces, mainly in the Outer Islands. Such a trend is cause for concern - the more so since it occurred during a period of spectacular performance in paddy production.

These findings are confirmed by Sajogyo and Wiradi (1985, pp. 36-40) who report that "the poorest 20 percent of the population in rural Java did improve their caloric intake in 1981, reaching 1 224 calories per person per day, although unfortunately it declines again by

8 percent in 1984". When national figures based on food balance sheets are examined for this period, however, the apparently disturbing declining trend in caloric consumption does not hold true. It is nevertheless apparent from Table 5.4 that disaggregated data for provincial level offer a micro-perspective of the food situation that merits closer monitoring by nutrition planners. There is a large discrepancy between the national average caloric consumption based on Food Balance Sheets (2 565 calories in 1983) and that based on SUSENAS data (1 798 in 1984). Although it is likely that systematic underreporting in SUSENAS may account for a large part of this discrepancy, this would not explain the downward trend in many provinces.

Next, we will examine Table 5.5 for national trends in per capita consumption of kilocalories, proteins and fats from both vegetable and animal sources:

Calories: Whereas in 1976 the per capita consumption of calories (available consumption at consumer level) was 2 117 (98 percent from vegetable sources), in 1983 the figures were 2 565 calories (98 percent). In 1983 cereals contributed most calories (i.e., 1 153 kcal/day or 68 percent of total calories consumed) (not shown in Table 5.5). Compared to 1976 (2 117 kcal/day), per capita consumption per day of calories in 1983 increased by 17 percent.

Protein: The per capita consumption of protein per day in 1976 was 42 gm versus 53 gm in 1983, showing a net increase in protein consumption of 11 gm or 21 percent. In both years, 89 percent of the protein consumed came from vegetable sources. Besides the cereal group, nut and pulses constitute the major source of proteins in the Indonesian diet.

Fats: The per capita consumption per day of fats was 31 gm in 1976, of which 93 percent were derived from vegetable sources. In 1983 the figures increased substantially to 40 gm per day, of which 92 percent were derived from vegetable sources. As compared to 1976, per capita fat consumption levels increased 21 percent.

Dependency on a Single Food

As a result of both tradition and economic limitations, in Indonesia rice and a few other basic staples (cassava, maize, sweet potatoes) make up a rigidly adhered to consumption pattern. The basic diet of the Indonesian population is heavily dependent on rice, except in Irian Jaya where sweet potatoes and bananas are preferred. (Teken and

Table 5.5: Trends in Per Capita Consumption of Kilocalories, Proteins and Fats from Vegetable (V) and Animal (A) Sources, 1976-83

	Kilocalories			Proteins			Fats		
	Total	V	A	Total	V	A	Total	V	A
1976	2 117	2 077	40	41.8	37.3	4.5	30.7	28.4	2.3
1977	2 186	2 150	36	42.8	38.4	4.4	32.4	30.1	2.4
1978	2 255	2 212	43	45.4	40.8	4.6	34.5	31.9	2.5
1979	2 330	2 282	48	46.4	42.3	4.1	34.3	31.4	2.7
1980	2 489	2 435	54	49.4	44.0	5.4	40.5	37.4	3.1
1981	2 542	2 489	53	49.3	43.8	5.6	44.7	41.7	3.1
1982	2 502	2 453	49	48.0	42.4	5.6	39.6	36.9	2.7
1983	2 565	2 512	53	53.0	47.3	5.7	40.5	37.3	3.2

Source: Government of Indonesia, Biro Pusat Statistik (1984b).

Suwardi note that the figure for rice consumption per capita for 1982 might have been as high as 152 kg.) In rural areas, the main source of animal protein is salted and dried fish and of vegetable protein is *tempe* and *tahu*, particularly in Java. In general, main sources of carbohydrates include rice, wheat, maize, cassava, sweet potatoes and sugar. Sources of protein include soyabean, fish and chicken and of edible oils include peanut, coconut, and palm oil. The limited availability of food is probably one of the most important reasons for Indonesia's undifferentiated pattern of consumption.

Seasonal influence on dietary patterns in East Java appears to have negligible effects. S. Kardjati et al. (1979) stress "the monotony of the diets of rural poor people and the irregularity of consumption of foodstuffs other than the staple foods". Interestingly enough they also noted that, contrary to the impression that a male child receives preferential treatment over a female, no gender differences were found in the dietary patterns of male and female children in East Java.

Teken and Suwardi report four prevailing patterns of carbohydrate consumption in 25 provinces in Indonesia (Irian Jaya and East Timor not included):

1. The *rice pattern* exists in 14 provinces (Aceh, North and West Sumatra, Riau, Jambi, South Sumatra, Bengkulu, Jakarta, West Java, West, Central, East and South Kalimantan, West Nusa Tenggara): involving 44.8 percent of the population.
2. The *rice-corn pattern* exists in five provinces (East Java, South, Southeast and North Sulawesi and East Nusa Tenggara): involving 29 percent of the population.

3. The *rice-cassava-sweet potatoes-corn pattern* exists in four provinces (Lampung, Central Java, Yogyakarta and Bali): involving 24.4 percent of the population.
4. The *rice-sago-cassava-corn pattern* exists in two provinces (Maluku and Central Sulawesi): involving sparsely populated areas with only 1.3 percent of the total population.

Obstacles to changing food habits from rice to a more diversified diet include the extra hours of work involved in processing food from other staples such as maize and the extra fuel (wood or coal) required to cook a more varied diet. Appropriate technology in the form of improved cooking facilities for Indonesian rural women may thus be a necessary element of nutrition education programmes.

Food Policy Issues

This section discusses major policy issues concerning food production, distribution and consumption in Indonesia.

Self-sufficiency in Rice

Given the inordinate preference of the Indonesian people for rice, coupled with the burden caused by rice importation, it is understandable why the GOI has strongly strived for rice self-sufficiency. Furthermore, economic, geographical and political reasons have justified the intensification of rice cultivation to reach self-sufficiency.

The emphasis on rice caused the Indonesian government and farmers to neglect secondary crops such as corn, cassava, soyabeans, peanuts and vegetables. Consequently, fewer of these crops were planted, especially in irrigated fields. A result of this situation is improved irrigation networks that increased double cropping and reduced secondary crops (Mubyarto 1982).

At the beginning of REPELITA II, the emphasis was changed slightly from self-sufficiency in rice to self-sufficiency in food to respond to overall nutritional needs for a varied diet.

Equity Implications of the Rice Policy

According to Teken and Suwardi (1982), during 1970-80 the food policy of the GOI focused on establishing food security and price stabilization to cut inflation. From the point of view of rice intensification, the policy was well accepted. From an equity point of view, however, the policy remains questionable. For example, non-rice farmers were an underprivileged group, receiving no credit for agricultural inputs, having low productivity due to underdeveloped technologies and having insecure markets for their products.

Another questionable aspect of the rice programme is that it tended to benefit privileged rice farmers with large holdings and greater access to facilities and inputs. These farmers also used more efficient techniques, such as tractors for soil preparation and sickles for harvesting, instead of the *ani-ani*, resulting in fewer landless and rural poor, particularly women, being employed.

In the context of the development plans and the seemingly genuine interest of the GOI to improve the welfare of its people, the two food policy issues we discussed, self-sufficiency in rice and equity implications, deserve close attention in Government policies. The final food policy issue relates to food diversification.

Food Consumption Diversification

The diversification of food consumption is a natural implication of the new food policy in which all sources of carbohydrates are included in the self-sufficiency objective. Whereas the GOI has been successful in satisfying the people's demand for rice, it has not had great success implementing its food diversification policy through persuasion.

Nevertheless, the 1984 GOI, BPS/UNICEF Report notes that "there is evidence of slowly increasing dietary diversification, with non-staple foods - fruits and vegetables, meat, sugar, eggs, and dairy products, etc, accounting for a growing share of total caloric intake". If the trend continues, it will help prevent some of the micronutrient deficiencies in the Indonesian diet that increased consumption of complex carbohydrates alone will not supply.

Table 5.6 shows that rice, corn, cassava and other starchy staples account for 76.78 percent and 79.37 percent of the total kilocalories consumed by the Indonesian population in 1976 and 1983, respectively.

Timmer, as quoted by Sajogyo (1980), reported that rice income elasticities are extremely high for the first two income classes in Indonesia and that even high income groups increase their rice intake with higher incomes, especially in the rural areas. Substitution away from rice because of higher incomes is occurring for less than 5 percent of the Indonesia population.

Table 5.6: Trends in Food Consumption Patterns, 1976 and 1983

Food Categories	1976 Kilocalorie	1976 Percent of Total	1983 Kilocalorie	1983 Percent of Total
Rice	1 165	52.22)		
Corn	175	7.84)	1 753	68.34
Cassava	204	9.14)		
Other starchy staples	169	7.58)	283	11.03
Sugar	105	4.71	94	3.67
Pulses, nuts, seeds	203	9.10	187	7.29
Fruits, vegetables	49	2.20	62	2.42
Meat, eggs, fish, milk	43	1.93	51	1.99
Oils and fats	118	5.29	135	5.26

Source: Government of Indonesia, Biro Pusat Statistik (1984d).

In spite of recent trends pointing to menu diversification, Table 5.6 shows that dependence on complex carbohydrates was higher in 1983 (79.37 percent) than in 1976 (76.78 percent). In addition, there are slight increasing trends in consumption of fruits, vegetables and animal protein.

Again, the question of efficient mechanisms and programmes for improving rural well-being, especially of the bottom one-third to one-half of the income distribution, becomes uppermost. Undoubtedly, not all nutritional problems will take care of themselves as incomes of the rural poor rise, but certainly a diversified diet will do much to solve the existing malnutrition problems of the poor.

Nutritional Status and Health-related Issues

The problems related to health and nutrition of any population group are increasingly recognized as a hindrance to the implementation of a national development plan. Because the etiology of nutritional problems is multifaceted, it follows that their solution needs to be multisectoral. In the case of the rural poor and other economically marginal groups, efforts to improve the nutritional status is done basically through agriculture and health. A dual preventative (increased food consumption) and curative (better health services) approach appears to be an effective means to reach the rural poor.

Nutritional Problems in Indonesia

During REPELITA III, major nutritional problems in Indonesia began to be identified with respect to their nature and magnitude. The underlying factors causing these problems were interrelated: economic, socio-cultural and environmental deprivation. On the basis of this diagnosis and the available resources, the main thrust of nutrition programmes in REPELITA III were (1) *institution building* to develop the existing Centre for Research and Development of Nutrition (CRDN) in Bogor and establish a new Food Technology Development Centre (FTDC) in the Institute of Agriculture in Bogor (IPB); (2) *nutrition personnel development* to expand the facilities and capacity of Academy of Nutrition to increase its enrolment and graduates; and (3) *community action* to organise and implement comprehensive direct nutrition intervention in the community, especially in rural areas. The concept of the nutrition programme is based upon self-help and community effort as in the old Applied Nutrition Program (ANP). Finally, (4) *inter-agency coordination* whereby serious efforts were undertaken to promote and establish inter-agency coordination to provide overall nutrition policy guidance. These included the MOA, MOH, and National Family Planning Coordinating Board (BKKBN). Also, the Ministry of Religion contributed substantially in ten provinces. Its role was to provide moral support for the Programme and, through its local organisation and village Islamic leaders, to encourage the active participation of the community (Soekirman 1983).

Several nutrition problems have been identified as affecting substantial segments of the population in Indonesia. PEM is the most prevalent problem. Thirty-three percent of all children under five, half a million pregnant women, and 200 000 nursing women are estimated to suffer from PEM. (Tarwotgo, et al, 1978.)

Brooks (1980) in his study of the problems of malnutrition in East Java and Hart (1980) in her study of labour allocation in rural Javanese households argue that there is some logic to the concentrated attention being given to the problem of PEM in Java, since about 65 percent of Indonesia's population is concentrated there and, as can be appreciated from Table 5.7, all parts of Java have high rates of PEM. Brooks, however, also notes that it may be misleading to assume that the problems are all in Java, since in the table it can also be appreciated that the two provinces with the highest rates are in Kalimantan.

Indonesian children have one of the highest rates of Vitamin A deficiency in the world. Brooks (1980) reports on an extensive

Table 5.7: Prevalence of PEM for Preschoolers in 23 Provinces of Indonesia, Based on Data from Vitamin A Survey (percent)

Province	Mild to Moderate PEM[1]	Severe PEM[2]	Total PEM	Vitamin A Deficiency
Sumatra				
D.I. Aceh	21.4	2.9	24.3	+
North Sumatra	18.2	1.5	19.7	-
Riau	23.0	0	23.0	-
West Sumatra	21.1	2.2	23.3	-
Jambi	14.5	1.2	15.7	-
Bengkulu	12.4	0	12.4	+
South Sumatra	21.8	4.2	26.0	+
Lampung	20.9	2.6	23.5	-
Java, Bali, Lombok				
West Java and D.K.I.Jakarta	22.9	3.6	26.5	+
Central Java and D.I.Yogyakarta	29.9	2.6	32.5	+
East Java	25.4	2.8	28.2	+
Bali	12.7	2.8	15.5	+
Lombok	26.4	6.9	33.3	+
Kalimantan				
West Kalimantan	33.7	7.9	41.6	-
Central Kalimantan	26.3	1.8	28.1	+
South Kalimantan	17.3	3.9	21.2	-
East Kalimantan	34.2	5.5	39.7	-
Sulawesi				
South Sulawesi	18.3	5.2	23.5	-
Southwest Sulawesi	20.2	2.6	22.8	-
Central Sulawesi	18.5	2.2	20.7	-
North Sulawesi	11.4	2.4	13.8	+
Maluku	23.8	2.4	26.2	+

[1] Weight for height between 80 percent and 90 percent of the standard.
[2] Weight for height less than 80 percent of the standard.
Source: Tarwotjo, et al. (1978).

Vitamin A project designed to assess the prevalence of xerophthalmia in different regions of Indonesia. More than 36 000 children were sampled and examined in 23 provinces. Preliminary results showed that during each year, an estimated 80 000 children suffer from potentially blinding corneal disease and 1.5 million from non-corneal disease due to Vitamin A deficiency. The highest prevalence rates of Vitamin A deficiency were found in Aceh, Lombok and throughout

Java. In total, 11 of the 23 provinces surveyed had rates of Vitamin A deficiency higher than those considered by WHO to be a significant community health problem.

Table 5.8 shows the estimated malnourished population by nutritional deficiency. We see that 700 000 pregnant and lactating women suffered from calorie and protein malnutrition and that the majority of the malnutrition in Indonesia is caused by iron deficiencies. Iron deficiency affected 41 million people, of which 14 million were pregnant women. When both pregnant and lactating mothers are considered, a 1984 GOI, BPS/UNICEF report notes that iron deficiency anaemia affects up to 70 percent of Indonesian women.

Table 5.9 presents data on the nutritional status of children roughly classified by the MOH as "good, fair, or bad". The number of children classified as exhibiting adequate nutritional status went up from 54.1 in 1980-81 to 59.3 percent in 1982-83. Similarly, the percentage of malnourished children declined from 8.4 to 6.4 percent in the same period. More than half the children in the provinces of Riau, East Nusa Tenggara, Central Kalimantan and Southeast Sulawesi who had fair or bad nutritional status in 1980-81 improved in the following years.

Nutritional deficiency has also been identified as an associated cause in 16 percent of the deaths of children ages 1 to 4. Low birth weight is another important contributing cause. About 14 percent of all Indonesian children weigh less than 2 500 gm at birth.

Table 5.10 shows significant comparative trends in the distribution of IMRs on a provincial level from 1971 to 1984, as well as the percentage decline for those periods. A number of observations can be made from these figures: (1) IMRs have dropped sharply from an estimated 140 per 1 000 live births in 1971 to about 90 per 1 000 live births in 1984; (2) regional variation rates calculated separately by province, based on the 1980 Census, showed a range in IMR from 63 in Yogyakarta to 188 in West Nusa Tenggara; (3) for 1984, infants born in urban areas have a considerably better chance for survival (Yogyakarta, 65; Jakarta, 69) than those born in more remote rural areas (Sumarno 1981). Moreover, with the exception of West Sumatra, the highest IMRs are located in the eastern part of the Indonesian Archipelago. Within Java Province, West Java exhibits the highest IMR. The Indonesian IMR is, however, two to three times higher than in some other Southeastern Asian countries.

Indonesia also had one of the world's highest incidences of nutritional anaemia among the adult male population. In a joint research project undertaken by the Indonesian Nutrition Research

Table 5.8: Estimated Malnourished Population by Nutritional Status, 1980

Nutritional Status	Numbers Affected (in thousands)
Calorie and protein deficiency	9 700
Children 0-4 years of age	9 000
Pregnant and lactating women	700
Vitamin A deficiency in preschoolers	1 500
Serious deficiency	100
Moderate deficiency	1 400
Iron deficiency	41 000
Preschoolers	12 500
School children	9 000
Pregnant mothers	14 000
Low-income earners	5 500
Iodine deficiency	12 100
Cretinism	100
Goitre	12 000

Source: Government of Indonesia, Biro Pusat Statistik (1985a).

Institute and the World Bank, between 28 percent and 52 percent of Indonesian male workers were found to be anaemic. Soekirman (1983) reported anaemia to be prevalent among pregnant women (50 to 92 percent) mostly due to iron deficiency. Other studies have ascertained that anaemia is an equally important problem. Martoatmodjo et al., as quoted in Sumarno (1981) using the WHO haemoglobin criteria, found that the incidence of anaemia ranged from 20 to 77 percent in pregnant women, from 0 to 48 percent in non-pregnant women and from 16 to 50 percent in men in rural Java and Bali. GOI, BPS/UNICEF 1984 notes that 27 infant deaths per 1 000 live births separate the urban and rural rates countrywide.

In summary, irrespective of different geographical regions or years of investigation, most findings point to a diet dangerously low in quantity as well as in quality for at least certain segments of the population. The following sections present some of the most salient nutritional problems in Indonesia, including what the GOI is presently doing to control, reduce or eliminate these problems.

Protein-Energy Malnutrition. PEM is the result of prolonged insufficient intakes of kilocalories and protein. It affects disease resistance, immunological resistance, physical activity and growth.

PEM afflicts all adults but is a particularly serious threat to young children and women. It has been identified as one of the reasons for

Table 5.9: Percentage of Children Under Five Years of Age by Nutritional Status and Province, 1980/81 to 1982/83 (percent)[1]

Province	Good 1980-81	1982-83	Fair 1980-81	1982-83	Bad 1980-81	1982-83
D.I. Aceh	56.5	56.9	37.5	41.0	6.0	2.1
North Sumatra	49.3	48.3	45.4	46.9	5.3	4.8
West Sumatra	55.2	53.4	38.0	41.0	6.8	5.6
Riau	33.3	51.9	55.3	40.3	11.4	7.8
Jambi	59.5	63.5	30.1	26.0	10.4	8.5
South Sumatra	58.4	72.7	30.4	20.3	11.2	7.0
Bengkulu	49.9	54.2	45.2	39.5	4.9	6.3
Lampung	59.5	61.7	33.4	34.4	7.1	4.1
D.K.I. Jakarta	-	64.0	-	27.2	-	8.8
West Java	56.7	64.9	35.3	28.1	8.0	7.0
Central Java	59.3	67.9	33.8	26.3	6.8	5.8
D.I. Yogyakarta	60.5	70.9	32.6	24.6	6.9	4.5
East Java	56.1	58.2	36.0	39.3	7.9	2.5
Bali	65.8	63.8	30.5	27.4	3.7	0.6
West Nusa Tenggara	63.3	64.7	28.2	27.2	8.5	7.1
East Nusa Tenggara	39.9	44.0	52.0	48.3	8.1	7.7
East Timor	-	-	-	-	-	-
West Kalimantan	48.6	53.1	40.9	48.0	10.5	6.9
Central Kalimantan	42.0	57.9	40.2	31.2	17.8	10.8
South Kalimantan	49.0	58.6	42.6	36.1	8.4	10.6
East Kalimantan	49.0	58.6	42.6	36.1	8.4	5.3
North Sulawesi	-	-	-	-	-	-
Central Sulawesi	45.5	55.2	41.2	35.0	13.3	9.8
South Sulawesi	51.0	58.4	42.3	35.1	67	6.5
S.E. Sulawesi	68.1	62.3	24.6	31.5	7.3	6.2
Maluku	-	56.1	-	35.1	-	8.8
Irian Jaya	56.1	55.3	38.7	39.8	5.2	4.9
Average	54.1	59.3	37.5	33.4	8.4	6.4

[1] The data was collected from UPGK (Family Nutrition Improvement Programme) only; nutritional status is determined based on age and weight.

Source: Based on data collected from the Ministry of Health, Government of Indonesia.

the high mortality rates among children in low-income countries. According to a nutrition survey by Tarwotjo et al. (1978), mild PEM afflicted 33 percent or 9 million preschool children (*balitas*) in Indonesia (based on 1978 Population Census). It was also prevalent

Table 5.10: Estimates of Infant Mortality, 1971-1980-1984

Province	Based on 1971 Census (1969)[1]	Based on 1980 Census (1978)[1]	Percentage Decline (1971-80)[1]	1984[2]	Percentage Decline (1980-84)
D.K.I. Jakarta	125	81	35.2	69	14.8
West Java	159	131	17.6	94	39.3
Central Java	147	108	26.5	81	33.3
D.I. Yogyakarta	147	63	57.1	65	3.2
East Java	133	113	15.0	84	34.5
Total Java	138	104	32.7	79	24.0
D.I. Aceh	130	91	30.0	76	19.7
North Sumatra	112	89	20.5	78	14.1
West Sumatra	142	122	14.1	102	19.6
Riau	116	113	2.6	98	15.3
Jambi	157	120	23.6	98	22.4
South Sumatra	153	98	35.9	80	22.5
Bengkulu	148	107	27.7	87	22.9
Lampung	145	98	32.4	81	20.9
Total Sumatra	139	93	49.5	89	4.3
West Kalimantan	138	117	15.2	98	16.2
Central Kalimantan	129	100	22.5	86	14.0
South Kalimantan	142	122	14.1	102	16.3
East Kalimantan	118	100	15.3	87	13.0
Total Kalimantan	139	106	23.7 $(31.1)^3$	93	12.2
North Sulawesi	112	96	14.3	85	11.4
Central Sulawesi	136	129	5.1	110	14.7
South Sulawesi	154	108	29.9	93	13.8
S.E. Sulawesi	160	117	26.9	107	8.5
Total Sulawesi	149	108	38.0	99	8.3
Bali	132	89	32.6	75	15.7
West Nusa Tenggara	170	188	(+10.6)	129	31.3
East Nusa Tenggara	136	125	8.1	106	15.2
Maluku	141	125	11.3	105	18.6
Irian Jaya	NA	125	NA	108	13.6
Total E. Islands	164	133	23.3	105	21.0
Total Indonesia	140	105	25.0 $(33.3)^3$	90	14.2

Source: [1] Biro Pusat Stastik estimates modified by the World Bank staff.

[2] Government of Indonesia, Biro Pusat Stastik (1985a).

[3] Mission calculations.

among pregnant and lactating women, with 7 percent and 3 percent, respectively, suffering from the mild form.

Since PEM is largely a problem of inadequate food consumption, improving the entitlement and purchasing power of those afflicted should reduce its prevalence significantly. Nutrition education strategies should not, however, be neglected, ensuring that additional income gets translated into real dietary improvements. The GOI's continued efforts to improve nutritional status, and eliminate PEM, will result in REPELITA IV improving, expanding and linking UPGK with other development programmes emphasising supplementary feeding accompanied by nutrition education.

Nutritional Anaemia. Nutritional anaemia is caused by insufficient intakes of one or more nutrients such as iron, folic acid and Vitamin B12. Anaemia caused by insufficient intake of iron represents the biggest portion of all nutritional anaemias. Symptoms of iron-deficiency anaemia include mental and physical sluggishness, reduced physical endurance and impaired work capacity and productivity. Some have suggested a link with impaired learning performance and school absenteeism. Nutritional anaemia in Indonesia is prevalent among pregnant (70 percent) and lactating women (40 percent), preschool (40 percent) and school children (31 percent) and male plantation workers and rural poor (40 percent) (Karyadi 1974).

The main strategy to control anemia is iron supplementation, which is provided in the UPGK activities. Particularly for pregnant women, iron or folate pills, along with nutrition education, are included in the distribution of nutritional first aid of UPGK type A.

Vitamin A Deficiency. Nutrition researchers have shown that Vitamin A deficiency is the critical etiological factor responsible for the development of xerophthalmia. At least half a million Asian children develop clinical xerophthalmia each year (Tarwotjo et al. 1982). In Indonesia more than 60 000 children develop the disease and about 100 000 children at risk become blind each year (Hellen Keller International, Inc. (HKII) 1980). Many children in Java suffer from xerophthalmia.

In 1973 the GOI initiated a programme to distribute Vitamin A capsules to children ages 1-4. At the same time, HKII evaluated the efficacy, cost and efficiency of the programme. On the basis of the magnitude of the disease, in 1975 the MOH set up a committee to explore the possibility of conducting a large research programme aimed at the prevention of nutritional blindness. As a result, in 1976 the Government collaborated with HKII to conduct research in 23 provinces, 11 of which showed a high prevalence of xerophthalmia.

These figures exceeded the WHO criteria (Tarwotjo et al. 1978). The simple way to identify Vitamin A deficiency is to observe the Bitot spot and night blindness among children. Figure 5.1 shows the 11 provinces where Vitamin A deficiency is prevalent.

Three approaches may prove to be valuable in improving Vitamin A status:

1. Through nutrition education, encourage increased consumption of natural dietary sources of Vitamin A and Vitamin A rich foods, such as green leafy vegetables, by children at risk.
2. Administer periodic massive doses of Vitamin A (HKII 1980).
3. Emphasize dietary diversification.

Iodine Deficiency. Iodine deficiency is the principal etiological factor in endemic goitre and in acute iodine deficiency and may also lead to deaf-mutism and cretinism. Recent studies show that iodine deficiency during pregnancy can result in impaired mental ability in children. In the village of Sengi in Central Java, 40 cretins were found out of a sample of 583 children. This is indicative of a severe shortage of iodine in the population. In most areas in which endemic goitre is prevalent, an insufficient intake of iodine through food and drinking-water has been shown to play a part. Goitre is considered endemic once it affects more than 10 percent of a population. In its early stages, goitre can be detected by palpation; in its severe stages it is shown by pathological alteration of the thyroid gland.

Studies on the prevalence of endemic goitre among school children reported increasing incidence. Between 50 and 80 percent of children surveyed in North and West Sumatra, East Java and Bali were found to have goitre. Data from 11 744 school children in an endemic goitre area in Central Java (1974) and study of 39 villages in another endemic goitre area revealed that 62 to 83 percent of the school children in these areas suffer from goitre as defined by the Pérez and WHO classifications, respectively.

Until 1972 endemic goitre was largely neglected in Indonesia. Attention was drawn to the problem when a large-scale survey was done by Djumadias et al. (as cited by Soekirman 1974), which revealed that goitre was prevalent among preschool children. Reasons for this neglect included the following:

1. Most nutrition problems are recognized from data obtained from hospitals, but goitre does not usually result in hospitalization.

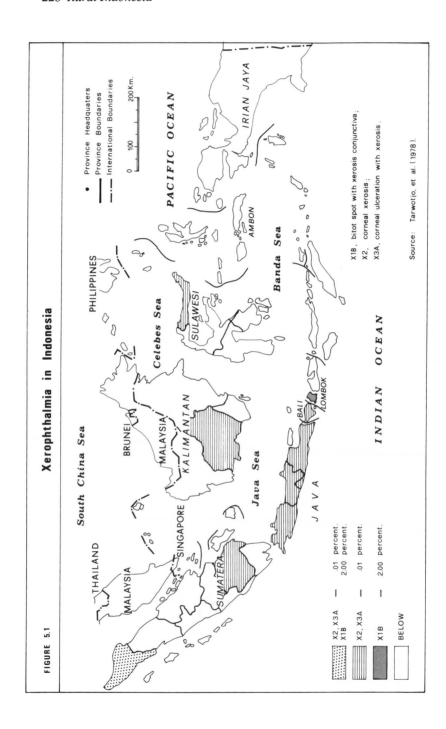

FIGURE 5.1

Xerophthalmia in Indonesia

X1B, bitot spot with xerosis conjunctiva;
X2, corneal xerosis;
X3A, corneal ulceration with xerosis.

Source: Tarwotjo, et al. (1978).

2. Goitre does not cause death or dramatic suffering, so attention from local health authorities was put off.
3. The people who suffer from goitre live in remote areas that are difficult to reach.

According to Djoko Mulyanto and other researchers in Indonesia (as cited by Tarwotjo et al. 1978), it was estimated that 12 million people live in endemic goitre areas. This includes 500 000 cretinoids and 100 000 cretins.

Goitre Control. In 1974 the GOI initiated an iodine deficiency control programme in order to reduce and/or eliminate goitre and cretinism in Indonesia. This was done through a prevention approach with salt iodization programme and a treatment approach by injection with iodinated oil in high-prevalence areas. A number of concrete steps was taken in REPELITA III to identify and control iodine deficiency. Prevalence mapping of endemic goitre was completed in 1982 for 25 provinces (excluding Jakarta and Irian Jaya). Iodation contractors (41) have set up plants to supply the country's salt needs. Domestic manufacturing of potassium iodate, initially imported with UNICEF assistance, is also underway.

There have been technical as well as marketing, distribution and cost problems in these approaches. Iodinated oil injections cost about US$ 0.70 per person. The GOI is now investigating an oral preparation, which if successful, should be less expensive and easier to administer.

Nutrition Programmes

This section present a review of UPGK, the basic instrument through which the most direct and intensive Indonesian nutrition activities and services are channelled.

Family Nutrition Improvement Programme. Nutrition improvement activities in Indonesia are carried out basically through the UPGK in the form of nutrition services to families at the village level. The main objectives of this programme are (1) to improve the nutritional status of the population (the primary targets are children under five and pregnant and lactating women in economically deprived families); (2) to promote food diversification away from rice; and (3) to reduce morbidity and mortality of diseases that are nutritionally related. The thrust of this programme is educational. It aims to provide mothers with increased awareness and knowledge to improve the nutritional status of their families. Following is a description of the main UPGK activities.

UPGK activities are classified as follows:

(a) *UPGK type A*, consisting of basic nutrition services such as monthly weighing of children under five; supplementary feeding; nutrition education; distribution of high doses of Vitamin A, iron and rehydration salts (Oralit); and home and village garden activities;

(b) *UPGK type B*, consisting of type A plus health services such as immunization; clean water supply; environmental sanitation; primary health centre; health education; and rehabilitation from severe PEM;

(c) *UPGK type C*, including A and B plus income-generating activities such as simple food technology; small food industry; village health insurance; cooperatives; and food storage.

UPGK type A is basically a nutrition education and rehabilitation programme. Once the activities are organized in a community and become accepted and established, the UPGK programme in the area is ready to be promoted to either B and C activities. When target children do not gain weight for three months, they are referred to the nearby health centre for further diagnosis and medication.

Table 5.11 shows the development of UPGK from its inception in REPELITA III through the beginning of REPELITA IV (1979-85). The programme's outreach and coverage are impressive: 3 000 villages are covered, 150 000 pregnant women, 890 000 children under five years of age and 34 692 children are given supplementary food. The prevention of goitre is carried out by administering Lipiodol injections, reaching 1.3 million in the first year of REPELITA IV.

Measures to control Vitamin A deficiency include the distribution of Vitamin A capsules. This programme in 1983-84 covered 15 provinces. The UPGK has managed to distribute Vitamin A capsules to 890 000 children under five. In a special programme, 10.5 million children received high doses of Vitamin A. The distribution of Vitamin A through Public Health Centres reached about 1.5 million children under five.

The programme to control nutritional anaemia is carried out by distributing iron (Fe) tablets to pregnant women. This effort reached 150 000 people in the beginning of REPELITA IV.

Other UPGK Activities. Child weighing posts, growth-monitoring charts, simple dietary counselling, home gardening and supplementary

Table 5.11: UPGK Programme, 1979-80 to 1984-85

Major Activities	Unit	1979-80	1980-81	REPLEITA III		REPELITA IV	
				1981-82	1982-83	1983-84	1984-85
UPGK							
Children age 1-4 years covered	Persons	900 000	2 000 000	2 750 000	1 900 000	1 200 000	890 000
Children age 1-4 years accepting supplementary food	Persons	35 917	70 165	77 692	124 893	38 800	34 692
Pregnant mothers covered[1]	Persons	3 017	3 850	1 074	-	-	150 000
Lactating mothers covered	Persons	3 533	3 566	1 744	-	-	-
Villages covered	Persons	4 521	9 917	12 056	9 278	4 313	3 000
Prevention on Endemic Goitre Lipiodol injections	Persons	434 488	1 763 496	1 711 521	690 884	16 426[2]	1 300 000
Deficiency Vitamin A Prevention							
Distribution of Vitamin A capsule (high dose)	1-4 years	73 788	592 935	1 052 061	1 256 065	979 404	10 502 800
Distribution through UPGK	Idem	900 000	1 983 400	2 411 200	1 855 600	862 600	890 000
Distribution through Public Health Centres	Idem	1 500 000	-	-	-	-	-
Anemia Prevention							
Distribution Fe tablets for pregnant mothers through UPGK	Persons	175 000	450 000	602 800	347 200	215 650	150 000

1 1982/83, 1983/84 - No servicer for pregnant women.
2 Only 11 provinces (preliminary figures, up to May 1984).
Source: Based on data collected from Ministry of Health, Government of Indonesia,

feeding are among the activities undertaken in REPELITA IV in 36 000 villages. Instructions in making salt and sugar oral rehydration solution at home and the promotion of this salt or packaged rehydration salts as a simple but effective treatment for childhood diarrhoea are also carried out.

Strengths and Weaknesses of UPGK. In spite of rapid programme expansion and substantial coverage, there are some areas for concern. Based on a recent evaluation of UPGK management and implementation (UN Economic and Social Council 1984), many factors behind its successes are also shown to be source of some of its weaknesses.

Whereas rapid expansion during previous REPELITAs brought direct nutritional assistance to millions of mothers and children in all 27 provinces of Indonesia, it also strained the resources and capabilities of all participating agencies. Although about 70 percent of the children under five years of age (*balitas*) live in villages reached by UPGK, only about 40 percent of them participated in or benefited directly from the programme. Constraints of rural poverty and low education among many of the programme volunteers and the limited training they are provided have made it difficult for the UPGK to achieve its full potential (GOI, BPS/UNICEF 1984).

REPELITA IV (1984-89). Efforts to increase food production have been a part of the agricultural development policy in REPELITA IV that has relied on intensification, diversification and extensification programmes. Because of the limited availability of land for wet paddy, special attention has been given to the intensification of dryland, with particular emphasis on secondary crops (*palawija*). To support the food diversification programme, food processing industries have been encouraged and more efforts have been directed toward improving post-harvest technology. On the consumption side, nutrition education programmes were intensified to promote diversification. In regions where consumption patterns have been successfully diversified, efforts have been made to maintain them through an appropriate pricing policy.

Steps taken regarding food and nutrition in REPELITA IV include (1) the expansion and improvement of the UPGK from 36 000 villages in REPELITA III to 64 400 villages; (2) intensification of food fortification with Vitamin A, iron and iodine; (3) intensification of nutrition education in communities and schools; (4) implementation of the Nutrition Surveillance System (NSS) in critical areas in 12 provinces. The NSS monitors probable occurrence of food crisis in certain areas due to drought, flood and pests.

Nutrition Trends, Overview and Recommendations

Clearly, increased nutrition education coupled with dietary behavioural changes are necessary elements in improving the nutritional status of the population. Thus, in addition to improving the income of the rural poor, significant changes must take place in three other sectors of the economy: health, agriculture and education.

Health. Adequate availability, easy access, low cost and frequent use of well-staffed health facilities are important in achieving the nutrition development objectives. Because of the vast, densely populated rural areas in certain provinces in Indonesia, public health centres, satellite dispensaries and mobile public health centres are important if effective medical care is to be provided. Underuse of present rural health facilities as well as a high percentage of rural people still treating their diseases by themselves are two major constraints that merit attention by health officers.

Agriculture. The improvement of people's nutritional status implies an adequate and equitably distributed supply of food, both in quantitative and qualitative terms. Increased food production and processing at the national level (supply) as well as increased efforts in home gardens, with particular emphasis on identified deficient nutrients (consumption), may contribute significantly to the eradication of malnutrition in Indonesia.

The GOI needs to be supported in its efforts toward food diversification programmes. Improvement of postharvest technology and low-level technology for home produce will increase food availability over a long period. Similarly improved food technology efforts can be directed toward exploring additional protein-rich foods, particularly for children. Fish flour, soyabean and its products such as soyabean milk, *tempe* and *tahu* are relatively inexpensive good protein sources that merit further consideration by Indonesian food technologists working on solving the food crisis. These sources are culturally familiar, thus their acceptability does not pose a barrier as has been the case in other countries eager to solve the protein gap.

In addition, efforts should be directed toward better coordination between the planning units of the MOA and MOH with respect to food and nutrition policy. It seems that food production policy and nutritional considerations are a natural match, and increased efforts to ensure coordination between planning agencies (particularly BAPPENAS and the MOA) that share the same goal (i.e., to improve the nutritional status of the Indonesian people) must merit priority in future government actions.

Education. Lastly, as the educational level of the population improves, in particular that of young women and their children, greater awareness of what constitutes an adequate diet and what constitutes desirable child-feeding practices needs to be emphasized. Admittedly, improved incomes, increased consumption of staples and increased knowledge *per se* will not guarantee adequate intake of all nutrients. But appropriate behavioural change with respect to adequate food intake based on informed choices are necessary elements required for high-risk groups - the poor landless, growing children and pregnant and lactating mothers - to achieve adequate nutritional status.

Rural Water Supply, Sanitation and Health Facilities

Relative to other Asian countries, access to clean water and sanitation facilities is low in Indonesia. According to a 1980 UN report, based on 15 reporting countries, Indonesia ranked eleventh in rural water supply coverage and thirteenth in urban water supply coverage.

Rural Water Supply and Sanitation

Indonesian ground water resources depend upon regional geological formation and variable rainfall. Large areas in Central and East Java have layers of highly porous limestone so that surface water rapidly disappears into relatively deep underground formations. Exploration for ground water under such conditions requires expensive and sophisticated technology.

During a long rainless period, many shallow dug wells dry up and springs and rivers become the only sources of water. Water fetching from distances of up to 6 km in the province of East Nusa Tenggara is sometimes necessary. Coastal areas of larger islands also face the problem of saline ground water, which is unsuitable for drinking or cooking.

Hand pumps (65 percent) and gravity-fed piped systems (15 percent) are the major sources of clean water. The rest comes mainly from artesian wells, spring protection systems, rain collection tanks and dug wells. Water availability on a per capita basis is not generally known. Each pump is assumed to serve 100 people, but variables such as population density and distance to point of supply affect the supply (UNDP, Report of the Water Supply and Sanitation Review and Programming Mission, Jakarta, 1984). Some estimates indicate availability as low as 10 litres/person/day from hand pumps. With respect to rainwater collection tanks, a 10 cubic metre tank should supply water for 15 people but, again, depending on variables such as length of rainless period, rainwater availability may fall as low as 5 litres/person/day. In designing a piped system, a per capita requirement of 60 litres per day is assumed (GOI, BPS/UNICEF 1984).

An analysis by Johnston (1986) in South Sumatra entitled, Clean Water at a Premium: The Case of Bandar Lampung notes that during the rainy season, when water is abundant, wells serve 80 percent of the population. But after only three weeks without rain the situation changes drastically. Wells dry up; the level of pollution increases in rivers in proportion to the dropping water level and rainwater supplies deplete rapidly. Johnston notes that people do not collect rainwater in large quantities because of the high cost of storage tanks and because they consider rainwater fit only for bathing and washing. An additional problem in Bandar Lampung is the cost of water. International standards set viable costs for water at 3 to 5 percent of household income. In the inner city of *kampung* Sawah Lama, an unskilled labourer's family with an income of Rp 60 000 a month spends 11.9 percent of its income on water.

At present, Johnston reports that in 40 percent of 58 *kampungs*, people complain of salty and mineral-contaminated well and pump water. In inner city areas of Bandar Lampung, many wells have reportedly ceased to function. In Kedaton *kampung* people complain there is virtually no ground left in which to sink a well. Still, with increasing urbanization, more wells will be sunk and existing wells deepened, a trend that will only put increasing pressure on the limited underground water supply.

Water uses are diverse in all communities, ranging from basic functions of sustaining human life and supporting personal and environmental cleanliness to non-domestic functions related to agriculture. In a country such as Indonesia, with a large Muslim population, water assumes a special significance with its role in the purifying rituals stipulating specific bathing procedures that precede prayers five times a day (Johnston 1986).

In the Indonesian rural countryside, water is used in many ways, including for bathing, drinking, washing clothes and dishes and for defecation. The deleterious impact of such multiple water use on rural health (diarrhoea, gastro-intestinal disease and skin infections) cannot be over-emphasized. A large number of mothers interviewed reported boiling water regularly.

The water and sanitation problem in Indonesia is one of the most complex within the development plan. The GOI has made substantial investments and continues to support water supply programmes.

According to a WHO report, at the beginning of REPELITA I (1969) rural water supply systems were "virtually nonexistent". Based on the GOI estimates at the end of REPELITA III only about 32 percent of the rural population and 60 percent of the urban population had access to clean water. Coverage estimates are based on the number of facilities constructed and number of people presumed served by each facility. The proportion of the population actually using clean water for drinking, cooking and other needs is probably lower than official estimates (GOI, BPS/UNICEF 1984).

Current Programmes. The INPRES programme for hygiene and sanitation is the basic instrument through which the GOI attempts to provide safe water supply and sanitation to its population. About 80 percent of all public funds for rural water supply and sanitation are channelled under this programme, although these budget allocations are used mainly as matching funds for outside funding. Although resources expended in village water supply and latrine construction have increased dramatically since REPELITA I, current budgetary allocations as a proportion of the total are still negligible compared with other Asian countries. Whereas Indonesia earmarked an average of about 0.5 percent of its budget for water and sanitation in REPELITA III, Bhutan, Nepal and Burma, for example, allocated 2-3 percent of their budgets for this programme (WHO 1983). At the end of REPELITA II rural population coverage was only 18 percent, at the end of REPELITA III coverage reached about 32 percent (against a target of 35 percent) (GOI, BPS/UNICEF 1984).

GOI plans for the UN Water Supply and Sanitation Decade call for safe water coverage of 60 percent of the rural population and 75 percent of the urban population. In sanitation, 40 percent and 60 percent of the rural and urban populations, respectively, were targeted for access to sanitary facilities by 1990. Although the major emphasis of INPRES has been on the construction of facilities, several of supportive activities, such as technical personnel development, have also been undertaken (GOI, BPS/UNICEF 1984). Schools for sanitarians increased from 9 to 13, and academies for health controllers from 2 to 6, each school graduating about 40 per year.

A World Bank Report summarizes the drinking-water and sanitation situation in Indonesia as follows:

Drinking-Water and Sanitation: Only 7 percent of the households in 1980 had access to piped water for drinking and 4.1 percent could boast of piped water for bathing. Only 9 percent of the households had a private toilet. A relatively large 26 percent had a private bath. The regional differentials are illustrated in Table 5.12. Because of the tremendous differences in access between urban and rural areas, the provinces with large urban areas have better access. Jakarta, East Java, North Sumatra, South Sumatra, South and East Kalimantan, North Sulawesi and Bali come under that category. East Nusa Tenggara, Maluku and Irian Jaya also have relatively high proportions of households with access to piped water. Those with insignificant access to piped drinking-water are Lampung, Central Kalimantan and West Nusa Tenggara. The patterns described with reference to piped water broadly hold with respect to private toilets (with septic tanks) also, since the availability of sufficient piped water could naturally induce people to go in for private toilet facilities. The urban-rural differentials are too striking to be ignored. However, urban needs may be more urgent and may need earlier attention. The issue should be tackled in the context of formulating an overall long-term strategy for developing drinking-water facilities.

Rural Health Problems as a Result of Lack of Water Supply and Sanitation. The multiple use of open rivers, streams and ponds may be a major reason for impaired rural health. High incidence of water-borne and water-related diseases, including diarrhoea, gastro-intestinal problems, dysenteries, hepatitis, cholera, typhoid and skin diseases has been reported in rural areas. Some of these diseases are among the leading causes of morbidity and death, especially among infants and young children.

Environmental contamination with fecal bacteria, viruses and intestinal parasites due basically to poor sanitation and inadequate human waste disposal is such that a large segment of the rural population is constantly exposed to infection. The problem is particularly acute in rural areas of Java, where domestic crowding and overall population densities are highest.

Programme Constraints. According to the WHO/German Technical Assistance report (WHO/GTZ 1982), there appear to be a number of problems in the attempt by the GOI to provide greater access to clean water supply and sanitation facilities in Indonesia. The GTZ reported that projects funded under INPRES are often subject to delays in implementation, a lack of accountability and control during implementation and poor supervision in regard to distributing hand-pumps to the field. Inadequate attention to health education and community participation and shortages of full-time personnel for planning and organizing at provincial and district levels were also

Table 5.12: Drinking-Water and Toilet Facilities, 1980

	Percentage of Households with Access to Piped Water for Drinking		Percentage of Households with Private Toilet with Spetic Tank	
	Urban	Rural	Urban	Rural
D.K.I. Jakarta	30.0	5.4	41.8	22.6
West Java	13.2	1.6	18.7	4.0
Central Java	23.4	1.6	23.7	2.8
D.I. Yogyakarta	11.3	1.2	30.3	6.5
East Java	35.8	2.0	27.7	3.5
D.I. Aceh	23.0	0.9	34.6	5.0
North Sumatra	35.2	3.9	37.1	3.5
West Sumatra	22.1	2.0	18.9	2.1
Riau	18.5	1.1	36.6	4.3
Jambi	6.0	1.4	24.5	4.1
South Sumatra	37.7	2.0	32.8	5.1
Bengkulu	10.4	2.1	12.4	4.6
Lampung	3.5	1.2	25.2	4.7
West Kalimantan	18.4	0.2	23.2	2.4
Central Kalimantan	2.7	0.1	23.2	1.3
South Kalimantan	49.1	2.7	18.1	3.5
East Kalimantan	22.6	1.1	38.1	4.4
North Sulawesi	31.3	4.5	32.4	10.5
Central Sulawesi	28.6	1.7	27.2	5.9
South Sulawesi	31.3	1.2	34.6	3.7
Southeast Sulawesi	15.5	1.7	23.4	2.8
Bali	42.8	7.7	37.2	7.7
West Nusa Tenggara	6.7	0.1	15.3	1.3
East Nusa Tenggara	57.6	10.1	32.5	3.1
Maluku	52.6	5.4	37.5	5.7
Irian Jaya	48.0	1.5	27.7	3.2
Total Indonesia	26.4	2.1	28.9	3.8

Source: Government of Indonesia, 1980 Census.

noted. The key problem, however, is the lack of an adequate system for proper maintenance and operation of piped systems, hand-pumps, dug wells and rain collectors.

Recommendations. Problems related to constructing water facilities, personnel constraints and financial issues are not easy to resolve. Efforts by GOI and bilateral and international agencies in terms of economic and technical assistance must continue so as to provide clean water and sanitary facilities to a large proportion of the rural population. Similarly, efforts to obtain greater community support and participation should continue. Training village volunteers to maintain hand-pumps and repair existing facilities must continue. At the same time, management efforts and education campaigns about adequate hygiene practices must be undertaken. This is especially important since access to or provision of improved water-supply and sanitary facilities does not guarantee improved health. Health education campaigns in the rural sector emphasizing increased awareness about the use of latrines is also a viable strategy.

Lastly, a suggestion by others concerned with access to clean water-supply in rural Indonesia is the possibility of increasing the number of simple rain collectors or other storage containers. Their construction could be done by village workers and the costs kept down if the basic construction materials are provided at the *kabupatens* or *kecamatans* level. The benefit-cost ratio of such rain collectors and/or water storage containers might be high.

Summary. Programmes to develop adequate water-supplies are relatively recent in Indonesia. In 1983, at the end of REPELITA III, nearly 70 percent of the rural population and 40 percent of the urban population still lacked access to clean water, and 65-75 percent were without proper waste disposal facilities.

The provision and effective use of clean water and sanitation facilities are fundamental prerequisites for achieving the goal of WHO - Health for All by the Year 2000. Given the rapid population growth in Indonesia, coupled with pressing demands for clean and accessible water and its serious financial implications, the water-supply situation in Indonesia does not appear comforting in the near future.

Health Facilities, Human Resources and Programmes

Beginning with REPELITA I in 1968, the GOI policy has been to achieve the widest possible coverage of basic health services. In view of continued population growth, however, improved coverage rates for immunization, maternal and child care and other services will depend on the ability to enlarge the health staff and its network delivery system.

A key element in the health infrastructure is the *puskesmas*, which serves as the focal point for comprehensive health-related activities. Beginning with REPELITA II, polyclinics and maternal and child health (MCH) centres were merged with the *puskesmas*. The growth in number of *puskesmas* has been dramatic: In 1969 there were about 1 000 such health centres in Indonesia; in 1973-74 there were 2 679; in 1980-81 there were 4 753; and by 1984 there were more than 5 250. On average, there is one *puskesmas* for every 30 000 people and a subcentre for every 11 800 people. In general, they are more evenly distributed throughout the country than hospitals, although quality, staffing levels and use by the public differ widely. Not all *puskesmas* have a physician, for example, and only 60 percent of them have adequate supporting staff (GOI, BPS/UNICEF 1984).

The regional differences in average populations served by *puskesmas* are striking. For example, Java's provinces have 41 000 people per health centre as compared to the national average of 31 000 people per centre. Similar patterns prevail in regard to population per subcentre, perhaps suggesting that greater density population means closer access. All the provinces in Java except Yogyakarta and the province of Lampung in Sumatra have more than 30 000 people per subcentre, much higher than the 20 000 of other provinces.

Number of Hospital Beds. Although there is an average of six hospital beds per 10 000 people, great variations exist among provinces. For example, Jakarta and North Sumatra have more than ten hospital beds per 10 000 people, while in Aceh, Jambi, Bengkulu, Lampung, West Java, Central Java, East Java, West Nusa Tenggara, East Nusa Tenggara, West Kalimantan and Central Kalimantan there are less than five beds per 10 000 people (World Bank 1990). Within the major islands, there are large interprovincial differences in the number of hospital beds per people. The private sector is quite active in some of the provinces. In Jakarta, Yogyakarta, Lampung, North Sulawesi and East Nusa Tenggara, the private sector provided more than 40 percent of the beds. The government hospitals in Java and Sumatra are relatively large, with 50 percent more beds than in Kalimantan, Sulawesi and eastern most islands. In contrast, the private hospitals in Java and Sumatra tend to be smaller than in other regions. The large demand for hospital accommodation in Java and Sumatra could be encouraging the growth of a number of small private hospitals and nursing homes.

Human Resources in the Health Sector. Understaffed health facilities still remain a major constraint, in terms of both quantity and quality, to the delivery of adequate health services. At the beginning of REPELITA III, there were about 12 000 physicians. During the Plan period almost 6 500 graduated, of whom 5 100 were appointed to government posts. Thus the population-to-physician ratio is about 9 000 to 1, well below the levels in India and Pakistan (3 500),

Thailand (8 200), Malaysia (7 500) and the Philippines (2 800)(GOI, BPS/UNICEF 1984). In addition, in 1983 the number of people providing health services was about 162 000, of which 40 percent were non-medical.

Traditional Birth Attendants. Of particular importance to rural maternal and infant health are the traditional birth attendants (TBAs) (*dukun bayi*) who attend about 80 percent of the child births in Indonesia. Table 5.13 shows their distribution by province and training status.

Health Policy in REPELITA IV. Specific objectives of health programmes in REPELITA IV included the eradication of contagious and common diseases, improvement in the population's nutrition, increased provision of adequate potable water for the population, improvement of the community's hygiene and sanitation, protection against narcotics and other dangerous drugs and increased awareness of hygiene. A brief review of major health programmes relevant to rural women and their children follows.

Village Community Health Department. The PKMD was designed to better meet the health needs of the poor. A key element of PKMD is to use and build upon the traditional Indonesian system of mutual self-help (*gotong-royong*) and, to a large extent rely on local resources. *Puskesmas* doctors, village leaders and local citizens are responsible for initiating PKMD. By 1983 approximately 1 800 villages had initiated PKMD activities in all 27 provinces with an average of 20 *prokesas* (health care promoters) per village. The effectiveness of this programme has been questioned since it has been plagued by lack of supervisors from trained health staff, as well as improper selection and training of *prokesas*.

Maternal Child Health. Because of the high incidence of perinatal deaths, particularly those due to neonatal tetanus, training TBAs was given emphasis during REPELITA III (25 000 TBAs were trained and 36 000 were retrained). The MCH programme emphasised teaching the DOs (such as referring at-risk mothers to *puskesmas*, practicing proper hygiene during delivery and supporting immunization to protect the newborn) and the DON'Ts (such as not pulling on the placenta and not examining internal organs). Major constraints faced by this programme have been shortage of staff and inadequate supervision of TBAs.

Expanded Programme of Immunization. Six diseases - neonatal tetanus (90 percent fatality rate), measles, whooping cough, diphtheria, polio and tuberculosis - are major causes of infant mortality and all are preventable by immunization. The long-term goal of the EPI is to

Table 5.13: Distribution of Traditional Birth Attendants and Training Status by Province, 1983

Province	Total	No. Untrained	Percent Untrained
D.I. Aceh	1 875	317	17
North Sumatra	4 004	1 274	32
West Sumatra	3 189	1 350	42
Riau	1 591	195	12
Jambi	1 180	474	40
South Sumatra	2 491	1 561	63
Bengkulu	1 470	741	50
Lampung	3 253	1 696	52
D.K.I. Jakarta	1 118	467	42
West Java	15 695	5 071	32
Central Java	21 871	4 214	19
D.I. Yogyakarta	1 885	238	13
East Java	18 524	4 866	26
Bali	646	-	0
West Nusa Tenggara	3 306	1 091	33
East Nusa Tenggara	1 219	-	0
East Timor	NA	NA	NA
West Kalimantan	2 319	1 046	45
Central Kalimantan	959	141	15
South Kalimantan	1 517	778	51
East Kalimantan	1 267	281	22
North Sulawesi	2 254	858	38
Central Sulawesi	1 506	56	4
South Sulawesi	5 898	1 366	23
Southeast Sulawesi	1 939	287	15
Maluku	876	204	23
Irian Jaya	815	-	0
All Indonesia	102 767	28 572	28

Source: Based on data collected from the Ministry of Health, Government of Indonesia.

make immunization accessible to every child in Indonesia and to ensure that at least 65 percent (aged 3-14 months) were fully immunized by 1990 and 80 percent by the year 2000. The GOI receives support for this programme from USAID and WHO as well as from UNICEF.

An evaluation of the programme carried out in 1982 noted that, although geographical expansion was improving, there was a disappointingly low rate of immunization-related issues such as inadequate collaboration and coordination within the MOH, low public awareness of the need for immunization and the ill-defined role of the health centre doctor who is expected to be the catalyst for local development of immunization services (GOI, BPS/UNICEF 1984).

School Health. The school health programme is seen as the main channel to reach children with basic messages on health and hygiene and to influence their attitudes toward health. By the end of REPELITA III, 90 000 primary schools and 15 000 junior and secondary schools were covered by the programme. Problems such as unclear division of responsibilities between participating departments were an initial constraint, but efforts to overcome these problems have been undertaken. The programme presently focuses on healthy living in school and health education and health care, but increased attention will be given to providing immunization to school children.

Family Planning. Indonesia's population planning and control programme has been recognized as one of the most effective in the world. This has been in part attributed to the strong political will and support from a president and Government unambiguously committed to fertility reduction as an integral part of overall national economic development. It is also widely acknowledged that USAID, with its technical and financial support, has been a major force in the programme's success to date.

Before REPELITA I, family planning was entirely a private sector activity. Since the formation of the BKKBN in 1970, more than 6 000 family planning service outlets in *puskesmas* and hospitals have been established. In addition, a network of 51 000 Village Contraceptive Distribution Centres (VCDC) have been developed, and 10 000 family planning field workers have been trained to recruit and supply participating couples.

Population Policy in REPELITA IV. Population policy in REPELITA IV, as a part of long-range population policy, sets the objectives of reducing fertility and mortality rates, increasing life expectancy and reducing the imbalance in population distribution. The achievement of the above objectives will be closely connected with the success of other development programmes such as food and nutrition as well as health and education.

During REPELITA IV, the scope of the Family Planning Programme (FPP) was expanded and the efforts intensified to promote the social acceptance of the norm of a small, happy and prosperous family. The programme expansion was planned not only in terms of geographical coverage, to reach all religions in Indonesia, but also in terms of social strata to reach new settlement areas, transmigration areas, and other specific community groups.

Extending Family Planning Services to the Outer Islands and the Urban Poor. There has normally been a deep division between Indonesia's Java-Bali heartland and its outer periphery. With only 7 percent of the total land area, Java and Bali have more than 65 percent of the total population. The differences in population densities are immense: More than 600 people per square kilometre in Java-Bali versus 50 per square kilometre in the Outer Islands. One criticism of the FPP is that since its inception, the programme strategically concentrated on Java and Bali, and thus its successes remain limited primarily to the rural areas of these two relatively small islands with large population density. Only recently has the need to extend the programme to the Outer Islands been recognized.

A second major criticism of the FPP has been its failure to reach the country's urban areas, particularly Jakarta, whose more than 5 million people constitute over 20 percent of Indonesia's entire urban population. This problem, however, does not appear to be recognized in REPELITA IV. Unless effective means to reach the urban poor population are planned in REPELITA IV, there could be a growing family planning service gap.

Chapter 6

Policies and Interventions in Agriculture and Rural Institutions: Pattern of Past and Present

Indonesia has undoubtedly achieved its most spectacular economic success in the area of rice production. During the period 1968-85, rice production increased from about 11.7 million tonnes per year to an estimated 26.3 million tonnes, corresponding to a growth rate of about 5 percent per year. Indonesia has made the transition from a country with chronic food deficits and large dependence on rice imports, to a nation in which self-sufficiency - and even a surplus - can be expected in normal years. In 1985, there were large rice surpluses for which there was not enough storage room.

At the aggregate level, the role of agriculture in the socio-economic development of Indonesia was analysed in Chapter 3. It was seen that agriculture has made important contributions toward alleviating poverty, ensuring food security and evening the balance of payments. The past contribution of that sector to employment is becoming increasingly more difficult; Java has already reached the turning point with the absolute size of the agricultural labour force declining (see Chapter 4). The sub-sectoral performance is described in Chapter 3.

In this chapter we review the pattern of planning, policies and interventions as well as rural institutions affecting agriculture. This review is divided into four main sections: (1) the planning process, macro-economic and agricultural policies and programmes; (2) government organizational instruments; (3) non-governmental development organizations; and (4) conclusion.

The Planning Process, Macro-economic and Agricultural Policies and Programmes

Development Plans, Performance and the Planning Process

Agricultural development has been a dominant force in each of Indonesia's five-year development plans. The primary aim of the first four REPELITAs was to increase food production, especially of rice, in which it was expected that the country would become self-sufficient. The stated main purposes of agricultural development were: (1) to increase per capita income; (2) to increase employment opportunities in both new and existing fields; and (3) to increase the equality of income distribution, among regions and among socio-economic groups in the population (REPELITA II, Book II, p. 33, quoted in Wiradi 1978, p. 2).

During the PELITA I (1969-73) period, the GOI introduced new high-yielding rice varieties on a large scale. (Note that PELITA indicates the planning period; REPELITA is the five-year plan.) The aim of increasing rice production was implemented through the BIMAS programme. As HYVs need large inputs of fertilizer and insecticide, as well as the proper and timely availability of water, the GOI had to provide these inputs as cheaply and efficiently as possible. The programme was successful right from the beginning - rice production started to increase rapidly. During this period, agricultural institutions and agrarian relationships underwent drastic changes. Owners of *sawah* land benefited from the Green Revolution, which led to a concentration of land ownership. In villages, larger and middle landowners reinforced their position *vis-à-vis* the smaller farmers and landless households. A decline in labour use, the closure of access to employment and the beginning of mechanization led to some displacement of rural labourers. Rural development tended to reinforce the existing inegalitarian social structure in the countryside.

In PELITA II (1974-78) two periods can be distinguished. During the first four years, from 1974 to 1977, production was levelling off. There was no production increase, due to a new plant disease affecting the HYVs, the *wereng* or brown plant hopper (*Nilaparata lugens*) and an extended period of drought. The last year of that plan, 1978-79, brought the start of the take-off. New varieties (IR36 and IR38) were introduced that were resistant to the *wereng* disease. Landless labourers faced a reduced demand for labour, and their position deteriorated initially. Rural development stagnated or diminished (Collier et al. 1982).

PELITA III (1979-83) witnessed a substantial acceleration in rice production. The new HYVs spread. Harvests were hit again by an extended drought in 1982-83, but in 1984 and 1985 production went up again. The shorter maturing period of the new HYVs allowed for an increase in the number of crops per year and provided more employment per year in rice cultivation per hectare because of the much higher annual yields per hectare. But employment per unit of output fell and the overall impact on employment appears to have remained steady - if not negative, as discussed in Chapter 4. As off-farm employment increased, some areas in Java experienced seasonal labour shortages at the same time. Rural development accelerated and the poorer strata were able to participate in the advance (Collier et al. 1982, p. 86). All socio-economic groups (including the landless agricultural workers) were better off in 1980 than they had been in 1970, as discussed in Chapter 4.

The first two years of PELITA IV (1984-1987) saw the realization of rice self-sufficiency. Planning officials in Indonesia consider this a turning point. Although there is still room for production growth in agriculture, the sector shows signs of levelling off, in terms of both production and labour absorption. It appears that it is time for moving relative emphasis away from rice toward secondary food and tree crops and a shift toward non-agricultural activities (i.e., to small-scale off-farm employment and to large-scale manufacturing).

The overall planning process in Indonesia is still highly centralized. BAPPENAS, which is the apex of policy making and national planning, is complemented at the provincial level by the various BAPPEDAs. (See for a useful summary of the planning system in Indonesia, FAO: *Toward Improved Multi-Level Planning for Agricultural and Rural Development in Asia and the Pacific*, Economic and Social Development paper 52, Rome, 1985, upon which this section draws.) In 1982, the GOI initiated another planning institution - called BAPPEDA II - at the district level, which is still evolving. BAPPEDAs, at the present time, have two weaknesses: (1) a lack of technical expertise and (2) a lack of adequate authority and control over the operation of ministries and departments at the subnational level. Within its own budget, BAPPEDA can select projects but it does not, typically, undertake any comprehensive assessment of total resource allocation at the regional level.

Funding of development projects comes from three main sources: (1) the national development budget, which is channelled through central line agencies; (2) the provincial development budget, which is allocated directly to the provinces with BAPPEDA as the body responsible for planning and programming; and, finally, (3) presidential grants (INPRES), which go directly to various levels, but mainly villages, as a stimulus to development. INPRES projects have been discussed briefly in Chapter 2, where it was shown that they serve as a major provider of basic social services and added income opportunities to low-income groups on the periphery. Although it is encouraging to note that the regional development outlays are currently the only category in which funds have been significantly increased within the present budget (from Rp 850 billion to Rp 939 billion - or from 7.8 to 11.3 percent of total development expenditures), their relative importance compared to projects in the national development budget is still quite low.

It is apparent that in spite of the stated intention to decentralize authority, the central Government continues to exercise much control over lower-level administrations. Investment programmes and projects at almost every regional and subregional level tend to be designed and selected by central ministries even though they have to be implemented at the local level.

There appears to be a growing consensus that the decentralization of the planning process needs to be pushed further if some of the envisaged reforms toward food production and consumption diversification and increased crop production in the Outer Islands are to succeed. The provincial BAPPEDAs must be given greater authority and technical competence to design and carry out regional development plans consistent with the overall national development plan (i.e., REPELITA) formulated by BAPPENAS. These issues are discussed in more detail in Chapter 8, where some recommendations are presented.

Macro-economic and Agricultural Policies and Programmes

Success in a number of agricultural sub-sectors can be attributed to GOI policies, both at the macro-economic and the micro-economic and sectoral levels. Glassburner (1985) has put forward the hypothesis that macro-economic policy lies at the base of the successful management of agriculture, as it has provided a favourable environment that enabled the implementation of sectoral policies, such as the BIMAS programme, the credit and fertilizer programmes and the rural extension service programme.

Glassburner points to two broad fields of macro-economic policy: monetary policy and the trade regime, the exchange rate policy and the intersectoral terms of trade. Indonesian monetary policy since the late

1960s has effectively combated the inflation problem, an inheritance from the Sukarno government. The GOI managed to bring inflation rates down from their extremely high levels in the early and mid-1960s and was able to maintain moderate inflation rates throughout the 1970s and early 1980s. Inflation has fluctuated between 3 percent and 47 percent per year, remaining most of the time at the level of 10-20 percent.

Interest rates in the formal banking sector were controlled by the Central Bank (BI), and, until the banking reforms of 1983, kept at relatively low levels after 1972. Credit was made available to farmers in the food sector at nominal interest rates (about 12 percent per year). With the decline of oil prices, the banking reforms of 1983 put an end to the low interest rate policy; interest rates rose to the more realistic level of 18-22 percent per year. As inflation went down during that period, the real interest rate went up substantially, with the result that in 1984 and 1985 deposits in banks increased sharply (Glassburner 1985).

Macro-economic policy in the field of trade and exchange rate policy has been instrumental in contributing to the sustained growth of agricultural exports. Many forms of overt export taxation were eliminated in the 1970s, though there have been periodic bans on exports of copra, coconut oil, logs and palm oil. On the import side, a number of important agricultural commodities have been substantially protected from international competition. In 1981, fairly high rates of effective protection could be observed for dairy products, fruits and vegetables, maize, soyabeans and peanuts, while cassava, palm oil and coconut oil were "anti-protected" (Glassburner 1985, p. 69).

Macro-economic policies provided the overall conducive setting for the successful implementation of a number of sectoral policies. In the remainder of this section a number of sectoral programmes and policies will be discussed briefly.

From 1969 to 1983 there has been a large extension of the irrigated area. A great deal of rehabilitation and expansion of existing irrigated systems has taken place. In the late 1960s, irrigation systems dating from the colonial period had lost much of their capacity as a result of the silting up of reservoirs and canals and the lack of maintenance of sluices, dams, and watergates. Rehabilitation was a first priority. With financial and technical assistance from the World Bank and other international agencies, several rehabilitation works were carried out. In addition, irrigation systems have been developed in swamp and tidal land. During each of the first three REPELITAs, the expenditures for irrigation development have gone up.

The improvement has been substantial. The share of total area irrigated rose from 64 to 72 percent during the period 1972-81, and the share of rehabilitated area rose from 4 to 21 percent (Dapice 1985, p. 14-5). The agricultural census of 1963 reported an irrigated area of 2.4 million ha; the 1983 agricultural census reported 7.9 million ha.

Although many large irrigation projects have been carried out, huge problems remain with the tertiary and smaller channels needed to bring water to the fields. The construction and maintenance of these systems is not only a technical problem but also a social one, as groups of farmers have to be mobilized to take responsibility for their maintenance. These farmers have to be organised on the basis of an irrigation zone, which turns out to be a difficult social problem as group and community formation in Java is based on the administrative unit, the *desa* and *dukuh*. Javanese farmers have never developed the type of water management organisations known, for instance, in Bali (*subak*). With the traditionally strong emphasis on the *desa* organization, the development of water management groups is sociologically a difficult problem. Improvement of these networks would, however, result in higher rice yields. Another major advantage of the rehabilitation of tertiary irrigation systems is that it is highly labour intensive.

The use of fertilizer in Indonesia has increased substantially. As shown in Table 6.1, in 1960 only 119 000 nutrient tonnes were used in the whole country; in 1981 it was estimated that the total amount of fertilizer used on food crops was 1 043 000 nutrient tonnes. The use of fertilizer per hectare has increased from 19 nutrient kg in 1960, to 127 kg in 1981 (Dapice 1985, p. 12). One of the main reasons for the increased demand for fertilizer was the steady decline in price during the period from 1968 until the early 1980s, especially during the late 1970s. There was no government monopoly and fertilizer was sold both through government and KUD channels, and through the private sector.

The real price of rice stayed the same from the early 1970s until the early 1980s, but the real price of fertilizer was halved during the same period. This means that it has become increasingly profitable for farmers to use fertilizer. The GOI has continued to subsidize fertilizer, keeping its retail price at about half the level of the world market price, even though this is an increasingly costly strategy, requiring a total expenditure of US $369 million in 1982 and about US $700 million in 1985. Subsequently, fertilizer subsidies were eliminated, as part of the package of adjustment measures.

Table 6.1: Use of Fertilizer on Food Crops, 1960-81 (In Thousands of Nutrient Tonnes)

Crop Year	Nitrogen	Potassium	Irrigated Rice Area Harvested, in Millions of Hectares	Use per Hectare (kg/ha)
1960	95	24	6.4	19
1970	157	34	6.5	28
1975	311	110	7.3	58
1980	731	263	7.8	127
1981	861	182	8.2	127

Source: Dapice (1985).

The GOI has controlled food prices during most of the period since the late 1960s. The government institution charged with this task is BULOG. In the 1960s, BULOG was a small rice agency mainly concerned with urban rice supplies. During the 1970s it grew into a multistaple national food organization (Dapice 1985, p. 20). BULOG buys rice from farmers, at a floor price, via the network of KUD, and also from private traders. It has built up a huge storage capacity all over the country, and maintains an extensive transportation system. In urban markets a ceiling price is maintained.

Of crucial importance has been the timely introduction of new seeds of HYVs in Indonesia. In the late 1960s and early 1970s the HYVs IR5 and IR8 were introduced. In the mid-1970s, however, these varieties were attacked by severe pest infestations and production remained stagnant for a couple of years. In 1977, the HYVs IR36 and IR38 were introduced, which were pest resistant, fast maturing, and fertilizer responsive. The rapid spread of these varieties in rice-growing areas brought about a new breakthrough in production, with increasing harvests, resulting in the achievement of self-sufficiency in 1985.

The spread of knowledge concerning new rice cultivation techniques has been an important factor. The MOA has a large extension service mainly working on the BIMAS rice programme. In 1985 this extension service covered only 13 provinces out of 26.

The BIMAS programme started as a pilot project in 1963, with university students demonstrating to farmers the use of fertilizer and of better cultivation methods. The programme turned into a nationwide campaign in 1967 and the GOI institutionalized it in 1969, harnessing it in the new government policy of modernizing the rice sector. The BIMAS programme provided farmers with a package of services that included seeds of HYVs, operating credit, guidance from extension workers, and fertilizer and pesticides at subsidized prices. The credit was provided by the local branches of Bank Rakyat Indonesia (BRI), that had been established in every *kecamatan* town, to handle credit for farmers participating in the programme. The extension services were provided by extension workers of the MOA. The *lurah*, (village head) was brought to exert pressure on the farmers to shift to the new rice technology. The whole BIMAS programme was under the authority of the Ministry of Home Affairs, rather than under the Ministry of Agriculture (Hardjono 1983, p. 50).

A second programme, known as INMAS (mass intensification), was introduced in 1973. Under this programme, the packages of services - with the exception of the operating credit - were provided to the farmers. This programme was intended to provide services to farmers who were in arrears on BIMAS repayments and were no longer acceptable as borrowers to BRI. In the second half of the 1970s, when fertilizer prices had gone down substantially, there was very little incentive for farmers to join the INMAS programme, as there was no credit available. Both the BIMAS and INMAS programmes saw their scope decrease in the course of the 1970s. While the number of participants had reached 3.6 million farming households in 1973-74, the number dropped to about 2 million in 1978-79 and to about 1 million in 1981-82. A large amount of the credit extended to farmers was never repaid. In 1984, the credit programme of BIMAS was abolished, but the extension activities continue.

In 1979, the GOI introduced a third programme, called INSUS. The basis of INSUS is group farming rather than individual farming. The programme grew out of the need to coordinate rice planting around the village in order to reduce pest damage, especially that caused by the *wereng*. It had been observed that *wereng* damage tended to be greatest where the insects could concentrate and attack one rice field after the other as crops ripened successively. The solution was to form farmers into groups who could plant an extensive area at more or less the same time (Dick 1982, p. 29). Under the INSUS programme, a large area - usually about 50 ha - is selected for intensification and all farmers owning land within that area are obliged to participate. As an incentive, the GOI buys rice from INSUS groups at a higher price than the current BIMAS floor price. In the early 1980s, INSUS groups obtained larger average yields than BIMAS farmers. But that can be attributed to the fact that *kecamatan* officials chose the best areas of rice land for the INSUS programme, with fertile soils, good irrigation and good drainage (Hardjono 1983, p. 51).

Until very recently Indonesia's agricultural policies focused on the fertile lowlands and toward rice production. Uplands and highlands received much less government attention. There has been a set of programmes, starting in 1969, which concentrated on tree crop development. The GOI has made large funds available for the rehabilitation of old estates and small holdings on which tree crops were grown, such as rubber, tea, coconuts and teak. The GOI has implemented tree crop development through various development schemes, such as the NES, the PMU and self-help schemes, which will be discussed later in this chapter. In implementing these schemes, various domestic and foreign fund sources, including the World Bank, have been tapped.

As indicated in Chapter 3, upland food production has been relatively neglected. The main agricultural programmes for the lowland, such as irrigation construction, agricultural research, the introduction of HYVs, cheap credit programmes, extension service and road-building, were not extended to the uplands. The consequence of this policy is visible in the record of production figures for upland crops, such as maize, cassava, potatoes, soyabeans and vegetables, which show some increase between 1969 and 1985, but by no means as spectacular as that of rice.

Governmental Organizational Instruments

Organizations for Horizontal and Vertical Integration of Small-scale Producers and Large-scale Enterprises

For a number of years the GOI has been trying to form production organizations based on the principle of horizontal and vertical integration, by tying small-scale producers, called the "plasma", to higher-level large-scale enterprises, called "nucleus". These systems of organization are known as NES.

The integration is horizontal in the sense that very different producers of the same product are grouped together in one unit. The underlying philosophy is that the plasma can benefit from economies of scale enjoyed by the nucleus (estate) in regard to inputs and extension of services and in processing and marketing the product. The principle of vertical integration can be recognized in various fields of the Indonesian economy, and is presently promoted as an organizational model, in accordance with the basic principles of the *Pancasila* and the Constitution. The combination of horizontal and vertical integration is the basis of new organizational structures introduced in the tree crop sector since the mid-1970s, known as the NES/PIR schemes, in which smallholders are linked to plantations. The principle has recently been recommended in various other fields, such as shrimp, fish, poultry, egg and dairy production, and can be recognized in various forms of contract growing in agriculture. It plays an important role in the cooperative system, where hierarchical structures have been developed between farmers, the KUD and higher level "cores", through which inputs flow downward and outputs upward.

Another programme to promote vertical integration is the *bapak angkat* (foster father) system, established by the MOI, under which larger industrial enterprises, especially assemblers and buyers of components, are encouraged to support small producers through subcontract mechanisms. There are a few designated *bapak angkat* industries in Indonesia, which have subcontracted with small producers to supply component parts. The small producers operate with low-level technology, and are given little technical assistance.

The GOI has declared the NES to be the principal institutional approach to the development of smallholder production in an effort to rationalize production and to increase employment. The nucleus can provide superior technology and managerial capabilities to the small-scale producers. Processing facilities and marketing channels are expected to help smallholders as well.

Integration structures can take various institutional forms. The nucleus can be a state enterprise, a private company or a cooperative owned by the producers. There are also different alternative arrangements possible between nucleus and plasma regarding the provision of inputs, credit and repayment schemes, and the degree to which the producers are obliged to sell their products to the nucleus.

In the existing literature on this subject, the acronyms NES and PIR are used more or less as synonyms. However, PIR has a somewhat wider meaning, reflecting the recent government strategy of applying the principle of vertical integration, via the "nucleus-plasma" model, to other economic fields as well.

However, reciprocal mutual benefit is not automatically guaranteed between nucleus-enterprise and small-scale producers. Their interests can diverge. The nucleus-level is bound to considerations of profit maximization, which can result in the use of price-fixing mechanisms, to the detriment of the small-scale producers. The nucleus can benefit from its near-monopolistic position in input supplying and its monopsony in output procurement. It is only in a cooperative organization, in which the smallholders own the enterprise, that this conflict of interest can perhaps be resolved. We address this issue in more detail later.

The Government uses two strategies for promoting tree crop development. The first is based on the use of PMUs. In 1970, the Government began providing support to smallholders for the rehabilitation and establishment of tree crops, under the supervision of PMUs. The Government identifies an area of geographic concentration of tree crop smallholders and then the organization of farmers is to implement the replanting programme. Assistance is given to the smallholders to obtain credit, planting materials, and agrochemicals as well as intensive extension support from the PMU. They also receive cost-of-living allowances. This approach is suited for developing existing small and scattered holdings. Currently there are about 925 PMUs in the whole country under authority of the Directorate-General of Estate Crops (DGEC).

The second strategy, the NES scheme, relies on large publicly owned estates (PTPs) to provide the managerial and technical expertise to promote and guide smallholder development. Using government funds, the PTPs clear tracts of forest land, which are to be planted with tree crops. Housing and infrastructural facilities are being set up for settlers. After a probation period during which they work as labourers, the settlers are given *hak milik* (full freehold title) to their land holdings, and they qualify for individual credit from government banks, using the land title as security. At this stage the smallholders assume full responsibility for their holdings. Smallholders are obliged to deliver their crops to the estate.

The two schemes, PMU and NES, are geared toward different social-spatial smallholder systems. The PMU scheme is suitable for far-flung smallholder farms at great distances from processing plants. As rubber and coconuts are not perishable, and consequently do not have to be processed immediately, there is no strong rationale to tie them too closely to processing plants. For this reason the PMU scheme is presently widely favoured.

The NES scheme is in principle suited for large-scale block farming in newly established settlement areas. The NES concept is not limited to public sector plantations, but is also meant to get the private sector to participate in developing activities through opening up new sites. According to a general formula under a NES scheme, 20 percent of the area constitutes the nucleus estate and 80 percent of the area is worked by smallholders.

In 1986, the GOI took steps (initiated by Presidential Instruction 1/1986) to link the Nucleus Estate and Smallholder Scheme more closely to the transmigration programme, known as PIR-TRANS. Government regulations provided for investment credits (at an annual interest rate of 16 percent) for state and private firms developing NES projects. This investment credit will also be extended to foreign investors already licensed to develop plantations under the NES scheme. However, only NES projects that are linked to transmigration programmes are entitled to the 16 percent interest investment loan, according to the ruling. The NES projects under this programme would be planted with one of the following tree crops: rubber, oil-palm, tea or cocoa. Under the last PELITA the plan was to open up 1.2 million ha of land, to be planted with plantation crops under NES schemes. This new policy reflects a general change in the transmigration programme, whose focus is gradually shifting toward a combination of food- and tree-crop cultivation.

The tree crop NES scheme is essentially a land-development programme with the intention to turn new settlers, both transmigrants and local population, into efficient cash crop smallholders. Under the NES scheme, the smallholders, in addition to the 2-3 ha for tree crops, receive 0.5-1 ha for food crops. The land for cultivating food crops should increase the farmers' income as well as their employment opportunities. This is in line with a general policy to increase the production of food crops (van der Kemp 1985a, p. 67).

The NES scheme for tree crops (rubber, coconuts) does not seem to function well, and a lot of criticism is being levelled against it. The PTPs seem to be rather dissatisfied with the schemes being imposed by the central Government. They find the smallholder sector too inefficient and too expensive, and they would prefer to work with contract labourers. The PTPs are financially not in good shape, and the GOI is presently considering the privatization of the plantation sector.

The smallholders experience difficulties in securing sufficient income, especially during the first few years. The food crop component seems to be rather unsatisfactory, with low yields due to poor soil conditions, the absence of extension service (BIMAS does not cover the tree crop regions), the lack of a market for food crops and so on (van der Kemp 1985a, p. 38).

On this ground it could be argued that the NES scheme would function better if the food crop component would be left out altogether. A counter-argument is that smallholder families' income would be reduced if the food crop land were to be excluded. Since food crop cultivation is usually done by women, the position and employment opportunities of the female population, as well as household food consumption, would probably be negatively affected by the removal of the food crop component in the programme.

Another issue relates to the optimal average size of the smallholding unit in a NES-PMU scheme. Raising the rubber smallholder's unit size from 3 to 5-6 ha might maximise the use of household labour inputs on these holdings and household income. Furthermore, abandoning the food crop component might also increase efficiency in the system. The main drawback of an enlargement in the average size of a holding is that the number of settlers (transmigrants) would accordingly be reduced, with consequent negative effects on employment and income prospects for the foregone settlers. The trade-off would be between a somewhat more efficient land allocation yielding higher employment and income levels to those smallholders fortunate to be chosen and foregone employment and income prospects for a large number of potential migrants. On the whole, the present land size can be defended as being most consistent with the equity and efficiency objectives.

Transmigration

The transmigration programme is a large-scale and ambitious scheme for land settlement and marginal land use. The term is used to indicate the voluntary movement of people from overcrowded areas in the Inner Islands to less developed areas in the Outer Islands. A distinction is made between *sponsored* migrants, who receive support from the government and move to selected sites, and *spontaneous* or *unassisted* migrants, who receive minimal government support. The Government prefers to use the term unassisted migrants to indicate that the difference between the two types is the level of support received (World Bank 1986b).

The administrative structure of the transmigration programme has undergone numerous changes over the course of time. During PELITA I, the Ministry of Transmigration (MOT) was responsible for national level activities concerning the programme. During PELITA II, transmigration became the responsibility of a directorate-general under the Ministry of Manpower, Transmigration and Cooperatives, assisted by coordinating bodies with representatives of other ministries involved in the programme. In 1978 a junior minister for transmigration was appointed, and in 1983 the directorate-general became a ministry again. The apparatus of the transmigration programme has expanded over time. In 1985 it consisted of more than 10 000 officials in the central department alone. The programme has a great deal of government funds at its disposal, and has received extensive financial support from the World Bank and other aid donors. However, in 1986 the budget for transmigration was cut sizeably and because of the adverse developments in public finances further limitations followed.

The transmigration programme has moved large numbers of people from Java to the Outer Islands. During PELITA I the numbers doubled annually, and amounted to more than 39 000 families over the whole period. During PELITA II a total of more than 44 000 families had been moved under the sponsored programme, and during PELITA III 301 000 families. If the local families and resettled families brought into the transmigration areas are added, a total of more than 365 000 families had been settled, or close to 1.5 million people (World Bank 1986b, p. xi). The REPELITA III target was 500 000 families. This has proved too ambitious and unattainable, but the programme came close to the target. Under REPELITA IV the Government originally intended to move 400 000 families under fully sponsored programmes, while another 300 000 migrant families were expected to move without assistance.

The GOI has pursued the transmigration programme to relieve the overcrowded areas in the Inner Islands, and to promote regional development in the Outer Islands. To achieve this purpose the GOI has made considerable investment in infrastructure, especially roads, irrigation and swamp reclamation.

Until the end of PELITA II, the main system, as practiced by the MOT, was to assign to each settler family 2 ha of land, consisting of 0.25 ha of house plot, 0.75 ha of dry land and 1 ha of *sawah*. The *sawah* land was usually not yet cleared and irrigated. If the settler family could not draw enough income from the dryland, its members had to look for other sources of income in the area, and they lacked the time necessary to carry out the burdensome task of clearing the *sawah* land. This meant that for the first few years the family had to cultivate food crops on the dryland. An additional problem was that the necessary agricultural inputs were usually not available in time.

For PELITA IV a gradual shift to tree crops was planned and initiated. While during PELITA III 90 percent of the migrants were settled in food crop areas, the plan for the PELITA IV envisaged settling half the number of transmigrant families on tree crop schemes.

Coordination between different government agencies remains a difficult problem. For instance, the research section of the MOA seems to have had limited influence over the choice of farm models, selection of sites and adoption of technology. The MOA favours complex farming systems, but the MOT has adhered more to the nuclear farm model and to food crop monoculture. The transmigration areas were to contribute to Indonesia's increase in rice production.

A criticism that has been made against the transmigration programme is that it has been based on a misconception about the capability of the land where farmers were settled to sustain a peasant scale of food crop production. Insufficient attention has been paid to soil capability assessments in the receiving areas.

Recently planners have experienced the need to pay more attention to soil conditions in transmigration areas. Most transmigration areas are located in dryland areas with red-yellow podzolic soils of low inherent fertility. These soils are acid and have a high aluminium toxicity. After a number of years, fertility declines to low levels. Yields of food-crop production on these soils are low, as has become clear in many of the older transmigration projects. This problem could be addressed by liming the soil, but this is a costly operation.

The main problem for the transmigration programme, as it has been carried out until very recently, is the shortage of suitable sites. There is not much land available that is suitable for agriculture. There are still areas in Sumatra, Kalimantan, Sulawesi and Irian Jaya with some agricultural potential, but they consist of soils of low fertility and that are highly susceptible to erosion. It is not advisable to introduce food cropping in these areas. As prospects for food-crop farming are limited, the World Bank recommends a shift to new settlement with tree crops (rubber, coconut), which are better suited to the low fertility soils in the Outer Islands. In addition, the World Bank advocates stronger emphasis on second-stage development of existing transmigration areas and an increase in assistance to spontaneous migrants. This change would have both institutional and per unit cost implications for the transmigration programme.

Rural Credit System

Within the financial system in Indonesia two kinds of credit markets can be distinguished: the informal and the formal. Each of these markets has two broad categories: those institutions with a social character and those with a commercial character.

In the informal credit market, a large number of interest-free transactions take place. Aside from regular borrowing and lending among relatives, neighbours and friends, there are several types of traditional institutions, organized on a voluntary basis, with the purpose of saving money and lending it to group members.

An important institution found in rural areas in Java is the *arisan*. An *arisan* consists of a group of people, more often women, numbering between 10 and 200, who meet at regular intervals and contribute a certain amount of money or goods to a common kitty, which is distributed to each member in turn (Williams and Johnston 1983, p. 69). The *arisan* is popular in Java. The original function of the *arisan* was more social than economic.

An institution with a more explicit economic purpose is the *kelompok simpan-pinjam* (savings-and-loan association), which provides loans to members at given interest rates, often in the field of specific local economic activities, such as trading or cottage industry. Interest rates are about 3-5 percent per month. This association lacks the social character and the unpredictability of the *arisan* and can be considered as a more rational credit institution (Williams and Johnston 1983, p. 69).

Rooted in the *arisan* tradition, but influenced by the modern cooperative philosophy, is the *usaha bersama*, a savings-and-loan cooperative or informal cooperative, a group formed to save money and/or to take a loan from a credit fund (often an NGO). Interest rates are usually 5 percent per month.

Commercial institutions in the informal credit markets have been declared illegal under various government laws and regulations, and it has been consistent government policy to suppress them by means of cheap government programmes with low interest rates. The informal markets still exist, although shrouded in secrecy. There are various types of commercial informal lending: merchants selling on an installment basis and charging high interest rates; moneylenders usually operating on a small scale (as their activities are illegal); contractual arrangements covering loans on the harvest (*tebasan, ijon*), or on land (*sewa, gadai*), with the tacit agreement that the debt can turn into a deed of sale in case of default.

A large number of formal credit institutions exist. In order to present a brief overview, we will discuss them in terms of organizational structure and operating procedure.

Credit programmes need an apparatus that reaches from the central headquarters down to the village level. There are presently three formal channels that have this structure:

1. The first category encompasses those institutions belonging to the banking system controlled directly by BI. These institutions include the state banks, development banks, commercial banks and

a number of foreign-owned banks. These institutions operate under close regulation by BI and the central government.

A difference between bank and non-bank financial institutions is that banks, particularly the state-owned deposit banks, are mandated to implement specific government credit programmes. Large funds from the World Bank and other international funding agencies are made available through the banking system. BI provides refinancing facilities at low interest rates and subsidies to defray the administrative costs. The non-bank institutions, such as provincial programmes, have to mobilise their own funds.

The most important bank is BRI, created in 1968 after the merger of a number of existing state-owned banks. BRI is wholly owned by the Government, and is the main source of rural credit in Indonesia. BRI operates on a decentralized branch banking basis, with its head office in Jakarta, 15 regional offices all over the country, 16 credit district offices, 287 branch offices and 3 600 unit *desa*, based in *kecamatan* towns and covering a number of villages at the local level.

BRI normally requires collateral (land, buildings, chattel mortgage) or, where assets are not available, requires the guarantee of a reputable third party, often one or more local officials.

The BRI is handling a large number of different credit programmes, such as Small-Scale Investment Credit and Permanent Working Capital Credit (KIK/KMKP), Petty Trading Credit (KCK), village general credit under the Indonesian General Cooperative Bank (BUKOPIN), and others, which will be discussed later in more detail. Until the 1983 banking reforms, credit programmes were subsidized by the Government through low interest (3-4 percent) liquidity credits from BI. This low rate allowed BRI to extend low interest credit under each of the different credit programmes (about 12 percent per annum). Since 1983 interest rates have been raised to about 22 percent.

2. A second channel is provided by the KUD, under the Ministry of Cooperatives (MOC). This system has a hierarchical structure, with centres in each of the provinces and more than 6 500 KUD at the *kecamatan* level (though not, as the name suggests, at the village level). Until recently the major credit programme administered by the KUD has been the KCK. The MOC is presently trying to build up its own credit system, using for this purpose the recently acquired Indonesian General Credit Union (KUPEDES). The system of cooperatives will be discussed in greater detail in the next section.

3. The third channel is a network of formal credit institutions in a few provinces only (Central Java, West Java and West Sumatra). These local financial institutions are not directly controlled by BI, but operate as independent units with funds from the Government. They are: the Kecamatan Credit Organization (BKK) in Central Java; the Business Bank for Village Production (BKPD), Subdistrict Credit Institution (LPK) in West Java; and the Regional Savings Institution (LPN) in West Sumatra. The BKK, LPK and LPN are connected with the Provincial Development Bank (BPD), under the Home Affairs Ministry. The BKPD is technically attached to and supervised by the BRI.

The BKK system in Central Java is incorporated into the structure of the provincial administration. The governor of Central Java presides over the programme, but operational responsibilities have been delegated to lower level officials. Administrative authority is at the *kecamatan* level. The BKK system in Central Java now operates about 500 units with 1 800 rotating posts. These units are staffed with employees from the *kecamatan* in which they operate, and may lend only to *kecamatan* residents.

The BKK credit programme has a number of features that set it apart from the main credit programmes of the banking system. The BKK programme lends without subsidy, responding to all kinds of credit requests. Loans are extended based not on a collateral basis, but on character references from local officials. Loans are generally small, but if borrowers have built up a good credit rating they can borrow larger amounts. There is personal contact between local officials and borrowers. A large percentage of borrowers are women using loans for production or for trade. Apparently the BKK programme has been doing well, with a relatively small proportion (14 percent) of unrecoverable loans. The BKK programme and other provincial level programmes have received a great deal of aid and technical support from USAID.

Following are some of the main current credit schemes:

From 1964 until 1984, the GOI extended rural credit to rice farmers through the BIMAS/INMAS programme, set up to increase rice production by providing farmers with cheap (subsidized) farm inputs such as fertilizer, HYV seeds and pesticides. The BIMAS/INMAS programme - through the extension service of the MOA - also provided technical advice and expertise to the farmers. The credit programme was terminated in 1984, but the extension work is being continued.

The BIMAS/INMAS programme was said to have the worst repayment rates of all the Indonesian credit programmes. In the early 1980s, over 60 percent of its total outstanding loans were thought to be unrecoverable, partly as a result of harvest failure due to droughts and plant diseases, but also because farmers felt this credit programme was a government handout, and loans did not need to be repaid. The defaults led the Government to abolish the BIMAS programme and to institute a new one, the KUPEDES, launched in 1984. The Village Banking Units (Bank Unit *Desa*) of BRI were transferred from the BIMAS programme to KUPEDES.

As the new banking regulations of 1983 eliminated most subsidies to government banks and freed them from BI control, BRI and the Village Banking Units generalized their lending practices, making working capital and investment capital available for virtually any kind of enterprise in rural areas. The BRI also charged higher interest rates than before. Funds for rural small and medium loan programmes (*Kredit Mini* and *Kredit Midi*) were shifted to KUPEDES (Glassburner 1986, p. 30).

The rationalization of interest rates stimulated savings in the rural areas and the Village Banking Units eagerly began mobilizing savings. By August 1985 the BRI Village Banking Units had accumulated savings accounts totalling Rp 95 billion, enough to finance 20 percent of total outstanding loans (Glassburner 1986, p. 30).

The KIK/KMKP scheme was first introduced in 1973 to provide medium-term credits for investment (KIK) and permanent working capital (KMKP) to small enterprises in all sectors of the economy. The objectives of the programme are: the creation of employment, geographic dispersion of investment; development of specific agricultural sectors, such as cloves, cattle fattening, fisheries, tobacco, poultry.

The distribution of KIK/KMKP credits according to economic sectors reveals that about 50 percent of the funds have been channelled into services (trade and transport), while 30 percent went to agriculture and 10 percent to industry. Small traders received the largest portion of KMKP, while transportation enterprises received large funding from KIK.

The KCK was started in 1976 to provide credit to small indigenous traders in the rural areas in order to free them from local usurers. Funds coming from central government budgetary sources are transferred to the MOC, which then channels them through BRI to the cooperatives (BUUD (Village Unit Enterprise Organization)/KUD).

An interesting question is to what extent these credit programmes are reaching the poorer strata in society. Some indication is available from data of the agricultural census of 1983, which reflect the situation in the early 1980s. The data show that in the early 1980s, 16.7 percent of agricultural households had received credit from BIMAS, KIK, KMKP or from other programmes, and therefore that 83.2 percent had not received any credit at all (see Table 6.2).

Table 6.3 reveals that of the total number of households that received BIMAS credit, 36 percent owned less than 0.5 ha, and 64 percent 0.5 ha and more. Because about 45-48 percent of farm households controlled or operated farms of less than 0.5 ha, this means that these households had relatively less access to BIMAS and other credit.

To what extent does the new KUPEDES programme serve agriculture? In contrast to the BIMAS programme, KUPEDES makes credit available to merchants, small-scale industries and builders as well as farmers. The lending distribution over the period March 1984-November 1985 shows that trade loans were the largest category, both by number of loans and by value of total lending - 72 percent. Agriculture received only 23 percent, industry and other types of lending absorbed only 5 percent of the total (Glassburner 1986, p. 31).

To what extent do women benefit from the government credit system? As we have seen, most of the credit goes to traders, many of whom are women. However, this does not mean that women receive most of the credit. The trade sector encompasses a great variety of activities and it has been pointed out by researchers (cf. White 1986a, pp. 56-57) that it has a stratified structure. The larger trading operations, requiring larger capital outlays, are increasingly dominated by men. Women are relegated to small-scale operations in the local setting. It is true that government credit programmes, such as the KCK, have benefited small traders, including women. However, it has not reversed the trend toward polarization among rural traders. Credit programmes with a much stronger focus on women traders would have to be designed to counterbalance this trend.

Credit programmes designed for the poor sometimes require the formation of joint liability groups among borrowers. The purpose of organizing people into small groups is to increase the probability of repayment in cases where borrowers cannot submit collateral for their loan. The joint liability group is supposed to substitute for the collateral, with each of the group members responsible for the other members' loans. If one of the members were unable to pay his or her debt, the other members would probably default and the group would

Table 6.2: Number of Agricultural Households Receiving Credit, for the Whole of Indonesia in 1983

	Number of Households	Percentage of Total
BIMAS	1 384 328	8.2
BIMAS and KIK	9 054	0.05
BIMAS and KMKP	3 903	0.02
Other credit	1 416 576	8.4
Does not know	14 281	0.08
Does not receive credit	13 991 660	83.2
Total number of agricultural households	16 819 802	100

Source: Government of Indonesia, Biro Pusat Statistik (1983a).

Table 6.3: BIMAS and KIK Credit Received by Agricultural Households in 1983, According to Landownership Category

	BIMAS	Percentage	BIMAS and KIK	Percentage
Less than 0.24	209 244	(15)	1 246	(14)
0.25 - 0.49	296 829	(21)	1 755	(19)
0.50 - 0.74	235 813	(17)	1 517	(17)
0.75 - 0.99	138 470	(10)	585	(6)
1.00 - 1.49	203 625	(15)	1 063	(12)
1.50 - 1.99	100 318	(7)	634	(7)
2.00 - 4.99	171 561	(12)	1 812	(20)
5.00 - 9.99	23 896	(2)	417	(4)
Greater than 10.00	4 572	(1)	25	(1)
Total	1 384 328	(100)	9 054	(100)

Source: Government of Indonesia, Biro Pusat Statistik (1983a).

disintegrate. Another objection to making group membership a requirement for securing a loan is that it gives group leaders a chance to levy an entrance fee on prospective group members. Finally, the strategy of forming joint liability groups of poor borrowers could discriminate between better-off and poor people at the village level, and is therefore doubtful on social and moral grounds.

Nevertheless there is a strong case for establishing joint liability groups, wherein, besides credit, additional collective activities such as training and transfer of technology are included. The performance of joint liability groups would also be improved if technical and financial guidance and advice were provided by expert personnel from credit institutions.

Cooperatives

One of the goals that the GOI has pursued over the years is the strengthening of cooperatives. The cooperative movement in Indonesia derives its ideological legitimation from a reference made in the Constitution to "cooperative principles". Also, the Indonesian national ideology *Pancasila* is interpreted as requiring cooperative organizations.

Since the late 1940s, the establishment of cooperatives has been regulated, revised and regulated again by a number of presidential decrees and instructions, laws and government regulations. Since the late 1960s the idea has been to make the cooperative movement an important instrument in the development thrust of the Government.

In 1970 the Government started to form new village organizations, known as BUUD, charged with the task of handling rice processing, marketing and the distribution of inputs. The BUUDs were harnessed to the new BIMAS programme, and were instructed to purchase rice from the farmers at low prices. This policy made farmers lose their confidence in the programme, which was more geared to the needs of urban consumers than to their own interests (Hardjono 1983, pp. 52-53).

Subsequently the Government started to establish and sponsor KUDs, which were officially recognized (i.e., legally incorporated) and entitled to receive government assistance. Since 1978 the KUDs have been located at the *kecamatan* level, so that their size is economically justifiable. Cooperatives serving only one village are considered too small. About 6 500 KUDs had formed by the mid-1980s, which means an average of two KUDs per *kecamatan*, each of them supposed to cover 4-6 villages. Table 6.4 presents the development of cooperatives in Indonesia over the 1968-84 period.

The primary function of the BUUD/KUD is to provide credit and agricultural inputs to the farmers and to collect the rice at harvest time. Rice purchasing was to take place on behalf of BULOG. By the late 1970s KUDs collected more than 50 percent of the total national rice production. The amount of credit channelled to KUDs increased over the years as did the sale of fertilizers and insecticides. In 1980 BULOG gave KUDs an increased role in the processing and storing of rice. For this purpose, KUD rice mills have been established with

Table 6.4: Development of Cooperatives in Indonesia, 1968-84

	1968	1973	1978	1983	1984
Cooperatives (Number)	9 339	19 975	17 430	24 791	26 179
Non-KUD	9 339	17 614	12 986	18 464	19 660
KUD	-	2 361	4 444	6 327	6 579
Members	1 509	2 972	7 610	13 612	16 404
Non-KUD	1 509	513	4 494	4 073	4 395
KUD	-	2 459	3 116	9 539	12 009
Savings (Million Rp)	259.9	6 797.5	20 074.2	124 991.0	131 958.5
Average number of members per cooperative					
All coop	161	148	436	549	626
Non-KUD	161	29	346	220	839
KUD	-	934	701	1 507	1 825
Average savings per cooperative (Million Rp)	0.02	0.34	1.15	5.04	5.04

Source: Rahardjo (1986).

mechanized dryers, drying floors and rice and fertilizer warehouses (Warr 1980, p. 11).

In the early 1980s the objective was to transform KUDs into cooperatives in order to handle all economic activities and needs in rural areas. KUDs were supposed to maintain the floor prices for maize, soyabeans, peanuts, mung beans and cloves. Since 1982 they have extended their activities to handle distribution of nine basic commodities (Hardjono 1983, p. 53). KUDs also administer one credit programme: the KCK.

On the other hand, the distribution of fertilizer has partly been moved from the KUDs to the private sector. The government-owned PT Pusri has a monopoly of the fertilizer trade down to district level. Prior to 1976 the distribution of fertilizer at lower levels was in the hands of the KUDs; since then it has been extended to the private sector but without credit. The private sector sells fertilizer for cash at less than the KUD floor price (Warr 1980, p. 11).

The official cooperatives are conceived of as economically viable, self-reliant organizations, which constitute not only a horizontally linked network, but are also vertically tied to a hierarchical organization. In the mid-1980s, the 6 500 KUDs were aggregated in 27 provincial centres (PUSKUD), each with an adjoining service center. The apex organization at the national level is INKUD (KUD Core). In 1982, an academic institution - the Indonesian Institute for Cooperative Management (IKOPIN), located in Sumedang, West Java - was established, specializing in cooperative affairs. The Institute offers courses in management, accounting, computer science, statistics and other topics relevant to prospective cooperative managers. In 1983, the Government set up a special MOC and made funds available for the cooperative system.

Although the KUDs are receiving all the official attention from the Government, it should be pointed out that they represent only one of the three types of cooperative in Indonesia:

(a) The BUUD/KUDs, established by the Government, which are recognized by the MOC and have acquired legal status.

(b) Cooperatives that comply with legal requirements concerning structure and organization, but have not yet acquired legal status and are indicated as *non-KUD*.

(c) Organizations that carry out activities in the socio-economic field, but do not have a cooperative identity or structure. These organizations are referred to as *kelompok usaha bersama*, joint effort groups (in the literature sometimes called "informal cooperatives"). These groups, with 10-50 members, undertake activities in saving, production, marketing, house construction, and so forth. They do not have legal status, have not been registered with the MOC, are not eligible for credit from the Government, operate on a small scale, do not maintain complete bookkeeping, do not have relationships with banks, and do not have a secretariat or office, using instead the home address of their leader or one of the members as the cooperative's address (Rahardjo 1986). These groups are sometimes affiliated with NGOs (discussed further later in this chapter).

The number of farmers who have become members of KUDs is small. Mubyarto et al. (1984, p. 11) in their analysis of the results of the Agricultural Census of 1983, have noted that out of a total of 17.1 million households engaged in food agriculture, fishery and animal husbandry, only 1.7 million households - or 10.1 percent - are members of KUD.

If one looks at households engaged in farming, stratified according to land controlled, the percentage of households for each stratum that does not join a KUD fluctuates between 85 and 97 percent. Observing figures on the regional distribution, the Yogyakarta area stands out with a high percentage of KUD members - 29 percent - probably because it was in this area that the KUDs were first established. East Java (14 percent), Central Java (10 percent) and West Java (7 percent) have much lower figures (Mubyarto et al. 1984, p. 14).

The KUD members do not receive services from their organization on an equal basis. It is reported that a relatively large number (of the total number of farming households) do not receive any service, although they are KUD members (Mubyarto et al. 1984, p. 12).

An interesting phenomenon is that it is the middle level farmers (0.50-0.99 ha) who most frequently use the services of the KUD. These services include the delivery of agricultural inputs, assistance during farming and the purchase of the harvest. It is reported in the 1983 Agricultural Census that KUD members mainly make use of inputs delivery. Relatively few farmers reported selling their output to the KUDs. Apparently most of them prefer to sell to private traders.

KUD management is often in the hands of traders, small entrepreneurs and better-off farmers. The social distance between these managers, who are based in the *kecamatan* town, and the farmers in the surrounding villages, can be fairly great. This explains the relatively low participation rates reported, and also the often heard complaint that many KUDs do not function well, do not serve the needs of the people and are characterized by mismanagement and corruption.

Several rural sociologists have argued that the KUD will probably not function well as long as its working area is the whole *kecamatan*, and that the formation of smaller cooperatives at the *desa* or even at the *dukuh* level should be considered.

The first cooperative established in Indonesia, in 1896, in Purwokerto, by Patih R. Aria Atmaja, was a savings-and-loan cooperative, intended to free farmers from moneylenders. The postwar cooperative movement in Indonesia similarly emphasized self-reliance via joint efforts at savings. It is therefore natural that the present-day MOC shows a keen interest in promoting credit programmes and reinforcing the savings-and-loan activities of KUDs.

The MOC is convinced that there is room for special credit programmes to be channelled via the KUDs. Some MOC officials point out that the government credit programmes through the banking system, and especially through BRI, have directed only about 32 percent of their funds to farmers, and the rest to other rural groups. The implication is that MOC credit programmes are intended to be more directly focused on small farmers and the landless poor. However, as of now it is not clear whether much credit does reach them.

There is a wide gap between KUDs and informal cooperatives. Current government regulations have turned the KUDs into multipurpose centres that have to incorporate all economic activities with a cooperative character at the local level, that is, in the *kecamatan*. Alongside these large KUDs there seems to be sufficient space for very small-scale cooperatives, of the *usaha bersama* type (joint-effort enterprise), involving a small number of people or households. As soon as these precooperatives expand and become *kecamatan*-level cooperatives, covering a certain field (e.g. trade in certain agrarian products), the KUD feels compelled to integrate them within its own structure. Government regulations do not allow specialized, single-purpose cooperatives to continue to operate at that level; they have to join the multipurpose KUDs. However, by doing so, the single-purpose cooperatives lose their autonomy and self-reliant character, and come under the control of KUD. To prevent this from happening, many non-KUD cooperatives attempt to avoid the name "cooperative" altogether (cf. White 1986a, pp. 80-82).

The MOC has entered into an arrangement with BUKOPIN, a bank that was established in 1970 by 12 national-level cooperatives and which now has a membership of 44 cooperatives, among which one finds the Cooperative Centres of the MOC and some non-KUD cooperatives. This increase in membership has reinforced the financial position of BUKOPIN. The head office is located in Jakarta; there are nine regional branch offices and a number of others will be established in order to cover all the 27 provinces. The MOC intends to strengthen BUKOPIN, and has called upon Bank Duta Ekonomi to assist BUKOPIN'S management in carrying out a rationalization and expansion programme. BUKOPIN is a small bank, and does not yet cover the whole of Indonesia. This prevents it from servicing the existing system of KUDs.

It is clear, however, that the MOC intends to build up a vertical organization reaching down to the village level to serve as a delivery system for credit, a marketing channel for agricultural products and a distribution system for consumption goods, all this in the name of the cooperative spirit sanctioned by the Constitution.

Agricultural Extension Service

Within the MOA the three directorates-general - food crops, livestock and fisheries - have their own extension services, as does the Ministry's Agency for Agricultural Education, Training and Extension (AAETE). AAETE has the task of developing extension methodology, producing extension material and managing agricultural education in schools and providing training to the other services.

The Directorate-General of Food Crops supervises about 23 000 extension workers; Estate Crops has about 10 000; Livestock, 2 000; and Fisheries, 1 000. The food crops extension service has been closely connected with the BIMAS programme, and is responsible to the BIMAS director. The service has played a pivotal role in the dissemination of new technologies in rice production. As a consequence, the service has mainly focused on wet rice areas.

The extension service operates as follows. Each Rural Extension Centre (REC) is located in a *kecamatan* town, and serves an area comprised of several *kecamatan*. The REC staff consists of two middle-level senior extension workers (PPMs) and 10-12 field extension workers (PPLs or FEWs), while at the *kabupaten* level a number of subject matter specialists (PPSs) are available to assist the FEWs with specialized knowledge. In lowland areas one FEW serves about 3 000 farmers. In upland areas the number of farmers per FEW is much higher. It can be roughly estimated that the extension service with its network of RECs reaches about one-half of the farmers, covering mainly the lowland areas.

Some structural features of the organizational set-up should be mentioned. It is a highly centralized organization, in which the local-level field workers are bound to follow strictly the guidelines coming from the central office. Field workers are trained to pass on a standardized package to the farmers, containing technical expertise, agricultural inputs and (often) credit. This delivery system is highly commodity-specific. Another aspect of this organizational set-up is that there is a lack of coordination between the different services. Apparently, the difficult links are those between the MOA extension service and the national Regreening Programme (*Penghijauan*), which is under the directorship of several ministries, but technically reports to the Ministry of Forestry.

The MOA extension service uses the so-called training and visit (T&V) system. Under this system the field extension worker visits the farmers to provide information, advice and service. The extension worker forms groups of around 100 farmers operating a contiguous field area. The groups meet regularly to discuss field problems and agricultural recommendations and decisions on the implementation of innovations. The extension worker initiates contacts with the group via the contact farmers and the group leader. The FEW cannot reach all the farmers directly, and therefore has to work via the contact farmers who are early adopters, are the informal leaders in their communities, and can serve as the links between the FEW and the other farmers. The role of the FEW is usually that of motivator, facilitator, educator, group worker, promoter and institution builder. He or she delivers a package of agricultural technology (*panca usaha* or five uses), relating to five farm principles: the use of HYVs, the use of water-management, the use of fertilizers, the use of proper pest control and the use of appropriate cropping techniques.

The GOI attempts to base the formation of farmer groups under the T&V system on pre-existing socio-cultural associations in Indonesian society, such as the *gotong-royong* groups in Java, the *subak* in Bali, and the *mapalus* in Minahasa. However, the problem is that agrarian changes in the 1960s and 1970s have tended to undermine traditional communal structures at least in many parts of Java. The strategy of group formation is presently carried out in a socio-economic setting of increased inequality, pronounced social stratification and economic diversification. The harmonious village community is no longer there. Yet, it seems that the group approach has been successful in many parts of Java, notwithstanding these drawbacks.

Interpretations of the effects of the new approach are open to discussion. The T&V system, with its corollary of group farming (INSUS), was introduced in 1977 and expanded in 1978. These years also witnessed a significant increase in rice production, which continued in subsequent years. The MOA has claimed that the two phenomena were causally related. However, there is a spurious third factor, the timely introduction of new types of HYVs, which were resistant to the dreaded *wereng* disease and were short-maturing, so that in a few years the cropping intensity in rice areas went up sharply. There is no doubt that the new extension approach has played an important role in improving rice production, although not the decisive role attributed to it.

The extension service is operating within a basically stratified society, with clearly observable differences in political and economic power, interest articulation and socio-cultural attitudes between the social strata. The extension agents explicitly make use of this stratified system. In forming farmers' groups, FEWs acknowledge the presence of an upper stratum of *petani maju*, the more progressive farmers, who are responsive to the new technology, and a lower stratum of *petani biasa*, or ordinary farmers, who are often more reluctant to adopt the novelties and are to be "educated" by the better-off farmers. This is essentially a harmonistic view of the village community. Extension workers, who are by training technical people, probably do not pay much attention to the sociological aspects of the social structure in which they work. They probably do not notice differences in risk perceiving and interest articulation between the upper and the lower social strata. The extension worker prefers to visit and work via the better-off farmers with whom they are most at ease. Small and poor farmers are often neglected, and their problems, which are more typically of a financial and social nature, are not given the attention they deserve.

Institutional Support Services for Women in Rural Development and Review of Existing Programmes

Various existing programmes in Indonesia provide institutional support to help rural women, including those in the areas of family planning, health and nutrition, agricultural extension, vocational and literacy skills training and, increasingly, those related to production/income-generation activities. At the Cabinet level, two ministries - Social Affairs and State for the Role of Women - are headed by women, and both are particularly involved in the development, integration and coordination of all activities for the enhancement of the role of women in development.

Following is a discussion of various formal and non-formal organizations providing support services for women in rural development.

In 1978 an Associate Ministry for the Role of Women was established, a post elevated to full ministry status in 1983. This change in status has some implications on its functions as well as its personnel and budgets. The primary functions of the ministry include: (1) preparing and planning the formulation of government policies pertaining to the enhancement of the role of women in all fields of development; (2) coordinating all activities in order to achieve a cooperative balanced and integrated efforts in their overall implementation; (3) coordinating the operational activities of various government institutions and agencies concerning programmes on the enhancement of the role of women; and (4) submitting reports, information and recommendations concerning the enhancement of the role of women in all fields of development (Sajogyo 1985).

Following the establishment of the office of the Ministry of State for the Role of Women, women's units and desks were established at a number of sectoral departments. At present almost every sector has a unit specifically handling women's programmes, and to see that women's issues are addressed.

Organized semi-governmental and non-governmental women's groups generally receive the full support of the central government. From the national, to the provincial, down to the *desa* level, women's organizations are gathered together under a number of umbrella organizations.

The Indonesian Women's Congress (KOWANI) was established in 1982. Through its representation in the working groups and other governmental committees, KOWANI participates in the planning and monitoring of government programmes. Its own programmes, which are complementary to and supportive of the government's, reach the community through its 55 member organizations (nationally based NGOs) and the Family Welfare Movement (PKK), or through the Provincial Women's Council (BKOW) and District Women's Council (GOW). These last two are also voluntary bodies with membership for women's organizations and groups at the provincial and district level, respectively (Muttalib 1985).

Two other types of NGOs that have been engaging in community development programmes are the Indonesian National Council for Social Welfare (DNIKS) and the Foundation for the Protection of Disabled Children (YPAC), both charity organizations; and Aisyiah Mahammadiyah, Fatayat Muslimat NU, the Islamic women's associations concerned with Muslim groups.

The Indonesian National Commission on the Status of Women (KNKWI), with its 45 members, draws membership from various GOI departments and women's organizations. It conducts surveys on women's issues at the national level and some of its recommendations have been implemented at the national and provincial levels. KNKWI has consultant status to the Government through the Ministry of State for the Role of Women (Sajogyo 1985).

Wives of civil servants and military personnel are organized into women's groups. *Dharma Wanita* with about 3 million members, is for the wives of civil servants. Sjahrir (1985) notes that *Dharma Wanita* is under the auspices of a government department, and its main function is to assist the husbands of its members in the performance of their duties. It has a similarity to the women's organizations of the 1950s in its affiliation with one social political force. *Dharma Wanita* is sheltered under the banner of GOLKAR (*golongan karya*, functional group). The difference is that the area of its movement is more restricted because of its orientation toward what is called the "nature" of women. *Dharma Pertiwi*, a similar association for wives of police and military personnel, is further subdivided by military service branch. The social hierarchy within these organizations generally corresponds to husbands' rank. Many of the groups are quite active and membership can confer high prestige in the community (Raharjo and Hull 1984).

Of these organizations, KOWANI probably exerts the greatest leadership in dealing with contemporary women's issues in Indonesia. Women in professional groups as well as various religious associations have, through their work in KOWANI, contributed significantly to helping to establish hundreds of schools, informal education courses, cooperatives and social welfare projects and presently their efforts are directed toward national development. In particular, KOWANI's role is now concentrated on the improvement of family health in rural areas, a nationwide project coordinated by the Ministry for the Role of Women. In REPELITA III a total of Rp 12 billion was allocated for the realization of the programmes of this organization.

Women's organizations in Indonesia aim mainly to improve the position of women through schooling and skill building. Also, the leaders within these organizations are usually highly educated women whose views prevail over a large segment of the population.

Concern for women in the sectoral programmes of technical ministries is concentrated basically under two programmes: the PKK and the Programme for the Improvement of Women's Social Welfare (P2W-KSS). Concentrated in the two lower ranks of villages (*rukun kampung* and *rukun tetangga*), its aims are to complement the PKK programme with additional funds and sectoral expertise.

Created in 1973 by the Ministry of Home Affairs as a non political women's movement, PKK is one of the most active and visible such organizations. Though not technically a woman's organization, PKK membership and leadership are predominantly female. PKK members are village-*kampung* adult females. The wife of the governor (or the *bupati* at the district level) is ex officio head of the PKK at the provincial level. The role of members is to motivate and mobilize women to participate in women's programmes at all levels, from the province to the village. Indonesian cultural values still hold firmly that the family is the foundation of society and the nation, and women are considered the pivot of family life.

Consequently the PKK programme seeks to instill in rural women the appropriate knowledge, attitudes and skills to perform this role to the best of their ability. The PKK covers ten basic segments of family life, which are inseparable and conceived as a unit, namely:

family relations
household economy
education and child guidance
household management
food and nutrition
physical and emotional security
housing
family planning
health
clothing and handicraft

PKK activities are funded from the regular budgets of national, provincial, and local-level governments. At the village level, women themselves contribute cash, kind, and time as well as some of the profits from their income-earning activities.

As noted earlier, the programme is stimulated and planned by teams usually headed by the wife of the ranking official at each level of government, to whom the team reports. At each of the administrative levels (*kabupaten, kecamatan* and *desa*), the teams select and train cadres and set up activity groups to oversee activities. Villages are ranked at three levels (*kelurahan, rukun kampung* and *rukun tetangga,* according to their level of development) and PKK activities are tailored to these rankings. Even though the programme is primarily directed at women, the entire village structure is expected to support and assist the PKK.

In spite of the broad scope listed under the described PKK programmes and activities, it is worth noting that food and nutrition and particularly family planning are receiving the most attention in this programme. Indeed the encouraging record of Indonesia's Family Planning Programme (FPP) is partly due to the PKK. It is noted that the FPP owes a great deal of its recent success to the work of women holding offices as KB promoters (cadres) within the PKK, especially in the KB-APSARI (Contraceptive Acceptors/Users) subsection in urban and rural areas. In general, it is fair to say that the PKK is training female leaders at all levels of society and that those leaders have definite effects on their society's development. The PKK volunteers have also been very active in the UPGK.

The P2W-KSS Programme is the integrated programme for the improvement of women's roles on behalf of a healthy and prosperous family. This programme is very much like the PKK. However, initially, P2W-KSS activities were concentrated on motivating development. Under P2W-KSS for example, programmes of the Ministry of Labour provide women with skills in order to increase their job opportunities. In the Ministry of Education and Culture the emphasis is on non-formal education, while in the MOA the emphasis is on an intensive programme for wives of poor fishermen. The home-gardens programme is considered a nutrition programme and comes under the MOH (Sajogyo 1985).

On the basis of advice from local representatives of sectoral departments, local government agencies and the PKK team, the provincial governor selects four villages from the most deprived subdistricts in the province for a two-year programme. The families that participate in P2W-KSS programmes are selected by the village head on PKK recommendations with referrals to the Minister of Defense body, the Village Security Institution (LKMD) guidance team, and daily coordination by the local officials (*bupati, camat, lurah*) who are also assisted by teams of the PKK and the LKMD. Thus, at village level, the P2W-KSS sectoral development programmes coordinated by the State Minister for the Role of Women are funnelled through the local administration and ultimately through the village headman's wife. In an effort to maximise the results, BAPPEDA has been charged with coordination at the provincial and district level and LKMD at the subdistrict and village level (Sajogyo 1985).

There are basically four categories of P2W-KSS activities, provided in a two-year programme. (1) *Basic activities* include literacy, home-gardens, immunization, maternal and child health, and construction of latrines - all designed to help meet basic needs. (2) *Follow-up activities* include income-generation for family planning acceptors (*kelompok akseptor*) to raise family incomes. They aim to increase skills of small entrepreneurs and petty traders in the informal sector, take account of local resources and markets, and build up cooperatives. (3) *Support activities* include research and development, village environmental protection and a special course for women to understand and internalize principles of *Pancasila*. (4) *Transmigration-related activities* include programmes planned, funded, and implemented by various GOI technical agencies aimed at women in transmigration areas.

While one does not deny the role and achievements of the women's organizations, there are various areas of concern, namely, the over integration of activities aimed at women's development, and the insufficient participation of rural women in the decision-making process of programmes aimed at benefiting them. Insufficient participation of women in training and skills development is quite evident in rural areas.

If rural development is to be accelerated, institutional supportive programmes aimed at eradicating rural poverty among women must consider various issues, such as: the impact of technological change and its relative effect on women's work and earning opportunities; the relationship among education, wage rates and employment; the consequences of seasonal labour, underemployment or long hours of unpaid work; consequences of divorce (which, incidentally, is higher in rural than urban areas; Raharjo and Hull 1984); abandonment for women supporting families without the help of men; and numerous other economic-related issues crucial to the role of women in rural development. In other words, since poor rural families are more dependent on women's earnings to survive, they are also more seriously hurt by the displacement of women from earning opportunities without provision of adequate substitutes.

If the facts argued by Pudjiwati Sajogyo (1985) - that nearly 40 percent of the rural Indonesian women from landless marginal poor households are presently confronting serious problems in the areas of nutrition and health, education and employment - it seems logical to conclude that time to take action is running short with respect to improving institutional supportive services for women.

Non-governmental Development Organizations

Private voluntary and non-governmental development organizations have been active in Indonesia since the mid-1970s. Since about 1984, these organizations have increased and have expanded their field of operations. In 1986 there were about 340 NGOs in Indonesia. They are known as Community Self-Reliance Development Organizations (LPSM). Before 1980 the term NGO was more common, but because of the negative connotations of this term, and the suggestion of antagonism to the government, the name has been changed.

LPSMs attempt to promote development and to overcome poverty and backwardness by focusing on the poor strata of the population, and by trying to increase participation at the grassroots level. LPSMs are engaged in a wide range of projects and activities, such as training of community workers, providing training and education to self-reliance groups, promoting health care projects, establishing savings and credit unions, assisting in low-cost housing projects, assisting groups (*kelompok usaha bersama*, or precooperatives) that are starting small-scale enterprises. They teach management skills, bookkeeping and technical knowledge. Many of these projects are income-generating.

LPSMs base their approach on several specific principles. Firstly, they take the *felt needs* of the poor local community as their point of departure; secondly, they emphasize that the surmounting of poverty can only be carried out through the poor community itself; thirdly, they emphasize that to overcome poverty poor people have to act through a group, and not individually. The group approach is an important element; it is based on the conviction that cooperative associations are the only organizations available to small-scale producers and small-scale traders to strengthen their economic position.

In a number of respects, LSPMs differ from official government programmes. They try to break with the top-down approach still prevalent in most parts of the bureaucracy. They try to increase people's participation, devise plans and projects in interaction with the community members and focus directly on the poor instead of waiting for "trickle down" via village elites. There is, of course, a big difference between government programmes and LPSMs when it comes to financial means. Government programmes are usually well-funded, while the LPSMs have very limited funds, which they use to start activities, rather than to finance them for an extended period.

A number of the LPSMs are larger organizations, operating at the national level, maintaining their headquarters in Jakarta, or in one of the other large cities. These LPSMs often attract funds from foreign donors, which enable them to start and manage several small-scale projects in various parts of the country. Other LPSMs are smaller, often located in the smaller cities, carrying out specialized activities that are more regionalized in scope. Often the specialized and regional LPSMs are connected with national LPSMs, which provide technical and financial assistance.

In some LPSM projects the cooperative philosophy becomes blended with the NES concept. One LPSM working in a larger city is promoting a cooperative of scavengers, who are collecting plastic. This group is tied to a plastic-recycling plant, which functions as the nucleus to the scavengers who form the plasma. What is new about this project is that the scavengers' cooperative acquired a share in the enterprise, which enables the members to participate in capital saving.

LPSMs operate within the framework defined by government regulations, which impose certain constraints. Nonetheless, some sort of *modus vivendi* seems to have been found, leaving enough scope to LPSMs to continue and expand their operations.

A new phenomenon appearing since 1985-86 is the cooperation in specific regional projects, of government agencies, a LPSM, a university institute, and grass-roots organizations. The cooperating partners in this set-up take care of different components of the project, with the government agencies handling the credit and extension service, universities providing scientific and technical guidance, the LPSMs getting involved in training, education and group formation. Projects of this type are presently being started in agriculture and in small-scale industries.

Some people involved in the LPSMs consider this a movement in the making. There seems to be a change in the perception of LPSMs among government officials. In the past, top-down development programmes were made possible by abundant oil revenues. The recent decline in government income has reduced the development budget and strengthened the awareness of the need for new approaches to support development.

Conclusions

Indonesia's success in agriculture can to a large extent be attributed to pragmatic macro-economic policies, which have created a favourable environment through which farmers have access to subsidized inputs and benefit from relatively stable prices. These general macro policies have been of even greater importance than the operation of agricultural service institutions, such as the extension service, BIMAS credit, village cooperatives and the delivery of packages to the farmers.

In organizational terms, the buildup of a government intervention apparatus in agriculture during the 1970s was extensive, covering a wide variety of fields from production to marketing and support institutions.

This apparatus exhibits a remarkably strong focus on rural areas and agricultural production, and is testimony to the absence - or possibly small presence - of urban bias in GOI policies. This orientation reflects the basic thrust of the four successive REPELITAs.

The organizational structure of the intervention apparatus is not a static one, but shows a great deal of dynamism and flexibility. Government agencies are continually being changed, expanded and rearranged in accordance with shifting policy emphasis, and one may add, probably also in connection with internal political shuffles.

Different programmes are increasingly fused. The NES scheme is expanded from the tree crop area to other economic fields, and is presently applied in transmigration schemes, while the cooperative idea is to some extent merged with NES schemes.

While government agencies are generally doing their jobs well, they also display a number of limitations. It has been mentioned in the sections on credit, cooperatives and extension that these organizations are strongly focused on larger, middle-level farmers, and do not reach very poor farmers and landless labourers to a sufficient degree. The main credit institutions channel credit to traders and middle-level farmers, and only to a much lesser extent to small farmers. Similarly, the extension service approaches the farmers via the upper stratum of better-off farmers who are supposed to educate the poorer ones.

These phenomena can be better understood if we analyse the functioning of these organizations within the context of the village social structure. The sociologist Tjondronegoro outlines the analytical framework for this presentation in his study, *Social Organization and Planned Development in Rural Java* (1984). He criticizes the assumptions of a number of present development programmes. The government agencies involved view the village unit as the smallest organizational entities, which constitute the basis of development programmes. The village is conceived of as a homogeneous community, where democracy rules and traditional institutions, such as *gotong-royong* prevail. However, in reality, an upper stratum of village high-ranking officials and better-off farmers dominate village affairs, in both a political and an economic sense. This upper stratum tends to promote the interests of the upper class in the village. It captures the development programmes reaching down from the national level, implying widespread non-participation of the lower strata. Tjondronegoro advocates the promotion of subvillage initiatives in order to mobilize traditional institutions and organizations for the implementation of development programmes.

Tjondronegoro's analysis enables us to get a clearer view of the interface between government organizations and village social strata. Each of the government's organizations has its lowest unit at the *kecamatan* level. These units deal via the village elites, which automatically step forward. Formal contacts between government organizations and villagers are dominated by the upper strata of officials and richer farmers. The poor and landless only have contact with the *kecamatan* level units via their "representatives".

Specially affected are the women in poorer households. Village administrations are usually male dominated, and the *kecamatan* units are also staffed with men. Poor women experience a double exclusion from whatever takes place in the *desa-kecamatan* nexus: as hamlet-based poor people and as women. One can presume that most of the credit, extended to women-traders in this context, goes to farmers' wives, who are active as local traders. But even these women, coming from the village elite and middle groups, are no match for the bigger merchant-truckers, who are mostly men, and who employ larger amount of capital in transportation and marketing networks of a regional scope.

This means that the rural poor are not only difficult to locate in a geographical sense, they are also difficult to reach with the existing apparatus. Programmes for the rural poor require a reorientation of the existing apparatus.

Extension services face a different problem. Extension has been mainly oriented toward the lowland rice areas, applying a commodity-specific approach and delivering a standardized package to the farmers. The extension service hardly covers the upland areas. A new focus on dryland and secondary crops would require a more differentiated approach, given the huge diversity and heterogeneity of soils, and replacing the commodity specificity with location specificity. This requires drastic organizational changes in the extension service.

An important feature of government programmes is the formation of more-or-less organized groups. The government cooperative movement is building a network of cooperatives, and is reaching down to lower-level "groups", as extensions of existing KUDs, possibly down to the hamlet level. Credit systems often use the joint liability group, by which borrowers assume collective liability for loans, which may be used for a collective purpose or for a variety of individual purposes. The extension service applying the T&V approach organizes farmers into farmers' groups reached via a contact farmer. The NES scheme equally fosters the formation of farmer's groups and cooperatives.

Indonesian policy makers are thus setting great store in cooperatives as a development instrument. Observers with worldwide experience of cooperatives may express some reservations.

Firstly, in a society characterized by uneven asset and income distribution, cooperatives or groups are usually dominated by better-off people who use the organization for their own private benefit. Although cooperatives appear to be horizontal and democratic, authority relationships can exist behind this façade. The poor can still be dominated within such organizations, as the history of the cooperative movement in many parts of the world has shown.

Secondly, it seems that smaller face-to-face groups, possibly built upon existing social relationships, function better than large-scale impersonal cooperatives such as the KUDs at the *kecamatan*-level. The small-scale groups are based on a number of social ties between the members (multistranded), which mutually reinforce each other, while the large-scale KUDs are based on single-stranded economic ties between members, which do not provide much binding force.

In this connection it can also be argued that groups of the joint liability type - which banks seem to prefer - do not have much of a group character. This character can and should be reinforced by adding other activities, such as training, education, decision making, technology transfer and mutual help, for example.

Thirdly, single-purpose cooperatives are bound to be more successful than multipurpose cooperatives of the KUD type. Single-purpose cooperatives, preferably based on multistranded social ties among the members, provide them with a clearer purpose for cooperation.

Chapter 7

Opportunities for Agricultural Development

In an analytical sense, agricultural development is the result of change: changes in the amount of land used for agricultural purposes, changes in those purposes, and changes in the way those purposes are achieved. By the same token, agricultural development policies are essentially concerned with bringing about desired changes. Macro-scale agricultural goals, whether relating to aggregate sector performance or to improvements in the socio-economic status of those living on the land, can only be achieved through changes in the overall agricultural system. Predictions of how and where development can or may occur therefore pivot on identifying the scope for changes within the operating milieu, which are likely either to reflect existing trends and policies or be altered through policy actions. Accordingly, in the context of this study, we undertake in this chapter to explore the technical opportunities for agricultural growth. Our discussion is subdivided into several sections: firstly, a discussion of the technical dimensions of possible changes, as set by the physical endowment and available technology; secondly, a discussion of the conditions that will need to be fulfilled if the changes sought are to occur spontaneously or if they will be induced; thirdly, a discussion of where and how those conditions will be, or can be, fulfilled; and, fourthly, a possible development scenario for a project-defined area is presented in terms of the various steps that may be required to design a successful location-specific project.

Technical Options

The opportunities for beneficial change, in technical terms, fall into four categories:

- opportunities for expansion of the land base, that is, to bring into agricultural production land that is presently not so utilized - for example, ungrazed grasslands, swamps, primary or secondary forest - and land where shifting cultivation has left a wholly unproductive climax flora (e.g., *alang-alang*);
- opportunities for reducing the land base, that is, to take out of direct agricultural production land in "critical areas" (or of similar physical marginality), where in sectoral terms the agricultural productivity is negative because of deleterious downstream effects attributable to upstream slope denudation, and so forth;
- opportunities to alter the output mix and cropping pattern, that is, to adjust or change the systems by which existing cropped or croppable land is utilized;
- opportunities for yield increase, that is, to increase the output, or improve returns, under the existing cropping or farming systems through changes in techniques and the amounts or mixes of input factors.

The perceptions of these technical opportunities necessarily lack specificity in terms of identified locations and the nature of location-specific changes that may be feasible because the determination of these details is essentially a planning task, and outside the scope of this book. But it will, perhaps, be opportune to emphasize here the view that many of the solutions to agriculture development problems in Indonesia are likely to be highly location - and/or situation-specific - due to the complexity of the resource endowment - and to record the opinion that unwarranted assumptions on the validity of generalized solutions may well have been the undoing of many of the developmental projects attempted in the past, both before and since the nation's independence.

The opportunities to open up new land for agricultural purposes are almost exclusively in the Outer Islands; although Java has 3 million ha of designated forest land, the proportion of this where the argument would hold that agriculture makes more sense than forestry must be very small.

The data for yields from forest exploitation indicate that over large tracts of forest in the Outer Islands - literally many millions of hectares - the actual production of marketable commodities does not exceed the equivalent of one cubic meter of timber per hectare per year. This is well below the yield that could be expected from well-managed forest plantations in the same locations, and in monetary terms worth only a small fraction of the value added that could be generated if the land were developed for plantation crops such as oil-palm, rubber, coconut and, in some locations, cocoa. Soils in many of these forest areas are acrisols and would not be suitable for the production of annual food crops on a long-term basis. Utilization systems concentrating on selected perennials are, therefore, indicated. Although much of this land is not of the highest intrinsic quality, it is on a par with much of the world's areas used for the crops in question; this is also true of the climatic environment. There are thus no prima facie reasons to suppose that perennial crops on this land would be non-competitive on world markets in terms of real cost.

The foregoing observations pertaining to forest zones also apply to the worked-over areas that are now covered by scrub/*alang-alang* vegetation complexes. In this instance the economic case for "reforestation" with crop perennials is even stronger, because present productivity is even lower than that of the forest areas, and developmental costs would, in many cases, be lower.

As explained earlier, tree crops such as oil-palm and rubber are, in cropping terms, the closest biological replication of the ecologically stable primeval forest that constitutes the climax flora of the rain forest areas of Sumatra and Kalimantan. Net fertility depletion rates are often much lower than those of tillage crops, particularly in the case of rubber, because the product, latex, is essentially a hydrocarbon, the constituents of which - carbon, hydrogen and oxygen - are derived from the atmosphere. Continuous cropping under perennials is thus more attractive agronomically than annual food staples.

The latter are a more practicable option where swamplands lend themselves to reclamation. Notwithstanding the successes achieved to date with this type of development, many uncertainties persist regarding investment cost-effectiveness, relative to other developmental options. It can be expected, however, that with experience, it will become easier to identify the physical parameters defining favourable long-term prospects of cost recovery, and that investment-worthy sites that will permit settlers to earn worthwhile incomes and make significant contributions to overall foodstuff supply can be selected.

In the lower rainfall areas, such as in parts of Sulawesi and the smaller eastern islands generally where the vegetation climax is savannah or grassland, the opportunities to bring presently unused land under cropping or managed livestock enterprises are not as good. Dryland farming is likely to be relatively unprofitable because of low yields, and feasible stocking rates under ranching are likely to be too low to make management costs easily recoverable.

On Java, the demographic pressure has been such that opportunities to bring unused land under agricultural production are virtually non-existent. An argument could possibly be made, however, to convert some limited areas presently under forest to tea plantations. There are, undoubtedly, some higher precipitation areas in Java where the soils would be highly suitable for growing tea, and where the returns from that crop would be much more rewarding economically than the present montane forest cover. With adequate attention to antierosion measures, it could be expected that under tea the runoff and erosion rates would not be significantly higher than at present.

Conversion opportunities on Java - or, more correctly, conversion requirements - run more in the opposite direction: for taking land out of agricultural production. The necessity for this is discussed in Chapter 3 and need not be repeated here.

The technical remedies are easily defined in principle, but less easy to specify in terms of systems that would ensure continuity of livelihood to those people who would be affected by their application. Reforestation is an obvious technical answer, but it cannot be expected that, on a smallholder basis, even the annualized returns to forestry investment - assuming this could be financed - would replicate those of exhaustive cropping *and* provide the needed social benefits in lower watershed areas.

This difficulty would not exist, of course, if the dispossession of farmers occupying critical areas could be arranged without inflicting hardship or creating risks of adverse socio-political repercussions. Unfortunately, this option is not available in most relevant circumstances, even where the present usufructural rights subsist only on unauthorised but tolerated incursions into forest areas. Although not a sine qua non for agricultural development, some retroactive substantiation of usufructural rights of the de facto occupiers of subcritical forest land may be expedient for both political and agricultural reasons. It can be argued that no system of utilization that is both agriculturally and ecologically sound is likely to be invested in without the farmers' confidence that their position is secure and that they will in fact be able to reap a reward from the time and effort put into their holdings. It is most unlikely that erosion-minimizing systems will be voluntarily adopted in the absence of tenurial rights, and it would seem that, if only as an exercise in damage limitation, legislation to award such rights must be a priority.

In the longer term, if reforestation of critical areas is not feasible, then systems of agroforestry or silvipasture may need to be adopted. It has been convincingly argued that agroforestry is not novel to Indonesia - it has its antecedents in the traditional *talun-kebun* system, in which a multistory stand of perennials, such as coconuts, sugar palm, bamboo, fruit trees, coffee, tea, is undercropped with annual food staples. It must be noted, however, that although agroforestry offers the prospect of multiple generators of farm income - timber, tree fodder, grazing fodder and food crops - much investigatory work needs to be done before satisfactory systems, adapted to the various rainfall regimes, can be recommended for widespread adoption. Much pioneer work in modern systems of agroforestry was not specifically oriented toward providing erosion-proof systems: The objective was more often a stable ecosystem which would replace systems that were not sustainable for reasons of fertility depletion rather than soil erosion. A requirement that soil stability is also catered for adds to the complexity of the research task, and may tend to limit the economic returns obtainable. The development of satisfactory silvipasture systems has to overcome the same difficulties, and it would be misleading to suggest or imply that the required systems are already proven and available. The required research and trial efforts will inevitably take time, and while the promise is there, realization is yet some way off.

The complete spectrum of opportunities to modify cropping systems and farming systems is so broad that it cannot be examined in detail here. But, in general terms, some important options can be outlined.

Although national food security is a valid macro-economic and political goal, attempting to grow food crops where the land is marginal for this purpose - due to edaphic characteristics - but would be suitable for perennial tree crops, can be in the best long-term interest of neither the country nor the cultivator. The arguments against doing this are essentially the same as those for preferring tree crops over food crops on the acrisols and it is, indeed, these and other soils that share their agronomic potentials, that considerations could well be given to switching from food crop systems (or subsystems) to plantation crops.

Opportunities can undoubtedly be found in many places to relegate staple foods production to a subordinate position relative to more rewarding cash crops, as indicated already by the concentration in some areas of tobacco, potatoes, peppers and other vegetables, as observed in the course of field visits. Subject to collateral developments, which could provide efficient processing and/or marketing facilities, opportunities to exploit comparative advantage in this way could probably be replicated in many places. More recent initiatives in the cultivation of asparagus and mushrooms provide examples of what might be done. Detailed investigations of both technical and economic aspects of such development are, of course, essential before cultivation is actively encouraged and investments made in supportive agroprocessing and/or marketing facilities.

In those areas where labour and not land is the major constraint, as in areas of North and West Sumatra, and probably in many areas of the Outer Islands, the arguments against investment in labour-saving machinery for the purpose of extending the sizes of farms under arable cropping, cannot be effectively countered by reference to labour-displacement efforts.

We can see few persuasive reasons why, in circumstances of labour constraint, greater use should not be made of mechanical power to overcome basic tillage bottlenecks, if this can lead to greater farm and labour productivity. Although the argument - advanced in some promechanization countries - that tractorization can increase demand for labour is often not substantiated by the available evidence, there are reasons to believe that where labour constraints prevail, mechanization is likely to permit a smallholder to increase his cropped area from, say, less than 1 ha to 2 ha, with a concomitant rise in total labour requirements and in per hour returns to labour. The elimination of drudgery can also be a social objective.

Any extension of the capability to apply supplementary water to farmland offers an opportunity to change the cropping system by including additional crops within the annual sequence, and thus facilitates an increase in land productivity. An evaluation of the technical possibilities to extend irrigation facilities necessarily requires examination of all relevant hydrological data and this we have not, of course, been able to do. There would seem to be evidence, however, to support the contention that improvements in the reticulation systems and in the actual use of these systems would permit greater overall water use efficiency. But the evidence is not all one way and generalizations could be misleading.

Observation suggests that there are probably a significant number of instances where irrigation of interfluve areas could be provided by the construction of contour channels. Minor irrigation work of this type would in most cases probably require somewhat longer, and better lined, channels than it has normally been the practice to construct.

The opportunities to extend irrigation by exploiting groundwater resources can only be speculated upon in the absence of exploratory data. But, as stated earlier, there are positive indications that this is a resource that could, in the future, make a significantly greater contribution to irrigation water supply in some of the lower rainfall areas.

The options available to adjust cropping systems and farming systems to intensify annual cropping intensities, by opening up "opportunity windows" through changing cultivation techniques, by adopting cultivars with shorter maturity periods and by phased intercropping, all tend to be location - and situation-specific. Changes at the micro-level that enable productivities to be increased in this way are more a matter of the exercising of management skills - which can be taught - by the farmer rather than following set recommendations. The options vary with the size of farm; in many cases the choice depends on the more precise value of the labour/land ratio. It also needs to be noted that yield and risk penalties often attach to the quicker-maturing cultivars, so from the farmers' point of view increased cropping intensity may not always be desirable.

Considerable attention is currently focused on the prospects for increasing domestic soyabean production, in an effort to reduce the heavy foreign-exchange outlays for imports of both beans and meal. The long history of cultivation in various parts of Indonesia has prompted many to believe that the crop does well. However, as mentioned elsewhere, high yields are difficult to achieve, and seed viability is often a problem. The short-term prospects for significant horizontal expansion of the hectarage under this crop do not, generally, appear to be exceptionally good. The expansion that does take place most likely follows local evolution of new cultivation systems, as occurred in Aceh, where a switch to zero-tillage sowing after rice proved very successful, and hectarage rose from 10 000 to 40 000 between 1981 and 1984. Whether this success can be replicated elsewhere remains to be seen.

Other "system changes" sought under current policies include more extensive plantings of perennials by smallholders on their dryland areas. It must be noted, however, that most of the more popular smallholder perennials, such as coffee, cloves, vanilla, nutmeg and various fruit trees, all require deep, well-drained soils if they are to thrive, and that in many localities, soils of this type do not exist. In the course of field visits in Java, many instances were observed where small plantings of coffee and cloves were failing to do well, and local professional staff confirmed that poor drainage was the probable cause. Opportunities to diversify cropping systems in this way are thus likely to be somewhat location-specific.

As implied earlier, farm models in the Indonesian context are not completely useful. Although the models are a necessary concept for quantifying prospective project benefits, and so on, in many circumstances this represents the limit of their utility. The idea that farmers' actual working practices can be best improved by adherence to a model is at best unrealistic and at worst often counterproductive. It is not at all clear that the success of the drive for rice self-sufficiency is attributable mainly to the adoption of packages, let alone models, since more plausible explanations are available that discount the idea that the success constitutes a validation of the model approach to farm management. This is not to say that at the local level examples of successful farm operations cannot serve as useful examples of what can be done and that features of practices can serve to demonstrate how similar results can be achieved by other farmers. This, indeed, is the approach we subscribe to, but is not farm modelling.

In the fourth category of technical opportunities - to improve yields under existing systems - the best example is the very extensive area of senile rubber plantations. Yields are low not only due to senility, but also because of suboptimal tree density and the trees themselves have low producing capabilities. Clearance, and replanting with improved stocks budded with selected clonal material, could be expected to provide a tenfold increase in per-hectare latex yields in many instances, provided proper tapping routines and techniques were practiced. The adoption of the appropriate methods of farm-level processing could be expected to increase substantially the producers' income per kilogramme of latex tapped. Even after meeting the amortized investment costs, net incomes would almost certainly be many times the current levels, although to achieve this, some reallocation of time between rubber-producing and other activities (e.g., those demanding longer-term absences) might be necessary.

Similar opportunities to obtain higher yields through the use of superior genetic material also exist on a large scale in the case of coconuts. Taking the country as a whole, the substitution of hybrids or improved cultivars for the existing trees would result, over the longer term, in at least a twofold increase in total annual yield, and a corresponding benefit to the producers' incomes. At the level of the individual farm, the costs of replanting would be minimal, being limited to that of the improved planting material and the loss of income while waiting for the new plantings to bear. Where the present stands are sparse, the latter cost would not be severe because replanting could be phased, with the most senile trees being replaced first.

Coffee is another crop that could yield significant dividends if there were a progressive introduction of improved varieties. The sectoral output quality would also be enhanced if more of the crop was bulked for processing (e.g., wet processing) and grading. If small-scale installations for these operations are owned by producer cooperatives, then the net returns to producers could be expected to be greater when all processing is performed at the household level.

The experience with rice has shown the manner in which yield increases can accrue following the introduction of improved plant material and, in principle, similar benefits can be expected in the case of most other field crops. This has already occurred to a limited extent where hybrid maize has been introduced. In practice, however, two factors are likely to limit the pace at which tangible benefits actually accrue to this process: firstly, the breeding, selection and testing of new cultivars or hybrids in the differing environmental conditions is inevitably time - and resource-consuming and, secondly, higher levels of management skill are often required to exploit the greater yield potential available. Additionally, prospective higher yields may be at the expense of quality - as has largely been the case, so far, with IRRI rice varieties - or at the expense of duality of crop function, as exemplified by the currently popular cultivars of cassava, of which both the roots and leaves can be used.

Currently, much effort and resources are being expanded in Indonesia to develop and test plant materials of better genetic quality and full advantage is taken - via ad hoc linkages - with relevant work being conducted in other countries under national and international auspices. For the crops mentioned earlier in this section, improved material is available and its widespread use is mostly a matter of adoption. In the case of rice, new cultivars combining high yield with good taste quality are in the offing. But for most other crops, only marginal increases in sectoral output could ensue from the adoption of the recommended available cultivars.

A more probable source of increased land productivity would seem to be a more widespread and more efficient use of chemical inputs: fertilizers, herbicides, insecticides, fungicides and rodenticides. But a necessary condition for the economic use of these inputs is good management skills: knowing when and how to use them. The past preoccupation of the extension services with the rice crop has, by most accounts, been at the expense of acquiring expertise relevant to the *palawija* and other non-rice crops. In this area, it is also likely that progress has been handicapped by insufficient agronomic research results pertaining to the various soil/cropping system combinations. It is therefore inevitable that a considerable time must elapse before the potential benefits available from the use of these modern inputs can be fully realised.

Elimination, or at least reduction, of post-harvest storage losses is one way to increase effective output under existing systems. Data on the magnitude of the existing levels of loss are not readily available, probably because these can usually only be generated by controlled experiments. Experience in analogous conditions suggests, however, that they are likely to be quite high, possibly over 10 percent in the case of grain stored for family consumption. Several cheap techniques have been developed in recent years to minimise this type of loss, and it would seem probable that some of them could usefully be applied in Indonesia. Precisely which techniques would be best in any given circumstance would depend on the actual cause of significant losses or spoilage.

With respect to livestock husbandry, the opportunities to increase output depend on whether the returns from resources used for animal production exceed the returns from those same resources used for alternative purposes. In densely settled areas in general and on Java in particular, there are few economic incentives for a smallholder to switch land from food or cash cropping to purposive fodder production. Therefore, in at least the shorter term, livestock husbandry would seem destined to continue mainly on the basis of using crop residues and such grazing as exists on uncropped land. This does not provide the conditions where high returns are realisable from genetic upgrading. So, although steps in this direction would be worthwhile, if only to reduce the proportion of animals that are poor converters of the available feed, overall gains in production from such action are likely to be marginal. Better prospects to increase output lie in a modest expansion in the numbers of small ruminants where carrying capacity is not yet fully used, which may be the case in East Java. Increased free range stocking rates are often accompanied by higher parasite burdens, so improved veterinary attention may be necessary if good animal productivity is to be maintained.

In the less densely settled areas, the use of cattle for draught purposes can help overcome labour availability constraints. Purposive planting of fodder species, for example, setaria grass and leucaena trees are manifestly worthwhile to enable cattle to be kept available for draught work. But it remains to be shown that such plantings can provide a satisfactory basis for a livestock raising enterprise having animal production, per se, as the principal economic objective. Attempts at ranging, for example, the IBRD-supported Cattle Ranching Project in Sulawesi, also have not met with much success. In the instance cited, some improvements of rangeland grazing were achieved initially by reseeding, but sward maintenance proved difficult. It is clear that further research inputs are needed before satisfactory ranching models can be evolved. Assessment of the prospects for livestock is made more difficult at the moment by uncertainties about the significance of a recently introduced pest of leucaena, the jumping leaf louse (*Heteropsylia sp.*), which has been spreading rapidly throughout Indonesia and causing much damage.

Prospects for the livestock sector is that although in many ways the natural resource base does not lend itself to animal husbandry, some potential exists to increase output from the present low base. Realisation of that potential, however, is likely to be largely dependent on the development of more productive and reliable systems of fodder supply and improved delivery of veterinary and livestock extension services. Visions of closely integrated intensive livestock-cum-cropping systems are probably illusory; the development of silvipasture systems probably holds more promise, but much research effort is needed before widely recommendable systems are in place.

The GOI recognizes the importance of developing the livestock sector, as it is highly desirable on nutritional grounds that there should be less dependence on vegetable protein. On Java, considerable emphasis will be given to poultry, which has high feed conversion capabilities. On the Outer Islands, where land is less of a constraint, there is considerable scope to increase the population of draught animals; this would yield benefits not only in terms of incremental cropping but also in beef production.

Detailed examination of the fisheries prospects was not included. The evidence presented in Chapter 3 suggests, however, that there is not much scope to expand output of the inshore sub-sector. Further development of brackish water aquaculture would, however, seem to be feasible. This should not take place at the expense of the remaining areas of mangrove swamp in Java, which provide, as noted elsewhere, the breeding habitat of marine prawns, which constitute an important proportion of the total marine catch.

To summarize this assessment of developmental opportunities, it can be said that the Outer Islands, and Sumatra in particular, have considerable potential for the establishment and/or rehabilitation of plantation crops. On Java, there is not much slack in the rice-production systems, and the opportunities to raise the output of other crops tend to be more location - and situation-specific.

Preconditions for Agricultural Sector Growth

It is abundantly clear that over a wide spectrum of agricultural activities the principal precondition for agricultural sector growth is substantially greater investment in productive capacity. Failure to make the investments needed to bring into full production land that is capable of carrying good stands of rubber, oil-palm, coconut, and so forth, simply means that total available resources are being underused. The same argument applies when lack of investment curtails the use of factors of production, such as irrigation water and mechanical power, where these are necessary inputs for the most efficient use of land. Investment is also needed in processing and storage facilities at the farm or near-farm level.

Apart from investments, institutional changes are also needed to upgrade the support services. A continuous flow of resources is further required to maintain appropriate levels of agricultural research, for example, plant breeding, agronomic trials, selection, pathogen investigations and cognate activities. When the research effort has to be directed toward finding multiple location-specific solutions to single agronomic problems, costs tend to rise exponentially. Further off-farm investments are probably also needed to improve the capabilities of the extension services and the performance of agencies supplying and delivering inputs to the farmers.

In a number of instances, farmers can contribute to the improvement of their economic environment by participating in supply and marketing cooperatives, thus ensuring that they retain the maximum proportion of the value added by the farm-based operations.

One precondition to realizing production growth opportunities is, of course, that available improved cultivars are used where appropriate, and recommended cultural practices followed. Some slack in the system in this respect can probably be taken up, but it is likely that collateral action to improve seed availability will also be needed.

Dealing with the "critical areas", particularly where there are tolerated incursions into posted forest areas, clearly calls for the exercise of statutory powers to define and enforce the boundaries of zones where sanctions must be imposed on damaging activities. Necessarily, these boundaries must to some extent be arbitrarily positioned, and it would be reasonable to make some provision to compensate those upon whom undue hardship may be inflicted.

Fulfilling the Preconditions for Growth

With respect to the smallholder sub-sector, developmental policies are in future likely to be more successful if they are more purposively directed toward improving farmers' incomes - which is a policy objective - and are less concerned about the achievement of physical targets. These were valid objectives when there was a yawning rice supply gap, but became rather less meaningful when expressed in such imprecise terms as intensification and diversification.

Policy makers will also have to learn to live with the fact that whereas in the case of rice, which tolerates wide variation in soil conditions, production technology can be treated almost as a given independent variable, this most certainly ceases to be true in respect of most palawija crops. The BIMAS programme approach implicitly assumes that growth is in large measure independent of soil characteristics: Where this is a valid assumption the programme may work, but where it is not valid then failure is predictable; hence, the relative failure of the soyabean BIMAS programme.

Where a sector or sub-sector manifestly does not perform satisfactorily in relation to the resources at its disposal, policies to upgrade performance are likely to be successful only when they are founded on an understanding of why underperformance occurs. To the extent that this can be identified as a result of insufficient financial incentives to make the risks associated with, say, higher levels of inputs worthwhile, policy clearly needs to seek, first and foremost, to create a more favourable economic environment.

Policies should reflect some attempt to exploit comparative advantage where this prevails. Weaknesses in this area probably stem from a lack, within the research establishment generally, of a well-developed communication system that has the specific function of advising top policy makers about the optimal ways to use the resource base.

Tangible actions suggesting themselves at the moment include substantial new investment in the NES and PIR-TRANS oil-palm projects and the PMU schemes for replanting rubber and coconuts. Possibly some adjustment of NES schemes for rubber, making systems more attractive to potential private investors, might be worthwhile. It is likely that opening such schemes to private enterprise might lead to some trade-off between capital and labour intensity. The increased efficiency and total output gains might be worth the reduced labour intensity.

Further investments in groundwater exploration would seem to be worthwhile. In public sector irrigation generally, it is an opportune time to start raising water charges with the aim of eventually being able to achieve full recovery of all operation and maintenance costs.

In agronomic research, the main need at present is to increase greatly the number of controlled trials of improved *palawija* crop cultivars, making sure that the representativeness of the trial sites is assessed and recorded. This effort is of crucial importance because the entire sequence of training extension workers, extending knowledge to farmers, investment in seed multiplication and so on, hinges on matching cultivars and cultivation techniques to the soil and climatic conditions.

Some special areas of research deserve attention. One is the cropping systems research relevant to the animal traction systems introduced under various livestock development projects. The other is the evaluation of proven workable agroforestry and silvipasture systems.

Chapter 8

Strategy and Recommendations

The starting point in formulating any strategy is to state the policy objectives the strategy seeks to attain. Here, the main objective is designing a development strategy oriented toward improving the standards of living of the rural poor. In addition, the strategy should be as consistent as possible with economic growth and efficiency.

The main vehicle of the strategy is to increase the incomes of the poor by creating additional and more productive employment opportunities. This goal requires the allocation of resources within the rural areas and an interregional cropping pattern within agriculture that pays particular attention to providing productive employment opportunities for the target group of landless, marginal and small farmers, including rural women. In turn, the GOI needs to establish institutions and policies that are conducive to realising such an allocation and a cropping pattern focused on creating employment opportunities responsive to the needs of the underprivileged rural groups.

It bears repeating that under the present conditions in Indonesia such a strategy need not conflict with economic growth and greater efficiency but, on the contrary, if properly conceived can be entirely consistent with Indonesia's pattern of comparative advantage and the process of agricultural adjustment already underway.

Employment Strategy and Reorientation of the Structure of Production

Given that employment is the key to the strategy, it is essential - at the outset - to review the prospects for the next decade or so. It was seen that the capacity of the agricultural sector on Java to absorb additional workers had become negative by the early 1980s, while its capacity to provide additional workdays of employment (through a rise in the labour intensity of the existing agricultural labour force) was still slightly positive. Future displacement of agricultural labour on Java, however, appears inevitable. In contrast, present and future transmigration projects in the Outer Islands continue to offer some limited scope for productive employment outlets in agriculture.

Evidence was presented in Chapter 4 that a process of agricultural adjustment toward more viable and economically sustainable farms appears to be underway on Java. Many truly marginal farmers must have felt the squeeze of low farm returns and rising indebtedness and must have been, more or less, pushed out of agriculture and forced to join the ranks of the landless. It is also likely that a number of small farmers had to dispose of some of their land and move down the stairs of land stratification to a lower farm size stratum. Besides these push factors, some pull factors were present even for the poorest rural groups of landless and marginal farmers. For some of them on Java, the transmigration projects offered an opportunity to improve their conditions. Some others were pulled into more remunerative off-farm activities in the rural areas (i.e., manufacturing, construction, and public administration), whereas a large share of the target groups must have ended up moving, almost residually, into service and household industries activities in the informal sector.

The first step in ascertaining the employment prospects for the next decade or so is to project the likely growth in the labour force. For Indonesia as a whole the annual growth rate of the labour force between 1986 and 1995 is estimated to be about 2.3 percent. Assuming a continuation of the transmigration programme with somewhat less ambitious targets than the present REPELITA IV plans, the labour force is projected to grow at 1.5 percent per annum in Java and Bali over the next decade and at about 3.5 percent in the Outer Islands. Even under favourable assumptions, including a slowing down of the process of mechanization in rice production and the realization of a relatively labour-intensive cropping pattern on Java, there is no doubt that the agricultural sector will continue to lose part of its labour force. The significance of this is that non-agricultural sectors on Java will have to absorb not only all of the new entrants into the Javanese labour force in the next decade but, according to one estimate, 15 percent of the agricultural employees and small farmers who will have been displaced from agriculture. In the Outer Islands, it is estimated that agriculture could productively absorb about half the new entrants to the labour force including the transmigrants.

Thus, the crucial question consists of attempting to match the projected new entrants into the labour force and transmigrants to prospective employment opportunities over the next decade, focusing especially on our target groups. Before exploring the future employment prospects, however, it is desirable to review the findings regarding the socio-economic characteristics of the target groups of poor since the prospective job opportunities should fit as much as possible these characteristics. Even though poverty is pervasive throughout Indonesia, it is possible to highlight the major characteristics of the rural poor. Poverty is strongly inversely related to the land and human capital (i.e., educational) endowment of the households. Among farmers there is a clear association between the amount of land owned or controlled and calorie consumption, whereas outside of agriculture it is also generally true that higher skill groups rank above the manual workers and more menial clerical, sales, and service workers. Furthermore, the greatest incidence of poverty was found among small upland (rain-fed) farmers producing typically secondary crops in contrast with rice producing farmers on *sawah* land. Using farm size and the relative incidence of rain-fed land as criteria, regencies on Java and Madura that constitute critical pockets of poverty could be located. The highest proportion of very smallholders and incidence of dryland occurs in the southern portion of West Java.

Given the socio-economic and locational characteristics of poor rural households, we can now explore the employment prospects that best match these characteristics. This analysis can best be undertaken within an interregional and intersectoral framework distinguishing between the Inner Islands (mainly Java) and the Outer Islands and between agricultural and non-agricultural activities in the rural areas. First, we have to identify the scope for new employment opportunities in the rural areas of the Outer Islands both within and outside agriculture for the additional local labour force and for the projected sponsored and spontaneous transmigrants. Second, the problem on Java is even more complex requiring that we identify a resource allocation and cropping pattern within agriculture that would slow down the inevitable exodus and yet be consistent with the pattern of comparative advantage and the ongoing process of agricultural adjustment toward more viable and sustainable farms. Furthermore, the scope for job creation in rural off-farm activities on Java of a type that is both labour intensive and economically efficient has to be explored.

Employment Opportunities on Java

In Java, a first key point to note is that the achievement of rice self-sufficiency has somewhat removed the justification for the high priority the GOI has attached to this crop in its planning and policies throughout the recent past. The attainment of rice self-sufficiency does not mean, however, that the nutritional requirements of all households are met. Lack of purchasing power, or entitlement, among the poor prevents many of them from satisfying their requirements for calories, which, given the dietary preferences, implies an inadequate rice consumption. The poor still display a relatively high income elasticity of demand for rice, and as their incomes increase (say through greater employment) they will be able to exercise a greater effective demand for rice. Since most other socio-economic groups continue to display a positive, although falling, income elasticity of demand for rice, the GOI cannot go too far in relaxing its efforts on the rice production front.

What is called for is a relative de-emphasis of rice production in favour of secondary food crops and other agricultural activities. It appears that rice production can continue to increase through higher yields rather than through land expansion. This will require a continuing research commitment to develop local HYVs that are resistant to the *wereng* pests. The main issue from an employment standpoint is that the present tendency toward mechanization in paddy production and rice processing be slowed down to reduce the exodus out of agriculture. In short, the big push in rice has already taken place and the apparatus is in place for a continuing growth trend in rice production so that on both macro-economic and distributional grounds - remembering that the rice farmers tend to be the better-off farmers - a relative tilt toward *palawija* food crops suggests itself.

Diversification into other agricultural activities, such as maize, soya, vegetables and livestock, makes sense at the present crossroad, both from a production and a consumption standpoint. Greater production of secondary crops would lead to greater employment and higher incomes for the small farmers in the rain-fed and upland areas (who constitute a significant part of the target group IFAD would like to reach). It would also help the balance of payments by import substitution of commodities such as soyabeans. Still another important advantage of some *palawija* crops is that they have to be processed, which strengthens the link between agriculture and rural industry.

The next step is to explore desirable employment prospects outside of agriculture on Java. Two promising types of activities under the control of the Government are in the areas of irrigation and rural road construction. Regarding the former, the large-scale investment in primary canal construction and dams that took place during the Big Push for rice self-sufficiency has produced a large irrigated land base and production capacity. At the present, the rehabilitation of existing facilities and the construction of tertiary and quaternary channels would appear to have the highest priority in terms of their impact on output and employment. These activities tend to be labour intensive and can have high economic rates of return.

Rural road construction, particularly farm-to-market roads, would have the advantages of being highly labour intensive and of improving the marketing of secondary food crops, particularly in the rain-fed and upland areas. Given the magnitude of the new jobs that have to be created to employ the new entrants into the labour force as well as those released from agriculture, it is clear that the informal sector will have an important role as a provider of productive jobs.

Employment Opportunities on the Outer Islands

We can now turn to an overview of the employment opportunities on the Outer Islands. For one thing, as we have seen in Chapter 7, employment opportunities based on tree crops rather than on food crops are available in the agricultural sector. Most of these alternatives rely on single crops (e.g., rubber) depending on the underlying soil characteristics, in contrast with the multiproduct, multi-activity farming systems that suggest themselves in the upland areas of the Inner Islands. It is clear that transmigration projects continue to have the potential to provide employment opportunities to a large number of migrants. In REPELITA IV the Government planned to move half a million households under the sponsored programme while it was hoped that a further one-fourth million households would move spontaneously. Even if these are somewhat exaggerated targets, it is clear that the agricultural sector can continue to absorb a large share (about half) of the incremental labour force including transmigrants in the Outer Islands over the next decade. One issue that needs to be highlighted is that the selection of transmigrants could be significantly improved upon. In a number of instances migrants who had little or no experience in agriculture were chosen out of the informal sector. The combination of having to adapt to an entirely new geographical environment and to new activities (e.g., growing tree crops) with no adequate training entailed both personal and social costs.

Outside of agriculture one activity that can help alleviate the employment problem is the complex of land clearing and preparation of settlement sites for transmigration projects. At times, project managers have tended to rely on relatively capital-intensive heavy machinery and equipment technologies. And as was indicated in

Chapter 7, not only do these techniques have unfavourable employment effects, in addition they may contribute to erosion. Through appropriate organizational arrangements and a greater degree of control over project managers, the GOI can encourage a shift toward the use of considerably more labour-intensive techniques.

A key concept that captures and underlies the essence of the above recommended strategy in terms of the structure of rural production is commodity and regional diversification. In Java it should take the form of greater emphasis on encouraging the cultivation of secondary food crops combined with other activities in the rain-fed upland areas. Likewise, the pattern of public expenditures on infrastructure projects should increasingly concentrate on the rehabilitation of existing irrigation schemes and the spatial extension of the downstream canal network to improve farmers' direct access to water through the building of tertiary and quaternary channels, the construction of rural farm-to-market roads linking upland and lowland areas better and conservation schemes in the so-called critical (mainly upland) watershed areas.

In the Outer Islands the selection of which crops to grow and which activities to undertake in transmigration projects should be dictated as much as possible by the principle of comparative advantage in the light of the underlying climatic and agronomic conditions. Concentration on specific individual tree crops depending on the location appears to be indicated in most instances. The land-clearing and preparation stage of new transmigration projects and settlement schemes should be as labour intensive as possible. The chosen technology should be based on the appropriate shadow prices reflecting the socio-economic input costs and benefits.

Now that we have described the major interregional and intersectoral features of an appropriate strategy from the standpoint of the structure of production, the next step is to examine the organizational requirements and major changes in policies and programmes needed to bring about the revised structure of production.

Organizational Requirements and Policy Recommendations

Under REPELITA IV and during the next five-year plans, GOI policy concerning the rural economy has faced increasingly complicated conditions and new problems. During the 1970s and early 1980s it was possible to increase rice production in irrigated lowland areas with pragmatic macro-economic and agricultural policies and a governmental apparatus split up along departmental lines, working with a top-down approach, and geared toward delivering standardized packages and introducing farming models to the rural population. This was possible because the irrigated lowland areas constituted a relatively homogeneous environment in which these macro-policies and organizational approaches worked effectively, exhibiting a strong impact in all regions in Java and in some of the Outer Islands, as well as on all social strata of farmers, with the possible exception of very small and marginal farmers and the landless. The rice ecology with its traditional emphasis on yield increase has been able to absorb the new technology in a relatively brief period of time.

During the next five-year plans further output growth in agriculture cannot be achieved along these lines. As the focus is shifting to less charted and more heterogeneous upland areas, as well as to newly opened areas in the Outer Islands, general policies have to give way to location-specific approaches. Synthetic models are not applicable in these areas in view of the heterogeneity of the environment.

To understand the need for new approaches, it is helpful to realise the contrast between lowland and upland areas in terms of ecology. That contrast can be described as follows (Nataatmadja, 1985): Lowland areas exhibit homogeneity of land resources, a relatively good infrastructure, concentrated settlement patterns, an imposed rhythm associated with the irrigation scheme of water allocation and monocropping of rice. Upland areas exhibit heterogeneity of land resources, a generally poor infrastructure, scattered settlement patterns, no particular imposed rhythm and a wide variety of crops and cropping patterns.

It was observed (see Chapter 6) that the success in rice production was even more attributable to proper macro-economic policies than to the impact of the agricultural service institutions. One can doubt whether a sizeable production increase can be achieved in the upland areas of Java and the new areas in the Outer Islands with similar macro-economic policies. General measures concerning subsidies on fertilizer, cheap credit and reasonably high commodity prices cannot be conceived for the wide range of products coming from those areas. These products are dependent on domestic and external markets, with sharply fluctuating prices. None of the products presently produced in the areas mentioned is in sufficiently short supply to warrant high commodity prices and large profits to the cultivators without technological and marketing improvements. All this means that the goal of production increase in the upland areas can only be achieved by strengthening the government apparatus charged with the task of promoting upland agriculture. This is not an easy task.

The shift to the new regions requires a new orientation of the agricultural service institutions. A commodity- or crop-specific approach has to give way to a location- or region-specific approach. A centralised programme structure is not appropriate, since the problems faced are unique for each area. Planning and implementation have to be carried out at the appropriate local level of administration. It has been strongly emphasised (in Chapter 3) that there is a long trajectory and consequently a big time gap between research on local conditions and local varieties, the drawing up of an agronomic profile of an area, fine-tuning agronomic research on plant breeding and viable cropping patterns, the testing of new cropping systems, and, finally, the introduction and dissemination of these systems in the field.

This region-specific approach requires organisational adjustments. At present there is strong sectoral and departmental segmentation in the government apparatus. The new approach has to be based on interdepartmental cooperation as well as on multidisciplinary research. The Government has to reinforce its emphasis on coordination of the different government agencies.

A location-specific approach requires not only a greater coordination, but also a much larger dedication of field workers to small-scale settings and a strong effort to cooperate with local farmers. The management of sustainable farming systems in upland regions requires the participation and cooperation of all villagers in planning, decision making and implementation of plans. The introduction of new techniques and information and the execution of local projects has to go hand in hand with changes in farmers' attitudes. This cannot be achieved with a top-down approach. It has been experienced time and again that the target groups of farmers often do not accept the models drawn up in research institutes, and if they accept them initially, they often do not maintain them in the long run. The new plans have to be anchored in the local community, which has to assume responsibility for their implementation and maintenance.

The GOI is presently undertaking steps toward further decentralization of government authority regarding budget allocation and programme management. Three trends are as follows: the first is the trend toward *deconcentration*, or transfer of specific responsibilities from the central offices to the field units of the central ministries. The second is further *devolution* of responsibilities to the provincial and district governments, specifically regarding resource mobilization and allocation, management and implementation of public expenditure. The third trend is the *introduction* of programmes at provincial and district levels.

During the past few year the BAPPEDAs have been reinforced and have extended their operations. It was noted that in many provinces BAPPEDA staff are highly motivated, deeply concerned with innovative planning and competent in the execution of these plans. At the same time, the BAPPEDAs are operating within the constraints imposed by national guidelines and centralised decision making.

Another recent development is the involvement of local community self-help organizations in implementing development programmes. In general, there is a more favourable attitude of Government toward cooperation with private voluntary or non-governmental development organizations. For example, there are new regional projects in which government agencies are cooperating with LPSM, a university institute and grass-root organizations. These forms of cooperation can create the framework and atmosphere in which the local population can participate in development projects.

Another possibility is the involvement of private capital in development projects. In Indonesia, however, private capital is being invested in lucrative enterprises in Jakarta and in Java, not in the Outer Islands. It is doubtful whether the uplands and the newly opened areas in the Outer Islands provide sufficiently profitable opportunities for investment. Even when this trend is being reinforced, the central role of the Government will still be needed.

The suggestions we made should not be viewed as an argument in favour of a complete shift of the focus of decision making from the national to the provincial or local level. They are rather a plea for a more rational division of labour by which the highest echelons are primarily dealing with the broader issues and long-term planning, the middle echelons with translating these concepts into specific policies and provincial and district level managers with adjusting these broadly formulated policies into location-specific measures and development plans.

Regional planning and implementation require imaginative interaction between provincial and district level managers, on the one hand, and village and community level leaders, on the other hand. The village unit approach, which was particularly suitable for homogeneous rice regions, is not the most appropriate for upland areas. In the upland areas the settlement pattern is more dispersed, and villagers are dealing with a variety of soil conditions and cropping patterns. Tackling heavily eroded areas may require cooperation structures involving a number of hamlets belonging to different *desas*, constituting a watershed ecosystem. Project managers will have to decide on the basis of practical experience and their knowledge of the socio-economic structure whether their entry point should be at the hamlet level, at the *desa* level or via some *desa* organization or even a supra-*desa* organization.

There are built-in tensions in this approach. Whereas projects have to be firmly rooted in the local community, probably at the hamlet level, in order to motivate people so they participate in and support the project, broader guidance and coordination need to be provided by *kecamatan* (subdistrict) and *kabupaten* (district) officials who are able to place the small-scale problems and activities in a wider perspective. The built-in tensions are often the result of conflicting interests. From the point of view of conservationists, the most appropriate measures might be reforestation of an eroded upland region and the complete replacement of food crops in the area. But local farmers who depend on food crop farming cannot be convinced to shift to tree planting if no alternative source of income is offered. It is in the interaction between local level researchers and field workers operating at the local level, farmers articulating their interests and agricultural researchers in research centres that solutions can be found that are specific enough to be acceptable to the local population.

In the process of shaping up a rural development strategy oriented toward production and regional diversification and organizational and policy decentralization, a key issue that has to be faced is that of the long-term viability and sustainability of individual farms and other quasi-private, quasi-public organizations such as the NES and PMU. Chapter 4 described and analysed the process of agricultural adjustment entailing the gradual elimination of marginal farms and the appearance of a higher proportion of farms of a size sufficient to provide a basic needs income to farm households.

It would be a losing battle to try to go against this trend. Instead the Government should try to ensure that this process occurs gradually and, throughout the transitional period, help the marginal farmers pushed out of agriculture acquire skills that would improve their chances of getting jobs outside of agriculture.

One serious difficulty at the present time is that the extension services under the MOA do not cover off-farm activities and skills. Rather, the training and teaching of off-farm skills fall within the domain of the extension service of the MOI. The dilemma is that the MOI extension service does not permeate into the rural areas and therefore does not reach the target clientele. An appropriate organizational coordination needs to be worked out between the two ministries so that vocational and non-agricultural skills be extended to the target group of marginal farmers and near landless who are being pushed out of agriculture. Increasingly, extension workers will have to become more polyvalent - not just in terms of being able to extend knowledge useful in activities outside of agriculture but also within agriculture - particularly to help upland farmers adopt the appropriate multicrop, multiactivity farming system. These generalists would have to be supported by a cadre of specialists.

Further, it might be desirable to design schemes that would link training marginal farmers and landless for non-agricultural activities together with access to credit to help them move into, or start off in, these activities. In a general sense, the credit system should try to encourage the development of productive projects outside of agriculture for marginal farmers and rural women.

One important qualification applying to all forms of rural credit is that the whole financial intermediation system should be designed in such a way that credit *not* be heavily subsidized so as not to conflict with the process of rural savings mobilization so crucial to any rural development strategy.

Another issue relating to the long-term viability of farm units is that of tenurial and ownership rights. This is particularly important in the upland regions of both the Inner and Outer Islands. As was discussed in Chapter 7, demographic pressures over the years have tended to push small farmers further uphill toward natural forest areas - sometimes so that they actually encroach on state forest land. In many areas of Java and the Outer Islands the tenurial question is clouded and is a serious obstacle to on-farm improvements and investment. In some of the NES tree crop projects, it was found that a number of farmers had great difficulty in obtaining clear titles to their plots, which made them ineligible for private formal credit after the three-year transitional period during which the nucleus (the estate) provided the credit to the plasma (the smallholder). Without land collateral, some farmers were put at a great disadvantage as compared to others and their viability endangered. A reorientation of agricultural development toward the upland areas will require the Government to focus on the tenurial question more seriously than in the past.

Chapter 6 examined the NES-PMU type of organization and found it to have great potential merits as long as a truly symbiotic relationship could be worked out between the nucleus and the plasma. Typically the nucleus provides, at least over a transitional period, inputs, credit and extension services to the plasma and, in turn, markets the output of the smallholders together with its own. It is essential that the terms applying to these various intra-NES transactions result in a positive sum game. Unless both sides stand to benefit from the new organizational arrangement, the incentive may not be there to make the projects succeed. It is clear that the design of mutually beneficial organizational structures and arrangements between smallholders and estates deserves serious attention.

Several recommendations were made on the basis of the analysis of the nutritional and health situation discussed in Chapter 5. The trend toward a varied and diversified diet could go a long way in reducing malnutrition, infant mortality and the incidence of a number of diseases such as anaemia and xerophthalmia (caused by Vitamin A deficiency). The reorientation in the structure of production, as described earlier in this chapter, should contribute to poverty alleviation and hence improvement in the nutritional status. Increased employment and income for the poor will, by itself, however, not suffice to eliminate malnutrition. Clearly, increased nutrition education coupled with dietary behavioural changes are also necessary elements in improving nutritional status. Parallel to improving the incomes of the rural poor, significant changes must also take place in the health sector and in education.

In the health sector, adequate availability, easy access, low cost and frequent use of well-staffed health facilities will be important components to achieve the nutritional development objectives. Because of the extremely high population density in the rural areas of certain provinces in Indonesia and the limited access to health delivery systems, supporting public health centres, satellite dispensaries and mobile public health centres become significant factors in the provision of quality medical care. One recommendation critical to the improvement in rural health lies in the area of training. The promotion of *health education* suited to a rural environment, together with the specific inclusion of rural *young* women in such training (both to break the cycle of traditionalism and also as an employment-creating scheme) and the provision of child care training facilities for young mothers (preferably near women's work places) has the potential of achieving greater social and economic welfare. A focus on health education training, including retraining of traditional midwives, may in the long run produce far-reaching success within the context of rural health.

Even though the envisaged process of socio-economic development based on crop and regional diversification of production will bring about a degree of diversification in the diet of the Indonesian people in an almost automatic and evolutionary way, there remains some concern regarding nutrition for the high preference (reflecting taste) and consumption (actual intake) of the Indonesian people for rice. To encourage changes in food habits and tastes is no small challenge. Two possible approaches to motivate consumers to modify their present eating patterns are as follows.

The first is a nutritional education approach that would focus on conveying a greater awareness of what constitutes an adequate diet and desirable child-feeding practices. The positive benefits of a varied diet could be made in relation to physical fitness (alertness, more energy, reduced school and job absenteeism, better body and muscle tone, healthy skin); the population being less prone to nutritionally related diseases (less anaemia, less night blindness), better growth of children; more varied diets in terms of colour, texture and taste that would please their families. A healthy, small, prosperous family - the GOI theme in family planning - can perhaps be the complementary vehicle to conduct such a nutrition education campaign.

The second approach would rely more on food technology and marketing. If rice is to be complemented or substituted in the diet, alternative food choices have to be produced. Intensive efforts in research development of new food technology is imperative, accompanied by effective marketing schemes. These complementary foods must be compatible with cultural food tastes, be attractive in appearance and be available at prices that are affordable to a large segment of the population. Efforts on the part of food technologists might be directed toward exploring additional protein-rich foods for the rural population, particularly for children. Fish flour, soyabean and its products such as soyabean milk, *tempe* and *tahu* are relatively inexpensive good protein sources that merit further consideration by Indonesian food technologies working to improving nutritional status.

It would seem that programmes and policies to increase and diversify food production and to improve nutrition should be as complementary as possible and, in principle, should form a natural match. This does not appear to be the case, however, at the present time in Indonesia. A potentially serious obstacle to the formulation of consistent policies and programmes in these two areas is the inadequate coordination that seems to exist between the planning units of the MOA, which is essentially in charge of the agricultural production pattern and its diversification, and other units in the MOH and BAPPENAS, which concentrate on nutritional and health issues in an attempt to encourage a more diversified diet from the consumption side. The whole process of agricultural production planning needs to be better coordinated with that of nutritional planning per se. One issue that is related to health that we examined is that of rural water supply and sanitation (see Chapter 5). The benefits in terms of rural health and resulting reduced disease and higher economic productivity of clean water and sanitary facilities appear high. Renewed efforts to obtain greater community support and participation such as training village volunteers in hand pump maintenance and repairing existing facilities merit emphasis. Parallel to these collective management efforts, education campaigns about adequate hygiene practices should be encouraged. One specific alternative regarding access to clean water supply in rural Indonesia is the possibility of increasing the number of simple rain collectors or other storage containers. The construction of them could be done by village workers and the cost kept down if the basic construction materials are provided at the *kabupaten* or *kecamatan* level.

In Chapter 4 as well as in other parts of this book, we argued that rural women constitute a target group of poor in the Indonesian context. Concentrating exclusively, or mainly, on the so-called "productive activities" in which rural women engage (i.e., activities that are counted as part of GNP in the national income accounts), leads to a serious underestimation of the economic contribution of women to the development process. By analysing the time allocation of women to the various tasks within as well as outside the household, it becomes evident that women fulfil a multiplicity of roles, functions and tasks (e.g., homemaker, wage labourer on farm and off farm, trader, household producers of handicrafts). If these various tasks are given proper recognition (i.e., assigned an imputed value consistent with what it would cost if they had to be contracted in the market), a significantly greater overall economic contribution of women would be registered.

For example, collecting water for drinking and other household uses, firewood and grass for feeding animals requires both time and energy without being adequately rewarded. The long hours women have to allocate to household and own-farm activities imply that rural women have no, or very little, time for access to educational activities or self-improvement or for learning practical skills or a new trade - let alone for participation in any political activity or leadership role that would help break the vicious circle of poverty, lack of education and social immobility in which they find themselves.

The contribution of rural women to the material welfare of rural households, when their household and own-farm activities are properly accounted for, looms essential in the broader development context. Since there is a significantly larger incidence of rural women among very small, marginal and landless rural households, the ongoing agricultural adjustment process of gradually pushing these households out of agriculture presents a serious challenge regarding the off-farm tasks the displaced women could perform to replace the tasks they are currently fulfilling within agriculture. It is crucial to provide them with opportunities for acquiring relevant skills of a vocational and practical nature. To prepare them for jobs in trading and service activities, a minimum training in business skills (e.g., some arithmetic and bookkeeping) might be very helpful. Paramedical training is an example of a practical skill that would have direct effects on the employment of women as well as contributing to rural health.

Evaluations of income-generating projects outside of agriculture reveals that illiterate women have great difficulty in participating in group projects other than as hired workers. Studying group business records and reading technical instructions appear to be necessary conditions for tackling more entrepreneurial tasks, at least among the literate or semi-literate women participating in income-generating projects. It has also been suggested that other aspects to look into are the capital requirements, the access to credit for poor rural women, where both collateral and legal regulations may be an obstacle. (Is the husband's consent needed or can credit only be given in the husband's name? Is the land only in the husband's name so the woman cannot obtain collateral credit?) Another potential risk is that men will take over the small business ventures once they become viable for women. In short, options for illiterate women would have to be carefully investigated and possibly linked to literacy programmes.

The underlying principle the Government has followed in reaching village people in areas such as rural credit, agricultural extension and research, cooperatives and adult literacy programmes is that of the "total family approach". There is some evidence that this approach does not permeate or reach rural women as far as it should. An approach focused more directly on the specific needs of women is called for. For example, there is a minimal representation of women among the staff of agricultural extension field workers, which handicaps the contact between the extension services and female farmers. It seems, therefore, appropriate to recommend that increasing female participation in the official staff of the MOA (preceded by increased agricultural and sociological training of young women to prepare them adequately as professional extension workers) deserves full attention in the near future. If there are more women among extension workers (both agricultural and non-agricultural), this would ensure that more women would be among the initial contact farmers who would disseminate these skills and techniques to other female farmers, starting a desirable snowball process among rural women.

In summary, the most important policy implication regarding rural women is the fact that since rural poor families are more dependent on women's contributions (both imputed and actual earnings) to survive, they are also subsequently more seriously hurt by the displacement of women from earning opportunities (within agriculture) without provision of adequate substitutes. In that sense, development policies that hurt women damage the poor more than the rich.

Annex to Chapter 4

A. Note on Identification of Poor Subdistricts (*Kecamatan*)

This note is a brief critique of the methodology used to construct the lists of poor *kecamatan* by the Directorate-General of Agrarian Affairs.

In Indonesia there are 3 539 subdistricts spread throughout 246 regencies (*kabupaten*) and 55 municipalities (*kotamadya*). The first step in the procedure to identify poor subdistricts was to select two sample subdistricts from each regency (on the basis of unclear selection criteria). All villages in the sample subdistricts were grouped into three categories on the basis of their "degree of development." One village was then randomly selected from each of these three categories. Gross income from all activities in the sample village was estimated (by undocumented procedures) and then divided by the village population.

Second, the per capita gross income estimates derived above were regressed on a variety of independent variables gathered from administrative sources at the local level. For example, in East Java the independent variables found significant in the regression on income (in order of importance) were ratio of land farmed to number of households, ratio of primary school children to children of school age, ratio of area harvested to area of dryland, ratio of household members to number of households, ratio of landowners to farmers, ratio of farmers to adult population, ratio of land damaged (by flood, etc.) to area of the subdistrict, ratio of children to household heads, population density, ratio of land owned to number of landowners, ratio of fishing income to number of households, and the productivity of land. Different sets of independent variables were used in the other provinces.

Third, on the basis of regression coefficients from the above step, the per capita income of each *kecamatan* in a given province was predicted.

Fourth, a poverty line was computed as the average consumption of nine basic commodities (rice, salted fish, sugar, cloth, cooking oil, kerosene, salt, soap, and *batik*) by a "few" households in each sample village.

Fifth, subdistricts with predicted income not greater than 75 percent of the above poverty line were identified as "very poor," those attaining 76 to 125 percent were designated as "poor," those in the range 126 to 200 percent were "almost poor," and those with more than 200 percent were "not poor."

The above process contains many weaknesses. The size of the samples, the methods for selecting them, and the use of *gross* income rather than *net* are certainly questionable. Perhaps more important is the prediction of per capita incomes on the basis of the regressions. No report is given as to how well the regressions fit. The dependent variables are also likely to display a great deal of multicollinearity.

Moreover, no reason is given as to why the average consumption bundles of the sampled households constitute a poverty line. The extent to which the results are comparable across provinces is also unclear.

These criticisms are not meant to disparage the ambitious efforts made to identify poor subdistricts, only to illustrate some of the difficulties involved. To the extent that these attempts are building up a data bank on a wide range of variables on the subdistrict level, they may lead to more useful exercises in the future. Perhaps it will be more useful to avoid attempting to measure income differences by a series of proxies and directly examine inequalities evident in the data from which the proxies are derived. For instance, information on such variables as the ratio of primary-school children to children of school age, or on the ratio of land damaged to total land are perhaps more valuable in their own right than as simply indirect predictors of income.

In short, these efforts to amass and analyze socio-economic inequalities on a subdistrict level should be encouraged, but the currently available lists of poor subdistricts are not recommended as a basis for selecting where policy interventions should be located.

B. Note on Annex Tables for Rural Farm Size and Land Use Status by Province and Regency (*Kabupaten*)

The final two columns of the following tables mark regencies with high concentrations of both smallholders and dryland. A "yes" indicates a regency with such high concentrations when compared with expected values either for the *province* (second column from right) or for the "*region*" (last column) where regions are defined as

1. Java and Madura
2. Bali and West Nusa Tenggara
3. Sumatra and Sulawesi
4. East Nusa Tenggara, Maluku, East Timor, Kalimantan.

The figure presented in Chapter 4 marked regencies with high concentrations of both smallholders and dryland when compared to a single, *national* set of criteria.

Annex Table 4.A: Worker Equivalents and Labour Force Participation Rates by Sex, Household Type and Occupation (1975) (Thousands)

Household Type	Agriculture		Production, Transportation		Clerical, Sales		Professional, Management		Total			Population	Workers per 1000 Potential Labour Force		
	Paid	Unpaid	Paid	Unpaid	Paid	Unpaid	Paid	Unpaid	Paid	Unpaid	Worker Equivalent	Labour force Age 10+	Paid	Unpaid	All
Female															
Agricultural labourers	1 346	85	117	125	86	206	5	13	1 555	430	1 985	5 240	297	82	379
Agricultural operators															
Rural:															
small	458	1 762	142	298	72	474	14	16	686	2 549	3 235	10 136	68	252	319
medium	94	1 111	30	99	16	198	7	5	147	1 413	1 560	5 487	27	258	284
large	35	1 504	15	62	34	152	15	4	99	1 722	1 822	6 126	16	281	297
Rural:															
lower level	251	96	365	303	261	983	15	41	893	1 423	2 316	6 767	132	210	342
inactive	36	42	32	24	20	74	14	9	101	149	251	1 721	59	87	146
higher level	22	45	39	195	75	403	74	20	210	662	872	2 614	80	253	333
Urban:															
lower level	9	8	196	63	322	522	33	34	559	627	1 186	4 267	131	147	278
inactive	1	0	21	6	55	38	10	1	87	45	132	885	98	51	149
higher level	9	7	32	30	308	276	116	29	465	343	808	2 854	163	120	283
All Female	2 262	4 662	989	1 206	1 249	3 325	302	171	4 801	9 364	14 166	46 097	104	203	307

Annex Table 4.A: Worker Equivalents and Labour Force Participation Rates by Sex, Household Type and Occupation (1975) (Thousands) (Cont'd)

Household Type	Agriculture		Production, Transportation		Clerical, Sales		Professional, Management		Total			Population	Workers per 1000 Potential Labour Force		
	Paid	Unpaid	Paid	Unpaid	Paid	Unpaid	Paid	Unpaid	Paid	Unpaid	Worker Equivalent	Labour force Age 10+	Paid	Unpaid	All
Male															
Agricultural labourers	2 928	177	171	75	102	149	83	14	3 283	415	3 698	4 776	687	87	774
Agricultural operators															
small	977	4 967	384	206	201	314	58	28	1 620	5 514	7 134	9 751	166	565	732
medium	271	3 152	143	123	81	135	35	12	529	3 422	3 952	5 533	96	619	714
large	183	3 720	88	88	63	126	60	25	395	3 958	4 353	6 466	61	612	673
Rural:															
lower level	260	248	1 656	696	789	1 407	115	135	2 821	2 486	5 307	6 224	453	399	853
inactive	50	86	68	35	43	72	81	5	241	198	439	1 224	197	162	359
higher level	58	89	93	307	193	501	546	91	890	988	1 878	2 533	351	390	741
Urban:															
lower level	28	41	1 418	355	786	738	36	105	2 268	1 239	3 507	4 184	542	296	838
inactive	3	5	44	6	38	8	12	2	97	21	117	740	131	28	159
higher level	15	23	98	117	464	307	714	108	1 290	555	1 845	2 782	464	199	663
All Male	4 772	12 508	4 163	2 008	2 760	3 756	1 740	524	13 435	18 796	32 231	44 213	304	425	729
All Indonesia	7 033	17 170	5 151	3 214	4 009	7 081	2 042	695	18 236	28 160	46 396	90 310	202	312	514
Female/Male Ratios	.472	.373	.238	.601	.453	.885	.174	.326	.357	.498	.267	1.043	-	-	-

Source: Government of Indonesia, Biro Pusat Statistik (1983w).

Annex Table 4.B: Rural Farm Size and Land Use Status by Province and Kabupaten

Province/Kabupaten	Households "Controlling" Less Than				Land Area Operated by Land Use Status				Number of Small Operators and % of Dry Land Area	
	0.25 ha		0.50 ha		Total	Percent Wet Land (Sawah)		Percent Dry Land	Average of:	
	'000	Percent	'000	Percent	'000 ha	Irrigated	Unirrigated		Province	"Region"
Jawa Barat	1 406.2	42.0	2 178.0	65.1	1 857.7	29.8	19.7	50.5	8	
Bandung	134.9	55.1	188.3	76.9	96.4	24.9	23.1	52.0	Yes	No
Kuningan	58.5	48.0	91.6	75.3	47.7	32.0	19.2	48.8	No	No
Garut	119.0	49.9	176.3	73.9	100.7	23.8	14.1	62.1	Yes	Yes
Sumedang	74.6	48.8	112.7	73.8	63.9	31.3	17.1	51.6	No	No
Majalengka	69.3	47.5	105.7	72.4	64.7	37.6	23.8	38.5	No	No
Bogor	115.5	52.2	159.6	72.1	92.9	24.3	20.5	55.2	Yes	Yes
Ciamis	118.5	41.9	192.8	68.1	140.3	16.5	15.5	68.0	Yes	Yes
Tasikmalaya	108.9	45.2	163.9	68.1	120.8	15.3	19.3	65.4	Yes	Yes
Sukabumi	109.9	49.1	152.4	68.0	115.1	17.9	18.8	63.3	Yes	Yes
Purwakarta	28.5	45.0	42.7	67.4	32.0	17.0	27.7	55.3	Yes	Yes
Cianjur	113.4	46.2	165.0	67.2	141.6	21.9	17.6	60.5	Yes	Yes
Cirebon	42.4	40.2	69.9	66.3	53.0	66.7	12.8	20.5	No	No
Subang	71.2	41.1	114.0	65.8	95.4	55.6	11.6	32.7	No	No
Tangerang	39.1	36.2	66.7	61.8	59.9	32.9	25.5	41.5	No	No
Indramayu	47.9	32.2	87.2	58.5	102.8	62.9	22.1	15.0	No	No
Bekasi	39.7	35.5	60.3	54.0	83.4	45.0	26.4	28.7	No	No
Serang	36.2	25.3	74.1	51.8	99.1	20.6	27.3	52.1	No	No
Karawang	36.2	26.6	64.6	47.6	109.8	69.8	5.8	24.4	No	No
Pandeglang	20.6	18.7	43.6	39.5	111.8	9.0	30.3	60.8	No	No
Lebak	21.9	17.1	46.6	36.4	126.5	6.2	23.5	70.3	No	No

Annex Table 4.B: Rural Farm Size and Land Use Status by Province and Kabupaten (Cont'd)

Province/Kabupaten	Households "Controlling" Less Than				Land Area Operated by Land Use Status				Number of Small Operators and % of Dry Land Area	
	0.25 ha		0.50 ha		Total	Percent Wet Land (Sawah)		Percent Dry Land	Average of:	
	'000	Percent	'000	Percent	'000 ha	Irrigated	Unirrigated		Province	"Region"
Jawa Tengah	1 149.7	34.1	2 040.7	60.6	1 908.6	24.3	21.2	54.6	No	3
Klaten	61.3	52.3	95.1	81.0	37.0	57.2	4.4	38.4	No	No
Kudus	21.3	46.0	33.8	72.9	21.3	30.4	43.9	25.8	No	No
Tegal	49.8	49.4	73.0	72.4	45.4	51.6	18.3	30.1	No	No
Kebumen	73.3	42.2	123.5	71.0	74.7	21.4	20.8	57.8	Yes	Yes
Brebes	65.5	45.3	100.9	69.9	74.2	43.7	21.8	34.5	No	No
Banyumas	74.2	44.7	114.6	69.0	78.5	27.1	11.8	61.1	No	Yes
Magelang	54.0	36.1	99.8	66.7	69.8	33.4	10.2	56.4	No	No
Sukoharjo	22.8	36.0	42.1	66.5	28.1	41.0	20.7	38.3	No	No
Pekalongan	30.2	43.4	46.2	66.3	36.3	39.8	20.1	40.1	No	No
Purbalingga	36.0	37.8	62.2	65.3	48.8	30.1	8.1	61.8	No	No
Jepara	33.4	38.3	56.9	65.3	47.8	37.0	12.2	50.8	No	No
Pemalang	40.9	40.7	65.1	64.8	51.9	37.1	18.2	44.6	No	No
Boyolali	46.4	33.4	89.6	64.5	65.5	12.9	19.0	68.2	Yes	Yes
Kendal	35.7	38.2	59.2	63.3	50.5	36.4	7.6	56.0	No	No
Batang	28.7	37.7	47.8	62.8	41.8	41.5	8.0	50.5	No	No
Semarang	42.8	36.4	73.8	62.7	60.1	22.1	12.7	65.2	Yes	Yes
Cilacap	65.6	34.1	118.1	61.4	111.8	14.5	35.6	49.9	No	No
Karanganyar	29.7	34.5	52.4	60.8	46.2	38.9	5.4	55.7	No	No
Purworejo	43.9	32.5	80.4	59.5	78.3	25.2	10.7	64.1	No	No

Annex Table 4.B: Rural Farm Size and Land Use Status by Province and Kabupaten (Cont'd)

Province/Kabupaten	Households "Controlling" Less Than				Land Area Operated by Land Use Status				Number of Small Operators and % of Dry Land Area	
	0.25 ha		0.50 ha		Total	Percent Wet Land (Sawah)		Percent	Average of:	
	'000	Percent	'000	Percent	'000 ha	Irrigated	Unirrigated	Dry Land	Province	"Region"
Sragen	36.1	29.6	69.7	57.1	73.1	22.6	29.5	47.9	No	No
Pati	38.9	28.3	75.9	55.3	93.2	20.8	34.2	45.0	No	No
Demak	25.9	26.2	53.6	54.3	66.3	28.4	36.1	35.5	No	No
Grobogan	51.3	25.4	109.3	54.2	120.1	11.1	42.9	46.0	No	No
Wonsobo	24.0	24.7	50.1	51.5	65.2	18.8	9.6	71.7	No	No
Banjarnegara	29.7	25.8	57.4	50.0	80.0	13.0	9.8	77.2	No	No
Temanggung	18.8	21.8	40.6	47.1	60.9	23.7	7.6	68.6	No	No
Wonogiri	36.0	20.8	75.6	43.6	132.8	12.6	12.1	75.3	No	No
Blora	20.5	17.6	48.9	42.0	89.3	4.8	44.3	50.9	No	No
Rembang	12.8	19.1	25.3	37.8	59.9	6.1	38.8	55.0	No	No
D.I Yogyakarta	161.8	39.8	247.6	60.9	231.6	14.7	6.9	78.4	0	
Sleman	54.5	57.0	78.2	81.9	30.8	55.4	2.8	41.8	No	No
Bantul	63.1	61.5	82.2	80.1	35.5	30.1	8.2	61.7	No	No
Kulon Progo	25.7	35.4	44.3	61.0	38.8	12.6	9.8	77.6	No	No
Gunung Kidul	18.5	13.6	42.8	31.5	126.6	1.1	6.7	92.2	No	No
Jawa Timur	1 330.6	35.4	2 312.4	61.5	2 106.2	28.8	16.4	54.8	6	
Pamekasan	45.0	45.1	73.7	73.8	41.2	5.0	19.5	75.5	Yes	Yes
Sumenep	81.5	42.1	140.1	72.5	78.5	6.8	17.3	75.9	Yes	Yes
Tulungagung	51.1	43.1	85.9	72.5	49.7	24.8	12.4	62.9	Yes	Yes

Annex Table 4.B: Rural Farm Size and Land Use Status by Province and Kabupaten (Cont'd)

Province/Kabupaten	Households "Controlling" Less Than				Land Area Operated by Land Use Status				Number of Small Operators and % of Dry Land Area	
	0.25 ha		0.50 ha		Total	Percent Wet Land (Sawah)		Percent	Average of:	
	'000	Percent	'000	Percent	'000 ha	Irrigated	Unirrigated	Dry Land	Province	"Region"
Bondowoso	50.1	45.8	77.6	70.9	49.4	44.3	4.9	50.8	No	No
Probolinggo	64.9	45.4	100.0	69.9	65.6	40.0	7.1	52.8	No	No
Jember	88.1	41.5	145.5	68.5	103.6	58.3	5.0	36.7	No	No
Sampang	41.3	35.7	79.0	68.2	50.9	2.1	21.5	76.3	Yes	Yes
Trenggalek	43.6	40.7	72.0	67.3	47.1	12.6	9.9	77.5	Yes	Yes
Situbondo	38.9	46.4	56.1	66.9	42.8	42.4	3.5	54.1	No	No
Magetan	37.1	38.9	62.6	65.7	46.5	44.7	9.0	46.3	No	No
Ponorogo	46.3	35.3	86.2	65.7	64.6	29.3	12.4	58.4	No	No
Jombang	43.9	42.1	67.8	65.0	60.1	52.6	13.4	34.1	No	No
Madiun	31.2	37.2	54.4	64.9	43.1	52.2	9.0	38.8	No	No
Kediri	62.8	40.7	100.0	64.7	86.3	44.3	4.4	51.3	No	No
Nganjuk	40.0	35.0	72.2	63.1	61.2	54.6	12.5	32.9	No	No
Ngawi	51.5	36.6	88.4	62.8	72.5	42.3	18.0	39.7	No	No
Lumajang	46.7	38.3	76.5	62.6	66.7	32.8	4.1	63.1	No	No
Pasuruan	50.5	36.5	86.1	62.1	75.9	36.2	5.9	57.9	No	No
Bangkalan	36.1	32.2	69.8	62.1	57.4	4.3	34.2	61.5	Yes	Yes
Sidoarjo	17.3	32.8	32.5	61.7	33.8	61.8	2.9	35.3	No	No
Blitar	64.6	37.3	105.1	60.6	93.0	22.5	4.7	72.8	No	No
Mojokerto	25.8	30.8	48.6	58.0	48.2	53.5	13.3	33.1	No	No
Banyuwangi	47.8	33.9	81.5	57.8	88.3	51.5	2.0	46.5	No	No
Malang	83.2	32.6	146.4	57.3	155.8	21.5	2.4	76.2	No	No

Annex Table 4.B: Rural Farm Size and Land Use Status by Province and Kabupaten (Cont'd)

Province/Kabupaten	Households "Controlling" Less Than				Land Area Operated by Land Use Status				Number of Small Operators and % of Dry Land Area	
	0.25 ha		0.50 ha		Total	Percent Wet Land (Sawah)		Percent	Average of:	
	'000	Percent	'000	Percent	'000 ha	Irrigated	Unirrigated	Dry Land	Province	"Region"
Gresik	28.5	30.5	49.8	53.3	69.0	18.2	29.6	52.2	No	No
Lamongan	40.6	24.5	86.4	52.2	107.1	14.4	59.3	26.3	No	No
Bojonegoro	31.6	17.9	81.4	45.9	124.8	14.3	49.9	35.8	No	No
Tuban	28.2	20.9	60.0	44.5	108.7	8.4	34.9	56.7	No	No
Pacitan	12.3	12.2	26.7	26.4	114.7	3.1	9.9	87.1	No	No
Bali	72.1	21.8	148.8	44.9	267.5	27.0	0.5	72.5	1	
Gianyar	11.8	28.0	27.4	64.9	20.6	55.9	0.1	44.0	No	No
Klungkung	6.0	28.8	12.5	59.7	10.9	29.2	0.0	70.8	No	Yes
Badung	10.4	25.1	21.6	51.9	27.3	44.4	0.2	55.4	No	No
Karangasem	14.6	25.9	28.3	50.2	35.3	12.6	0.7	86.6	Yes	Yes
Buleleng	11.6	18.9	22.2	36.4	60.1	16.5	0.9	82.7	No	No
Tabanan	7.7	14.3	18.7	34.9	54.0	40.7	0.4	58.9	No	No
Bangli	4.4	15.4	9.3	32.8	28.6	8.1	0.0	91.9	No	No
Jembrana	5.7	20.7	8.9	32.3	30.8	21.8	1.2	77.0	No	No
Nusatenggara Barat	97.9	25.9	175.5	46.4	321.0	33.9	18.3	47.8	0	No
Lombok Timur	32.3	33.9	56.4	59.3	56.6	53.0	7.5	39.4	No	No
Lombok Tengah	25.4	26.4	49.2	51.2	63.8	31.4	43.3	25.3	No	No
Bima	16.5	26.5	29.4	47.3	45.8	36.7	13.2	50.1	No	No
Lombok Barat	17.4	26.8	28.7	44.3	55.6	25.3	7.3	67.4	No	No

Annex Table 4.B: Rural Farm Size and Land Use Status by Province and Kabupaten (Cont'd)

| Province/Kabupaten | Households "Controlling" Less Than | | | | Land Area Operated by Land Use Status | | | | Number of Small Operators and % of Dry Land Area | |
| | 0.25 ha | | 0.50 ha | | Total | Percent Wet Land (Sawah) | | Percent | Average of: | |
	'000	Percent	'000	Percent	'000 ha	Irrigated	Unirrigated	Dry Land	Province	"Region"
Dompu	2.2	14.9	4.1	27.8	16.2	43.1	7.8	49.1	No	No
Sumbawa	4.2	9.4	7.6	16.8	82.8	25.3	18.6	56.1	No	No
Nusatenggara Timur	32.4	7.2	73.9	16.5	680.6	5.8	4.6	89.6	3	No
Ende	4.2	13.8	8.7	28.6	39.1	6.3	2.0	91.7	No	No
Kupang	8.3	13.8	17.2	28.5	63.8	10.8	7.6	81.6	No	No
Timor Tengah Sel.	5.1	9.4	10.3	19.0	66.9	1.7	0.8	97.5	Yes	Yes
Sikka	1.7	5.1	6.1	18.4	45.4	1.8	0.2	97.9	Yes	Yes
Flores Timur	3.0	7.5	7.2	18.1	59.8	0.1	0.2	99.7	Yes	Yes
Ngada	1.5	6.5	4.0	17.0	37.3	9.6	4.6	85.7	No	No
Manggarai	3.8	6.1	8.5	13.6	107.0	12.2	8.8	79.0	No	No
Alor	1.6	7.3	2.6	12.0	46.3	0.6	0.0	99.4	No	No
Sumba Timur	1.1	5.3	2.6	11.9	34.8	9.3	13.5	77.2	No	No
Timor Tengah Utara	0.8	3.2	2.6	10.3	41.9	3.2	2.0	94.8	No	No
Sumba Barat	0.7	1.8	2.5	6.2	70.2	6.6	8.9	84.5	No	No
Belu	0.5	1.5	1.6	4.7	68.0	3.1	2.5	94.4	No	No
Kalimantan Barat	16.7	4.5	38.0	10.2	1 572.0	3.2	15.6	81.2		
Sambas	6.1	6.3	19.5	20.1	182.1	-	-	-		
Pontianak	4.6	5.1	9.3	10.2	323.7	-	-	-		
Ketapang	2.0	4.3	4.1	9.0	124.5	-	-	-		

Annex Table 4.B: Rural Farm Size and Land Use Status by Province and Kabupaten (Cont'd)

Province/Kabupaten	Households "Controlling" Less Than				Land Area Operated by Land Use Status				Number of Small Operators and % of Dry Land Area	
	0.25 ha		0.50 ha		Total	Percent Wet Land (Sawah)		Percent Dry Land	Average of:	
	'000	Percent	'000	Percent	'000 ha	Irrigated	Unirrigated		Province	"Region"
Kapuas Hulu	1.3	5.9	1.6	7.6	99.3	-	-	-		
Sintang	2.0	3.3	2.5	4.3	284.5	-	-	-		
Sanggau	0.8	1.3	0.9	1.6	558.0	-	-	-		
Kalimantan Tengah	5.7	4.0	10.4	7.3	468.5	0.0	19.7	80.3	5	
Barito Selatan	1.2	15.3	1.6	19.4	24.3	0.0	13.9	86.1	Yes	Yes
Barito Timur	0.5	5.7	1.2	14.4	22.3	0.0	15.4	84.6	Yes	No
Katingan	1.0	9.2	1.4	12.3	41.9	0.0	8.7	91.3	Yes	No
Kotawaringun Timur	1.1	4.1	2.4	9.4	74.6	0.0	19.6	80.4	Yes	No
Barito Utara	0.6	5.9	0.8	8.3	25.2	0.0	6.6	93.4	Yes	No
Kotawaringin Barat	0.4	2.8	0.8	6.3	24.9	0.0	23.3	76.7	No	No
Kapuas	0.9	1.8	2.1	4.4	96.1	0.0	61.3	38.7	No	No
Gunung Mas	0.1	0.8	0.2	1.6	126.0	0.0	0.5	99.5	No	No
Murung Raya	0.0	0.0	0.0	0.0	33.3	0.0	0.4	99.6	No	No
Kalimantan Selatan	48.0	15.9	111.2	36.8	325.6	5.9	48.0	46.0	1	
Hulu Sungai Selat.	7.3	24.8	16.6	56.8	19.0	3.6	58.2	38.2	No	No
Tabalong	5.3	26.1	11.3	55.6	15.1	2.3	26.3	71.5	Yes	No
Hula Sungai Utara	10.8	24.7	23.0	52.3	32.9	0.0	61.5	38.5	No	No
Hulu Sungai Tengah	7.4	19.5	19.7	52.2	24.7	2.8	54.8	42.4	No	No
Banjar	7.0	13.9	17.3	34.1	59.2	0.3	53.6	46.2	No	No

Annex Table 4.B: Rural Farm Size and Land Use Status by Province and Kabupaten (Cont'd)

Province/Kabupaten	Households "Controlling" Less Than				Land Area Operated by Land Use Status				Number of Small Operators and % of Dry Land Area	
	0.25 ha		0.50 ha		Total	Percent Wet Land (Sawah)		Percent Dry Land	Average of:	
	'000	Percent	'000	Percent	'000 ha	Irrigated	Unirrigated		Province	"Region"
Tapin	1.7	7.6	6.2	28.3	29.0	36.5	27.8	35.8	No	No
Kotabaru	4.9	12.3	7.6	19.0	58.8	0.6	22.0	77.4	No	No
Tanah Laut	1.7	7.8	3.7	16.9	34.5	0.0	46.9	53.1	No	No
Barito Kuala	1.9	5.2	5.8	16.1	52.3	2.9	80.2	16.9	No	No
Kalimantan Timur	8.7	9.8	14.6	16.6	157.0	1.4	21.3	77.3	0	No
Berau	0.5	10.6	1.2	24.6	5.7	0.0	29.9	70.1	No	No
Bulongan	2.4	15.7	3.4	21.6	24.5	6.8	18.8	74.4	No	No
Kutai	4.4	8.1	8.3	15.3	101.1	0.5	19.5	80.0	No	No
Pasir	1.3	9.8	1.8	12.9	25.8	0.0	28.7	71.3	No	No
Sulawesi Utara	38.7	14.1	75.6	27.6	375.6	6.7	4.1	89.2	1	
Gorontalo	29.1	41.7	64.6	9.5	10.1	80.4	No	Yes		
Sangihe Talaud	11.0	31.4	50.5	0.0	0.0	100.0	Yes	Yes		
Minahasa	30.9	25.1	176.4	5.4	1.1	93.5	No	No		
Bolaang Mongondow	4.7	10.2	84.0	11.3	8.2	80.5	No	No		
Sulawesi Tengah	13.0	6.4	27.0	13.4	422.2	0.0	14.4	85.6	0	No
Buol Tolitoli	1.9	7.2	4.4	16.8	47.4	0.0	18.7	81.3	No	No
Donggala	6.6	8.1	13.6	16.8	152.3	0.0	21.3	78.7	No	No

Annex Table 4.B: Rural Farm Size and Land Use Status by Province and Kabupaten (Cont'd)

Province/Kabupaten	Households "Controlling" Less Than				Land Area Operated by Land Use Status				Number of Small Operators and % of Dry Land Area	
	0.25 ha		0.50 ha		Total	Percent Wet Land (Sawah)		Percent Dry Land	Average of:	
	'000	Percent	'000	Percent	'000 ha	Irrigated	Unirrigated		Province	"Region"
Poso	2.8	6.3	5.5	12.3	91.8	0.0	14.2	85.8	No	No
Banggai	1.7	3.4	3.6	7.0	130.7	0.0	4.8	95.2	No	No
Sulawesi Selatan	117.2	15.3	233.9	30.6	858.7	17.9	24.9	57.2	3	
Tana Toraja	17.3	32.5	28.4	53.5	35.5	8.0	34.2	57.8	Yes	No
Takalar	9.2	35.5	13.6	52.7	20.7	7.6	53.4	39.0	No	No
Pangkajene Kepulaua	8.7	29.8	14.8	50.5	22.4	8.1	47.3	44.6	No	No
Barru	4.2	23.0	8.0	43.4	16.0	9.9	42.2	47.8	No	No
Polewali Mamasa	11.9	22.6	22.1	42.2	43.7	16.3	4.6	79.0	Yes	No
Gowa	10.6	20.4	20.7	39.6	51.0	22.8	20.5	56.7	No	No
Maros	4.4	16.5	9.5	36.0	25.1	57.6	22.3	20.1	No	No
Jeneponto	6.8	15.8	14.3	33.4	40.3	16.8	15.9	67.4	Yes	No
Enrekang	2.5	12.0	6.5	30.5	20.3	3.3	21.3	75.4	No	Yes
Majene	2.2	13.9	4.8	30.0	17.4	0.9	4.4	94.7	No	Yes
Bulukumba	5.0	10.6	12.9	27.2	47.9	24.1	3.9	72.1	No	No
Pinrang	5.2	15.4	9.1	26.9	46.2	14.1	14.2	44.6	No	No
Sinjai	3.4	13.9	6.5	26.4	27.7	10.4	22.1	67.5	No	No
Selayar	1.9	12.0	4.1	25.9	21.4	0.0	1.9	98.1	No	No
Sidenreng Rappang	2.7	10.2	6.3	23.8	35.2	34.3	27.0	38.7	No	No
Soppeng	2.7	8.2	7.9	23.8	34.4	31.2	10.4	58.4	No	No
Bantaeng	1.7	8.7	4.4	21.8	22.4	20.3	3.5	76.1	No	No

Annex Table 4.B: Rural Farm Size and Land Use Status by Province and Kabupaten (Cont'd)

Province/Kabupaten	Households "Controlling" Less Than				Land Area Operated by Land Use Status				Number of Small Operators and % of Dry Land Area Average of:	
	0.25 ha		0.50 ha		Total	Percent Wet Land (Sawah)		Percent Dry Land	Province	"Region"
	'000	Percent	'000	Percent	'000 ha	Irrigated	Unirrigated			
Bone	7.0	8.3	16.3	19.3	98.8	9.4	42.2	48.5	No	No
Luwu	5.4	7.2	14.0	18.5	113.4	20.6	18.1	61.4	No	No
Mamuju	0.8	4.9	2.4	14.9	31.7	2.2	11.8	86.0	No	No
Wajo	3.5	7.0	7.4	14.9	87.2	0.8	56.9	42.3	No	No
Sulawesi Tenggara	14.2	9.7	28.3	19.3	213.7	0.0	12.9	87.1	1	No
Buton	8.0	16.9	14.9	31.5	48.9	0.0	6.2	93.8	Yes	Yes
Muna	2.4	8.7	4.8	17.7	37.4	0.0	0.9	99.1	No	No
Kolaka	1.7	8.8	2.9	14.8	32.9	0.0	24.6	75.4	No	No
Kendari	2.1	4.1	5.7	10.9	94.5	0.0	17.0	83.0	No	No
Maluku	16.1	9.0	27.2	15.2	422.0	0.2	0.0	99.8	1	No
Maluku Tengah	9.9	14.5	15.7	23.1	111.4	0.8	0.0	99.2	No	Yes
Maluku Tenggara	3.6	9.5	7.0	18.6	100.8	0.0	0.0	100.0	Yes	Yes
Maluku Utara	2.4	4.1	3.8	6.5	175.1	0.0	0.0	100.0	No	No
Halmakera Tengah	0.2	1.7	0.7	4.8	34.7	0.0	0.0	100.0	No	No
Irian Jaya	46.5	30.2	70.0	45.5	152.7	0.1	3.6	96.2		
Jaya Wijaya	21.6	40.9	31.4	59.4	31.4	-	-	-		
Sorong	3.9	33.4	5.3	45.3	17.3	-	-	-		
Paniai	5.7	19.3	12.3	41.5	24.5	-	-	-		

Annex Table **4.B:** Rural Farm Size and Land Use Status by Province and Kabupaten (Cont'd)

Province/Kabupaten	Households "Controlling" Less Than				Land Area Operated by Land Use Status				Number of Small Operators and % of Dry Land Area	
	0.25 ha		0.50 ha		Total	Percent Wet Land (Sawah)		Percent Dry Land	Average of:	
	'000	Percent	'000	Percent	'000 ha	Irrigated	Unirrigated		Province	"Region"
Manokwari	2.2	25.0	3.6	40.8	9.5	-	-	-		
Fak-Fak	1.6	27.0	2.4	40.5	5.7	-	-	-		
Merauke	6.9	33.9	8.0	39.1	27.2	-	-	-		
Jayapura	2.5	23.1	3.9	36.0	16.5	-	-	-		
Teluk Cendrawasih	1.3	17.7	2.1	29.4	8.4	-	-	-		
Yapen Waropen	0.7	11.7	1.0	15.5	12.2	-	-	-		
Timor Timur	14.4	12.6	20.8	18.3	239.9	0.0	15.0	85.0	3	
Dili	3.2	41.9	3.7	49.1	8.5	0.0	13.3	86.7	Yes	No
Ainaro	2.5	30.2	3.0	36.8	14.6	0.0	20.1	79.9	No	No
Aileu	0.7	19.1	1.3	34.3	4.5	0.0	10.3	89.7	Yes	No
Ambeno	1.1	13.9	2.6	32.1	6.7	0.0	11.2	88.8	Yes	No
Baucau	3.7	22.8	4.1	25.4	26.7	0.0	33.0	67.0	No	No
Covalima	0.4	7.9	0.9	17.8	5.0	0.0	5.1	94.9	No	Yes
Liquica	0.7	10.3	1.2	16.8	15.6	0.0	0.4	99.6	No	Yes
Lautem	0.8	10.4	1.1	13.9	20.2	0.0	13.3	86.7	No	No
Viqueque	0.5	4.5	1.3	11.4	22.3	0.0	33.8	66.2	No	No
Manatuto	0.2	4.0	0.4	8.4	11.8	0.0	20.3	79.7	No	No
Ermera	0.4	2.6	0.8	5.2	47.8	0.0	4.3	95.7	No	No
Manufahi	0.1	2.0	0.3	4.8	28.6	0.0	2.3	97.7	No	No
Bobonaro	0.0	0.4	0.1	1.3	27.5	0.0	23.0	77.0	No	No

Annex Table 4.B: Rural Farm Size and Land Use Status by Province and Kabupaten (Cont'd)

Province/Kabupaten	Households "Controlling" Less Than				Land Area Operated by Land Use Status				Number of Small Operators and % of Dry Land Area	
	0.25 ha		0.50 ha		Total	Percent Wet Land (Sawah)		Percent Dry Land	Average of:	
	'000	Percent	'000	Percent	'000 ha	Irrigated	Unirrigated		Province	"Region"
Daerah Istimewa Aceh	58.2	15.0	128.5	33.2	426.0	16.3	19.7	63.9	1	No
Pidie	11.1	19.1	26.4	45.2	40.0	48.3	5.6	46.1	No	No
Aceh Utara	21.5	22.2	43.1	44.4	85.5	15.7	17.8	66.5	Yes	No
Aceh Selatan	7.2	16.8	15.5	36.3	44.1	20.3	17.1	62.7	No	No
Aceh Besar	4.6	13.3	12.5	36.2	29.9	9.8	26.6	63.6	No	No
Aceh Timur	8.0	14.7	16.1	29.6	63.4	5.0	29.1	65.8	No	No
Aceh Tenggara	1.2	5.2	5.9	24.8	21.6	42.4	8.6	49.0	No	No
Aceh Barat	4.0	8.4	7.7	16.4	91.7	5.6	32.9	61.5	No	No
Aceh Tengah	0.6	1.9	1.4	4.8	49.7	15.0	1.2	83.7	No	No
Sumatera Utara	204.2	21.5	366.3	38.6	897.0	14.2	19.7	66.0	1	No
Deli Serdang	47.6	32.1	75.7	51.2	110.4	19.6	26.1	54.3	No	No
Tapanuli Utara	32.1	27.9	52.4	45.5	94.4	22.2	8.7	69.1	No	No
Simalungun	23.9	24.0	44.1	44.2	70.6	36.3	2.7	61.0	No	No
Asahan	26.1	27.4	41.1	43.2	92.0	9.5	31.5	59.1	No	No
Langkat	24.1	25.7	38.9	41.5	99.3	4.7	28.8	66.5	Yes	No
Tapanuli Tengah	4.8	14.7	12.0	36.5	30.5	15.9	21.9	62.2	No	No
Tapanuli Selatan	19.5	15.7	43.7	35.1	115.0	24.0	13.7	62.3	No	No
Dairi	4.6	10.4	12.5	28.4	36.0	13.0	0.4	86.6	No	No
Labuhan Batu	12.3	16.2	20.0	26.2	108.2	1.3	38.5	60.3	No	No

Annex Table 4.B: Rural Farm Size and Land Use Status by Province and Kabupaten (Cont'd)

Province/Kabupaten	Households "Controlling" Less Than				Land Area Operated by Land Use Status				Number of Small Operators and % of Dry Land Area	
	0.25 ha		0.50 ha		Total	Percent Wet Land (Sawah)		Percent Dry Land	Average of:	
	'000	Percent	'000	Percent	'000 ha	Irrigated	Unirrigated		Province	"Region"
Nias	6.5	8.2	17.3	21.9	99.4	3.3	14.4	82.2	No	No
Karo	2.7	6.5	8.5	20.6	41.2	10.4	5.0	84.6	No	No
Sumatera Barat	76.2	16.5	174.2	37.7	385.9	25.7	15.3	59.0	2	
Padang Pariaman	11.5	16.5	26.3	37.7	67.6	16.0	15.8	68.2	Yes	No
Limapuluh Koto	8.6	16.5	19.7	37.7	41.3	24.2	20.7	55.2	No	No
Solok	10.7	16.5	24.4	37.7	61.1	30.7	12.4	56.9	No	No
Pasaman	10.5	16.5	23.9	37.7	55.3	29.3	12.2	58.5	No	No
Tanah Datar	9.2	16.5	21.0	37.7	43.1	33.8	11.3	54.9	No	No
Pesisir Selatan	8.3	16.5	18.9	37.7	32.5	23.7	26.2	50.2	No	No
Agam	10.7	16.5	24.6	37.6	39.8	35.6	13.3	51.1	No	No
Sawahlunto	6.7	16.5	15.4	37.7	45.2	15.0	15.5	69.5	Yes	No
Riau	28.4	10.6	46.6	17.4	674.0	0.0	9.1	90.9	3	
Kepulauan Riau	7.8	19.2	10.2	25.1	95.1	0.0	2.3	97.7	Yes	No
Indragiri Hulu	4.4	10.3	8.9	20.7	86.3	0.0	10.3	89.7	No	No
Bengkalis	7.2	12.3	11.7	19.9	122.9	0.0	8.9	91.1	Yes	No
Kampar	7.3	10.6	13.0	19.0	156.8	0.0	6.3	93.7	Yes	No
Indragiri Hilir	1.7	3.0	2.8	5.0	213.0	0.0	13.9	86.1	No	No

Annex Table 4.B: Rural Farm Size and Land Use Status by Province and Kabupaten (Cont'd)

Province/Kabupaten	Households "Controlling" Less Than				Land Area Operated by Land Use Status				Number of Small Operators and % of Dry Land Area	
	0.25 ha		0.50 ha		Total	Percent Wet Land (Sawah)		Percent	Average of:	
	'000	Percent	'000	Percent	'000 ha	Irrigated	Unirrigated	Dry Land	Province	"Region"
Jambi	20.5	9.1	38.2	17.1	641.3	3.8	15.8	80.4	1	
Kerinci	7.0	13.9	15.6	31.2	52.5	17.5	9.2	73.2	No	No
Batanghari	6.8	20.9	9.9	30.6	57.9	0.3	15.0	84.6	Yes	Yes
Bungotebo	3.6	8.7	6.7	16.1	128.3	2.2	6.1	91.8	No	No
Sarko	1.5	3.4	3.5	7.9	259.6	4.6	2.8	92.6	No	No
Tanjung Jabung	1.6	2.9	2.5	4.5	143.1	0.0	50.8	49.2	No	No
Sumatera Selatan	32.8	6.1	74.5	14.0	981.7	0.0	25.0	75.0	2	
Belitung	3.5	30.7	5.2	45.0	9.8	0.0	0.1	99.9	Yes	Yes
Bangka	4.9	10.0	9.9	20.2	61.3	0.0	0.4	99.6	Yes	No
Ogan Komer. Ilir	6.1	7.6	14.5	18.1	122.3	0.0	44.7	55.3	No	No
Musi Banyuasin	8.0	7.6	14.8	14.0	224.7	0.0	38.0	62.0	No	No
Ogan Komering Ulu	4.5	4.0	14.1	12.5	191.4	0.0	25.9	74.1	No	No
Lahat	2.6	3.5	7.6	10.3	122.4	0.0	18.0	82.0	No	No
Musi Rawas	1.7	3.3	4.8	9.7	108.9	0.0	15.7	84.3	No	No
Liot	1.4	2.8	3.6	7.0	140.8	0.0	11.7	88.3	No	No
Bengkulu	6.4	4.9	16.1	12.3	210.7	11.6	12.8	75.6	0	
Rejang Lebong	3.6	7.6	9.1	19.3	54.8	19.4	5.4	75.2	No	No
Bengkulu Utara	1.7	4.0	3.9	9.4	84.5	6.5	11.1	82.4	No	No
Bengkulu Selatan	1.1	2.7	3.0	7.3	71.5	11.7	20.3	67.9	No	No

Annex Table 4.B: Rural Farm Size and Land Use Status by Province and Kabupaten (Cont'd)

Province/Kabupaten	Households "Controlling" Less Than				Land Area Operated by Land Use Status				Number of Small Operators and % of Dry Land Area	
	0.25 ha		0.50 ha		Total	Percent Wet Land (Sawah)		Percent Dry Land	Average of:	
	'000	Percent	'000	Percent	'000 ha	Irrigated	Unirrigated		Province	"Region"
Lampung	44.3	6.4	139.7	20.2	881.5	8.4	9.2	82.4	0	
Lampung Selatan	19.5	7.5	61.9	23.9	289.6	8.1	14.7	77.2	No	No
Lampung Tengah	20.3	7.1	63.9	22.4	324.8	13.7	8.5	77.8	No	No
Lampung Utara	4.5	3.0	14.0	9.4	267.1	2.2	4.2	93.7	No	No
All Indonesia	5 060.9	27.5	8 818.1	47.9	17 679.1	14.9	16.1	69.0	46	8

Source: Government of Indonesia, Biro Pusat Statistik (1983a).

Bibliography

Alarcon Rivero, J.V., J. Van Heemst, S. Keuning, W. De Ruijter, and R. Vos. 1986. *The Social Accounting Framework for Development: Concepts, Construction and Applications*. The Hague: Institute of Social Studies.

American Embassy. 1985. *Labor Trends in Indonesia*. Jakarta: American Embassy.

Anderson, A. Grant. 1980. "The Rural Market in West Java." *Economic Development and Cultural Change*. 28 (4): 753-777.

Arifin, Bustanil. 1975. *Fungsi Badan Urusan Logistik*. (Functions of the National Stock Authority.) Jakarta: Badan Urusan Logistik.

Azis, I.J. 1980. *Future Development Planning Techniques in Indonesia: The Need for a New Framework and the Incorporation of Regional Dimension*. Seminar Sistem Neraca Sosial Ekonomi Indonesia, 23-24 July 1986, Project RTA-104. Jakarta: Sistem Nanaca Sosial Ekonomi.

—. 1986. "Banking on Disaster - Indonesia's Transmigration Programme." *The Ecologist*. 16 (2/3).

Baharsyah, S., and S.S. Hadiwigeno. 1982. "The Development of Commercial Crop Farming." In Mubyarto (ed.). 1982. *Growth and Equity in Indonesian Agricultural Development*. Jakarta: Yayasan Agro Ekonomika.

Barlow, C., and Muharminto. 1982. "The Rubber Smallholder Economy." *Bulletin of Indonesian Economic Studies*. 18 (2): 86-119.

Bina, Swadaya. 1984. *Working Report 1984*. Jakarta: Community Self Reliance Development Agency.

—. 1985. *Working Report 1985*. Jakarta: Community Self Reliance Development Agency.

Binswanger, H., R. Evenson, C. Florencio, and B. White. 1980. *An Anthropological Approach to the Study of Economic Value of Children in Java and Nepal*. Rural Household Studies in Asia. Singapore: Singapore University Press.

Birowo, A.T. 1979. "The Big Problem of the Small Farmer: The Indonesian Case." *The Big Problem of the Small Farmer*. Amsterdam: ILACO.

Birowo, A.T., and D. Prabowo. 1985. "Pressure on Natural Resources in Indonesian Agricultural Development." Paper presented at the International Conference of Agricultural Economists, Malaga, Spain.

Booth, Anne. 1984. "Survey of Recent Developments." *Bulletin of Indonesian Economic Studies.* XX (3): 1-35.

Brooks, Markhan, R. 1980. *The Problem of Malnutrition Within the Agricultural Economy of Bojonegoro, East Java.* Ph.D. dissertation. Ithaca, New York: Cornell University.

Chernichovsky, Dov, and Oey A. Meesook. 1984. *Poverty in Indonesia: A Profile.* Staff Working Paper 671. Washington D.C.: World Bank.

Chitman, P., and G.S. Tan (eds.). 1984. *The Progress and Development of Rubber Smallholders.* Proceedings of the Fifth Seminar held in Kuala Lumpur, Malaysia, 4-10 December 1982. Kuala Lumpur: The Association of Natural Rubber Producing Countries.

Collier, William L. 1979. "Food Problems, Unemployment and the Green Revolution in Rural Java." *Prisma.* No. 9.

Collier, William L., *et al.* 1982. "Acceleration of Rural Development in Java." *Bulletin of Indonesian Economic Studies.* 18 (3): 84-101

Colter, M. Jusuf. 1984. *Ciri-Ciri Dan Pola Tenaga Kerja Migran Dari Daerah Pedesaan, Studi Dinamika Pesesaan.* Bogor, Indonesia.

Dapice, David. 1985. "Indonesian Food Policy Since 1967: Surprising Progress." Washington, D.C.: World Bank.

Dent, F.J., and M. Sukardi. 1981. "The Photomorphic Approach to Intermediate Screening of Land Resources in Indonesia." *Indonesian Agricultural Research and Development Journal.* 3 (2).

Desaunettes, J.R. 1977. "Land Capability Appraisal Project. Catalogue of Landforms for Indonesia: Examples of a Physiographic Approach to Land Evaluation for Agricultural Development." Working Paper 13. Rome: Food and Agriculture Organization; Bogor: Soil Research Institute, Land and Water Development Division.

Development Alternatives, Inc. (DAI). 1985. *Central Java Enterprise Development Project (Design).* Semarang: DAI for United States Agency for International Development.

Development Studies Centre. *"Women's Work and Women's Roles, Economics and Everyday Life in Indonesia, Malaysia and Singapore.* Monograph No. 32. Canberra: The Australian National Unversity.

Dick, Howard. 1982. "Survey of Recent Developments." *Bulletin of Indonesian Economic Studies.* XVIII (1): 1-38.

Downey, R.A. 1984. *Indonesian Inequality: Integrated National Accounting of Who Gets What.* Vols. I and II. Ph.D. dissertation. Ithaca, New York: Cornell University.

Edmunson, Wade. 1981. "Nutrition and the Household Economy." In Hansen. 1981. 255-269.

Effendi, S., Inu G. Ismail, and J.L. McIntosh. 1982. "Cropping Systems Research in Indonesia." In International Rice Research Institute. 1982. *Cropping Systems Research in Asia.* Report of a Workshop held in Los Baños, Laguna, Philippines. Manila: International Rice Research Institute. 203-210.

Esterik, Penny van (ed.). 1982. *Women of Southeast Asia.* Occasional Paper No. 9. Dekalb: Northern Illinois University, Center for Southeast Asian Studies.

Fajans, P., and H. Sudiman. 1984. *The Indonesian National Family Nutrition Improvement Programme (UPGK): A Case Study of Seven Villages.* Jakarta: United Nations Children's Fund.

Falcon, W.P., W.O. Jones, S.R. Pearson, J.A. Dixon, G.C. Nelson, F.C. Roche, and L.J. Unnevehr. 1984. *The Cassava Economy of Java.* Stanford: Stanford University Press.

Food and Agriculture Organization of the United Nations (FAO). 1985. "Toward Improved Multilevel Planning for Agricultural and Rural Development in Asia and the Pacific." Economic and Social Paper 52. Rome: Food and Agriculture Organization.

—. 1986a. *Growth, Equity and Poverty in the Far East - Performance of Countries.* Rome: Food and Agriculture Organization.

—. 1986b *Reference List of Some Programmes, Projects and Reports (1949-85). Annex I.* Rome: Food and Agriculture Organization.

Food and Agriculture Organization/United Nations Development Programme. 1985. *Improving and Developing Mixed Farming Systems under Rainfed Conditions in West Java and South Sumatra.* Draft Terminal Project Report. Rome: Food and Agriculture Organization.

Gasser, F. 1983. *The State of Nutrition Among Children Below Five Years in Three Villages in West Pasaman, North Sumatra.* Report of field work. Mimeographed.

Geertz, Clifford. 1962. "The Rotating Credit Association: A Middle Rung in Development." *Economic Development and Cultural Change.* 10 (3): 241-263.

Glassburner, Bruce. 1985. "Macroeconomics and the Agricultural Sector." *Bulletin of Indonesian Economic Studies.* 21 (2): 51-73.

———. 1986. "Survey of Recent Developments." *Bulletin of Indonesian Economic Studies*. 22 (1): 1-33.

Government of Indonesia, BAPPENAS. 1984. *Policies and Prospects for Sustained Development Under Challenging Conditions, REPELITA IV: The Fourth Five-Year Development Plan of Indonesia 1984/85-1988/89 (A Summary)*. Jakarta: Ministry of Planning.

Government of Indonesia, Biro Pusat Statistik. 1972. *Statistik Pendidikan 1971-1972, Diluar lingkungan Departemen P&K*. No. 04330.8403. Jakarta: Central Bureau of Statistics.

———. 1975. *Sosial Accounting Matrix: Indonesia 1975*. No. 04420.8402, Vol. II. Jakarta: Central Bureau of Statistics.

———. 1976. *National Labour Force Survey*. Jakarta: Central Bureau of Statistics.

———. 1980a. *Analisa Keadaan Perumahan di Indonesia Berdasarkan Data Sensus Penduduk 1980*. No. 03320.8601. Jakarta: Central Bureau of Statistics.

———. 1980b. *Analisa Ringkas Hasil Sensus Penduduk 1980*. No. 03320.8411. Jakarta: Central Bureau of Statistics.

———. 1981a. *Keadaan Angkatan Kerja di Indonesia 1961-1980*. VP.KK.0662.8301. Jakarta: Central Bureau of Statistics.

———. 1981b. *Peta Konsumsi Pangan di Indonesia 1981*. No. 04110.8406. Jakarta: Central Bureau of Statistics.

———. 1982a. *Analisa Kesejahteraan Rumah Tangga di Indonesia Berdasarkan Survei Sosial Ekonomi Nasional 1982*. No. 03320.8605. Jakarta: Central Bureau of Statistics.

———. 1982b. *Indikator Pembangunan Pertanian 1982*. (Indicators of Agricultural Development 1982.) No. 04150.8410. Jakarta: Central Bureau of Statistics.

———. 1982c. *Statistik Industri Rumahtangga 1982*. (Statistics of Cottage Industry 1982.) No. 04150.8411. Jakarta: Central Bureau of Statistics.

———. 1982d. *Survei Sosial Ekonomi Nasional, Statistik Kesejahteraan Rumah Tangga, September-Desember 1982*. No. 04340.8402. Jakarta: Central Bureau of Statistics.

———. 1983a. *Agricultural Census 1983*. Series A2 and B. Jakarta: Central Bureau of Statistics.

———. 1983b. *Agricultural Census 1983, Land Utilization by Province and District*. Seri D. Jakarta: Central Bureau of Statistics.

———. 1983c. *Agricultural Survey: Agricultural Machinery by Province and District, 1981-1983*. No. 04110.13. Jakarta: Central Bureau of Statistics.

——. 1983d. *Food Balance Sheet in Indonesia 1983.* No. 04150.8601. Jakarta: Central Bureau of Statistics.

——. 1983e. *Indikator Pertanian 1983.* (Agriculture Indicators 1983.) No. 04150.8602. Jakarta: Central Bureau of Statistics.

——. 1983f. *Keadaan Koperasi non KUD di Indonesia 1983.* No. 04240.8507. Jakarta: Central Bureau of Statistics.

——. 1983g. *Land Area by Utilization Outer Jawa 1983.* Jakarta: Central Bureau of Statistics.

——. 1983h. *Land Area by Utilization in Jawa 1983.* Jakarta: Central Bureau of Statistics.

——. 1983i. *Luas dan Intensitas Serangan Jasad Pengganggu Terhadap Tanaman Bahan Makanan di Indonesia 1983.* Jakarta: Central Bureau of Statistics.

——. 1983j. *Produksi Buah-Buahan di Jawa, Tahun 1983.* Jakarta: Central Bureau of Statistics.

——. 1983k. *Produksi Tanaman Sayuran di Jawa 1983.* Jakarta: Central Bureau of Statistics.

——. 1983l. *Sensus Pertanian 1983 (Agricultural Census), Land Utilization by Province and District.* No. 04100.8502, Seri D. Jakarta: Central Bureau of Statistics.

——. 1983m. *Sensus Pertanian 1983 (Agricultural Census), Report on Households' Listing by Province and District.* No. 04100.8501, Seri A2. Jakarta: Central Bureau of Statistics.

——. 1983n. *Sensus Pertanian 1983, Angka Sementara, Sensus Sampel Perikanan Laut Dan, Sensus Sampel Perikanan Tambak.* No. 04120.8502, Seri H1. Jakarta: Central Bureau of Statistics.

——. 1983o. *Sensus Pertanian 1983, Analisa Pendahuluan Hasil Pendaftaran Rumahtangga.* No. 03310.8504, Seri J.1. Jakarta: Central Bureau of Statistics.

——. 1983p. *Sensus Pertanian 1983, Banyaknya Koperasi Unit Desa di Indonesia 1982 (Angka Sementara).* No. 04100.8402, Seri C.1. Jakarta: Central Bureau of Statistics.

——. 1983q. *Sensus Pertanian 1983, Daftar nama Dan Alamat Koperasi Unit Desa (KUD) 1983, Sumatera.* No. 04100.8405, Seri C.2.2. Jakarta: Central Bureau of Statistics.

——. 1983r. *Sensus Pertanian 1983, Daftar nama Dan Alamat, Koperasi Unit Desa (KUD) 1983, Luar Jawa Tanpa Sumatera.* No. 04100.8406, Seri C.2.3. Jakarta: Central Bureau of Statistics.

——. 1983s. *Sensus Pertanian 1983, Hasil Pendaftaran Rumahtangga Dalam Gambar.* No. 03300.8515, Seri A3. Jakarta: Central Bureau of Statistics.

——. 1983t. *Sensus Pertanian 1983, Koperasi Unit Desa di Indonesia 1982.* No. 04150.8506, Seri C.3. Jakarta: Central Bureau of Statistics.

——. 1983u. *Statistik Potensi Desa, Sensus Pertanian 1983.* No. 04340.8602, Seri E2. Jakarta: Central Bureau of Statistics.

——. 1983v. *Statistik Potensi Desa, Sensus Pertanian 1983.* No. 04340.8601, Seri E1. Jakarta: Central Bureau of Statistics.

——. 1983w. *Indonesian System of Socio-economic Accounts, 1975.* Vol. II. Jakarta: Central Bureau of Statistics.

——. 1984a. *Agricultural Survey: Agricultural Machinery by Province and District 1984.* No. 04110.8601. Jakarta: Central Bureau of Statistics.

——. 1984b. *Food Balance Sheet in Indonesia in 1982.* Jakarta: Central Bureau of Statistics.

——. 1984c. *Ikhtisar Statistik Sosial dan Kependudukan 1984.* No. 04300.8501. Jakarta: Central Bureau of Statistics.

——. 1984d. *Konsumsi Kalori dan Protein Penduduk Indonesia per Provinsi 1984, Survei Sosial Ekonomi Nasional.* No. 04340.8604, Seri 2. Jakarta: Central Bureau of Statistics.

——. 1984e. *Land Area by Utilization Outer Jawa 1984.* Jakarta: Central Bureau of Statistics.

——. 1984f. *Land Area by Utilization in Jawa 1984.* Jakarta: Central Bureau of Statistics.

——. 1984g. *Luas dan Intensitas Serangan Jasad Pengganggu Terhadap Padi Dan Palawija di Indonesia 1984.* Jakarta: Central Bureau of Statistics.

——. 1984h. *Luas Tanah Menurut Pneggunaannya di Luar Jawa.* (Land Area by Utilization - Outer Java.) No. 04110.8608 ISSN.0216-7220. Jakarta: Central Bureau of Statistics.

——. 1984i. *Pengeluaran Untuk Konsumsi Penduduk Indonesia 1984.* No. 04340.8603, Seri 1. Jakarta: Central Bureau of Statistics.

——. 1984j. *Pengeluaran Untuk Konsumsi Penduduk Indonesia per Provinsi 1984.* No. 04340.8605, Seri 3. Jakarta: Central Bureau of Statistics.

——. 1984k. *Produksi Buah-buahan di Jawa 1984.* Jakarta: Central Bureau of Statistics.

——. 1984l. *Proyeksi Angkatan Kerja Indonesia per Propinsi 1983-1990.* No. 04320.8407. Jakarta: Central Bureau of Statistics.

——. 1984m. *Statistical Profile of Mothers and Children in Indonesia 1983.* Jakarta: Central Bureau of Statistics.

——. 1984n. *Statistical Profile of Mothers and Children in Indonesia 1984.* Jakarta: Central Bureau of Statistics.

——. 1984o. *Statistik Energi (Energy Statistics) 1984.* No. 04140.8601. Jakarta: Central Bureau of Statistics.

——. 1984p. *Statistik Keuangan (Financial Statistics) 1983/1984.* No. 04240.8506. Jakarta: Central Bureau of Statistics.

——. 1984q. *Statistik Lingkungan Hidup Indonesia 1984.* No. 04340.8502. Jakarta: Central Bureau of Statistics.

——. 1984r. *Statistik Perkebunan Besar 1984.* No. 04120.8503. Jakarta: Central Bureau of Statistics.

——. 1984s. *Statistik Sosial Budaya, Hasil Susenas 1984.* No. 04339.8605. Jakarta: Central Bureau of Statistics.

——. 1985a. *Indikator Kesejahteraan Rakyat, Welfare Indicators, 1985.* Jakarta: Central Bureau of Statistics.

——. 1985b. *National Income of Indonesia 1983-1984, Main Tables.* Jakarta: Central Bureau of Statistics.

——. 1985c. *Statistical Profile of Mothers and Children in Indonesia 1985.* Jakarta: Central Bureau of Statistics.

——. 1985d. *Statistik Lingkungan Hidup Indonesia 1985.* No. 04340.8606. Jakarta: Central Bureau of Statistics.

——. 1986a. *Indikator Ekonomi, Januari 1986, Monthly Statistical Bulletin.* No. 03300.8601. Jakarta: Central Bureau of Statistics.

——. 1986b. *Sensus Pertanian 1983, Pembahasan Hasil Analisa, 17-18 Maret 1986, Pengelolaan Pasca Panen Dan Pemasaran.* Jakarta: Central Bureau of Statistics.

——. 1986c. *Sensus Pertanian 1983, Pembahasan Hasil Analisa, 17-18 Maret 1986, Laporan Analisis Sensus Pertanian 1983 Perkreditan Dan KUD.* Jakarta: Central Bureau of Statistics.

——. 1986d. *Sensus Pertanian 1983, Pembahasan Hasil Analisa, 17-18 Maret 1986, Aplikasi Teknologi Pertanian Di Indonesia.* Jakarta: Central Bureau of Statistics.

——. 1986e. *Sensus Pertanian 1983, Pembahasan Hasil Analisa, 17-18 Maret 1986, Distribusi Penggunaan Tanah Pertanian di Indonesia.* Jakarta: Central Bureau of Statistics.

——. 1986f. *Sensus Pertanian 1983, Pembahasan Hasil Analisa, 17-18 Maret 1986, Pola Pemilikan Tanah di Indonesia.* Jakarta: Central Bureau of Statistics.

——. 1986g. *Sensus Pertanian 1983, Pembahasan Hasil Analisa, 17-18 Maret 1986, Intensifikasi Pertanian Tanaman Pangan.* Jakarta: Central Bureau of Statistics.

——. 1986h. *Sensus Pertanian 1983, Pembahasan Hasil Analisa, 17-18 Maret 1986, Pola Pertanian Dan Usaha Tani.* Jakarta: Central Bureau of Statistics.

—. 1986i. *Indonesian System of Socio-economic Accounts, 1980.* Jakarta: Central Bureau of Statistics.

—. 1987. *Agricultural Indicators.* Jakarta: Central Bureau of Statistics.

—. 1989. *Statistik Lingkungan Hidup Indonesia 1989.* Jakarta: Central Bureau of Statistics.

Government of Indonesia, Biro Pusat Statistik/United Nations International Children's Fund. 1984. *An Analysis of the Situation of Children and Women in Indonesia.* Jakarta: United Nations International Children's Fund.

Government of Indonesia, Directorate-General of Fisheries, Ministry of Agriculture. 1986. "Small-Scale Fishermen's Development in Indonesia." Jakarta. Mimeographed.

Government of Indonesia, Directorate-General of Water Resources Development, North Sumatra. 1985. *Simalungun Irrigation Sector II Project, 1985.* Directorate of Irrigation-I. Jakarta: Directorate General of Water Resources Department.

Gusti Bagus Teken, I., and H. Suwardi. 1982. "Food Supply and Demand and Food Policies." In Mubyarto (ed.). 1982. *Growth and Equity in Indonesian Agricultural Development.* Jakarta: Yayasan Agro Ekonomika.

Hadid Soesastro, M. 1984. "Policy Analysis of Rural Household Energy Needs in West Java." In Islam, Nurul M., R. Morse, and M. Hadid Soesastro (eds.). 1984. *Rural Energy to Meet Development Needs - Asian Village Approaches.* Boulder, Colorado: Westview Press.

Hansen, Gary E. (ed.). 1981. *Agricultural and Rural Development in Indonesia.* Boulder, Colorado: Westview Press.

Hardjono, J. 1983. "Rural Development in Indonesia: The "Top-Down" Approach." In Lea, D., and D.P. Chaudhri (eds.). 1983. *Rural Development and the State: Contradictions and Dilemmas in Developing Countries.* London: Methuen.

Hart, G. 1980. "Patterns of Household Labour Allocation in a Javanese Village." In Binswanger, H., R. Evenson, C. Florencio, and B. White (eds.). 1980.

—. 1983. "Productivity, Poverty and Population Pressure: Female Labor Deployment in Rice Production in Java and Bangladesh." *American Journal of Agricultural Economics.* 65 (5): 1037-1042.

—. 1984. *Agrarian Labour Arrangements and Structural Change: Lessons from Java and Bangladesh.* World Employment Programme Research Working Paper. Geneva: International Labour Organisation.

Hartoyo, Sri, Makali. 1984. *Perubahan Pola Pengeluaran Rumah Tangga di Pedesaan Jawa, Studi Dinamika Pedesaan.* Bogor, Indonesia. Mimeographed.

Heiby, J., G.D. Ness, and B.L.K. Pillsbury. 1979. *AID's Role in Indonesia Family Planning: A Case Study with General Lessons for Foreign Assistance.* United States Agency for International Development, Bureau for Asia. Washington, D.C.: United States Agency for International Development.

Helen Keller International Incorporated (HKII). 1980. *Indonesia Nutritional Blindness Prevention Project, Final Report.* Jakarta: Helen Keller International Incorporated.

Hull, T.H., and Valerie J. Hull. 1984. "Population Change in Indonesia: Findings of the 1980 Census." *Bulletin of Indonesian Economic Studies.* XX (3): 95-119.

Hull, Valerie J. 1982. "Women in Java's Rural Middle Class: Progress or Regress?" In Esterik, Penny van (ed.). 1982.

Huppi, Monika, and Martin Ravallion. 1990. "The Sectoral Structure of Poverty During an Adjustment Period. Evidence from Indonesia in the mid-1980s." Policy, Research and External Affairs Working Papers (IBRD). No. 529. Washington, D.C.: World Bank.

Husein Sawit, M., and Triono Dkoko. 1984. *Pola Musiman Dan Tingkah Laku Rumah Tangga Buruh Tani Dalam Pasar Tenaga Kerja Di Pedesaan Jawa, Studi Dinamika Pedesaan.* Bogor, Indonesia. Mimeographed.

Informasi Perkoperasian (INFOKOP), Media Pengkajian Perkoperasian. 1984. *Nomor 1, Tahun ke I, Desember 1984.* Jakarta: Informasi Perkoperasian.

——. 1985. *Nomor 4, Tahun ke II, Oktober 1985.* Jakarta: Informasi Perkoperasian.

——. 1986. *Nomor 5, Tahun III, April 1986.* Jakarta: Informasi Perkoperasian.

International Fund for Agricultural Development. 1985. *Rural Women in Agricultural Investment Projects 1977-1984.* Nairobi, Kenya, 15-26 July 1985. Rome: International Fund for Agricultural Development.

——. 1986. "Women in Development." In IFAD. 1986. *1985 Annual Report.* Rome: International Fund for Agricultural Development.

International Labour Organisation/Asian Development Bank. 1985. *ILO/ADB Regional Workshop on Training for Entrepreneurship and Self-Employment, Country Study.* Indonesia: International Labour Organisation/Asian Development Bank.

International Monetary Fund. 1990. *Government Finance Statistics Yearbook 1990.* Washington, D.C.: International Monetary Fund.

—. 1991. *International Financial Statistics Yearbook 1991.* Washington, D.C.: International Monetary Fund.

Jayasuriya, S.K., and R.T. Shand. 1986. "Technical Change and Labour Absorption in Asian Agriculture: Some Emerging Trends." *World Development.* 14 (3): 415-428.

Johnston, M. 1986. "Clean Water at a Premium: The Case of Bandar Lampung." *Prisma.* 39.

Jones, G.W. 1984. "Links Between Urbanization and Sectoral Shifts in Employment in Java." *Bulletin of Indonesian Economic Studies.* XX (3): 120-157.

Kantor Statistik. 1985. *Lampung Dalam Angka 1984-1985.* (Statistik Tahunan 1984-1985.) Bandar Lampung: BAPPEDA, Kantor Statistik Propinsi Lampung.

Kardjati, S., *et al.* 1979. *Food Consumption and Nutritional Status of Mothers and Preschool Children in Sidoarjo and Madura, East Java.* Report III. Surabaya: University of Airlangga.

Karyadi, D. 1974. "Hubungan Ketahanan Fisik Dengan Keadaan Gizi dan Anemi Gizi Besi." Doctoral dissertation.

Kasryno, F. 1985. "Efficiency Analysis of Rice Farming in Java 1977-1983." *Jurnal Agro Ekonomi.* 4 (2).

Kasryno, F., D. Budianto, and A.T. Birowo. 1982. "Agriculture - Non-agriculture Linkages and the Role of Agriculture in Overall Economic Development." In Mubyarto (ed.). 1982. *Growth and Equity in Indonesian Agricultural Development.* Jakarta: Yayasan Agro Ekonomika.

Keuning, S.J. 1984. "Farm Size, Land Use and Profitability of Food Crops in Indonesia." *Bulletin of Indonesian Economic Studies.* XX (1): 58-82.

Khan, H.A., and Erik Thorbecke. 1986. *Macroeconomic Effects and Diffusion of Alternative Technologies within a Social Accounting Matrix Framework: The Case of Indonesia.* Geneva: International Labour Organisation.

Kikuchi, M. and Y. Hayami. 1982. "Growth and Equity in New Rice Technology. A Perspective from Village Studies in Rice Research Strategies for the Future." In papers presented at the Symposium on *Rice Research Strategies for the Future.* 21-23 April 1980. Manila: International Rice Research Institute.

Lastario, Arie. 1983a. *Analisa Perbandingan Peningkatan Pendapatan dan Pemerataan.* Vol. I (Pulau Jawa), Vol. II (Pulau

Sumatera), Vol. III (Pulau Kalimantan), Vol. IV (Pulau Sulawesi), Vol. V (Kepulauan), Nusantara 1983. Jakarta: Unpublished.

——. 1983b. *Kompilasi Analisa Data.* Vol. I (Pulau Jawa), Vol. II (Pulau Sumatera), Vol. III (Pulau Kalimantan), Vol. IV (Pulau Sulawesi), Vol. V (Kepulauan), Nusantara 1983. Jakarta: Unpublished.

Lee, Eddy. 1983. "Agrarian Change and Poverty in Rural Java." In International Labour Organisation. 1983. *Poverty in Rural Asia.* Geneva: International Labour Organisation.

Maamun, Y. 1985. "Resource Utilization Efficiency of Rice Production in South Sulawesi." *Jurnal Agro Ekonomi.* 4 (2).

Manderson, Lenore (ed.). 1983. *Women's Work and Women's Roles: Economics and Everyday Life in Indonesia, Malaysia and Singapore.* Development Studies Centre Monograph No. 32. The Australian National University, Canberra, Australia and New York. Canberra: Australian National University.

Mintoro, Abunawan, Sugairto, Waluyo. 1984. *Hubungan Kerja Dalam Usahatani Padi, Kasus di Dua Desa: Wargabinangun (Kabupaten Cirebon) dan Gunungwangi (Kabupaten Majalengka).* Bogor, Indonesia: Studi Dinamika Pedesaan.

Mubyarto. 1980. *Ilmu Ekonomi, Ilmu Sosial Dan Keadilan: Analisa Trans-disiplin dalam Rangka Mendalami Sistem Ekonomi Pancasila.* Jakarta: Yayasan Agro Ekonomika.

——. 1985. *Peluang Kerja dan Berusaha di Pedesaan.* Yogyakarta: BPFE untuk P3PK UGM. (P3PK UGM - Pusat Penelitan Pembangunan Pedesaan Dan Kawasan Universitas Gadjah Mada.)

——. 1986. *Perkreditan dan KUD: Laporan Analysis Sensus Pertanian 1983.* Jakarta: Biro Pusat Statistik dan Universitas Gadjah Mada.

——. 1987. *Ekonomi Pancasila: Gagasan dan Kemungkinan.* Jakarta: Lembaga Penelitian, Pendidikan dan Penerangan Ekonomi dan Sosial.

Mubyarto, Sajogyo, and S. Tjondronegoro. 1982. "Poverty, Equity and Rural Development." In Mubyarto (ed.). 1982. *Growth and Equity in Indonesian Agricultural Development.* Jakarta: Yayasan Agro Ekonomika.

Mubyarto, L. Soetrisno, and M. Dove. 1984. *Nelayan dan Kemiskinan, Studi Ekonomi Antropologi di Dua Desa Pantai.* Jakarta: Rajawali.

Muttalib, J.A. 1985. *Women as the Driving Force in Development: Why and How?* Jakarta: Kowani.

Nataatmadja, H. 1985. "Indonesia: Soyabean Marketing in Indonesia: A Constraint to Production." *Research Implications of Expanded*

Production of Selected Upland Crops in Tropical Asia. Proceedings of a Workshop, Bangkok, 27-30 November 1984. Bogor, Indonesia: CGPRT Centre.

Nirwoan, and A. Rofi'ie. 1984. *Profil Indonesia 1983. Lembaga Studi Pembangunan.* Jakarta: Lembaga Studi Pembangunan Anggota IKAPI.

Paauw, Douglas S., and S. Stavenuiter. 1986. *Government Budgeted Expenditures and Employment.* Working Paper. Geneva: International Labour Office.

Palmer, Ingrid. 1977. "Rural Poverty in Indonesia with Special Reference to Java." In International Labour Organisation. 1977. *Poverty and Landlessness in Rural Asia.* Geneva: International Labour Organisation.

Pandjaitan, M., and I.G.N. Gde Pemayun. 1985. "Rural Energy Systems in Indonesia." In Elmahgary, Y., and A.K. Biswas (eds.). 1985. *Integrated Rural Energy Planning.* Guildford, United Kingdom: Butterworth.

Papanek, H. 1975. *Marriage, Divorce and Marriage Law Reform in Indonesia.* Boston: Harvard University, Center for the Study of World Religions.

—. 1979a. *Implications of Development for Women in Indonesia: Selected Research and Policy Issues.* D.P. No. 8. Boston: Boston University, Center for Asian Development Studies.

—. 1979b. "Family Status Production: The Work and Non-work of Women". *Signs: Journal of Women in Culture and Society.* 4 (4).

Papanek, H., P. Hendrata, Y. Rahardjo, M.G. Tan, T.O. Ihromi, and A. Way. 1976. "Women in Jakarta: Family Life and Family Planning." In a report to the Interdisciplinary Communication Program of the Smithsonian Institution. Occasional Monograph Series, No. 6, Cultural Factors and Population in Developing Countries, ICP Work Agreements Reports, December 1976, pages 129-166. Washington, D.C.: ICP, Smithsonian Institution.

Partadiredja, Ace. 1982. "Farm Organization, Technology and Employment." In Mubyarto (ed.). 1982. *Growth and Equity in Indonesian Agricultural Development.* Jakarta: Yayasan Agro Ekonomika.

Penny, D.H., and M. Ginting. 1984. *Pekarangan Petani dan Kemiskinan: Suatu Studi Tentang Sifat dan Hakekat Masyarakat Tani di Sriharjo Pedesaan Jawa.* Yogyakarta: Gadjah Mada University Press and Jakarta: Yayasan Agro Ekonomika.

Postma, N., Z. Hadad, and B. Sudarsono (compilers). 1985. *Bibliography of Women in Indonesia, Suplemen 2.* Jakarta: Kantor

Menteri Muda Urusan Peranan Wanita bekerja sama dengan Pusat Dokumentasi Ilmiah Nasional, Lembaga Ilmu Pegatahuan Indonesia.

Prabowo, Dibyo. 1985. "Methodological Considerations on the Analyses of the Demand for Maize in Indonesia." *In Research Implications of Expanded Production of Selected Upland Crops in Tropical Asia.* Proceedings of a Workshop, Bangkok, 27-30 November 1984. Bogor, Indonesia: CGPRT Centre.

——. 1986. *Some Issues on Informal Credit Markets in Indonesia.* Yogyakarta: Gadjah Mada University.

Prabowo, D., and A. Anwar. 1982. "Natural Resources, Agriculture and the Environment." In Mubyarto (ed.). 1982. *Growth and Equity in Indonesian Agricultural Development.* Jakarta: Yayasan Agro Ekonomika.

Project RTA-104. 1986a. *Modelling the Indonesian Social Accounting Matrix.* Seminar Sistem Neraca Sosial Ekonomi Indonesia 1980. Jakarta: Biro Pusat Statistik and The Hague: Institute of Social Studies.

——. 1986b. *Sistem Neraca Sosial Ekonomi Indonesia 1980.* Seminar Sistem Neraca Sosial Ekonomi Indonesia 1980. Jakarta: Biro Pusat Statistik and The Hague: Institute of Social Studies.

Rahardjo, Dawam a.o. 1986. *Laporan Baseline Survey Koperasi Non-KUD dan Koperasi Informal, Hasil kersajama antara Cooperative Union of Canada (CUC), Dewan Koperasi Indonesia (DEKOPIN) dan Lembaga Pengembangan Swadaya Masyarakat (LPSM).* Jakarta: Unpublished.

Raharjo, Y., and V. Hull. 1984. *Employment Patterns of Educated Women in Indonesian Cities.* Development Studies Centre Monograph No. 3, The Australian National University. Canberra: Australian National University.

Rao, B. 1984. *Poverty in Indonesia 1970-1980: Trends, Associated Characteristics and Research Issues.* Washington, D.C.: The World Bank, East Asia and Pacific Programs Department.

Ravallion, Martin, and Monika Huppi. 1989. "Poverty and Undernutrition in Indonesia during the 1980s." Policy, Planning and Research Working Papers. Washington, D.C.: World Bank.

Repetto, R. 1986. "Soil Loss and Population Pressure on Java." *Ambio.* 15 (1): 14-18.

Rietveld, Piet. 1986. *Non-Agricultural Activities and Income Distribution in Rural Java.* Amsterdam: Satya Wacana Christian University of Free University, Department of Economics.

Rucker, R.L. 1985. *A Preliminary View of the Employment Problem: Indonesian Options and Realities (Revised Draft).* Jakarta: United States Agency for International Development.

Sabrani, M., and A.P. Siregar. 1981. "The Role of Small Ruminants in Traditional Indonesian Farming Systems." *Indonesian Agricultural Research and Development Journal.* 3 (4): 99-104.

Sajogyo, Pudjiwati. 1976. *Action Research on Community Nutrition in Villages in West Java, Indonesia 1975-1976.* Prepared for the Workshop on Household Studies. Bogor, Indonesia: Bogor Agricultural University.

———. 1980. "Basic Human Needs Approaches in Development Efforts to Improve Nutritional Status of the Poor." In Sastrapradja, D.S., S. Adisoemarto, and S. Sastrapradja (eds.). 1983. *Proceedings of the Third Asian Congress of Nutrition, Jakarta, 6-10 October, 1980.* Jakarta: Lembaga Ilmu Pengetaluan Indonesia, for the Indonesian Food and Nutrition Association.

———. 1981. *The Role of the Women in the Family, Household and Wider Community in Rural Java.* Centre for Rural Sociological Research, Bogor Agricultural University. Bogor, Indonesia: Bogor Agricultural University.

———. 1983. *Women in Food, Animal and Plant Production in Indonesian Rural Development.* Paper presented at the Expert Consultation on Women in Food Production, Rome, Italy, 7-14 December 1983, FAO, Bogor Agricultural University. Rome: Food and Agriculture Organization

———. 1984. *Women and Food: Production, Processing and Marketing (Indonesian Case).* Bogor, Indonesia: Bogor Agricultural University.

———. 1985. *Local Level Organization in Planned Development: An Analysis of Women's Participation in Rural Indonesia.* Center of Development Studies, Bogor Agricultural University. Bogor, Indonesia: Bogor Agricultural University.

———. 1986a. *Laporan Penelitian, Monitoring Dan Evaluasi Pembangunan Pedesaan, 1983/84, Kegiatan: Peningkatan Pusat Studi Pengembangan Pedesaan, Penanggungjawab Kegiatan.* Lembaga Penelitian: Institut Pertanian Bogor, Departemen Pendidikan Dan Kebudayaan.

———. 1986b. *Roles Played by Women in Rural Development: An Indonesia Case.* Presented at Dutch Cultural Centre, Jakarta. Bogor, Indonesia: Bogor Agricultural University.

——. 1986c. *Some Notes on Women's Work and Family Strategies from Case-studies on the Role of Rural Women in Development: An Indonesia Case.* Bogor, Indonesia: Bogor Agricultural University.

Sajogyo, Pudjiwati, and G. Wiradi. 1985. *WCARRD Follow-Up Programme: Series of In-depth Studies on Rural Poverty Alleviation, Rural Poverty and Efforts for Its Alleviation in Indonesia, a Sociological Review.* Rome: Food and Agriculture Organization.

Sanjur, Diva. 1982a. *Sociocultural Determinants of Protein-energy Malnutrition in Indonesia.* Bogor, Indonesia: Center for Research and Development in Nutrition, Komplex Gizi.

——. 1982b. *Social and Cultural Perspective in Nutrition.* New Jersey: Prentice-Hall, Inc., Englewood Cliffs.

Saragih, B., P.C. Huszar, and H.C. Cochrane. 1986. *Model Farm Program Benefits: An Elaboration of the Beneficiary Impact Study - Citanduy Watershed Area.* Jakarta: United States Agency for International Development.

Sen, Amartya, K. 1982. *Poverty and Famines: An Essay on Entitlement and Deprivation.* Oxford: Clarendon Press.

Sjahrir, Kartini. 1985. "Women: Some Anthropological Notes." *Prisma.* Vol. 37.

Smith, C.L. 1984. *Evaluation of "Development of the Productive Role of Rural Women."* Prepared for UNDP. Jakarta: United Nations Development Programme.

Soekirman, Sri Wahjoe. 1974. *Priorities in Dealing with Nutrition Problems in Indonesia.* Cornell International Nutrition Monograph Series 1. Ithaca, New York: Cornell University.

——. 1983. *Akademi Gizi - Its Origins, Development and Present Role in Nutrition Manpower Training in Indonesia.* M.P.S. Thesis. Ithaca, New York: Cornell University.

Soemardjan, S. 1985. "Influence of Culture on Food and Nutrition: The Indonesian Case." In Biswas, M., and P. Pinstrup-Andersen (eds.). 1985. *Nutrition and Development.* Oxford, New York: Oxford University Press.

Soemarwoto, O., L. Christanty, Henky, Y.H. Herri, J. Iskandar, Hadyana, and Priyono. 1985. "The Talun-Kebun: A Man-made Forest Fitted to Family Needs." *Food and Nutrition Bulletin.* 7 (3): 48-51.

Soemarwoto, O., I. Soemarwoto, Karyono, E.M. Soekartadiredja, and A. Ramlan. 1985. "The Javenese Home Garden as an Integrated Agro-ecosystem." *Food and Nutrition Bulletin.* 7 (3): 44-47.

Sommer, A. 1982. *Nutritional Blindness, Xerophthalmia and Keratomalacia.* Oxford: Oxford University Press.

Speare, Alden, Jr., and J. Harris. 1986. "Education, Earnings and Migration in Indonesia." *Economic Development and Cultural Change.* 34 (2): 223-244.

Stohler, Ann. L. 1979. *In the Company's Shadow: A History of Plantation Women and Labour Policy in Sumatra.* Colombia University, Department of Anthropology. Unpublished Paper.

Sumarno, Iman. 1981. *Food Crisis Prediction as Part of National Surveillance in Indonesia.* MPS Thesis. Ithaca, New York: Cornell University.

Suzuki, S., Soemarwoto, O., and T. Igarashi. 1985. *A Project Report, Human Ecological Survey in Rural West Java in 1978 to 1982.* Department of Public Health, Japan. Tokyo: Ministry of Public Health.

Tampubolon, S.M.H., and B. Saragih. 1986. *"Model Farm" Upland-Farming Technology, Citanduy River Basin: A State of the Art.* Pengembangan Wilayah Daerah Aliran Sungai Citanduy. Ciamis: Unit Studi dan Evaluasi Sosial Ekonomi.

Tarwotjo, I., A. Sommer, T. Soegiharto, D. Susanto, and Muhilal. 1982. "Dietary Practices and Xerophthalmia among Indonesian Children." *American Journal of Clinical Nutrition.* 35: 574-581.

Tarwotjo, I., I.J. Susanto, and A. Sommer. 1978. *Characterization of Vitamin A Deficiency and Design of Intervention Program.* Paper presented at the XI International Congress of Nutrition, 28 August-1 September 1978, Rio de Janeiro, Brazil. Mimeographed.

Teken, I., and H. Suwardi. 1982. "Food Supply and Demand and Food Policies." In Mubyarto (ed.). 1982. *Growth and Equity in Indonesian Agricultural Development.* Jakarta: Yayasan Agro Ekonomica.

Thorbecke, Erik. 1992. *Adjustment and Equity in Indonesia.* Paris: Organisation for Economic Cooperation and Development (OECD). 1992.

Tjondronegoro, Sendiono M.P. 1984. *Social Organization and Planned Development in Rural Java: A Study of the Organizational Phenomenon in Kecamatan Cibadak, West Java, and Kecamatan Kendal, Central Java.* Singapore: Oxford University Press.

United Nations Conference on Trade and Development (UNCTAD). 1991. Handbook of International Trade and Development Statistics. 1990. New York: United Nations.

United Nations Development Programme. 1984. "Report of the Water Supply and Sanitation Review and Programming Mission". Jakarta: United Nations Development Programme.

——. 1986. "System Analysis for Agricultural Development in Indonesia". Jakarta: United Nations Development Programme.

United Nations Economic and Social Commission for Asia and the Pacific-Regional Research and Development Centre for Coarse Grains, Pulses, Roots and Tubers Centre (ESCAP-CGPRT). 1984. *Cassava in Asia, its Potential and Research Development Needs.* Proceedings of a Regional Workshop held in Bangkok, 5-8 June 1984. Bangkok: United Nations Economic and Social Commission for Asia and the Pacific.

——. 1985. The Soybean Commodity System in Indonesia. Bogor, Indonesia: ESCAP-CGPRT.

United States Agency for International Development. 1983. *Composite Report of the Watershed Assessment Team GOI/USAID.* Jakarta: United States Agency for International Development.

——. 1984. *Project Paper: Upland Agriculture and Conservation Project.* Report No. 4501A:6/13/84. Jakarta: United States Agency for International Development.

van der Kemp, Oda. 1985a. *The Nucleus Estate Smallholders Development Programme: An Overview of the Programme's Operation and Implementation, and its Impact on Income and Employment.* Unpublished paper.

——. 1985b. *The NES/PIR Programme in North Sumatera: A Case Study on the Progress in Implementation of Two Oil Palm Projects and Their Employment and Income-generating Effects.* Unpublished paper.

Warr, Peter G. 1980. "Survey of Recent Developments." *Bulletin of Indonesian Economic Studies.* 16 (3): 1-31.

White, Benjamin. 1986a. *Rural Non-farm Employment in Java: Recent Developments, Policy Issues and Research Needs.* Report prepared in the framework of the UNDP/ILO Department of Manpower Project INS/84/006. Jakarta: United Nations Development Programme/International Labour Office.

——. 1986b. *Implementation of an Employment Strategy.* The Hague: Institute of Social Studies.

White, B., and E.L. Hastuti. 1980. *Decision-making Pattern: Male and Female in the Household and Community Affair in Two Javanese Villages.* Paper presented at Village Economy and Institutions, International Rice Research Institute, Philippines, 25-27 August, 1980. Manila: International Rice Research Institute.

—. 1983. *Measuring Time Allocation, Decision-making and Agrarian Changes Affecting Rural Women: Examples from Recent Research in Indonesia.* The Hague: Institute of Social Studies.

Wigna, W. 1982. *Women's Subordination and Emancipation: The Case of Indonesia.* The Hague: Institute of Social Studies.

Williams, Glen, and May Johnston. 1983. "The Arisan: A Tool for Economic and Social Development?" *Prisma.* 2: 69-73.

Williamson, David. 1984. *Household Buffering of Seasonal Food Availability in a Crisis-Prone Area of Lombok, Indonesia: Implications for Timely Warning and Intervention Systems.* Ithaca, New York: Cornell University.

Wiradi, Gunawan. 1978. *Agro-economic Survey, Rural Development and Rural Institutions: A Study of Institutional Changes in West Java.* Rural Dynamics Study. Bogor, Indonesia: Bogor Agricultural University.

Wiradi, G., and C. Manning. 1984. *Landownership, Tenancy and Sources of Household Income: Community Patterns from a Partial Recensus of Eight Villages in Rural Java.* Bogor, Indonesia: Bogor Agricultural University.

World Bank. 1990. *Indonesia: Strategy for a Sustained Reduction in Poverty.* Washington, D.C.: World Bank.

—. 1985. *Indonesia: Wages and Employment, A World Bank Country Study.* Washington, D.C.: World Bank.

—. 1991a. Trends in Developing Economies 1991. Washington, D.C.: World Bank.

—. 1991b. *World Tables.* 1991 Edition. Baltimore, Maryland: The Johns Hopkins University Press.

World Health Organization/Deutsche Gesellschaft Technische Zusammenarbeit (WHO/GTZ). 1982. *Rural Water and Sanitation Sector Review.* Geneva: World Health Organization.

Yayasan Ilmu-Ilmu Social. 1984. *Wanita Indonesia Sai Karangan 1.* Jakarta: Yayasan Ilmu-Ilmu Social.

Yusuf, A.S. 1980. *An Analysis of Farm Household Income in West Java, Indonesia.* Paper presented at the symposium, Village Economy and Institutions, International Rice Research, Philippines. Manila: International Rice Research Institute.

Index

DATE DUE